A unique and unusual verse by verse commentary on the book of

The Revelation of Jesus Christ

Dr. R. G. Kammar
Th.D. in Systematic Theology

COPYRIGHT 2021 BY DR. R. G. KAMMAR

ALL RIGHTS RESERVED. NO PART OF THIS BOOK MAY BE REPRODUCED OR USED IN ANY MANNER WITHOUT THE PRIOR WRITTEN PERMISSION OF THE COPYRIGHT OWNER, EXCEPT FOR THE USE OF BRIEF QUOTATIONS IN A BOOK REVIEW.

TO REQUEST PERSMISSIONS, CONTACT THE PUBLISHER AT: DRKAMMAR@GMAIL.COM

COVER DESIGNED BY R. HODALEH

First Edition February, 2021
eBook ASIN: B08WYW9L64
Paperback ISBN: 978-0-578-90131-2

INTRODUCTION

You are about to embark on a compelling and enjoyable study of the book of Revelation that I am confident will be a source of spiritual blessing to you and many others around you. I have taught this book multiple times before and it has resulted in the salvation of several souls. Therefore, I pray you will experience the same fruit. This time around I will strive to go into more detail and deeper exegesis that I hope will foster a clearer and better and a more complete understanding of this grand prophetic book of the Bible.

We cannot ignore the fact that the book of Revelation is a book of difficult prophecies; therefore it requires three basic elements for proper and sound interpretation:

(1) The first element needed is "logical sequencing of events", as it is necessary to tie the text being delved into with the previous and following passages.

(2) The second element needed is "clarifying the text itself" by expounding on the meaning of the text itself and understanding its intent.

(3) The third element needed is "simplicity of interpretation" to allow the believer to understand the interpretation and apply

it to himself and be blessed by it. We notice this simple yet profound clear and uncomplicated method of teaching in the Sermon on the Mount where Jesus uttered the most profound words in the entire world, in the Bible.

The book of Revelation contains difficult theological concepts which first appear in the book of Genesis and then culminate in the book of Revelation. For example, in the book of Genesis we study of the creation of the universe, the creation of Adam and Eve, and their subsequent fall. We see that God created five cherubims who formed the seat or The Throne of God. One cherub embraced pride and fell: "Therefore I will cast thee as profane out of the mountain of God: and I will destroy thee, O covering cherub, from the midst of the stones of fire. Thine heart was lifted up because of thy beauty, thou hast corrupted thy wisdom by reason of thy brightness: I will cast thee to the ground" (Ezekiel 28:16-17). Then God cast that prideful cherub to planet Earth and gave him authority over it. That is why the devil, on the mount of temptation, said to Jesus "All this power will I give thee, and the glory of them: for that is delivered unto me" (Luke 4:6). Consequently, and finally in chapter 5 of the book of Revelation we see God using the four cherubims to reclaim the Earth's Title Deed of ownership from Satan, who is Lucifer the fallen cherub.

There are some great and beautiful comparisons between the books of Revelation and Genesis some of which are:

(1) Genesis: Creation of the earth and the sea.
Revelation: Earth and sea pass away.
(2) Genesis: Creation of the Sun and the Moon.
Revelation: No more need for Sun or Moon
because the Light of God shines and brightens
the Eternal abode.
(3) Genesis: A river that waters the Garden of Eden.
Revelation: A new river that proceeds out of the
Throne of God for the blessing of the new earth.

(4) Genesis: The prideful rebellion of Satan.
Revelation: God's final Judgment upon Satan.
(5) Genesis: Beginning of sin, curse, and death.
Revelation: End of sin curse and death.
(6) Genesis: A cherub guards the Garden of Eden.
Revelation: Four cherubims guard the throne of God.
(7) Genesis: Man is cast out of paradise.
Revelation: Man lives in paradise for eternity.
(8) Genesis: Tree of Life is forbidden.
Revelation: Tree of Life is accessible and blessed.
(9) Genesis: Nimrod the symbol of the antichrist founds Babylon.
Revelation: Jesus the true Christ destroys Babylon.
(10) Genesis: Rainbow is a sign of the peace of God in the sky of the earth.
Revelation: Rainbow is around God's heavenly throne.
(11) Genesis: Marriage of the first Adam.
Revelation: Marriage of the last Adam.
(12) Genesis: we find a physical bride.
Revelation: we find a spiritual bride.
(13) Genesis: Bride is Eve.
Revelation: Bride is the Church of Christ.

Between the fall of man into sin and his arrival in the end to heaven after a great conflict, the Bible speaks of "the mystery of iniquity" (2 Thessalonians 2:7), which no man currently comprehends. There is a great struggle between good and evil that begins in Genesis and ends in Revelation. This struggle culminates in victóry for the good by the complete defeat and eradication of all evil. Therefore, the study of prophecy in the book of Revelation provides insight into how the end of this struggle unfolds.

Ahead of us there are three future events that unfold and are addressed in the prophecies of Revelation:

The first event is the ascension of the Body of Christ, the true Church into heaven in the "Rapture", where "the dead in Christ shall rise first. Then we which are alive and remain shall be caught up together with them in the clouds, to meet the Lord in the air: and so shall we ever be with the Lord" (1 Thessalonians 4:16-17). "Rapture" is the "Appearing" of the Lord Jesus (1 Timothy 4:1) who will gather the righteous from the earth prior to the start of the tribulation.

The second event is the return of the Lord Jesus and all his redeemed people of all the ages to the earth for the "Millennial reign", when the Lord Jesus will return to earth to establish his Kingdom for a thousand years: "And they lived and reigned with Christ a thousand years" (Revelation 20:4). "And the Lord my God shall come, and all the saints with thee" (Zechariah 14:5). The return of the Lord Jesus to earth is in two phases:

(1) First, at His "Appearing" the Church is caught up or "raptured" to heaven.

(2) Second is the "Return" of the Lord Jesus Christ from heaven and with him all the believers, from Adam on, to earth to set up "the Kingdom": "and the Lord Jesus Christ, who shall judge the quick and the dead at his Appearing and his Kingdom" (1 Timothy 4:1). Return = Appearing + Kingdom !

(3) The third event is entering "Eternity". After one thousand years of the Millennial reign, there will be cast forever into the fires of hell:

(a) Satan;

(b) Antichrist;

(c) False prophet;

(d) Fallen angels;

(e) All unsaved sinners.

All of them will rise to be judged at the end of the millennium and doomed to eternal burning in torment and suffering in the Lake of Fire: "So man lieth down, and riseth not: till the heavens be no more" (Job 14:12). "And many of them that sleep in the dust of the earth shall awake, some to everlasting life, and some to shame and everlasting contempt" (Daniel 12:2)."The heavens shall pass away with a great noise, and the elements shall melt with fervent heat, the earth also and the works that are therein shall be burned up" (2 Peter 3:10). "And the devil that deceived them was cast into the lake of fire and brimstone, where the beast and the False prophet are, and shall be tormented day and night for ever and ever"; "And I saw a new heaven and a new earth: for the first heaven and the first earth were passed away; and there was no more sea" (Revelation 20:10; 21:1). At that point in time we shall enter Eternity and live in righteousness and peace forever and ever with God and our Beloved Lord Jesus Christ. "For the Lamb which is in the midst of the throne shall feed them, and shall lead them unto living fountains of waters" (Revelation 7:17). "Behold, the tabernacle of God is with men, and he will dwell with them" (Revelation 21:3).

The entire Book of Revelation revolves around the Second Coming or Return of the Lord Jesus in glory to earth to establish the Kingdom of Heaven on Earth. This is subsequent to his first coming in humility to die on the cross for us. His sacrifice for our redemption is the repeated prominent emphasis throughout the Book of Revelation as the "Slain Lamb":

(1) In chapter one Jesus is the glorified Lamb, the Son of God.

(2) In chapters two and three he is the Lamb who walks among the seven churches and holds their pastors in his right hand.

(3) In chapter five Jesus the Slain Lamb, comes forward to open the seven seals of God's scroll.

(4) In chapter six he is the Lamb who opens the first seal releasing the great wrath of God upon the earth.

(5) In chapter seven we see that the redeemed have washed their clothes and made them white in the Blood of the Lamb.

(6) In chapter twelve we see the righteous overcome Satan with the Blood of the Lamb.

(7) In chapter thirteen we see most of the human race in bondage to the Antichrist because their names are not written, from the foundation of the world, in the Slain Lamb's Book of Life.

(8) In chapter fourteen we see the Lamb standing on Mount Zion. In chapter fifteen we see the redeemed singing the song of the Lamb.

(9) In chapter seventeen the Lamb vanquishes the antichrist and his allies: "And the Lamb shall overcome them: for he is Lord of lords, and King of kings: and they that are with him are called, and chosen, and faithful" (Revelation 17:14).

Jesus Christ is the (1) Purpose, (2) Means, and (3) Goal of all the redeemed that are comprised of: (1) Israel, (2) Gentiles, and (3) Church.

The Lord Jesus Christ is the Regal authority of the entire Bible; of all the Old Testament; and in the New Testament:

(a) Church age
(b) Rapture
(c) Great Tribulation
(d) Millennium
(e) Eternity past and future world without end.

Glory to His name: JESUS CHRIST, SON OF GOD !

Jesus has many attributes and names in the book of Revelation:

1- The Faithful Witness
2- First Begotten of the Dead
3- King of Kings
4- Lord of Lords

5- Prince of the kings of the earth
6- The Alpha and Omega
7- The First and Last
8- He who Is and Was and Is to Come
9- The Lord God Almighty
10- Son of Man
11- Son of God
12- Word of God
13- The Holy One
14- The True
15- The Beginning of the Creation of God
16- The Slain Lamb
17- The Lion of the Tribe of Judah
18- The Root of David
19- The Key of David
20- Having a Voice as the voice of many waters with thunder
21- Having a Countenance as the Sun
22- Having the Seven Spirits of God
23- Searcher of the reins and hearts
24- He who opens and no man shuts, and shuts and no man opens
25- Has a Sword proceeding out of his Mouth
26- The Bridegroom
27- Has Knowledge of our works
28- God of the holy prophets
29- The Judge
30- The Bright and Morning Star

The key verse of the Book of Revelation is: "The kingdoms of this world are become the kingdoms of our Lord, and of his Christ; and he shall reign forever and ever" (Revelation 11:15).

Divisions of the Book of Revelations are as follows:

(I) The first three chapters of Revelation speak of the church age.

(II) Chapters four and five describe the scene in Heaven following the lifting up of the church into heaven.

(III) Chapters six through nineteen describe what happens on Earth following the rapture of the church into heaven; that being the great tribulation when God

pours out his wrath upon the world through the:

(1) Seals,
(2) Vials,
(3) Trumpets.

The wrath of God will be directed at the evil structures of the world:

(1) Political,
(2) Military,
(3) Economic,
(4) Religious.

(IV) Chapter twenty describes Jesus' reign during the Millennium where the devil will be bound for a thousand years. After that the devil will be loosed and a great final war begins. Then the Lord Jesus will exterminate Satan and throw him in the fires of hell forever. At that point in time, the Great White Throne of God appears in heaven to judge all the wicked of all ages.

(V) Chapters twenty one and twenty two describe the commencement of the wonderful Eternal State in the New Jerusalem in the Third Heaven before the Great Throne of God.

The sequence of events of the last days may be summarized as follows:

1- Rapture of the church
2- In Heaven: BEMA seat of Christ for rewards, and his bride prepares herself
3- On Earth: Tribulation for seven years
4- Christ returns to earth and his bride, the church. with him
5- Antichrist and False prophet are slain and cast into

the lake of fire
6- Kingdom of Christ commences and peace prevails on earth
7- Satan is bound for a 1,000 years
8- Marriage of the Lamb and Wedding Supper of the Lamb
9- New human beings are born on earth
10- Christ rules the nations with rod of iron
11- Millennium comes to an end and Satan is unbound and the world revolts
12- Russian invasion with all the evil forces of this world
13- Destruction of Satan and evil is thrown into the lake of fire
14- Great White throne of God to judge all sinners
15- Eternity or the eternal state

The book of Revelation beautifully wraps up the whole Bible and brings down the curtain on the story of the creation and fall and redemption of the human race, that leads up to and ends in eternal bliss.

The Lord Jesus Christ is returning very soon and he will reward each faithful follower of his. Watch and be prepared like the 5 wise virgins teach us to do!

1
THE MEETING BETWEEN JESUS AND JOHN

(1) "The Revelation of Jesus Christ, which God gave unto him, to shew unto his servants things which must shortly come to pass; and he sent and signified it by his angel unto his servant John"

- The Revelation - This book is given to us with the purpose of unveiling something hidden, or previously undeclared, about the end of the world.

- of Jesus Christ - The giver of the prophesies in this book is JESUS himself, the Lord of glory.

- Which God gave unto him – The verse does not say that the "Father" gave unto him, but that "God" gave unto him. When we read the word "God" in the Bible, it incorporates the three persons of the Triune God, who are the Father, the Son, and the Holy Ghost. The word "God" speaks collectively of the three in one entity, in a heavenly family that is made up of the "Father" that refers to the first person of the Trinity, the "Son" that refers to the second person of the Trinity, and the Holy Ghost that refers to the third person of the Trinity. Each person of the triune divine persons possesses the same divine attributes, the same divine characteristics, and the same divine capabilities, of God.

The second person of the trinity, God the Son, came down to earth and took on the form of flesh. The Bible describes further this unfathomable and unabsorbable doctrine of incarnation of Jesus Christ that took place in Bethlehem: "[6]Who, being in the form of God, thought it not robbery to be equal with God: [7]But made himself of no reputation, and took upon him the form of a servant, and was made in the likeness of men: [8]And being found in fashion as a man, he humbled himself, and became obedient unto death, even the death of the cross" (Philippians 2:6-8); "Great is the mystery of godliness: God was manifest in the flesh" (1Timothy 3:16); Forasmuch then as the children are partakers of flesh and blood, he also himself likewise took part of the same; that through death he might destroy him that had the power of death, that is, the devil (Hebrews 2:14).

Thus Jesus Christ has two entities, the divine heavenly nature and the human earthly nature in one person. Jesus Christ is fully God and fully Man. Jesus Christ is God the Son and the Son of God. In theology, this union of two natures is called the: "Hypostatic Union" of His Deity & His Humanity. That is why the Christian creed of Faith states about the birth of Jesus states that he is: "begotten, not made" , "consubstantial with the Father"; that is to say: "For in him dwelleth all the fulness of the Godhead bodily" (Colossians 2:9).

The relationship of the divine nature with the human nature is like the relationship of a father with his son. So does the Spirit within us cry: "And because ye are sons, God hath sent forth the Spirit of his Son into your hearts, crying, Abba, Father (Galatians 4:6): "Abba, Father". The father is seen in two ways: first, in God the Father, the first person of the Trinity; second, the Father is seen in the divine nature of the second person of the Trinity, God the Son, in relation to his human nature, Son of man. To simplify it even further, in the second person of the Trinity, in God the Son Jesus Christ, the word "Father" relates to his Deity in connection with his humanity within the same person. Whereas the word "Son" speaks of his humanity, the Son of man in relation to his deity within the same person. The Bible calls the Son of God "The everlasting Father" (Isaiah 9:6), speaking of the Divinity of the second person of the Godhead, that he is the father of his human nature. The divine nature of Jesus Christ is the fathership of his human nature; and the human nature of Jesus Christ is the sonship of his divine nature. In his fatherly nature, that is in his divine nature, Jesus is God, Holy, Sovereign, Creator, Omnipresent, Omnipotent, Omniscient, Immutable (unchanging), and all Knowing. In his sonly human nature, that is in his human nature, Jesus is encompassed by weakness and limitation in his fleshly human soul, spirit, and body. An example of that is the story at the well: "Now Jacob's well was there. Jesus therefore, being wearied with his journey, sat thus on the well: and it was about the sixth hour" (John 4:6). Great is the mystery of such verses as: "Blessed be the God and Father of our Lord Jesus Christ (Ephesians 1:3).

We can also notice the distinction between these two natures in some of the Bible verses that add light to this truth, such as: "No man hath seen God at any time, the only begotten Son, which is in the bosom of the Father, he hath declared him"; "And no man hath ascended up to heaven, but he that came down from heaven, even the Son of man which is in heaven" (John 1:18; 3:13); Jesus is present both in heaven and on earth at the same time. We see Jesus Christ waking among men on earth in his humanity; and at the same time; he in his deity is in heaven and filling the whole universe and all existence: "For in him in Jesus we live, and move, and have our being" (Acts 17:28). Also, in his human nature Jesus was standing by Philip at a certain place by the sea of Galilee, and in his divine nature he saw Nathanael in a different location under the fig tree:

"Nathanael saith unto him, Whence knowest thou me? Jesus answered and said unto him, Before that Philip called thee, when thou wast under the fig tree, I saw thee. Nathanael answered and saith unto him, Rabbi, thou art the Son of God" (John 1: 48-49); "to feed the church of God, which he hath purchased with his own blood." (Acts 20:28); "[17]That the God of our Lord Jesus Christ, the Father of glory, ... hath put all things under his feet, and gave him to be the head over all things to the church, [23] Which is his body, the fulness of him that filleth all in all"; "[10] He that descended is the same also that ascended up far above all heavens, that he might fill all things" (Ephesians 1:17, 22-23; 4:10).

There are verses that are more difficult to expound, such as: "But of that day and that hour knoweth no man, no, not the angels which are in heaven, neither the Son, but the Father" (Mark 13:32). In this verse, the Father denotes the "deity" of Jesus Christ and the Son points to the humanity of Jesus Christ. If the Father were to be interpreted as the first person of the trinity and the Son as the second person of the trinity, then the second person would be limited in knowledge and lacking in deity and that would constitute a theological heresy.

"Son" refers to the "human nature" which is "Jesus", and "Father" refers to the "divine nature" which is "Christ". This makes interpreting the verse clear and logical and understandable: Jesus Christ two natures in one. In his divinity he is all knowing but in his humanity his knowledge has earthly limitations as he is fully Man just like he is fully God in his hypostatic union.

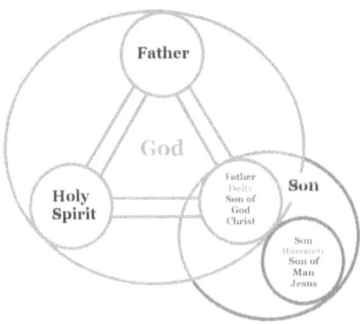

Another very important similar reference can be seen in the following text: "And when all things shall be subdued unto him, then shall the Son also himself be subject unto him that put all things under him, that God may be all in all" (1Corinthians 15:28) where his humanity is subject to his divinity; for the verse does not say that the Son will be subject to the "Father" but the Son will be subject to the triune "God". Jesus is fully God and fully Man in one person, and Jesus the man is subject to Christ the God. Jesus adds light to this fact in the gospel of John saying: "I and my Father are one"; "Believe me that I am in the Father, and the Father in me" (John 10:30; 14:11).

The meaning of this verse in Revelation is that his humanity is submissive to his divinity, like a case in point would be in: "Though he were a Son, yet learned he obedience by the things which he suffered" (Hebrews 5: 8). In his humanity, on the cross he cried: "And about the ninth hour Jesus cried with a loud voice, saying, Eli, Eli, lama sabachthani? that is to say, My God, my God, why hast thou forsaken me?" (Matthew 27:46). Theological heresy comes from taking verses that speak of the human nature of Christ and attributing them to his divine nature, in an attack to undermine his divinity; and that is the core of the heresy of the Jehovah's Witnesses. Also the Moslems and the Mormons; all of them use verses that speak about his humanity and try to attribute them to his deity in an attempt to discredit his humanity or to undermine his deity. This is a far cry from the truth that in Jesus Christ: "dwelleth all the fulness of the Godhead bodily" (Colossians 2:9). Jesus is fully God and fully Man. His divine and human natures united in one person, who is Jesus Christ the Son of God: "¹¹Believe me that I am in the Father, and the Father in me: or else believe me for the very works' sake", "Believe me that I am in the Father, and the Father in me" (John 10:30; 14:11); "¹God, who at sundry times and in divers manners spake in time past unto the fathers by the prophets, ²Hath in these last days spoken unto us by his Son, whom he hath appointed heir of all things, by whom also he made the worlds; ³Who being the brightness of his glory, and the express image of his person, and upholding all things by the word of his power, when he had by himself purged our sins, sat down on the right hand of the Majesty on high: ⁴Being made so much better than the angels, as he hath by inheritance obtained a more excellent name than they. ⁵For unto which of the angels said he at any time, Thou art my Son, this day have I begotten thee? And again, I will be to him a Father, and he shall be to me a Son?" (Hebrews 1:1-5).

One of the most important doctrines of the Bible is the pre-existence, or even the eternal existence of Christ Jesus. The eternal existence of Christ Jesus is one of the most beautiful doctrines in the Bible: "But thou, Bethlehem Ephratah, though thou be little among the thousands of Judah, yet out of thee shall he come forth unto me that is to be ruler in Israel; whose goings forth have been from of old, from everlasting" (Micah 5:2); "¹In the beginning was the Word, and the Word was with God, and the Word was God. ²The same was in the beginning with God. ³All things were made by him; and without him was not any thing made that was made…. ¹⁰He was in the world, and the world was made by him, and the world knew him not…. ¹⁴And the Word was made flesh, and dwelt among us, and we beheld his glory, the glory as of the only begotten of the Father, full of grace and truth. ¹⁵John bare witness of him, and cried, saying,

This was he of whom I spake, He that cometh after me is preferred before me: for he was before me" (John 1:1-3, 10, 14-15); "Jesus Christ the same yesterday, and to day, and for ever" (Hebrews 13:8). Jesus confounded the Jewish leaders with regard to his eternal existence saying: "³⁸For I came down from heaven, not to do mine own will, but the will of him that sent me", "⁴²And they said, Is not this Jesus, the son of Joseph, whose father and mother we know? how is it then that he saith, I came down from heaven?", "⁶²What and if ye shall see the Son of man ascend up where he was before?"; "⁵⁶Your father Abraham rejoiced to see my day: and he saw it, and was glad. ⁵⁷Then said the Jews unto him, Thou art not yet fifty years old, and hast thou seen Abraham? ⁵⁸Jesus said unto them, Verily, verily, I say unto you, Before Abraham was, I AM" (John 6: 38, 42, 62; 8:56-58). Jesus Christ is the eternal I AM ! Jesus Christ says: "The Lord possessed me in the beginning of his way, before his works of old" (Proverbs 8:22); "Behold my servant, whom I uphold; mine elect, in whom my soul delighteth; I have put my spirit upon him: he shall bring forth judgment to the Gentiles. ²He shall not cry, nor lift up, nor cause his voice to be heard in the street. ³A bruised reed shall he not break, and the smoking flax shall he not quench: he shall bring forth judgment unto truth. ⁴He shall not fail nor be discouraged, till he have set judgment in the earth: and the isles shall wait for his law" ; "Come ye near unto me, hear ye this; I have not spoken in secret from the beginning; from the time that it was, there am I: and now the Lord God, and his Spirit, hath sent me" (Isaiah 42:1-4 ; 48:16); "While the Pharisees were gathered together, Jesus asked them, ⁴²Saying, What think ye of Christ? whose son is he? They say unto him, The son of David. ⁴³He saith unto them, How then doth David in spirit call him Lord, saying, ⁴⁴The Lord said unto my Lord, Sit thou on my right hand, till I make thine enemies thy footstool? ⁴⁵If David then call him Lord, how is he his son? ⁴⁶And no man was able to answer him a word, neither durst any man from that day forth ask him any more questions" (Matthew 22:41-46).

This subject of humanity and deity cannot be understood by man. Speaking of it Jesus declares: "All things are delivered unto me of my Father: and no man knoweth the Son, but the Father; neither knoweth any man the Father, save the Son, and he to whomsoever the Son will reveal him" (Matthew 11:27). The verse means that it is possible to know the Father, but it is impossible to know the Son! Likewise Paul describes this doctrine to Timothy saying: "And without controversy great is the mystery of godliness: God was manifest in the flesh" (1 Timothy 3:16). Deity in Humanity, we accept it and believe it simply by faith.

To simplify understanding this principle even further; each one of us regenerated converts of Christ is born of the Flesh and born of the Spirit "by the Holy Ghost which dwelleth in us" (2 Timothy 1: 14); two natures a spiritual divine nature and an earthly physical nature in one person.

In this verse we see that Jesus Christ in his human nature did not know future events until his divine nature declared them to his human nature. Divinity revealing to Humanity both in the same one person Jesus Christ.

- To show unto his servants - In the Bible, the phrase the "servants of Christ" refers most frequently to the prophets and the apostles. At other times, all of the Lord's children are described as servants of the Lord. As Peter the Apostle says concerning the Lord's children "As free, and not using your liberty for a cloke of maliciousness, but as the servants of God" (1 Peter 2:16). Directing his words to the church of Thyatira, Jesus says "Notwithstanding I have a few things against thee, because thou sufferest that woman Jezebel, which calleth herself a prophetess, to teach and to seduce my servants to commit fornication, and to eat things sacrificed unto idols" (Revelation 2:20). And the angel ascending from the east says "till we have sealed the servants of our God" (Revelation 7:3), who are the witnesses of the Lord Jesus. We who have believed in the Lord Jesus Christ are all the servants of the Lord Jesus. Every person who has repented, believed, and been baptized in the name of the Lord Jesus is His servant. We were the servants of sin, but now we have become the servants of Jesus Christ.

- He sent and signified it by his angel - After the Lord Jesus rose from the dead, he ascended in the heavens and sat down at the right hand of Majesty. The Lord uses his angels, who obey his commands. But he himself does not move from the right hand of Majesty: "Thousand thousands ministered unto him, and ten thousand times ten thousand stood before him" (Daniel 7:10). Paul was praying when the ship he was on was in the midst of the storm when the angel of the God appeared to him with a message of salvation: "For there stood by me this night the angel of God, whose I am, and whom I serve" (Acts 27:23). But of a truth, the Lord does appear in person yet without leaving his throne. He did that with Stephen: "being full of the Holy Ghost, looked up stedfastly into heaven, and saw the glory of God, and Jesus standing on the right hand of God" (Acts 7:55). Also Saul of Tarsus: and with Saul of Tarsus: "But Barnabas took him, and brought him to the apostles, and declared unto them how he had seen the Lord in the way, and that he had spoken to him, and how he had preached boldly at Damascus in the name of Jesus" (Acts 9:27). Jesus sent an angel to his servant, John. The Lord Jesus used an angel to bring the revelation to John, who was in exile, and to every believer who is suffering for the cause of Christ.

(2) "Who bare record of the word of God, and of the testimony of Jesus Christ, and of all things that he saw."

(i) First, in his gospel John bore witness to the Word of God. "In the beginning was the Word, and the Word was with God, and the Word was God. And the Word was made flesh, and dwelt among us, (and we beheld his glory, the glory as of the only begotten of the Father,) full of grace and truth" (John 1:1, 14).

(ii) Second, John bore witness at the cross. "But one of the soldiers with a spear pierced his side, and forthwith came there out blood and water. And he that saw it bare record, and his record is true: and he knoweth that he saith true, that ye might believe" (John 19:34-35).

(iii) Third, John bore witness at the empty tomb. "And the other disciple did outrun Peter, and came first to the sepulcher. And he stooping down, and looking in, saw the linen clothes lying; yet went he not in. Then cometh Simon Peter following him, and went into the sepulcher, and seeth the linen clothes lie, And the napkin, that was about his head, not lying with the linen clothes, but wrapped together in a place by itself. Then went in also that other disciple, which came first to the sepulcher, and he saw, and believed". "And many other signs truly did Jesus in the presence of his disciples, which are not written in this book: But these are written, that ye might believe that Jesus is the Christ, the Son of God; and that believing ye might have life through his name (John 20:4-8, 30-31).

(iv) Fourth, in his epistles, John states: "That which was from the beginning, which we have heard, which we have seen with our eyes, which we have looked upon, and our hands have handled, of the Word of life; (For the life was manifested, and we have seen it, and bear witness, and shew unto you that eternal life, which was with the Father, and was manifested unto us;) That which we have seen and heard declare we unto you, that ye also may have fellowship with us: and truly our fellowship is with the Father, and with his Son Jesus Christ. And these things write we unto you, that your joy may be full" (1 John 1:1-4).

(v) Fifth, we see the witness here in the book of Revelation at a time when John, for the sake of the name of the Lord Jesus, is exiled on the island of Patmos. Then Jesus gave him this heavenly revelation and commanded that he communicated it to us. "I John, who also am your brother, and companion in tribulation, and in the kingdom and patience of Jesus Christ, was in the isle that is called Patmos, for the word of God, and for the testimony of Jesus Christ. I was in the Spirit on the Lord's day, and heard behind me a great voice, as of a trumpet, Saying, I am Alpha and Omega, the first and the last: and, What thou seest, write in a book, and send it unto the seven churches which are in Asia; unto Ephesus, and unto Smyrna, and unto Pergamos, and unto Thyatira, and unto Sardis, and unto Philadelphia, and unto Laodicea" (Revelation 1:9-11).

God has divine plans and as always, he wishes to reveal his will to us in advance: "And the LORD said, Shall I hide from Abraham that thing which I do?" (Genesis 18:17). "The secret of the Lord is with them that fear him" (Psalms 25:14). "Surely the Lord GOD will do nothing, but he revealeth his secret unto his servants the prophets" (Amos 3:7).

(3) "Blessed is he that readeth, and they that hear the words of this prophecy, and keep those things which are written therein: for the time is at hand."

Here we see here the following three blessings:

(i) The first blessing is for the man who reads. Such a person has the privilege of coming to know God's thoughts. It is not through reading only but reading and meditating. Thus he possesses understanding and depth in spiritual matters. There are many who read and mock, and others who read but do not care and therefore, do not comprehend. Here the blessing is for the person who reads and absorbs the material being explained, that is the prophecies concerning the last days). Blessed is the person who understands God's sovereign plan for this world and sees the end from afar off and so gets comforted in the Lord Jesus by the fact that there is an end to this earthly toil. Our comfort is that after the toils and pains of this world we are going to rest and enjoy an eternity that exceeds description and even imagination; an eternity where: "Eye hath not seen, nor ear heard, neither have entered into the heart of man, the things which God hath prepared for them that love him" (1 Corinthians 2:9).

(ii) The second blessing is for those who are attentive and purpose to apply what they read. The phrase "Who hath ears to hear, let him hear" is mentioned by Jesus fourteen times in the New Testament. There are those who read and hear but then turn a blind eye, and by doing so, do not receive this blessing. This second blessing is reserved for he who listens to the voice of the Lord speaking to his heart; and makes a conscious decision to apply what he hears.

(iii) So follows the third blessing, which is for the man who keeps the words of the prophecy, for after reading and understanding comes implementation. Blessed is the one who receives exhortation from what he reads and decides to live a life of consecration which glorifies the name of the Lord Jesus: "for thou wast slain, and hast redeemed us to God by thy blood out of every kindred, and tongue, and people, and nation" , "Worthy is the Lamb that was slain to receive power, and riches, and wisdom, and strength, and honour, and glory, and blessing" (Revelation 5: 9 , 12).

- The time is short - This phrase has a double meaning: First, you have a short, golden opportunity to serve the Lord Jesus. Second, the phrase basically points to a sequence of events occurring very rapidly. This is what we see in our lives today since Israel's return to existence in 1948. Since then events have been moving at an astonishing pace, and the end times prophecies are being fulfilled before our very eyes on daily basis. This is true beatitude or blessing because the literal fulfilment of these prophecies is the greatest comfort and blessing and motivation to live faithfully, truthfully, and loyally for the Lord Jesus. When a person understands that the end of the world is near, he begins to prepare himself for living for the

Lord because his return is imminent. The Christian that lives a life of stand by because the end of the world is near, prepares himself to meet the Lord Jesus because his appearing in imminent and we could hear the trump of the rapture any time now. Jesus deserves our allegiance and loyalty because he purchased us with his blood and made us kings and priests unto God our Father. This is what Jesus is trying to teach us in the parables of the gospels such as: The wise virgins, the faithful steward, and the watchful servant expecting his master's return to reward him.

(4) "John to the seven churches which are in Asia: Grace be unto you, and peace, from him which is, and which was, and which is to come; and from the seven Spirits which are before his throne."

- John to the seven churches which are in Asia - John directs his words to seven churches. The seven churches represent seven stages in the development of the church through the ages of the new testament. The church of Christ passes through seven ages. In each of these seven ages, we see churches of all seven types in existence. But in each age, there is one type which is prevalent. For example, we are now in the age of the church of Laodicea. This church is characterized by the fact that believers in it consider themselves to be rich spiritually and in need of nothing, while the Lord is ready to spew them out of his mouth for their spiritual lukewarmness, for they are neither hot nor cold. This is our Christian world in this day. With this, we see some churches in these days like the churches of Thyatira, Sardis, and Philadelphia. The seven types of churches are present today, but the vast majority is of the type of Laodicea. It is important to note that the church of Laodicea is a believing, regenerate church; however, she lives a life that is lacking in consecration. She behaves as if she does not know the Lord Jesus. and ignores him to the extent that he has become an outsider knocking on the door of their church. Today's Christians are placing Christ out of their plans and the undertakings of their lives.

The words are addressed to the seven churches, but, at the same time, they convey lessons and morals by which our spiritual lives should be exhorted. In each of the seven churches, we see a spiritual condition. We see a spiritual problem which has a specific spiritual remedy.

All the problems of churches today are found in one way or another in the seven churches. They are lessons and solutions for the problems of all the churches of Christendom today. Also they are precious lessons with applications to our own personal lives so that we may be nourished and grow in the grace of our Lord and Saviour Jesus Christ.

- Grace be unto you, and peace, from him which is, and which was, and which is to come; and from the seven Spirits which are before his throne - The Lord Jesus Christ is the God of all grace, the Lord of all peace, and the Prince of peace. He is God the Son, the one who is and was and is to come. God the Holy Spirit shares with God the Son in sending grace and peace. The phrase "the seven Spirits of God" speaks of the divine perfection of the Holy Spirit.

(5) "And from Jesus Christ, who is the faithful witness, and the first begotten of the dead, and the prince of the kings of the earth. Unto him that loved us, and washed us from our sins in his own blood".

- From Jesus Christ, who is the faithful witness, and the first begotten of the dead - This revelation reaches us from the divine family by way of Jesus Christ, the only mediator between God and man. "For there is one God, and one mediator between God and men, the man Christ Jesus" (1 Timothy 2:5). He is the faithful witness, since no one else can testify to the salvation of God which was completed in his own body on the cross. "Moreover it is required in stewards, that a man be found faithful," (1 Corinthians 4:2) and no one is as faithful as the Lord Jesus who rose victorious over death. He is the first to rise from the dead as proof of the salvation of God. "But now is Christ risen from the dead, and become the firstfruits of them that slept" (1 Corinthians 15:20).

- The prince of the kings of the earth - Jesus is the prince of the kings of the earth. He rules in our hearts over our lives, and when he returns he will rule the whole world for eternity. The Lord Jesus says, with all right and merit, that he is the "prince of the kings of the earth". He is the "King of kings and the Lord of lords" (Revelation 19:16), and the "God of gods" (Joshua 22:22).

- That loved us, and washed us from our sins in his own blood – What regal deed did Jesus do for us? Out of the greatness of his lovefor us, he humbled himself, gave his life, washed us from our sins in his own blood, and made us kings and priests unto God and his Father; to him be glory and dominion forever and ever. Amen. Who loved us?! Jesus!! Only he loved us before we were born and only he will remain with us forever. We begin our lives with parents. After that, there is marriage and children. But the time comes when all leave us. However, the true Friend stays with us and never leaves us. He loved us as we were, in our shape, our form, our character, and our sins. He loved us, went to the cross for us, and shed his blood for our sins. The Bible says: "and without shedding of blood is no remission" (Hebrews 9:22). "If we confess our sins, he is faithful and just to forgive us our sins, and to cleanse us from all unrighteousness" (1 John 1:9). Here we see that he loved us and washed us from our sins in his own blood. The wages of sin is death, but Jesus died in our place on the cross. Because he is God's Son, he rose again the third day, opening to us the door of salvation, the door of hope, the door of everlasting life.

(6) "And hath made us kings and priests unto God and his Father; to him be glory and dominion for ever and ever. Amen."

Why kings and priests? Because a king serves the people, and a priest serves God. Jesus made us kings so that we, in his name, will reign over the whole world. When Jesus comes and descends to the Mount of Olives, we will descend with him, enter Jerusalem with him, and reign over the whole world. Each one of us will reign in a certain place, in some country or some specific location. Even though we will reign with him, we will remain his priests, serving in his heavenly temple and presenting worship and adoration to him forever. No matter how much our earthly station increases, we will remain servants and priests to the Lord Jesus forever.

(7) "Behold, he cometh with clouds; and every eye shall see him, and they also which pierced him: and all kindreds of the earth shall wail because of him. Even so, Amen."

- Behold, he cometh with clouds - As he ascended with the clouds, so also will he come: "And when he had spoken these things, while they beheld, he was taken up; and a cloud received him out of their sight. And while they looked steadfastly toward heaven as he went up, behold, two men stood by them in white apparel; Which also said, Ye men of Galilee, why stand ye gazing up into heaven? this same Jesus, which is taken up from you into heaven, shall so come in like manner as ye have seen him go into heaven" (Acts 1:9-11).

- And every eye shall see him, and they also which pierced him: and all kindreds of the earth shall wail because of him. Even so, Amen - His return will be the opposite of his first coming, when the world was not aware of his arrival. But now, all the world will see him. Who pierced him? The Romans pierced the Lord Jesus. The Jews pierced him. The Gentiles pierced him. All the world pierced him. We pierced the Lord Jesus with our sins. And the day will come in which all the armies of the world, Europe, Africa, the East, Russia, and the Middle East, will be gathered together against Jerusalem for war, and the Jewish people will be facing the prospect of another captivity. But this time, before Jerusalem falls, the Lord Jesus will return in the clouds to deliver his city Jerusalem. The

Jews and all the peoples of the world will see Jesus returning in the clouds. "Every eye shall see him," and they will wail over one whom they crucified with their own hands.

Zechariah asks and Jesus answers: "What are these wounds in thine hands? "Those with which I was wounded in the house of my friends" (Zechariah 13:6).

The Lord is returning very soon. The Lord God returned the Israelites to the land of Canaan after the captivity of Babylon in preparation for the first coming of the Lord Jesus Christ. He died on the cross, rose from the dead, and ascended back up to heaven, completing the work of redemption. The Israelites were dispersed a second time, and their diaspora was quite lengthy. In 1948 they returned in preparation for the second coming of the Lord Jesus. The Lord Jesus gave us a sign, namely the return of the Jews to the land of Canaan. This marks the commencement of the end of the world; and the return of the Lord Jesus to earth is at hand.

Jesus says, "Now learn a parable of the fig tree; When her branch is yet tender, and putteth forth leaves, ye know that summer is near: So ye in like manner, when ye shall see these things come to pass, know that it is nigh, even at the doors. Verily I say unto you, that this generation shall not pass, till all these things be done" (Mark 13:28-30). We are now in the last days.

Elisha told Gehazi his servant: "Is it a time to receive money, and to receive garments, and oliveyards, and vineyards, and sheep, and oxen, and menservants, and maidservants?" (2 Kings 5:26). The answer comes from the book of Psalms which says, "It is time for thee, LORD, to work" (Psalm 119:126). So let us lay treasures up for ourselves in heaven. By our faithfulness, let us ensure that when the Lord comes to rapture us to the heavenly glories, we will not be ashamed of him but rather be glad at his appearing. The book of Proverbs warns us saying, "If thou scornest, thou alone shalt bear it," and then it asks, "But a faithful man who can find?" (Proverbs 9:12; 20:6). The Lord requires faithfulness to himself. The end of the world is near. This is the best motivation for us to live for him who died for us, rose again, and washed away every one of our sins. The world will wail at the return of Christ, but we will rejoice. We should comfort and encourage each other to be watchful for the day when we will meet Christ in the clouds at the rapture.

(8) "I am Alpha and Omega, the beginning and the ending, saith the Lord, which is, and which was, and which is to come, the Almighty."

The Lord Jesus tells us that he is the beginning and the end. Before him there was no God formed, neither shall there be after him. Without him, no man ever lifts up his hand upon the earth. The Lord Jesus is eternal; he has existed from eternity past, and he will continue to exist in eternity future. He is "I am that I am". He is Jehovah. He is Elohim. He is the Lord God, the Creator in whom we live and move and have our being. He is the Almighty who can do all things, for all things exist by the might of his Word; and he desires to be the first and the last in every matter in your life. He is able to do anything for you. He wants to be the first and the last in your plans and undertakings, in your thoughts, in your decisions, and in your entire life; for your own well being. Why not come to Jesus? Because you are entangled in your problems and do not bring them to Jesus. You have thorns which obstruct your way and choke your spiritual life. Remove these thorns so that you can be a fruitful branch in Jesus the vine. According to the parable of the sower, most believers are carnal because the thorns and cares of this life choke them, keeping them from fruitfulness for the Lord. And thus the Lord Jesus tells you to come to him with all the problems and cares which you have, and which make your yoke heavy. As for the Lord Jesus, his yoke is easy and his burden is light. He is the Lord Almighty. When the Lord appeared to Abraham, the latter did not know his name. But Abraham knew that the Lord Jesus was almighty. He is the beginning and the end, the one who kills and makes alive, and beside him there is no god. He destroys all those who play the harlot in departing from him. Make the Lord Jesus "The Lord of your life". Start you day with him. Greet him. Say to him "Good morning, my Lord Jesus"! Speak to him throughout the day. Share with him, and ask him for guidance. Make him the central axis of your breaths. Make him first and last in your life, and he alone is able to meet all your needs. He is able to bestow all things upon you, for he is God Almighty. Place him first in your personal life, your family life, and your social life. Then end your day with him, and close your day resting in his protection.

The basic purpose of studying the book of Revelation is for us to know that God will bring down his wrath upon the world that refuses to worship the Lord Jesus. We must be faithful until his coming so that we will not be ashamed at his appearing. We want to be watchfully studying the words of this book of Revelation because the motive of this book is to keep those things which are written therein, so that we can remain faithful to the end, because the times are at hand. Jesus says: "Verily I say unto you, that this generation shall not pass, till all these things be done. Heaven and earth shall pass away: but my words shall not pass away" (Mark 13:30-31).

Knowledge has increased greatly, as the Lord Jesus told Daniel: "But thou, O Daniel, shut up the words, and seal the book, even to the time of the end: many shall run to and fro, and knowledge shall be increased" (Daniel 12:4). In addition to that, take, for example, the worship of the beast in the book of Revelation. John wrote of it without understanding it. Today, computers and the diverse social networking applications like Facebook are widely used allowing people to easily connect with each other and be secretly supervised by higher authorities. Through such means, the Antichrist will control the masses of the world. These are matters which would not have entered our minds fifty years ago, and yet here they are between our hands. Consider another occurrence in the kingdom of Western Europe which speaks of the preparation of the throne of the Antichrist and of the last days. The Bible says that people will be sealed, meaning that people will accept the seal of the beast on their hands and foreheads.

Things that were once unimaginable to people are now commonplace. Today we have a lower volume of transactions in cash, and a replacement of these transactions with the use of credit cards (which tend to limit the carrying of cash and the direct use of currency). Shortly, all buying will become through a computer microchip grafted in your hand between the thumb and the index finger. In the great tribulation all the dealings of people will move from the use of credit cards to the use of a seal on the hand and on the forehead or this microchip. Whatever one wants to buy, all he will have to do is swipe his hand through a scanner, and the required sum of money will be deducted from his account. If a person does not submit and obey all that is asked of him in that new world system, then the Antichrist will mess his your chip and he will not be able to buy or sell: "[16]And he causeth all, both small and great, rich and poor, free and bond, to receive a mark in their right hand, or in their foreheads: [17] And that no man might buy or sell, save he that had the mark, or the name of the beast, or the number of his name" (Revelation 13:16-17). Such a person becomes like a robot without free will or liberty; or the Antichrist may remotely disrupt his microchip and thus control him via computers. In the Great Tribulation, man must not accept the microchip or else he will be doomed to hell: "[9]And the third angel followed them, saying with a loud voice, If any man worship the beast and his image, and receive his mark in his forehead, or in his hand, [10] The same shall drink of the wine of the wrath of God, which is poured out without mixture into the cup of his indignation; and he shall be tormented with fire and brimstone in the presence of the holy angels, and in the presence of the Lamb: [11] And the smoke of their torment ascendeth up for ever and ever: and they have no rest day nor night, who worship the beast and his image, and whosoever receiveth the mark of his name. [12] Here is the patience of the saints: here are they that keep the commandments of God, and the faith of Jesus" (Romans 14:9-12).

This will enhance the capability of the Antichrist to control people; and to persecute those who put their trust in Christ and bear the seal of the Lord Jesus: "Hurt not the earth, neither the sea, nor the trees, till we have sealed the servants of our God in their foreheads" (Revelation 7:3). With all deviousness, the Antichrist will put a mark like a cross or any such sign next to the name of every believer in the Lord Jesus. By so doing he will persecute them because they do not worship him, and he will make them the scum of the earth and the outcasts of the world.

To John the Beloved at the time of writing the book of Revelation, these things which he was beholding were as like a fantasy to him, but today they have become a reality to us who are in the world today and have begun to live and witness them.

We are at the doors of the rapture and Jesus is coming very soon for our deliverance! Our beloved Lord Jesus gives this declaration to John the Beloved to send comfort to our hearts, for all these things are for the good for the believers. Amen. Even so come Lord Jesus!

(9) "I John, who also am your brother, and companion in tribulation, and in the kingdom and patience of Jesus Christ, was in the isle that is called Patmos, for the word of God, and for the testimony of Jesus Christ."

- I John, who also am your brother - John introduces himself by saying that he is our brother. He is the brother of all believers in the Lord Jesus. The Lord Jesus says that we are all brethren in Christ. "But be not ye called Rabbi: for one is your Master, even Christ; and all ye are brethren" (Matthew

23:8). "We know that we have passed from death unto life, because we love the brethren. He that loveth not his brother abideth in death", "Hereby perceive we the love of God, because he laid down his life for us: and we ought to lay down our lives for the brethren" (1 John 14,16). "Behold, how good and how pleasant it is for brethren to dwell together in unity!" (Psalm 133:1).

Spiritual brotherhood in Christ is more sacred than physical blood brotherhood, for it is heavenly and eternal; not earthly temporal transient; as is the case with this passing world. Thus, we must be protective of the sanctity of this love for the brethren in the Lord Jesus Christ.

- And companion in tribulation - John says that he is our companion and our partner. As brethren in Christ, we share in bearing the sufferings of the persecutions for the name our Lord Jesus and his kingdom. For Jesus in the Bible tells us "Remember the word that I said unto you, The servant is not greater than his lord. If they have persecuted me, they will also persecute you; if they have kept my saying, they will keep yours also" (John 15:20). "Yea, and all that will live godly in Christ Jesus shall suffer persecution" (2 Timothy 3:12). If you do not suffer persecution, it is because you are not living for the Lord. Go visit and witness and persecution will begin.

- And in the kingdom and patience of Jesus Christ - If you are a faithful witness to Jesus, you will share in reign of the kingdom of Christ at the end of the great tribulation. It is the fruit of your patience for the sake of the kingdom. There is a direct correlation between patience and spiritual perception. One of the strongest incentives for striving and patience side by side with faithful brethren, is the hope of receiving the blessed promise given by the Lord Jesus Christ that we will reign with him. Thus Paul comforts Timothy, saying "If we suffer, we shall also reign with him" (2 Timothy 2:12). Paul also encourages Titus, saying "Looking for that blessed hope, and the glorious appearing of the great God and our Saviour Jesus Christ" (Titus 2:13).

And to the Hebrews, Paul says in affirmation "That by two immutable things, in which it was impossible for God to lie, we might have a strong consolation, who have fled for refuge to lay hold upon the hope set before us" (Hebrews 6:18).

- Was in the isle that is called Patmos, for the word of God, and for the testimony of Jesus Christ - Notice here that the Holy Spirit does not begin a new verse but continues the same verse 9. The phrase we are considering is firmly connected to the first part of verse 9 for it shows that John truly practices what he says to us: "Your brother, and companion in tribulation... in the isle that is called Patmos, for the word of God, and for the testimony of Jesus Christ." John loved the Lord Jesus and was faithful to him from the day he was converted to the last day of his life. He was faithful to the word of God and to the testimony of Jesus Christ when he wrote "In the beginning was the Word, and the Word was with God, and the Word was God. ... And the Word was made flesh, and dwelt among us, and we beheld his glory, the glory as of the only begotten of the Father, full of grace and truth." John continued to bear witness faithfully when he was the bishop of the church of Ephesus. Then the emperor Trajan boiled him in oil, but John did not die; so he removed him from the cauldron and exiled him to the island of Patmos. John was in his nineties when he faced this persecution! His whole life was characterized by love, faithfulness, patiently bearing trials, and spreading the message of the kingdom of Christ.

(10) "I was in the Spirit on the Lord's day, and heard behind me a great voice, as of a trumpet."

Note the setting we are now in. We are about to consider a personal dialogue between Jesus and John in the presence of the angel who will dictate to John what he should write.

- I was in the Spirit on the Lord's day - There is victory and triumph for those who want to live unto the Lord Jesus. John was vibrant in the Spirit when he was passing though these difficult circumstances. He was exiled alone on a Greek island named Patmos. The width of the island is three kilometres, and the length is ten kilometres as well. The island has no river and no agriculture. If a king or a ruler wanted to crush anyone, they would exile him to Patmos, an island that was not visited by anyone and in which there is was life.

Similarly, every person who takes a stand for the Lord Jesus will suffer persecution. The least that you will receive from others is derision and mocking. A life of consecration requires you to carry "your cross daily" and live for the Lord Jesus. "Your cross" represents "sacrifice" and "daily" or "every day" means perseverance.

The devil will fight you and try to stop you from reading the Bible and from praying. He will try to obstruct you from going to church. He will try to place before you matters that will captivate your thoughts and distract you from a commitment to Christian living. He will also try to entice you to cheat on your tithes and offering that you ought to put in your local church where Christ has placed you. These matters in themselves are trials in the flesh, but you can have spiritual victory in facing them. John was happy spiritually refreshed on Sunday, the Lord's day!

"Patmos" means "crushed". The lesson here is that even if you are crushed in your soul because of the problems of this life, learn always to rejoice in the Lord and in his day, and to renew strength like an eagle, from before his presence: "The law of the LORD is perfect, converting the soul" (Psalm 19:7); "they that wait upon the Lord shall renew their strength; they shall mount up with wings as eagles" (Isaiah 40:31). John was in the island of crushedness, but he was in the presence of the Lord sky high rejoicing in the spirit. The question is, are you in the Spirit on the Lord's day? Do you feel revival on the day of the

Lord? Do you feel a spiritual blessing on Sunday, the Lord's day?! Without offense I ask you: Do you feel glad on Saturday because tomorrow is Sunday, the Lord's day?!

- And heard behind me a great voice, as of a trumpet - This great and mighty voice is the voice of the Lord Jesus Christ. "The voice of the LORD is upon the waters: the God of glory thundereth: the LORD is upon many waters. The voice of the LORD is powerful; the voice of the LORD is full of majesty. The voice of the LORD breaketh the cedars; yea, the LORD breaketh the cedars of Lebanon. He maketh them also to skip like a calf; Lebanon and Sirion like a young unicorn. The voice of the LORD divideth the flames of fire. The voice of t he LORD shaketh the wilderness; the LORD shaketh the wilderness of Kadesh. The voice of the LORD maketh the hinds to calve, and discovereth the forests: and in his temple doth every one speak of his glory" (Psalm 29:3-9).

In spite of the fact that the voice of the Lord Jesus is mighty, yet that voice remains sweet and tender, more tender than that of many waters. As is said of the cherubimss: "And when they went, I heard the noise of their wings, like the noise of great waters, as the voice of the Almighty" (Ezekiel 1:24). "And his voice as the sound of many waters" (Revelation 1:15).

As he was in an exalted spiritual state, John heard the mighty, pure, and tender voice of the Lord Jesus!

The lesson here is that we should lose ourselves in the Lord Jesus on Sunday, the Lord's day, far from the concerns and problems of our daily lives. This is how we enjoy his presence and hear his voice.

(11) "Saying, I am Alpha and Omega, the first and the last: and, What thou seest, write in a book, and send it unto the seven churches which are in Asia; unto Ephesus, and unto Smyrna, and unto Pergamos, and unto Thyatira, and unto Sardis, and unto Philadelphia, and unto Laodicea."

- Saying, I am Alpha and Omega, the first and the last - Jesus is all in all as we previously noted in verse eight.

- What thou seest, write in a book, and send it unto the seven churches which are in Asia - The Lord Jesus directs his words to the churches in Asia minor, the center of the world at the time. He speaks of seven churches, seven being the number of divine perfection, as we have already explained in the introduction.

- Unto Ephesus, and unto Smyrna, and unto Pergamos, and unto Thyatira, and unto Sardis, and unto Philadelphia, and unto Laodicea - The names of these churches have meanings from which spiritual lessons can be drawn:

1- Ephesus = Desired
2- Smyrna = Bitter tribulation
3- Pergamos = Marriage
4- Thyatira = Theatrical acting
5- Sardis = Faithful remaining remnant
6- Philadelphia = Brotherly love
7- Laodecia = Rule of the people

The successive prophetic lessons are that the church age will develop as follows:

(i) Ephesus begins the age of preaching and of
spreading Christianity

(ii) That is followed by Christian martyrs in Smyrna, who experience the atrocities of the Roman persecution

(iii) King Constantine embraces the Christian religion, and the church marries the Roman state in Pergamos

(iv) So true Christianity weakens in the days of Jezebel in Thyatira

(v) A barely small faithful remnant remains in Sardis

(vi) The church of Philadelphia flourishes in her love for the Lord Jesus Christ and missionary work is revived

an age of a final spiritual awakening,

(vii) Finally, Christianity falls into a state of deep spiritual lukewarmness as a result of replacing Theocracy (the rule of God) with Democracy (the rule of the people).

(12) "And I turned to see the voice that spake with me. And being turned, I saw seven golden candlesticks."

- And I turned to see the voice that spake with me - John turned to see who was speaking with him from behind him. Lo and behold, he found himself in the presence of the Lord Jesus himself, the one on whose chest he leaned on the eve of the last supper. The Lord Jesus spoke to John from behind in order to prepare him with his blessed voice for the surprise that he was going to see Jesus in his greatness.

We too should be in the Spirit and expect declarations (that is, spiritual guidance) from him. We should turn to hear, and carefully heed, the voice of the Lord when he calls us, like the Holy Spirit says: "To day if ye will hear his voice, harden not your hearts" (Hebrews 3:15). The question today is, are you in a spiritual situation that allows you to hear the voice of the Lord Jesus when he speaks to you?

- And being turned, I saw seven golden candlesticks - When John turned around, he saw seven candlesticks made of gold that represented the seven churches, and their light shone and glittered like gold. The Lord Jesus considers every church a candlestick, and so every church should shine the light of Christ like a lighthouse in order to bring ships to the haven of safety. So is the role of the church in a world of spiritual darkness to bring people to Jesus. We must preach the soon return of the Lord Jesus. We must tell people that his coming back is at hand. Our mindset should always be that the coming of the Lord is nigh. Our motto and banner should always be "Amen. Even so, come Lord Jesus."

(13) "And in the midst of the seven candlesticks one like unto the Son of man, clothed with a garment down to the foot, and girt about the paps with a golden girdle."

This description is figurative and symbolic, presenting Jesus as the just Judge. In his first coming he wore a girdle about the waist is for service, as he did when he washed the feet of the disciples. Now, the same Lord Jesus wears a golden girdle around the chest as the heavenly, righteous, and just Judge.

(14) "His head and his hairs were white like wool, as white as snow; and his eyes were as a flame of fire."

- His head and his hairs were white like wool, as white as snow - His head speaks of his eternality, as well as his complete purity and holiness. Jesus is holy. Jesus is holy, Jesus is righteous; and his head and his hair shine with white light as they did on the Mount of Transfiguration: "And his face did shine as the sun, and his raiment was white as the light" (Matthew 17:2).

- And his eyes were as a flame of fire - The eyes of the Lord Jesus are examining and inspecting. When we, as God's people, sin, the Lord chastises us. He is the Good Shepherd. He is our Father. Every father who loves his children chastises them. "Thy rod and thy staff they comfort me" (Psalms 23:4). And the opposite is true as everyone who does not love his children does not chastise them. "He that spareth his rod hateth his son: but he that loveth him chasteneth him betimes" (Proverbs 13:24). "The rod and reproof give wisdom: but a child left to himself bringeth his mother to shame" (Proverbs 29:15). This is the principle which we will see the Lord Jesus applying in the midst of his seven churches in chapters 5 and 6.

(15) "And his feet like unto fine brass, as if they burned in a furnace; and his voice as the sound of many waters."

- And his feet like unto fine brass, as if they burned in a furnace - If the eyes of the Lord Jesus examine us God's people whom he loves and chastises us, how much more severity will be expected from him when he comes to this sinful world to bring judgment upon them. With regards to this same subject the Apostle Peter says: "For the time is come that judgment must begin at the house of God: and if it first begin at us, what shall the end be of them that obey not the gospel of God?" (1

Peter 4:17). Brass is the symbol of judgment, the judgment of Jesus on the world of the ungodly. This is what we will see Jesus doing to the sinful world in chapters 6 through 19.

- And his voice as the sound of many waters - The voice of the Lord Jesus is awesome, just as the voice of many waters has an awe to it.

(16) "And he had in his right hand seven stars: and out of his mouth went a sharp twoedged sword: and his countenance was as the sun shineth in his strength."

- And he had in his right hand seven stars - The seven stars are the pastors of the churches. We will explain the candlesticks and the stars in verse 20.

- And out of his mouth went a sharp two edged sword - The sword is the Word of God as we read in the Word of God: "And take the helmet of salvation, and the sword of the Spirit, which is the word of God" (Ephesians 6:17). The word of God is the words which proceed out of the mouth of Jesus; and by them are examined and judged the thoughts of believer and church: "For the word of God is quick, and powerful, and sharper than any two edged sword, piercing even to the dividing asunder of soul and spirit, and of the joints and marrow, and is a discerner of the thoughts and intents of the heart. Neither is there any creature that is not manifest in his sight: but all things are naked and opened unto the eyes of him with whom we have to do" (Hebrews 4:12-13). Jesus is called the Word of God: "In the beginning was the Word, and the Word was with God, and the Word was God", "And the Word was made flesh, and dwelt among us" (John 1:1, 14); "And he was clothed with a vesture dipped in blood: and his name is called The Word of God" (Revelation 19:13). The believer who loves the Lord Jesus reads the Word of God and studies it daily: "For thou hast magnified thy word above all thy name" (Psalms 138:2).

- And his countenance was as the sun shineth in his strength - The light of the face of the Lord Jesus is greater than the light of the sun as Paul the Apostle testifies: "At midday, O king, I saw in the way a light from heaven, above the brightness of the sun, shining round about me and them which journeyed with me. And when we were all fallen to the earth, I heard a voice speaking unto me, and saying in the Hebrew tongue, Saul, Saul, why persecutest thou me? it is hard for thee to kick against the pricks. And I said, Who art thou, Lord? And he said, I am Jesus whom thou persecutest" (Acts 26:13-15). The light of Jesus emits into us reverence, fear, respect, holiness, submission, and spiritual warmth when we come into his presence.

(17) "And when I saw him, I fell at his feet as dead. And he laid his right hand upon me, saying unto me, Fear not; I am the first and the last."

Before the greatness of Jesus, God's Son, the first and the last, no man can stand. This applies even to beloved ones, such as Daniel and Ezekiel who all shared this experience. "Then I lifted up mine eyes, and looked, and behold a certain man clothed in linen, whose loins were girded with fine gold of Uphaz: His body also was like the beryl, and his face as the appearance of lightning, and his eyes as lamps of fire, and his arms and his feet like in colour to polished brass, and the voice of his words like the voice of a multitude. Yet heard I the voice of his words: and when I heard the voice of his words, then was I in a deep sleep on my face, and my face toward the ground. And, behold, a hand touched me, which set me upon my knees and upon the palms of my hands. And he said unto me, O Daniel, a man greatly beloved, understand the words that I speak unto thee, and stand upright: for unto thee am I now sent. And when he had spoken this word unto me, I stood trembling" (Daniel 10:5-6, 9-11). Ezekiel had the same experience too. "This was the appearance of the likeness of the glory of the LORD. And when I saw it, I fell upon my face, and I heard a voice of one that spake" (Ezekiel 1:28).

John the Beloved fell to the ground on his face before the

greatness of Jesus even though he had passed through a similar experience on the Mount of Transfiguration. "And after six days Jesus taketh Peter, James, and John his brother, and bringeth them up into a high mountain apart, And was transfigured before them: and his face did shine as the sun, and his raiment was white as the light. And, behold, there appeared unto them Moses and Elias talking with him. Then answered Peter, and said unto Jesus, Lord, it is good for us to be here: if thou wilt, let us make here three tabernacles; one for thee, and one for Moses, and one for Elias. While he yet spake, behold, a bright cloud overshadowed them: and behold a voice out of the cloud, which said, This is my beloved Son, in whom I am well pleased; hear ye him. And when the disciples heard it, they fell on their face, and were sore afraid. And Jesus came and touched them, and said, Arise, and be not afraid" (Matthew 17:1-7). No creature made of dust can stand before the greatness of Jesus, the Lord God, the creator who is the beginning and the end of all things in the universe. "For in him we live, and move, and have our being" (Acts 17:28).

The day will come when all of creation, in heaven and on earth, will worship the Lord Jesus Christ forever. "And I beheld, and I heard the voice of many angels round about the throne and the beasts and the elders: and the number of them was ten thousand times ten thousand, and thousands of thousands; Saying with a loud voice, Worthy is the Lamb that was slain to receive power, and riches, and wisdom, and strength, and honour, and glory, and blessing. And every creature which is in heaven, and on the earth, and under the earth, and such as are in the sea, and all that are in them, heard I saying, Blessing, and honour, and glory, and power, be unto him that sitteth upon the throne, and unto the Lamb for ever and ever. And the four beasts said, Amen. And the four and twenty elders fell down and worshipped him that liveth for ever and ever." (Revelation 5:11-14). Today, when we go the house of the Lord, we actually enter into the presence of the Lord as the Bible says, "Serve the Lord with gladness: come before his presence with singing" (Psalms 100:2). We would be then in the presence of the Lord and he works with us through the indwelling of the Holy Spirit within us: "[17] And if he shall neglect to hear them, tell it unto the church: but if he neglect to hear the church....[20] For where two or three are gathered together in my name, there am I in the midst of them" (Matthew 18:17...20); "He that raised up Christ from the dead shall also quicken your mortal bodies by his Spirit that dwelleth in you" (Romans 8:11); "That good thing which was committed unto thee keep by the Holy Ghost which dwelleth in us" (2 Timothy 1:14).

(18) "I am he that liveth, and was dead; and, behold, I am alive for evermore, Amen; and have the keys of hell and of death."

- I am he that liveth, and was dead; and, behold, I am alive for evermore, Amen - Jesus is alive from eternity past to eternity future. The language and logic of this verse in the original Greek indicate that Jesus "became" dead, meaning that by his own choosing and by his own will, he died. He died, he arose, and he is alive forevermore. He is the eternal "I AM"!

- And have the keys of hell and of death - His resurrection from the dead gave him power over death and hell. "And declared to be the Son of God with power, according to the spirit of holiness, by the resurrection from the dead" (Romans 1:4).

Note the order of the verses, which is in harmony with the principle that the victory of the Lord Jesus over hell and death springs from his sacrifice of himself and his resurrection: "And they sung a new song, saying, Thou art worthy to take the book, and to open the seals thereof: for thou wast slain, and hast redeemed us to God by thy blood out of every kindred, and tongue, and people, and nation" (Revelation 5:9).

(19) "Write the things which thou hast seen, and the things which are, and the things which shall be hereafter."

- Write the things which thou hast seen - The glory of Christ and his greatness in the midst of the church, the world, and history.

- And the things which are. The age of the church.

- And the things which shall be hereafter. The tribulation, the millennium, and the eternal state.

(20) "The mystery of the seven stars which thou sawest in my right hand, and the seven golden candlesticks. The seven stars are the angels of the seven churches: and the seven candlesticks which thou sawest are the seven churches."

- The mystery of the seven stars which thou sawest in my right hand, and the seven golden candlesticks. The seven stars are the angels of the seven churches - Who are the seven angels? Are they really angels or are these angels symbols representing human beings? The answer is that the angels represent the bishops and pastors of the churches. Some of whom were chosen by Paul and Barnabas in Lystra, Lycaonia, and Antioch of Pisidia: "And when they had ordained them elders in every church, and had prayed with fasting, they commended them to the Lord, on whom they believed" (Acts 14:23); "And from Miletus he sent to Ephesus, and called the elders of the church" (Acts 20:17).

The Lord Jesus sent the twelve two by two, and he sent the seventy two by two. The apostles served two by two such as Peter and John, Paul and Barnabas, Paul and Silas, Paul and Timothy. In every church it is better to have more than one pastor for accountability and responsibility sharing.

Why do we say that the angels are pastors? Because in hermeneutics, the science of Biblical interpretation, we must compare spiritual things with spiritual. Here, it says candlestick and angel. However, the candlestick is not a candlestick but rather refers to a church. By the same token the same is true of the angel. So the angel here is not an angel but rather the pastor. Or senior pastor of every church in a concept similar to the "high priest" in the temple of God in the Old Testament. So we conclude that the angel here is not a literal angel, but is a person; which is the case on many occasions in the Bible: in Genesis Jacob said of Esau: "If now I have found grace in thy sight, then receive my present at my hand: for therefore I have seen thy face, as though I had seen the face of God" (Genesis 33:10); The Tekoite woman said to David: "For as an angel of God, so is my lord the king" (2 Samuel 14:17); Paul the Apostle said to the Galatians: "And my temptation which was in my flesh ye despised not, nor rejected; but received me as an angel of God, even as Christ Jesus" (Galatians 4:14). And regarding Stephen, the Word of God says: "And all that sat in the council, looking steadfastly on him, saw his face as it had been the face of an angel" (Acts 6:15).

The important lesson here is that the Lord Jesus deals with us through the church and through the pastor or pastoral staff of the church. The church and the church members are all in the right hand of the Lord. Take heed from the Word of the Lord: "For thy people are as they that strive with the priest" (Hosea 4:4).

- And the seven candlesticks which thou sawest are the seven churches - The Lord Jesus deals with us through the institution of the church. The Lord always looks upon the believers as individuals and as a church. Jesus said to Peter, "Thou art Peter, and upon this rock I will build my church" (Matthew 16:18); he did not say, I will build believers nor did he say, I will build my children, nor did he say, I will build my family. Rather, he said, "I will build my church" "This is he, that was in the church in the wilderness" (Acts 7:38); "Unto him be glory in the church" (Ephesians 3:21). We see Jesus walking in the midst of the churches. The text does not say that he walks in the midst of our houses, stores, schools, or workplaces. Rather, he walks in the midst of our churches. The Lord expects every individual to be converted, baptized, and a member of a church.

At home the believer meets the Lord every day; this is part of the priesthood of the believer. On Sunday, the day of the Lord, the believer meets the Lord at church as well (this is in addition to the daily individual and family meetings at home).

Jesus walks in the midst of the churches on Sunday and we see him proclaim the book of Revelation to John on a Sunday. Even in exile, John observed Sunday. Sunday the Lord's day is very important to the Lord Jesus, and it is important to all who love the Lord Jesus. When we meet in the name of the Lord Jesus, he comes among us. "But if he neglect to hear the church, let him be unto thee as an heathen man and a publican .... For where two or three are gathered together in my name, there am I in the midst of them" (Matthew 18:17,20). Jesus examines his children to see he who is present and he who is absent, he who is in a state of spiritual revival and he who carries the cares of this world and its thorns with him into the church.

The Holy Spirit speaks in this text not of one church but of seven churches in seven different cities in Asia Minor. He reveals to us the history of each church and its independence as a local church. Spiritually, we have neither a hierarchy nor a pyramidal structure. We do not have spiritual hegemony. We do not believe in interfering in the affairs of other churches. Rather, we believe that the Lord Jesus is the head of each church! Each church has its own existence and sovereignty. Jesus is the foundation and the founder of every local church. He is the head of every true, local, Christian church. So if any church is facing a problem or a concern, then that church, with fasting and prayer, should bring it to the Lord Jesus Christ. "Looking unto Jesus the author and finisher of our faith" (Hebrews 12:2).

It is interesting and delightful to read the book of Revelation and to see throughout it that Jesus is always ready to meet with his children. Jesus is truly alive and walks in the midst of his churches; and interacts with our lives and bestows his blessings on when we go to church. More importantly, we must come to church to see the beauty of the Lord and to worship him! He deserves all worship, prostration, and submission. He deserves our adoration as we gaze upon his beauty and majesty. "Holy, holy, holy, is the Lord of hosts: the whole earth is full of his glory" (Isaiah 6:3).

2
THE CHURCHES AT EPHESUS, SMYRNA, PERGAMOS, AND THYATIRA

John described in chapter one: what was. We now see him describing: What is, that is the church age; from the ascension of Christ to the day of the rapture. The history of Christianity passes through seven periods of time which are:

1- The church of Ephesus: 29 - 100 A.D.
2- The church of Smyrna: 100 - 313 A.D.
3- The church of Pergamos: 313 - 500 A.D.
4- The church of Thyatira: 500 - 1517 A.D.
5- The church of Sardis: 517 - 1648 A.D.
6- The church of Philadelphia: 1648 - 1945 A.D.
7- The church of Laodicea: 1945 - Current

The seven churches are representative. Each of these churches is first a representative (or picture) of the spiritual condition of different churches existing at the time of the writing of the book of Revelation. Second, each church represents an age of the seven successive ages which constitute the church age, the age of grace, the New Testament.

In each of these churches, we see that the Lord Jesus is the one who controls their affairs. He is the one who walks in the middle of every church. He examines each church if it is doing its duty in her utmost towards him or not? He directs each church in the right direction and he rebukes each church that deviates. Then, he promises reward that awaits each church that obeys his voice.

The association of Jesus with his church holds important spiritual lessons concerning the relationship between the Lord Jesus and his church today. Of these lessons is the relationship of the believer with the person of the Lord Jesus, and with the Bible. The focus is on the real, living, direct relationship with:

(a)The Name of Jesus, and

(b) The Word of Jesus which is the Bible.

Chapters 2 and 3 present a wealth and a depth of beautiful, spiritual material, which we delight in. For this reason we endeavor to study this book repeatedly to derive from it living spiritual lessons for our Christian lives today. Additionally, we receive the blessings that are promised to those who study this book: "Blessed is he that readeth, and they that hear the words of this prophecy, and keep those things which are written therein: for the time is at hand" (Revelation 1:3). So let us start meditating:

(1) "Unto the angel of the church of Ephesus write; These things saith he that holdeth the seven stars in his right hand, who walketh in the midst of the seven golden candlesticks."

These words are directed to the church of "Ephesus" which means "desired." The church age it represents goes from AD 29 to AD 100; that is, from the ascension of the Christ, to the death of John the Beloved, who was the longest-lived of the twelve apostles of Christ.

It is worth stating that each of these churches, with all its pastors. are as gold in the eyes of the great Shepherd of the sheep, the Lord Jesus. In spite of all our short comings and flaws and mistakes and weaknesses, Jesus does not see any blemish in us. Rather, we are pure like pure gold in Jesus estimation just like we see him wooing his church in the Song of Solomon saying: "Thou art all fair, my love; there is no spot in thee" (Song of Solomon 4:7). Jesus rises to our defense: "And the great dragon was cast out, that old serpent, called the Devil, and Satan, which deceiveth the whole world: he was cast out into the earth, and his angels were cast out with him. And I heard a loud voice saying in heaven, Now is come salvation, and strength, and the kingdom of our God, and the power of his Christ: for the accuser of our brethren is cast down, which accused them before our God day and night" (Revelation 12:9-10).

The most important point to make in this regard is that the messages found in Revelation 2 and 3 are directed towards real, born again converted Christian churches, and each is tightly bound to the Lord Jesus in a personal relationship. The traditional nominal Christian churches, who have adopted the adulterous worship of virgin Mary and the saints, have no place in the framework set forth in chapters two and three of the book of the Revelation of John the beloved apostle.

(2) "I know thy works, and thy labor, and thy patience, and how thou canst not bear them which are evil: and thou hast tried them which say they are apostles, and are not, and hast found them liars:"

Notice that these statements:

(i) "I know they works",

(ii) "To him that overcometh", and

(iii) "He that hath an ear, let him hear what the Spirit saith unto the churches";

These three remarks are repeatedly addressed by the Lord Jesus to each and every church of the seven churches. Each time he gives the church the counsel she needs, in accordance with her spiritual state. Since the Lord Jesus is the one who tries the hearts and the reins he knows each church's true problem. He is the one holding each church in his hand, and his eyes examine the inner being and the real motives. He is the healing physician who can cure every spiritual malady because he has the authority, dominion, and power. He is the Almighty who is able to correct situations.

The church of Ephesus was founded by Paul the Apostle, Aquila, Priscilla, and Apollos (Acts 18:18- 19:7). The church of Ephesus was very well known in Asia as it was the center of great spiritual activity and blessing and explosive growth the Christian Faith during the time when Paul was in the city. "And this continued by the space of two years; so that all they which dwelt in Asia heard the word of the Lord Jesus, both Jews and Greeks. And God wrought special miracles by the hands of Paul" (Acts 19:10-11). This led to the demise of the worship of the goddess Diana, also known as Artemis of the Ephesians.

Notice that because Paul the Apostle founded this church, he remained its primary spiritual leader even after he appointed local pastors at the time of his departure:"And from Miletus he sent to Ephesus, and called the elders of the church" (Acts 20:17).

Timothy also served in the church of Ephesus based on the directive of Paul: "As I besought thee to abide still at Ephesus, when I went into Macedonia, that thou mightest charge some that they teach no other doctrine" (1 Timothy 1:3). Then John the Beloved himself became pastor of the church of Ephesus which remained spiritually vibrant, and produced spiritual giants of Christianity like Trophimus the Ephesian: "they had seen before with him in the city Trophimus an Ephesian" (Acts 21:29).

The Lord Jesus knew well condition of the church at Ephesus because: "all things are naked and opened unto the eyes of him with whom we have to do" (Hebrews 4:13); so he says:

(3) "And hast borne, and hast patience, and for my name's sake hast labored, and hast not fainted."

The church of Ephesus was distinguished by the following:

(i) Sound doctrine,

(ii) Spiritual diligence,

(iii) Forbearance and patience,

(iv) Unwavering service,

(v) Rejection of evil,

(vi) Intolerance towards evil-doers,

(vii) Spiritual discernment,

(viii) Examining new proselytes to discover their true identity,

(ix) Following the path of the Lord Jesus in the life of

consecration. It is very important for us to have spiritual perseverance in our Christian walk. "Take up your cross" means to sacrifice; and "daily" means to do so with perseverance and persistence without fainting. Unfortunately, many do faint, behave shamefully, and exit the race. "Know ye not that they which run in a race run all, but one receiveth the prize? So run, that ye may obtain" (1 Corinthians 9:24). Even worse is the condition of: "Demas hath forsaken me, having loved this present world, and is departed unto Thessalonica" (2 Timothy 4:10). Or worse even are those described in: "For many walk, of whom I have told you often, and now tell you even weeping, that they are the enemies of the cross of Christ" (Philippians 3:18).

(4) "Nevertheless I have somewhat against thee, because thou hast left thy first love."

Ephesus means desired and loved. Yes, the church of Ephesus had the blessed Christian characteristics which Jesus desires of our churches today: hard work, patience, and love for Jesus. All these characteristics stem from a loving heart. Paul the Apostle in his letter to the Ephesians highlights the love that the church at Ephesus had for the Lord Jesus. In it, the word "love" is mentioned fourteen times and is repeatedly emphasized. "As I besought thee to abide still at Ephesus ... Now the end of the commandment is charity out of a pure heart, and of a good conscience, and of faith unfeigned" (1 Timothy 1:3-5).

Sadly, a slight coldness entered into the heart of the Church at Ephesus and so her love for Jesus somewhat laxed. This was a basic and essential spiritual problem that the Lord Jesus pointed out and counselled the church to treat. Thus is the case with many believers today who begin with great spiritual fervor, but after a while, their love for the Lord declines and wanes; as the devil enters in and starts messing up their spiritual lives with: "the lust of the flesh, and the lust of the eyes, and the pride of life, is not of the Father, but is of the world" (1 John 2:16). This is an important lesson and we out to heed well for the well being of our spiritual lives. This lesson is to keep Jesus first in our lives and prioritize him and give him the priority in our daily living. This will keep the flame of our first love for Jesus kindled.

(5) "Remember therefore from whence thou art fallen, and repent, and do the first works; or else I will come unto thee quickly, and will remove thy candlestick out of his place, except thou repent."

The Lord Jesus always has the solutions to your problems. These solutions consist of three stages. 1- Remember, 2- Repent, and 3- Work.

Every church, and this applies to individuals as well, should remember the day or the circumstances which drew it away from the love of the Lord. Remembering is not such a difficult task, and when the church remembers the reason, then three fourths of the problem is solved. All that is required at that point is a quick decision in heart and in the mind to return to the first love for the Lord Jesus. Jesus is a jealous God who demands our absolute love that we might be revived spiritually.

In this verse, Jesus, the true physician, gives us the proper prescription for our spiritual ailment: " do the first works", of which are:

1. Return to daily reading of the Bible.

(b) Return to fervent prayer life.

(c) Return to fasting.

(iv) Return to the love of the brethren – the simplest way to rekindle this love is to pray for your brethren individually by name.

(v) Return to testifying to the grace of Christ Jesus in your life. Tell about your personal experiences with Jesus in your life others will be attracted to him: "And I, if I be lifted up from the earth, will draw all men unto me" (John 12:32).

The Lord Jesus had previously counselled through Jeremiah. "Thus saith the LORD, Stand ye in the ways, and see, and ask for the old paths, where is the good way, and walk therein, and ye shall find rest for your souls. But they said, We will not walk therein" (Jeremiah 6:16). Stand, see, ask, and walk, and ye shall find. You will find spiritual rest. Walk in the way of the Lord and make your heart worship him; and not only your heart, but also your soul, your mind, and your strength; and you will be the winner.

The first two commandments, which summarize the entire Bible are: "And thou shalt love the Lord thy God with all thy heart, and with all thy soul, and with all thy mind, and with all thy strength: this is the first commandment. And the second is like, namely this, Thou shalt love thy neighbor as thyself. There is none other commandment greater than these" (Mark 12:30-31). Fearful is the threat of the Lord that he will remove your candlestick as he removed the candlestick of the church of Ephesus. The church of Ephesus continued for around five centuries. But if you go now to see this church in Turkey, you will find its debris and its walls. The Lord Jesus is jealous concerning his name, his church, and his children. Be faithful, so that your candlestick will not be removed. Many are the believers that we see in the world today who are shaken and unstable because they did not keep their first love for the Lord Jesus.

(6) "But this thou hast, that thou hatest the deeds of the Nicolaitans, which I also hate."

The word "Nicolai" means "the victory of the people" or "The victor of the people, or "loved by all". The Lord Jesus, and the church of Ephesus, hated the core of this teaching which focused on the will of the people above the word of God. This seed of teaching began to be planted in the early church and grew to fruition in the seventh church, Laodecia; and completely controlled it. The heart of the teaching of the Nicolaitans was that they believed in the existence of hierarchy within the church. This viewpoint prized worldly popularity regardless of a person's spiritual level. The church according to the Bible should be shepherded by a spiritual group of people, well-reported of regarding their words and deeds, under the theocracy of Christ. Theocracy comes from a Greek word "Theos" which means God and points to the rule of God. This is what the church of Ephesus practiced and so received the praise of Christ, for he hates the usurpation of authority in the church by carnal Christians.

(7) "He that hath an ear, let him hear what the Spirit saith unto the churches; To him that overcometh will I give to eat of the tree of life, which is in the midst of the paradise of God."

- He that hath an ear, let him hear what the Spirit saith unto the churches – In spite of the Lord's commendation to the church at Ephesus for their sound stance with regard to the teachings of the Nicolaitans; yet he also enjoined them to have hearts filled with the fervent first love. He tells them "he that hath an ear, let him hear" because there are many who hear and then turn a deaf ear to what they have heard.

- To him that overcometh will I give to eat of the tree of life, which is in the midst of the paradise of God - Adam and Eve did not eat of the tree of life for they were expelled from paradise after their fall into sin. "So he drove out the man; and he placed at the east of the garden of Eden Cherubimss, and a flaming sword which turned every way, to keep the way of the tree of life" (Genesis 3:24). But if you remain faithful to the Lord to the end, you overcome, and will return to your first friendship with the Lord Jesus in the garden of Eden, the paradise of God, and you will eat of the tree of life: "Blessed are they that do his commandments, that they may have right to the tree of life, and may enter in through the gates into the city" (Revelation 22:14).

These promises of special privileges await all those who overcome. "The sufferings of this present time are not worthy to be compared with the glory which shall be revealed in us" (Romans 8:18).

(8) "And unto the angel of the church in Smyrna write; These things saith the first and the last, which was dead, and is alive."

"Smyrna" means "bitter tribulation". This church represents the period from the 100 to 313 AD, the period from the death of John the Beloved, the last of Christ's twelve apostles, to the time when the Roman emperor Constantine embraced Christianity. Smyrna was a beautiful, rich, cultured city. The city remains to this day under the name of "Izmir" in Turkey and has a population of two hundred thousand people, of whom one third are Armenian Christians. It was around 35 miles north of Ephesus, and its population was comprised of Romans, Greeks, and Jews, most of whom were wicked. The Jews who lived there were among the greatest enemies of the Christians in the first century. The church of Smyrna suffered violent persecution at the hands of the Jews, the Greeks, and especially the Romans.

This verse gives comfort to the church of Smyrna in that Jesus "is alive" forever and is "the same yesterday, and to day, and for ever" (Hebrews 13:8). He is the one that says: "I am he that liveth, and was dead; and, behold, I am alive for evermore, Amen; and have the keys of hell and of death" (Revelation 1:18); and so the church at Smyrna is assured that they will overcome in the end, just like the Lord Jesus Christ overcame.

(9) "I know thy works, and tribulation, and poverty, (but

thou art rich) and I know the blasphemy of them which say they are Jews, and are not, but are the synagogue of Satan."

The church of Smyrna was suffering on two different fronts: an external earthly physical persecution, and internal problems arising from Christians who claimed that they were born again believing brethren while they really were children of darkness. Of such had spoken John the Beloved earlier: "They went out from us, but they were not of us; for if they had been of us, they would no doubt have continued with us: but they went out, that they might be made manifest that they were not all of us" (1 John 2:19). In spite of these challenges, the church of Smyrna remained faithful and spiritually rich for the Lord Jesus.

(10) "Fear none of those things which thou shalt suffer: behold, the devil shall cast some of you into prison, that ye may be tried; and ye shall have tribulation ten days: be thou faithful unto death, and I will give thee a crown of life" (Revelation 2:10).

- Fear none of those things which thou shalt suffer - It seems that the element of fear- specifically, the fear of death- had entered the hearts of the members of the church, and Jesus encourages them to be faithful.

- Behold, the devil shall cast some of you into prison, that ye may be tried; and ye shall have tribulation ten days - The source of every persecution is Satan, the enemy of souls. This is what happened historically, even started in the days of the church of Ephesus. Paul and Peter were martyred by Nero the Roman emperor. Gaius and Aristarchus the Macedonian, companions of Paul in travel and in bondage; and Erastus the treasurer of the city of Corinth, and many other heroes of the Christian Faith, were martyred at the hands of Nero. Even Ananias, who baptized Saul of Tarsus who became Paul the Apostle, when visiting the brethren in Rome, was martyred as well at the hands of Nero. In a similar vein, ten Roman emperors continued with the terrible persecution of Christians. They were bloodthirsty butchers in their persecution of Christ's church. Ignatius, the pastor of the church of Antioch, was taken to Rome by the Roman emperor Trajan for the express purpose of casting him to the lions there to tear up his flesh and eat him alive. Once Ignatius knew that he was going to be cast to the lions, he wrote a letter to the believers in Rome asking them not to intervene by asking for a pardon based on his advanced age because he was in his eighties; for it was his yearning to die a martyr for the Lord Jesus. What sublime faith, boldness, and love for the Lord Jesus, who tasted death on the cross for our sake and lived that we may live faithful to him.

After that, in one single day, ten thousand believers were martyred by crucifixion with crowns of thorns on their heads, and each one of them being pierced by a spear-thrust in imitation of Christ. As they were being crucified, these Christians sang with their loudest voices, and many of them were burned with grease and fire. And as the Roman soldiers were carrying out these orders, one of their centurions cried out with a loud voice saying, "Great is the God of these men" What a beautiful testimony for the most wonderful saviour: Jesus!

- Be thou faithful unto death, and I will give thee a crown of life - The Lord Jesus here encourages them, urging them to faithfulness unto death, which will lead to a crown that does not fade away. This crown will be the portion of all those whom heaven considers worthy of being martyrs for the Lord Jesus. From a heavenly perspective, it is great privilege when the Lord Jesus Christ allows a man to suffer a beating or to be a martyr and to receive an eternal crown as a reward for his faithfulness and his laying down his life for the name of JESUS; exactly as was the case with Peter and John who "Departed from the presence of the council, rejoicing that they were counted worthy to suffer shame for his name" (Acts 5:41).

(11) "He that hath an ear, let him hear what the Spirit saith

unto the churches; He that overcometh shall not be hurt of the second death."

The one who dies the first death belonging to the Lord Jesus will not see the spiritual death which is the second death for the wicked: "But the fearful, and unbelieving, and the abominable, and murderers, and whoremongers, and sorcerers, and idolaters, and all liars, shall have their part in the lake which burneth with fire and brimstone: which is the second death" (Revelation 21:8). The Lord's statement is highly encouraging to this church for he died for us, but is now alive. So, the members of the Smyrna church who were martyred for the name of Jesus will not die again but will live forever in heaven with him. The Bible teaches us that martyrdom is a heroic deed in heaven's eyes: "And they overcame him by the blood of the Lamb, and by the word of their testimony; and they loved not their lives unto the death" (Revelation 12:11).

Why did Jesus suffer and shed his blood? Why did Christianity prosper through the shed blood of the martyrs of Jesus? Why does the Lord Jesus allow the believer to suffer persecution and even martyrdom? Why should the ministry be watered with blood? It is because blood gives birth to spiritual life:

(i) Firstly, "the soul that sinneth, it shall die" (Ezekiel 18:4).

(ii) Secondly, "For the life of the flesh is in the blood for it is the blood that maketh an atonement for the soul." "For the blood is the life" (Leviticus 17:11; Deuteronomy 12:23).

(iii) Thirdly, "and without shedding of blood is no remission" (Hebrews 9:22). Blood gives birth to spiritual life. That is why when Paul the Apostle was

converted, the Lord Jesus said "I will shew him what great things he must suffer for my name's sake." The Christian life is a life of spiritual striving in reading the Bible, fasting, praying, witnessing, taking stands for the Lord Jesus, and enduring persecution. It culminates in martyrdom in watering the ministry with the blood of the martyrs during a spiritual drought so that souls will be saved! And the Lord Jesus is with us till the end: "and, lo, I am with you always, even unto the end of the world" (Matthew 28:20).

The Christian faith was founded on the blood of the Lord Jesus; and he allowed Christianity to prosper and grow being watered by the blood of the heroic martyrs. In the eyes of heaven, it is a tremendous privilege when a Christian ends his life as a martyr for the Lord Jesus Christ; for in that he will participate in a vital way in the salvation of the souls of men and the entire earth.

(12) "And to the angel of the church in Pergamos write; These things saith he which hath the sharp sword with two edges"

"Pergamos" means marriage. This church's represents the period from 313 to 500 AD, from the Emperor Constantine embracing Christianity to the beginning of the Middle Ages. Pergamos was a small city about 125 miles north of Ephesus, a 95 miles north of Smyrna. Its people were cultured, and it had a university.

Spiritually speaking and after the persecution that the Smyrna church faced, the Pergamos church enjoyed wide Christian prosperity especially after king Constantine embraced Christianity around the year 315 AD, thus ending the Roman persecution. Now the church is yoked to the world, so the Lord Jesus reminds her of the importance of purity. He demands purity based on the Bible, which is the Lord's two-edged sword.

(13) "I know thy works, and where thou dwellest, even where Satan's seat is: and thou holdest fast my name, and hast not denied my faith, even in those days wherein Antipas was my faithful martyr, who was slain among you, where Satan dwelleth."

At the beginning of the church of Ephesus we saw how it had "first love". Then the church of Smyrna suffered death for the name of the Lord Jesus. Now we see in the age of the church of Pergamos that Christianity flourishes and fills out the world. When Constantine embraced Christianity, the state married the church, and the church married the state, for crying out loud. This marriage made many heathen people embrace Christianity simply to please Emperor Constantine. At that time the pagan priests secretly practiced their pagan baal and idol worship by giving their practices a Christian cover. Their Christianity was a facade for the continued practice of their pagan rites. This practice lives on today in the nominal Christian churches, whether by way of dress uniforms or idols or vain rituals. Spiritual corruption began to dominate the outer framework of Christianity and most of the world became Christian, but in name only.

Thus Satan set his chair and sat on the throne of the Roman empire and the nominal traditional Christianity; and where he failed in his external assault on the Church, he resorted to attacking it from within. In history, the greatest number of Christians martyrs for Christ, around 40 million of them, suffered martyrdom at the hands of the nominal traditional Church.

Instead of attacking it like a roaring lion, Satan resorted to appearing like an angle of light, a wolf in sheep's clothing. "Be sober, be vigilant; because your adversary the devil, as a roaring lion, walketh about, seeking whom he may devour" (1 Peter 5:8). "And the great dragon was cast out, that old serpent, called the Devil, and Satan, which deceiveth the whole world: he was cast out into the earth, and his angels were cast out with him" (Revelation 12:9). "And no marvel; for Satan himself is transformed into an angel of light" (2 Corinthians 11:14).

As true Christians, we believe in a life of sanctification and separation from the world. We see the church of Pergamos holding fast to its faith despite the murder of Antipas, whose name means "against all". Antipas was a true separatist who was opposed to all, including carnal Christians, as the Apostle Paul and the Lord Jesus were. The Lord Jesus used to have meals with sinners so that he could have the opportunity to speak to them and heal them; however, he did not "walk" with them nor did he befriend anyone except the apostles and other dedicated Christians. He teaches us in his word saying, "Be ye not unequally yoked together with unbelievers: for what fellowship hath righteousness with unrighteousness? and what communion hath light with darkness? And what concord hath Christ with Belial? or what part hath he that believeth with an infidel?" (2 Corinthians 6:14-15); "Now I beseech you, brethren, mark them which cause divisions and offences contrary to the doctrine which ye have learned; and avoid them" (Romans 6:14-15); "And if any man obey not our word by this epistle, note that man, and have no company with him, that he may be ashamed. Yet count him not as an enemy, but admonish him as a brother" (2 Thessalonians 3:14-15).

Let us look at some examples of this. Abraham, a consecrated believer, separated himself from Lot, a carnal believer. Paul separated himself Barnabas because of John Mark, a believer who was weak in the front lines of missions. The Lord was angry with Jehoshaphat, a spiritual believer, because of his fellowship with Ahab, who was of the carnal kingdom of Israel. Nehemiah cast out the son of the great high priest Joiada because this son married the daughter of Sanballat the Horonite.

All of these are examples to us of the direct relationship between separation and a fruitful Christian life. Separation constitutes sanctification and leads to a life of holiness which, in turn, leads to blessings and fruitful soul winning. Jesus teaches us this principle in how he lived his own life. He kept away from any fellowship with sinners beyond that which afforded him the opportunity to win their souls. Jesus said: "And for their sakes I sanctify myself" (John 17:19) ; "For such an high priest became us, who is holy, harmless, undefiled, separate from sinners, and made higher than the heavens" (Hebrews 7:26); "Wherefore come out from among them, and be ye separate, saith the Lord" (2 Corinthians 6:17); Abraham said to Lot, "Separate thyself, I pray thee, from me" (Genesis 16:26); and Moses said to the Israelites, "Depart, I pray you, from the tents of these wicked men" (Numbers 16:26). Paul said: "But when divers were hardened, and believed not, but spake evil of that way before the multitude, he departed from them, and separated the disciples" (Acts 19:9). Separation and sanctification lead us to the strength and blessing of the Spirit of God: "He shall be a vessel unto honour, sanctified, and meet for the master's use" (2 Timothy 2:21); "Who hath saved us, and called us with an holy calling" (2 Timothy 1:9). "And purify unto himself a peculiar people" (Titus 2:14); "But ye are a chosen generation, a royal priesthood, an holy nation" (1 Peter 2:9); "Follow peace with all men, and holiness, without which no man shall see the Lord: Looking diligently lest any man fail of the grace of God; lest any root of bitterness springing up trouble you, and thereby many be defiled" (Hebrews 12:14-15).

Both the world and the carnal Christian defile and sadden the Holy Spirit who abides in the converted Christian. We should strive for the name of the Lord and not compromise with the world, a compromise that brings corruption into our lives and into the church. Antipas was against all and was lonely; it is the same for the person who is dedicated to, and loves Jesus. All may reject you, but the Lord Jesus will praise you!

(14) "But I have a few things against thee, because thou hast there them that hold the doctrine of Balaam, who taught Balac to cast a stumblingblock before the children of Israel, to eat things sacrificed unto idols, and to commit fornication."

Balaam was a very wicked man for he was a sorcerer who loved money without the love of God. He used religion and sorcery and witchcraft for profit and personal gain: "There shall not be found among you any one that maketh his son or his daughter to pass through the fire, or that useth divination, or an observer of times, or an enchanter, or a witch. Or a charmer, or a consulter with familiar spirits, or a wizard, or a necromancer. For all that do these things are an abomination unto the Lord" (Deuteronomy 18:10-12).

Balaam taught Balac to make the Israelites intermarry with the Moabites. In so doing, the Israelites lost their separation, and the worship of idols infected them deeply, which would anger God and bring judgment and death. The situation in the church of Pergamos was similar, where there were people who wanted to accommodate nominal Christianity. This type of compromise is a great evil which the Lord Jesus warns us of. It is forbidden for a child of the Lord, a believer, to marry an unbeliever. This was the very cause for Noah' flood; God's wrath as a result of the intermarriage of his children with the daughters of men: "That the sons of God saw the daughters of men that they were fair; and they took them wives of all which they chose" (Genesis 6:2). The believer brings upon himself God's anger when he marries a woman who does not believe in the Lord Jesus as her personal Lord and Saviour.

(15) "So hast thou also them that hold the doctrine of the Nicolaitans, which thing I hate."

The Lord Jesus hates hierarchy in the church, which is the teaching of the Nicolaitans about religious hierarchies and about democracy in the congregation of the believers. This teaching opposes the God-centered theocracy. Note that the Nicolaitan's teachings continued to grow in the true church, even today.

This doctrine was planted in the church of Ephesus. It continues to grow, and it will reach the pinnacle of its glory in the last church, the church of Laodecia.

(16) "Repent; or else I will come unto thee quickly, and will fight against them with the sword of my mouth."

The authority of Jesus to in our fight is his Word, the sword of the Spirit that teaches us that we are all brothers and there is no place for religious hierarchies. The church does not conduct itself according to the viewpoint of the majority but according to the Word of God. For instance, suppose that a church decides, by majority vote, to elect a woman as pastor. This is an evil deed, since it is opposed to God's word, which says that a pastor should be a man. "A bishop then must be blameless, the husband of one wife", that is, a man. None of Christ's twelve apostles was a woman.

(17) "He that hath an ear, let him hear what the Spirit saith unto the churches; To him that overcometh will I give to eat of the hidden manna, and will give him a white stone, and in the stone a new name written, which no man knoweth saving he that receiveth it."

Everyone who is like Antipas and overcomes in the name of the Lord Jesus Christ, will receive blessings and spiritual rewards. The first of these rewards is the Heavenly Manna, the joy we derive from the Bible. This manna, which the Israelites ate in the wilderness, tasted like: "wafers made with honey" (Exodus 16:31), and "fresh oil" (Numbers 11:8).

We learn from this Heavenly Manna, the Bible, some important lessons:

(i) It is the Lord Jesus who always supplies our needs.

(ii) We learn to depend on him daily.

(iii) We learn the importance of obedience to Jesus and his commandments.

(iv) At the end of the day, we learn that Jesus is faithful to the end, just as he was until he entered the people into Canaan.

(v) We learn how good Jesus is: "O taste and see that the Lord is good: blessed is the man that trusteth in him" (Psalms 34:8).

In the New Testament, Jesus used manna as an illustration of the living bread, who is the Lord Jesus himself. The portion of the faithful believer is the sweetest portion; it is Jesus himself. When we get to Heaven, each faithful Christian will receive a stone on which is written a name which describes his special, personal relationship with Jesus. What an honour it is that each of us true Christians should have a personal privileged relationship with the Lord Jesus, Lord of Glory, Lord of Heaven and Earth and the Universe!

(18) "And unto the angel of the church in Thyatira write; These things saith the Son of God, who hath his eyes like unto a flame of fire, and his feet are like fine brass."

- And unto the angel of the church in Thyatira write - "Thyatira" means "theater". The church represents the period from 50-0 to 1517 AD, from the beginning of the middle ages to the reformation of Martin Luther.

Located in Asia, Thyatira was a very prosperous city. It was founded by Alexander the Great upon his return from his great victory over the Persians in 331 B.C. Thyatira was a small but very rich city. It was surrounded by fertile, agricultural ground and had a prosperous dyeing industry. Acts 16:14 tells us that Lydia, the seller of purple, was from Thyatira.

The church of Thyatira represents the fourth age in the history of the church. This period, from 500 to 1500 AD, is known as the Middle Ages. It is also referred to as the Dark Ages because it was characterized then by the spiritual darkness and violent oppression of the nominal Christian church over the true believing Christian church.

There is no doubt that the role of women in Thyatira was strong; women like Lydia and Jezebel were prominent. Lydia's role was positive and constructive in the founding of the church of Philippi while Jezebel's role was negative and destructive. Jezebel was an unknown person in the history of the church. She might have been the wife of one of the pastors of the church, or she might have been a strong-willed woman who emerged within the church. Jezebel may have been her real name, or it may have been used to liken her to Jezebel of the Old Testament, who was the daughter of Ethbaal, king of the Sidonians, and the wife of Ahab, the evil king of Israel. She was a very wicked woman who was steeped in the worship of Baal. It could be that because of that, Jesus speaks to Thyatira more severely than to the other churches, causing John to see the Lord Jesus as a stern strong judge.

- These things saith the Son of God. "For the Father judgeth no man, but hath committed all judgment unto the Son" (John 5:22).

- Who hath his eyes like unto a flame of fire - His eyes examine and test human beings: "The Lord is in his holy temple, the Lord's throne is in heaven: his eyes behold, his eyelids try, the children of men. The Lord trieth the righteous" (Psalms 11:4-5); "That the trial of your faith, being much more precious than of gold that perisheth, though it be tried with fire, might be found unto praise and honour and glory at the appearing of Jesus Christ" (1 Peter 1:7).

- And his feet are like fine brass - Brass is the symbol of judgment in the temple: "Thou shalt make an altar ... and thou shalt overlay it with brass" (Exodus 27:1-2). Jesus judges and condemns all who betray him: "Whom have I in heaven but thee? and there is none upon earth that I desire beside thee ... thou hast destroyed all them that go a whoring from thee" (Psalms 73:25-27).

(19) "I know thy works, and charity, and service, and faith, and thy patience, and thy works; and the last [to be] more than the first."

This church had Christian qualities similar to those of the church of Ephesus such as works, patience, labor, and love.

(20) "Notwithstanding I have a few things against thee, because thou sufferest that woman Jezebel, which calleth herself

a prophetess, to teach and to seduce my servants to commit fornication, and to eat things sacrificed unto idols."

But the members of the Thyatiran church practiced a great sin by accommodating the people of world in their celebrations of worship to the idols and images and statues. As we saw previously in this chapter, the Lord demands of us to be separate and isolation and a live a life of holiness far removed from any compromise at the expense of our testimony for the Lord.

In the days of Ahab, Jezebel attempted to mix the worship of idols with the worship of the Lord. She killed many of the Lord's faithful prophets and she tried, assiduously, to kill Elijah the Tishbite, the great prophet. Jezebel has always been a symbol of spiritual corruption, spiritual adultery, and spiritual debauchery. She vehemently opposed the Word of God, which commands sanctification by separation. Sanctification requires separation between the worship of God and isolation from the worship of idols; between the spiritual world and the world of the flesh; the world of the Lord Jesus Christ and the world of Satan. Jezebel's end was that as a result of her wickedness, the Lord judged her and she died like a dog and the dogs ate her flesh: "This is the word of the Lord, which he spake by his servant Elijah the Tishbite, saying, In the portion of Jezreel shall dogs eat the flesh of Jezebel" (2 Kings 9:36).

The teaching of Jezebel emerged in the church of Thyatira. This teaching espouses compromise at the expense of the Lord as it seeks to unite all denominations. It is worth noting that idols are not always of stone or wood, neither are they necessarily of a physical image. An idol is anything which stands between you and the Lord Jesus. Your idol could be your work, your house, or your car; anything that distracts you or keeps you from worshipping and serving our Lord Jesus Christ.

(21) "And I gave her space to repent of her fornication; and she repented not."

O the greatness of the meekness and gentleness of the Lord

Jesus who gave Jezebel a chance to be pure and loyal to him, and to return to him. There is nothing more difficult than stubbornness. When coldness creeps into the heart and the believer's love for Jesus grows weak; the believer becomes infected with rebellion, mutiny, and an insistence on sin. The Lord knows whether the rudder of your life is pointed towards him, as was the case with Abraham, or away from him, as was the case with Lot. The Lord Jesus asks you to repent and return to him.

(22) "Behold, I will cast her into a bed, and them that commit adultery with her into great tribulation, except they repent of their deeds."

In case there is no repentance, the penalty of the Lord begins. Then the Lord Jesus begins to chastising: "For this cause many are weak and sickly among you" (1 Corinthians 11:30).

(23) "And I will kill her children with death; and all the churches shall know that I am he which searcheth the reins and hearts: and I will give unto every one of you according to your works."

The devil tries to trick you into compromising with others on your stands and tries to blind you from observing positional and doctrinal differences. In the end, he destroys your testimony for the Lord and damaging the spiritual lives of your wife and children who are your responsibility: "But the seventh day is the sabbath of the Lord thy God: in it thou shalt not do any work, thou, nor thy son, nor thy daughter, thy manservant, nor thy maidservant, nor thy cattle, nor thy stranger that is within thy gates" (Exodus 20:10); "thou mightest fear the LORD thy God, to keep all his statutes and his commandments, which I command thee, thou, and thy son, and thy son's son" (Deuteronomy 6:2); "For if we would judge ourselves, we should not be judged. But when we are judged, we are chastened of the Lord, that we should not be condemned with the world." (1 Corinthians 11:31-32); "For the time is come that judgment must begin at the house of God: and if it first begin at us, what shall the end be of them that obey not the gospel of God?" (1 Peter 4:17).

(24) "But unto you I say, and unto the rest in Thyatira, as many as have not this doctrine, and which have not known the depths of Satan, as they speak; I will put upon you none other burden."

- But unto you I say, and unto the rest in Thyatira, as many as have not this doctrine - The Lord Jesus in his earthly ministry, as on the Bible, always calls us to a life of separation and dissociation from the world and of consecration to him and him alone: "And for their sakes I sanctify myself, that they also might be sanctified through the truth" (John 17:19); "Be ye not unequally yoked together with unbelievers: for what fellowship hath righteousness with unrighteousness? and what communion hath light with darkness? And what concord hath Christ with Belial? or what part hath he that believeth with an infidel? And what agreement hath the temple of God with idols? for ye are the temple of the living God; as God hath said, I will dwell in them, and walk in them; and I will be their God, and they shall be my people. Wherefore come out from among them, and be ye separate, saith the Lord, and touch not the unclean thing; and I will receive you, And will be a Father unto you, and ye shall be my sons and daughters, saith the Lord Almighty" (2 Corinthians 6:14-18): "separate from sinners, and made higher than the heavens" (Hebrews 7:26).

Calling on the names of the saints is spiritual adultery. Calling on the name of Mary and referring to her as "the mother of God" or as "mediator", is spiritual adultery. The use of the name of any god other than Jesus, the Son of God, is spiritual idolatry. Your friendship with those who practice such worshipping and your participation in their traditional rituals is spiritual adultery; and the Lord will make you pay a high price for the sin of apostating from him: "Their sorrows shall be multiplied that hasten after another god"; "thou hast destroyed all them that go a whoring from thee" (Psalm 16:4; 73:27). You and your children will receive a severe punishment from the Lord Jesus like says to the church of Thyatira in v.23, that he will kill her children with death.

- And which have not known the depths of Satan, as they speak -What is the depth of Satan? The depth of Satan is the accommodation of religions and false denominations that have no solution for the problem of man's sins; for there is no remission of sins and no salvation without the blood of Jesus. Salvation is only in Jesus. If you do not witness to them of the wonderful salvation of Jesus, then it is as if you are casting them into the depths of the devil's hell.

- I will put upon you none other burden - The Lord Jesus does not ask much of us. He only asks of us a life of purity and testimony to him.

(25) "But that which ye have already hold fast till I come."

Persevere in the life of holiness and in soul winning till the end of your life; or until Jesus returns.

(26) "And he that overcometh, and keepeth my works unto the end, to him will I give power over the nations."

The Lord Jesus says that if you remain faithful all your life in sanctification and holiness and soul winning, then you will reign with him over the entire world. Such were the words of consolation which Paul shared with Timothy: "Therefore I endure all things for the elect's sakes, that they may also obtain the salvation which is in Christ Jesus with eternal glory. It is a faithful saying: For if we be dead with him, we shall also live with him: If we suffer, we shall also reign with him: if we deny him, he also will deny us" (2 Timothy 2:10-12).

(27) "And he shall rule them with a rod of iron; as the vessels of a potter shall they be broken to shivers: even as I received of my Father."

This is the promise of the Father to the Son, and it is also the promise of the Son to us: "Ask of me, and I shall give thee the heathen for thine inheritance, and the uttermost parts of the earth for thy possession. Thou shalt break them with a rod of iron; thou shalt dash them in pieces like a potter's vessel" (Psalm 2:8-9). We shall reign over the whole world and rule over the nations with Christ in his kingdom.

(28) "And I will give him the morning star."

Who is the bright and morning star? Jesus!: "I am the root and the offspring of David, and the bright and morning star" (Revelation 22:16). The greatest gift is Jesus. Jesus is greater person in the world and history and eternity. Jesus is greater than the whole universe. He is the "desire of all nations" (Haggai 2:7); the "treasure hid in a field" (Matthew 13:44); the "pearl of great price" (Matthew 13:46); he is "the Son of God" (1 John 5:5), and we will be with him forever in a "world without end" (Ephesians 3:21).

(29) "He that hath an ear, let him hear what the Spirit saith unto the churches."

Not all understand these things, and that is why Jesus calls attention to this matter. Every person has ears but the question is, are you a hearer or have you stopped your ears from hearing? The Lord is trying to obtain an answer from you whether you are going to work according to these words or not? Will you live a life of consecration and holiness or not? Will you live a life of service the brings lost souls to Jesus: "And he said to them all, If any man will come after me, let him deny himself, and take up his cross daily, and follow me" (Luke 9:23). The Word of God counsels us to: "put ye on the Lord Jesus Christ" (Romans 13:14); and as Paul the apostle affirms: "Be ye followers of me, even as I also am of Christ" (1 Corinthians 11:1)!

3
THE CHURCHES AT SARDIS, PHILADELPHIA, AND LAODECIA

(1) "And unto the angel of the church in Sardis write; These things saith he that hath the seven Spirits of God, and the seven stars; I know thy works, that thou hast a name that thou livest, and art dead" (Revelation 3:1).

- And unto the angel of the church in Sardis write - Sardis means "Faithful remaining remnant" and it represents the period from 1517 to 1648 AD; from the time of Martin Luther's reformation to the age of the wide spreading of the KJV Bible and revival of missionary work. Sardis was a prosperous city in Asia Minor that served as a link between the east and the west. Today, Sardis is a small village in Turkey known by the name "Sart".

- These things saith he that hath the seven Spirits of God, and the seven stars - How glorious are these words! Jesus is the Son of God and the Son of Man. He is the central link between God and man, and between heaven and earth.

- I know thy works, that thou hast a name that thou livest, and art dead – Thus because he is this central link between the spiritual and the physical, he is the one capable of examining the hidden and inner reality of the church; that although it might appear to be alive and active, yet its heart is cold having lost the first love.

Sometimes we see that some church members are outwardly active and appear to be spiritually enthused, but their hearts would be cold in their love towards the Lord Jesus. Their relationship the Lord Jesus is tenuous; he who is able to examine the hearts of men and know the true motives of each individual, no matter what their outward visible level of spiritual activity is. If your heart is not warm towards the Lord, then external appearances will pass away and you will become without fruit for him. For everything there is a foundation; and if the foundation is not in the heart, then fruit will fade away. This was the case with the church at Sardis.

(2) "Be watchful, and strengthen the things which remain, that are ready to die: for I have not found thy works perfect before God" (Revelation 3:2).

- Be watchful - There is an Arabic proverb which says "He who seeks the highest should study till late at night." This saying is true. Any person who desires to be successful in his ministry and his spiritual life, must pour time and effort into reading God's Word and meditating on God's Word with prayer and fasting.

- Strengthen the things which remain - Be a blessing to others and stir them up. Encourage them to persevere in witnessing and in living for the Lord Jesus.

- That are ready to die - This small faithful remnant's testimony will eventually be extinguished if there is no spiritual awakening in the church.

- For I have not found thy works perfect before God. The Lord is not pleased; and if the church is demised then the fault and burden of responsibility falls on the pastor and the church leadership.

(3) "Remember therefore how thou hast received and heard, and hold fast, and repent. If therefore thou shalt not watch, I will come on thee as a thief, and thou shalt not know what hour I will come upon thee".

The pastor and the church must return to their former level of spiritual consecration in fasting and prayer; they must persevere in witnessing and preaching and soul winning. The Lord Jesus examines the pastor of the church, represented symbolically as the star and after examining concluded that its members appear to be alive but are almost dead spiritually. They need a spiritual awakening in drawing back near to the Lord.

Why don't Christians run to the Lord Jesus Christ at all times? It is because they have inner emptiness in that he occupies a small corner of their hearts, and the rest is filled with the world. We must strive, along with the Lord, for him to fill every corner of our hearts. The Lord Jesus teaches us that, though we are in the world, we are not of the world: "I have given them thy word; and the world hath hated them, because they are not of the world, even as I am not of the world. I pray not that thou shouldest take them out of the world, but that thou shouldest keep them from the evil. They are not of the world, even as I am not of the world." (John 17:14-16).

The greatest enemy of the believer is the world. Why? Because the believer cannot love the Lord and love the world. The Holy Spirit advises us: "Love not the world, neither the things that are in the world. If any man love the world, the love of the Father is not in him. For all that is in the world, the lust of the flesh, and the lust of the eyes, and the pride of life, is not of the Father, but is of the world. And the world passeth away, and the lust thereof: but he that doeth the will of God abideth for ever." (1 John 2:15-17). From the dawn of history to this day, this has been the problem of man: "And when the woman saw that the tree was good for food, and that it was pleasant to the eyes, and a tree to be desired to make one wise, she took of the fruit thereof, and did eat, and gave also unto her husband with her; and he did eat" (Genesis 3:6). Eve fell into the very first sin when she saw that the tree was good for food (lust of the flesh), was pleasant to the eyes (lust of the eyes), and was a tree to be desired to make one wise (pride of life). She ate of the tree, she fell, and Adam fell with her. And we still suffer from the same enticements and lures of the world. There is a spiritual war raging inside us against the whims of the flesh. From the moment of spiritual birth, this spiritual struggle begins!

Jesus faced these three temptations when: "the tempter came to him" (Matthew 4:3); and Jesus was victorious over the devil in all three respects:

(i) The lust of the flesh: "If thou be the Son of God, command that these stones be made bread"; Jesus answered "It is written, Man shall not live by bread alone, but by every word that proceedeth out of the mouth of God".

(ii) The lust of the eyes: from the pinnacle of the temple, "If thou be the Son of God, cast thyself down: for it is written, He shall give his angels charge concerning thee: and in their hands they shall bear thee up, lest at any time thou dash thy foot against a stone."; "Jesus said unto him, It is written again, Thou shalt not tempt the Lord thy God";

(iii) The pride of life: "All the kingdoms of the world, and the glory of them; ...will I give thee, if thou wilt fall down and worship me"; "Then saith Jesus unto him, Get thee hence, Satan: for it is written, Thou shalt worship the Lord thy God, and him only shalt thou serve" (Matthew 4:1-10).

Jesus defeated the devil and had victory over him, and only Jesus can give us victory because he says, "For without me ye can do nothing." (John 15:5). Paul the Apostle experienced this when he said, "I can do all things through Christ which strengtheneth me" (Philippians 4:13). It is asked of us to live a life of dependence on the Lord Jesus that we may always be victorious over the desires of the flesh.

(4) "Thou hast a few names even in Sardis which have not defiled their garments; and they shall walk with me in white: for they are worthy" (Revelation 3:4).

We thank the Lord that there were a few members in Sardis who were living a life of consecration and holiness. With these, the Lord is very pleased. We must not be defiled with the people of the world; and as a reward, we will wear white clothes too, for we will inherit with Christ.

The Christian life is a life of striving and perseverance, a life in which we should continue to the very end. Every believer is required to have stamina to the very end. Everyone is required to strive and to strive lawfully according to the rules. Salvation and entrance into heaven is by the Blood of Christ. But it is consecration that secures us the crowns, prizes, rewards, treasures and reign with Christ in the kingdom. All these rewards are the lot of:

(i) Faithful soldiers: "Thou therefore endure hardness, as a good soldier of Jesus Christ. No man that warreth entangleth himself with the affairs of this life; that he may please him who hath chosen him to be a soldier. And if a man also strive for masteries, yet is he not crowned, except he strive lawfully" (2 Timothy 2:3-5);

(ii) Sowers and plowers who farm and labor hard in the fields: "Behold, there went out a sower to sow" (Mark 4:3); "The husbandman that laboureth must be first partaker of the fruits" (2 Timothy 2:6);

(iii) The runner who perseveres and completes the race: "Know ye not that they which run in a race run all,

but one receiveth the prize? So run, that ye may obtain. And every man that striveth for the mastery is temperate in all things. Now they do it to obtain a corruptible crown; but we an incorruptible" (1 Corinthians 9:24-25). The crowning is for those who run; for we shall walk with Jesus in the procession of the victors and reign with him over the entire world.

This is the portion of everyone who overcomes spiritual weakness, watches after and strengthens others, walks in the path of piety, and wins souls. Not only will he receive eternal life, but he will also receive rewards before God before angels and before the assembly of saints in the kingdom: "Whosoever therefore shall confess me before men, him will I confess also before my Father which is in heaven" (Matthew 10:32); "Also I say unto you, Whosoever shall confess me before men, him shall the Son of man also confess before the angels of God" (Luke 8:12). Paul says to Timothy, "It is a faithful saying: For if we be dead with him, we shall also live with him: If we suffer, we shall also reign with him: if we deny him, he also will deny us: If we believe not, yet he abideth faithful: he cannot deny himself" (2 Timothy 2:11-13).

(5) "He that overcometh, the same shall be clothed in white raiment; and I will not blot out his name out of the book of life, but I will confess his name before my Father, and before his angels."

This is a difficult verse to interpret, but I will try my best. Our God is a God or management and organization. Every human being who is born is numbered in the depths of the earth. For instance, Adam 1, Eve 2, Cain 3, Abel 4, and so on with regard to the billions of people who have been created up to this day; for the Bible says: "My substance was not hid from thee, when I was made in secret, and curiously wrought in the lowest parts of the earth" (Psalm 139:15). At the moment of fertilization, a human being is born and is recorded in the book of the living. When a man dies, his name is erased from the book of the living and is recorded in the book of the dead: "Yet now, if thou wilt forgive their sin; and if not, blot me, I pray thee, out of thy book which thou hast written. And the LORD said unto Moses, Whosoever hath sinned against me, him will I blot out of my book" (Exodus 32:32-33). The name of the person who experiences the salvation of Jesus Christ is written in the book of the Lamb, though this name, in God's knowledge, is written there from the foundation of the world. "And all that dwell upon the earth shall worship him (the Antichrist), whose names are not written in the book of life of the Lamb slain from the foundation of the world" (Revelation 13:8). "And the books were opened: and another book was opened, which is the book of life"; "And there shall in no wise enter into it any thing that defileth, neither whatsoever worketh abomination, or maketh a lie: but they which are written in the Lamb's book of life" (Revelation 20:12; 21:27). In heaven there are books and one of them is called the "Book of Life" which Paul and other believers were aware of: "And I intreat thee also, true yokefellow – Silas, from Acts 15:40; & 16:19 – help those women which laboured with me in the gospel, with Clement also, and with other my fellowlabourers, whose names are in the book of life" (Philippians 4:3).

When a converted Christian dies, his name is erased from the book of the living; and is confirmed in the Book of the Lamb. He goes on from life to life. The person who has Jesus in his heart does not see death, but is translated to heaven; because his sins have been washed away by the blood of Christ. So to him absence from the body is presence with the Lord: "We are confident, I say, and willing rather to be absent from the body, and to be present with the Lord" (2 Corinthians 5:8). Such a Christian does not see death for his soul ascends into the presence of the Lord Jesus; but his body sleeps temporarily until Christ returns for him. Then the Holy Spirit who raised Jesus from the dead will raise our bodies to eternal life: "But if the Spirit of him that raised up Jesus from the dead dwell in you, he that raised up Christ from the dead shall also quicken your mortal bodies by his Spirit that dwelleth in you" (Romans 8:11); "For this we say unto you by the word of the Lord, that we which are alive and remain unto the coming of the Lord shall not prevent them which are asleep. For the Lord himself shall descend from heaven with a shout, with the voice of the archangel, and with the trump of God: and the dead in Christ shall rise first: Then we which are alive and remain shall be caught up together with them in the clouds, to meet the Lord in the air: and so shall we ever be with the Lord. Wherefore comfort one another with these words." (1 Thessalonians 4:15-18). When the believer departs this earth, the Lord Jesus confirms his name in the book of the Lamb; but the man that is without Christ has his name erased from the book of the living and written in the book of the second death.

(6) "He that hath an ear, let him hear what the Spirit saith unto the churches."

Repetition helps in the teaching of those who are mentally slow. The Lord Jesus urges us repeatedly to read and listen, meditate, and then implement what we read. He is the one who led James to write "But be ye doers of the word, and not hearers only, deceiving your own selves" (James 1:22). If you are not living for the Lord then you are deceiving yourself. The Lord knows, sees, examines, and will bring into account, as he did with Israel in the days of Jeremiah who warned them saying: "For ye dissembled in your hearts, when ye sent me unto the LORD your God, saying, Pray for us unto the LORD our God; and according unto all that the LORD our God shall say, so declare unto us, and we will do it" (Jeremiah 42:20). The people did not heed, and consequently lost badly.

(7) "And to the angel of the church in Philadelphia write; These things saith he that is holy, he that is true, he that hath the key of David, he that openeth, and no man shutteth; and shutteth, and no man openeth."

- And to the angel of the church in Philadelphia write - Philadelphia means "brotherly love". This church represents the period from 1648 to 1945 A.D. These years were characterized by revival, the flourishing of missionary work, and a revolution in thoughts and ideas which led to changes in moral, religious, musical, social, and democratic political values.

Philadelphia was located in Turkey to the southeast of Sardis in an area known for volcanoes and earthquakes; an area which had experienced its most recent earthquake in 17 A.D. As a result, the region of Philadelphia was famous for its wheat harvests. It was therefore natural for the inhabitants of Philadelphia and its vicinity to worship the god of wheat, Dionysius. This god's name appears in the Bible through his namesake, Dionysius the Areopagite, who became a Christian brother, a believer on the name of the Lord Jesus Christ (Acts 17:34).

When World War I began, Philadelphia was a very little town that had ruins from the days of the Romans. It was inhabited by a small number of adherents of Eastern Greek Orthodox Church. During the war, these inhabitants emigrated to Greece, and today the city of Philadelphia exists only as rubble.

- These things saith he that is holy, he that is true - The beautiful words which the Lord Jesus addresses to the church of Philadelphia serve as evidence of this church's spiritual state. It was steadfast and was holding firmly to his teachings, and it had borne much persecution. The Lord Jesus introduces himself as the one who is holy and true. We always see holiness and truth associated with each other, so he shows us the church of Philadelphia as living a life of holiness in faithfulness to God. There is a direct connection between sound doctrine and upright conduct. When a church teaches the truth, its conduct also will be true. When a church errs doctrinally, its conduct will be crooked. There is a strong bond between the way a man thinks and how he behaves. His mind dictates his behavior. The thoughts of a person will determine his behavior.

- He that hath the key of David, he that openeth, and no man shutteth; and shutteth, and no man openeth - The Lord Jesus is returning to the earth to establish his kingdom and sit upon the throne of David and rule over the whole world. Jesus has the key of the kingdom of David and he has the keys of the kingdom; the key of truth, the key of holiness, and the keys of the most beautiful heavenly gates. Every believer will overflow with joy forever and ever in the eternal paradise of the heavenly Jerusalem. The faithful, such as the church of Philadelphia, will reign with Jesus. This is what comforts the person that is faithful to the Lord Jesus: "For I reckon that the sufferings of this present time are not worthy to be compared with the glory which shall be revealed in us"(Romans 8:18).

(8) "I know thy works: behold, I have set before thee an open door, and no man can shut it: for thou hast a little strength, and hast kept my word, and hast not denied my name."

We live in a world full of evil; but the Lord Jesus protects and blesses each individual who holds fast to his name and his Word. For the Bible that which invigorates our hearts and helps our faith to grow: "faith cometh by hearing, and hearing by the word of God" (Romans 10:18); "Is not my word like as a fire? saith the LORD; and like a hammer that breaketh the rock in pieces?" (Jeremiah 23:29). The Lord says to the church of Philadelphia that he knows her works, that her strength is limited and little and weak; opposite of the church of Sardis which had much activity, but, on the inside, was cold and deA.D. The church of Philadelphia did not have great activity; but she had love, zeal, and a heart overflowing with a desire to live for the Lord Jesus and according to his word.

Indeed the world knew a sweeping spiritual revival in the days of the church of Philadelphia. The yoke of the papal church was broken by the Reformation of the 1500s, now long over. The spiritual darkness of the Middle Ages was gone, and the world was filled with spiritual enlightenment anew, and the principles of the Christian religion were wide spread and the teachings of the Bible prevailed.

You might be in the same condition as the church of Philadelphia: Your power may be weak, but your faithfulness is firm. This was the distinctive feature of the church of Philadelphia, her steadfast faithfulness to the Lord. So the Lord assured her that her door was going will remain wide open and no one was going to be able to shut it down. As a result, over three centuries, the world witnessed unprecedented missionary work. Christians supported one another materially so that the word would be preached; so that the message of salvation would reach the entire world.

There were many heroes of preaching and missionary work during this time. One such hero was David Livingstone, who went to Africa; another was William Carey, the famous Baptist who is considered the "father of modern missions, went to India and translated the Bible into many of its languages, including Sanskrit. Another great hero was Hudson Taylor, who went to China, adopted the customs of its people, and had a highly successful ministry there.

(9) "Behold, I will make them of the synagogue of Satan, which say they are Jews, and are not, but do lie; behold, I will make them to come and worship before thy feet, and to know that I have loved thee."

And so the door of Christ was opened to the world, and no man could shut it thereafter. A huge number of souls received salvation by grace through faith in Jesus Christ. Moreover, in 1611 the King James of England ordered the compilation on the entire Bible based on the Textus Receptus of the oldest manuscripts in their original languages. For the first time the average Christian could acquire the entire Bible and read it for himself the gospel message that saves his soul. The word of God spread to the four corners of the world and the power of the traditional, papal, Christian church receded gradually. It is a historical truth that wherever the gospel spreads and evangelical churches multiply, and the traditional churches are weakened.

(10) "Because thou hast kept the word of my patience, I also

will keep thee from the hour of temptation, which shall come upon all the world, to try them that dwell upon the earth."

This Reformation did not prevail without a high cost at the hands of the papal church, whose reprisals resulted in the martyrdom of forty million believers throughout the Middle Ages. This papal church is identified in the Bible: "And I saw the woman drunken with the blood of the saints, and with the blood of the martyrs of Jesus" (Revelation 17:6).

(11) "Behold, I come quickly: hold that fast which thou hast, that no man take thy crown."

We must not be afraid. Rather, we must remain faithful in the race and strive to be the first, not the second or third, in the service of the Lord Jesus. The Lord asks us to have a zeal for his ministry.

(12) "Him that overcometh will I make a pillar in the temple of my God, and he shall go no more out: and I will write upon him the name of my God, and the name of the city of my God, which is new Jerusalem, which cometh down out of heaven from my God: and I will write upon him my new name."

We will be pillars in the temple of the Lord. Jesus remains faithful, and he will not allow any of us to be lost outside. Rather he will write his name JESUS on our foreheads, and the name of the New Jerusalem, just like:

(i) Jesus "had a name written, that no man knew, but he himself" (Revelation 19:12);

(ii) Jerusalem: "shalt be called by a new name, which the mouth of the Lord shall name" (Isaiah 62:2). Jesus will write his blessed name on our foreheads so that:

(a) We will not be lost;
(b) We will not forget that he owns us;
(c) All will know that we belong to Jesus;
(d) We will have special relationships and
heavenly blessings with the Lord of glory
Jesus, the living Son of God, forever, world

without end. Amen.

(13) "He that hath an ear, let him hear what the Spirit saith unto the churches."

The question of the Holy Spirit is "Who has an ear to hear? Who is faithful:

(a) To the Word of the Lord,

(b) The Name of the Lord, and (c) the House of

the Lord?

Who wants to:

(a) Love the Lord and love the brethren,

(b) Take spiritual stands, and (c) live loyal to the

Lord like the church of Philadelphia?!"

The answer is that the Holy Spirit desires to help you; are you willing?!

(14) "And unto the angel of the church of the Laodiceans write; These things saith the Amen, the faithful and true witness, the beginning of the creation of God."

- And unto the angel of the church of the Laodiceans write - Laodicea means "the rule of the people". This church represents the period from the year 1945, from the end of the second world war, until the time of the rapture when: "In a moment, in the twinkling of an eye, at the last trump: for the trumpet shall sound, and the dead shall be raised incorruptible, and we shall be changed" (1 Corinthians 15:52). "For the Lord himself shall descend from heaven with a shout, with the voice of the archangel, and with the trump of God: and the dead in Christ shall rise first: Then we which are alive and remain shall be caught up together with them in the clouds, to meet the Lord in the air: and so shall we ever be with the Lord" (1 Thessalonians 4:16-17).

The church of Laodicea, which represents the church in our current age, differed from the other churches in that it did not receive any praise from Jesus, but on the contrary received only rebuke from him. That is because the teachings of Nicolaitans, which were first planted in the church of Ephesus and then grew in the church of Smyrna and all the subsequent churches, have now flourished and taken center stage in the Laodicean church and brought its spiritual destruction.

- These things saith the Amen, the faithful and true witness, the beginning of the creation of God - The Lord Jesus Christ is the spring of God's creation and its source: "Who is the image of the invisible God, the firstborn of every creature: For by him were all things created ... all things were created by him, and for him: And he is before all things, and by him all things consist" (Colossians 1:15-17); "In whose hand is the soul of every living thing, and the breath of all mankind" (Job 12:10); He is "upholding all things by the word of his power ... And, Thou, Lord, in the beginning hast laid the foundation of the earth; and the heavens are the works of thine hands: They shall perish; but thou remainest; and they all shall wax old as doth a garment; And as a vesture shalt thou fold them up, and they shall be changed: but thou art the same, and thy years shall not fail" (Hebrews 1:3,10-12). Thus, he is Amen at the beginning and the Faithful one at the end. Therefore, this is what he desires of the members of the church of Laodicea;, namely faithfulness till the end of the church age.

(15) "I know thy works, that thou art neither cold nor hot: I would thou wert cold or hot."

Alas, the church of Laodicea has neither faithfulness nor truthfulness. The believers of these days do not have faithfulness to God's word, the Holy Bible, nor to God's house, the local church that they belong to. We now live in times when it is hard to find a church that is faithful to the Lord; or to find a Bible college that is sound in its teachings. We cannot find spiritual fervor these days but mostly spiritually bankruptcy and fearful lukewarmness prevailing in true Christendom of true believers in the grace of or Lord and Saviour Jesus Christ.

The Bible speaks of believers being in one of three states of spiritual fervor:

(i) Fervency in the spirit: Paul the Apostle was "fervent in the spirit"(Acts 18:25). The Emmaus disciples said: "Did not our heart burn within us?" (Luke 23:32);

(ii) Cold spiritually: "And because iniquity shall abound, the love of many shall wax cold" (Matthew 24:12);

(iii) Lukewarm:

(16) "So then because thou art lukewarm, and neither cold nor hot, I will spue thee out of my mouth."

When there is spiritual warmth, there is love for the Lord Jesus. When there is spiritual coldness, there is love for the world. The one who lingers between the two is neither hot nor cold for he is lukewarm. He is perplexed whether to love the Lord Jesus or to love the world, as if this decision needs any thought. For this reason, the Lord desires to spew him out of his mouth because he rejects spiritual hypocrisy and game playing Christianity.

The majority of Christians today are in an extremely poor spiritual condition. Today's generation is lukewarm in its love for Jesus and is spiritually confused and disoriented and perplexed in either loving Jesus or embracing self and world indulgence. Either love the Lord who bought us with his own precious blood and is preparing a place for us in heaven, or love the world of sin that Jesus Christ freed us from. This reminds us of what happened with the people of Israel after God freed them from slavery in Egypt: "And they said one to another, Let us make a captain, and let us return into Egypt" (Numbers 14:4). The choice is obvious and the remedy is a return to the Bible to renew spiritual fervor, as happened with the disciples in Emmaus: "And they said one to another, Did not our heart burn within us, while he talked with us by the way, and while he opened to us the scriptures?" (Luke 24:32). Spiritual strength comes from reading the Bible: "The law of the Lord is perfect, converting the soul (as in refreshing the soul)" (Psalm 19:7); "Thy words were found, and I did eat them; and thy word was unto me the joy and rejoicing of mine heart"; "Is not my word like as a fire? saith the Lord" (Jeremiah 15:16; 23:29); "So then faith cometh by hearing, and hearing by the word of God" (Romans 10:17).

(17) "Because thou sayest, I am rich, and increased with goods, and have need of nothing; and knowest not that thou art wretched, and miserable, and poor, and blind, and naked."

The world had moved in and dwelt inside the church of Laodicea leaving little room for the love of the Lord Jesus. The church of Laodicea had become contrary to the Philadelphia which had been poor materially but rich spiritually, rich in her love for the Lord Jesus Christ, and received great praise from him. The church of Laodicea was poor spiritually and rich materially. She is in a state of spiritual ailment, and the Great Physician, the Lord Jesus Christ, has come to treat her illness, lead it, and direct it. The hearts of the believers today are plunged in the love of the world. They think that their relationship is very good with the Lord who examines the hearts and reins. He looks inside and sees inner spiritual poverty and misery, spiritual nakedness, and sickness of hearts.

Many times when a Christian gets materially rich he rejects the Lord. This is what the Bible teaches. The Lord Jesus warns Israel in the Old Testamentsaying: "When thou hast eaten and art full, then thou shalt bless the Lord thy God for the good land which he hath given thee. Beware that thou forget not the Lord thy God, in not keeping his commandments, and his judgments, and his statutes, which I command thee this day: Lest when thou hast eaten and art full, and hast built goodly houses, and dwelt therein; And when thy herds and thy flocks multiply, and thy silver and thy gold is multiplied, and all that thou hast is multiplied; Then thine heart be lifted up, and thou forget the Lord thy God ... And thou say in thine heart, My power and the might of mine hand hath gotten me this wealth" (Deuteronomy 8:10-14,17). Unfortunately, this is exactly what happened with the people of Israel then. After receiving spiritual blessing, material blessing came to the people of Israel so they turned away from the Lord: "And he made him to suck honey out of the rock, and oil out of the flinty rock; Butter of kine, and milk of sheep, with fat of lambs, and rams of the breed of Bashan, and goats, with the fat of kidneys of wheat; and thou didst drink the pure blood of the grape. But Jeshurun waxed fat, and kicked: thou art waxen fat, thou art grown thick, thou art covered with fatness; then he forsook God which made him, and lightly esteemed the Rock of his salvation" (Deuteronomy 32:13-15) ; "According to their pasture, so were they filled; they were filled, and their heart was exalted; therefore have they forgotten me" (Hosea 13:6). This is the church of Laodicea today, and these are spiritual lessons for the New Testament churches of our day.

Jesus says: "I am come that they might have life, and that they might have it more abundantly" (John 10:10). When a person gets saved, the Lord blesses his life with what is best upon the earth; however, with prosperity, man faces a spiritual danger. That is why the wisdom of God says: "Give me neither poverty nor riches; feed me with food convenient for me: Lest I be full, and deny thee, and say, Who is the LORD?" (Proverbs 30:8-9); "Vanity of vanities; all is vanity" (Ecclesiastes 1:2). The Lord Jesus teaches us to pray saying: "Give us this day our daily bread ... And lead us not into temptation" (Matthew 6:11,13).

The world is currently very prosperous, materially speaking. Means of entertainment are increasingly accessible. We do not see poverty and misery as we did in the past. Any time of the year, you can eat all that your eye desires of earthly bounty. Foods, that used to be seasonal, are now available all year round and in large quantities. Every house if filled with electrical appliances. The poorest people have televisions and cell phones. All this led to poor communion with the Lord Jesus, and lukewarm spiritual living, and impoverished seeking for the kingdom of heaven.

(18) "I counsel thee to buy of me gold tried in the fire, that thou mayest be rich; and white raiment, that thou mayest be clothed, and that the shame of thy nakedness do not appear; and anoint thine eyes with eyesalve, that thou mayest see."

- I counsel thee to buy of me gold tried in the fire, that thou mayest be rich - The Lord Jesus gives the church of Laodicea three spiritual words of advice that are useful for remedy and recovery:

(I) The first word of advice is to return to preaching the Word of God, which is like gold purified with fire. It will inflame the life and heart of the believer and will bring persecution upon him. For it is written: "Yea, and all that will live godly in Christ Jesus shall suffer persecution"; "Preach the word; be instant in season, out of season" (2 Timothy 3:12; 4:2). Persecution is beneficial, for the Apostles Paul and Peter both describe it as: "For unto you it is given in the behalf of Christ, not only to believe on him, but also to suffer for his sake" (Philippians 1:29); "Wherein ye greatly rejoice, though now for a season, if need be, ye are in heaviness through manifold temptations: That the trial of your faith, being much more precious than of gold that perisheth, though it be tried with fire, might be found unto praise and honour and glory at the appearing of Jesus Christ: Whom having not seen, ye love; in whom, though now ye see him not, yet believing, ye rejoice with joy unspeakable and full of glory: Receiving the end of your faith, even the salvation of your souls" (1 Peter 1:6-9).

It is very good for a believer to pass through trials and tribulations that lead him to deny the self and to depend on the Lord Jesus. They polish our faith, making it like pure gold, and thus they would yield many dividends and great treasures when we stand before the BEMA seat of Christ for valuable rewards: "And the fire shall try every man's work of what sort it is. If any man's work abide which he hath built thereupon, he shall receive a reward. If any man's work shall be burned, he shall suffer loss: but he himself shall be saved; yet so as by fire" (1 Corinthians 3:13-15); "For we must all appear before the judgment seat of Christ; that every one may receive the things done in his body, according to that he hath done, whether it be good or bad" (2 Corinthians 5:10);

The Lord Jesus counsels you to pass through difficulties and trials so that your faith will be purified and you will prosper spiritually. All you must do is share the message of the gospel with others. Inevitably, persecution will come your way, and your life will be purified as gold; you will rise from your spiritual poverty to spiritual wealth.

- And white raiment, that thou mayest be clothed, and that the shame of thy nakedness do not appear -

(II) The second word of advice is to improve your spiritual clothing, because a ragged dress shows the person's nakedness and shame and testifies to spiritual defeat and humiliation.

White clothing of good works reveals the true righteousness of real Christians: "For the fine linen is the righteousness of saints" (Revelation 19:8). The Lord Jesus counsels to wear a robes whose names and colours are "good works" of . holy living, righteousness, justice, truth, mercy, faith, soul winning, and love for our brethren. Such traits show Jesus in our lives. We must strive to show Christ in our homes, our churches, on the job and in our society. It is our greatest sense of honour to be the disciples of the Lord Jesus, and his servants, and bearing his cross, and following him daily. We are not followers of men but the Creator of men, the Lord Jesus Christ, the Lord of Glory!

- And anoint thine eyes with eyesalve, that thou mayest see -

(III) The third word of advice is that the believer needs is sharp spiritual vision: "But he that lacketh these things is blind, and cannot see afar off, and hath forgotten that he was purged from his old sins" (2 Peter 1:9). The believer should forsake the life of sin and of loving of the world, and acquire sharp spiritual insight into the future and judge correctly where will his path lead him for: "Where there is no vision, the people perish" (Proverbs 29:18); "And we know that the Son of God is come, and hath given us an understanding, that we may know him that is true, and we are in him that is true, even in his Son Jesus Christ. This is the true God, and eternal life" (1 John 5:20). Walk in the truth as he is in the truth, and your eyes will be enlightened. "Because as he is, so are we in this world" (1 John 4:17).

These words of advice are sound and beneficial for every believer. Applying them is not difficult if we continue to deny ourselves daily in spiritual joy that we can draw from immersing ourselves in God's word, which gives real joy that far exceeds that of the world. King David says: "Thou hast put gladness in my heart, more than in the time that their corn and their wine increased" (Psalm 4:7).

(19) "As many as I love, I rebuke and chasten: be zealous therefore, and repent."

Here we see three consecutive stages in which Jesus puts us back on track:

(i) "Love" - "I love": "I drew them with cords of a man, with bands of love" (Hosea 11:4); "Or despisest thou the riches of his goodness and forbearance and longsuffering; not knowing that the goodness of God leadeth thee to repentance?" (Romans 2:4).

(ii) "Rebuke" - "I rebuke": "These things hast thou done, and I kept silence; thou thoughtest that I was altogether such an one as thyself: but I will reprove thee, and set them in order before thine eyes" (Psalms 50:21).

(iii) "Chastise" - "chastise": "But if ye be without chastisement, whereof all are partakers, then are ye bastards, and not sons" (Hebrews 12:8). In his jealousy for his son's life wise King Solomon counsels him saying: "My son, despise not the chastening of the Lord; neither be weary of his correction: For whom the Lord loveth he correcteth; even as a father the son in whom he delighteth" (Proverbs 3:11-12). As to the father, Solomon says: "Correct thy son, and he shall give thee rest; yea, he shall give delight unto thy soul" (Proverbs 29:17).The purpose of the dealings of the Lord Jesus with you is to deliver you from spiritual neglect, rebellion, and loss. So be humble and submissive and repent.

The Lord is compelled to chasten us in order to purify us and be a people of his own, because he is jealous for our spiritual state. Our God is a jealous God; therefore: "And ye have forgotten the exhortation which speaketh unto you as unto children, My son, despise not thou the chastening of the Lord, nor faint when thou art rebuked of him: For whom the Lord loveth he chasteneth, and scourgeth every son whom he receiveth ... Now no chastening for the present seemeth to be joyous, but grievous: nevertheless afterward it yieldeth the peaceable fruit of righteousness unto them which are exercised thereby" (Hebrews 12:5-6,11).

(20) "Behold, I stand at the door, and knock: if any man hear my voice, and open the door, I will come in to him, and will sup with him, and he with me."

Not all want to return from their spiritual backsliding to fellowship with the Son of God, the Lord Jesus; most do not want this. That is why we see him saying to the church of Laodicea: "If any man hear my voice". The Lord Jesus is now outside of the church and is not included in their personal plans. They are walking in the flesh. They have no desire to go back and sup with the Lord Jesus, which represents having spiritual fellowship with him.

The medicine is Jesus, the water of life, and the word of God, which cleanses our hearts, just like water cleanses our bodies from the dirt which had adhered to us: "Even as Christ also loved the church, and gave himself for it; That he might sanctify and cleanse it with the washing of water by the word, That he might present it to himself a glorious church" (Ephesians 5:25-27).

Jesus is standing at the door to our hearts: "The heart is deceitful above all things, and desperately wicked: who can know it? I the Lord search the heart" (Jeremiah 17:9-10). For the mind is spiritually sick: "The whole head is sick, and the whole heart faint." (Isaiah 1:5). Therefore, it is important that every believer today pray as the prophet David prayed saying: "Search me, O God, and know my heart: try me, and know my thoughts: And see if there be any wicked way in me, and lead me in the way everlasting" (Psalms 139:23-24). We should accept the wisdom of King Solomon: "Keep thy heart with all diligence; for out of it are the issues of life" ; "My son, give me thine heart, and let thine eyes observe my ways" (Proverbs 4:23; 23:26). The Lord Jesus reminds us of an important truth when he says: "For where your treasure is, there will your heart be also" (Matthew 6:21).

Jesus knocks on the heart's door of each one of us. He is the Lord Jesus who saved us from the judgment of sin and made heaven our eternal destination. He wants us to return, with an honest and a pure heart, to a life of blessed fellowship with him.

(21) "To him that overcometh will I grant to sit with me in my throne, even as I also overcame, and am set down with my Father in his throne."

We thank God that there always is found a small faithful remnant: "Esaias also crieth concerning Israel, Though the number of the children of Israel be as the sand of the sea, a remnant shall be saved ... Even so then at this present time also there is a remnant according to the election of grace" (Romans 9:27; 11:5).

This small remnant faithful to the Lord Jesus will rule with him as he has promised.

(22) "He that hath an ear, let him hear what the Spirit saith unto the churches."

It is strange that Jesus directs this motivation to each of the seven churches: "He that hath an ear, let him hear". Only a small minority hears and listens. Are you listening today? Are you determined to live faithfully for the Lord Jesus in a continuous living in blessed fellowship with him?!

4
THE THRONE IN HEAVEN

(1) "After this I looked, and, behold, a door was opened in heaven: and the first voice which I heard was as it were of a trumpet talking with me; which said, Come up hither, and I will shew thee things which must be hereafter."

In this chapter the scene moves from earth to heaven when John hears a voice, like a trumpet, asking him to ascend into heaven. This scene is similar to the experience of the Apostle Paul when he was caught up to the third heaven, the future abode that awaits the righteous who are saved by the precious blood of Jesus: "It is not expedient for me doubtless to glory. I will come to visions and revelations of the Lord. I knew a man in Christ above fourteen years ago, (whether in the body, I cannot tell; or whether out of the body, I cannot tell: God knoweth;) such an one caught up to the third heaven ... How that he was caught up into paradise, and heard unspeakable words, which it is not lawful for a man to utter" (2 Corinthians 12:1-2...4). Paul describes the location and beauty of paradise, whereas John describes the grandeur and greatness of God's throne that is in paradise.

Here the church disappears from the earth to heaven until it returns in glory with Jesus Christ in chapter nineteen. John's call to ascend to heaven is a picture of the ascension of the church directly into heaven at the end of its age.

Now begins the period of "things which are to come". That is when the Church age on earth ends with the age of the church of Laodicea; and the entire Body of Christ disappears from the earth and ascends into heaven in the Rapture. This events includes every born again Christian, dead or alive, from the days of Jesus' public ministry on earth, some two thousand years ago, until the last saved convert at the end of the age of the church of Laodicea. They are all children of light, children of the Lord Jesus Christ who are washed with his blood.

Those that remain on earth are children of darkness, children of the devil, wicked people from all denominations and religions. They are not converted but some of them with experience the salvation of Christ in the Great Tribulation.

The nation of Israel remains upon the earth, as do all other peoples and nations. God will resume his dealings with the nation of Israel fulfilling the seventieth week of Daniel ($7 + 62 = 69 - 70 = 1$). The is the last week remaining of the seventy weeks that are appointed by God for the chastisement of Jerusalem; as we shall see later in the explanation of this verse.

God pours out his wrath on the nation of Israel and on the whole world for seven years on account of their crucifying Jesus and of their refusal to worship him. This is a period known as "Jacob's trouble", during which the church will not be present. The church does not pass through the great tribulation. The Lord always teaches us that, when he pours out his wrath on a people or nation, he first delivers his own chosen people, as he did at the time of Noah's ark. He delivered Noah and his family, and, after that, he brought the flood upon the earth. We see the same pattern in the Lord's dealings with Lot. The Lord brought

Lot and his family members out, and then he poured fire and brimstone upon Sodom and Gomorrah. Also, Paul the Apostle says to the people of Thessalonica "Jesus, which delivered us from the wrath to come" (1 Thessalonians 1:10).

So there is a wrath which will come! We believe that the rapture will occur before the great tribulation; and here are some convincing defenses. In studying the book of Leviticus chapter twenty three, we find seven holy convocations which had a literal interpretation in Israel, and a spiritual application in the church. These holy convocations or feasts were:

(i) Sabbath: Day of temporary earthly rest, which the church celebrates on Sunday, because: "Jesus was risen early the first day of the week" (Mark 16:9), opening the doors of eternal heavenly rest.

(ii) Passover: "Christ our passover is sacrificed for us" (1 Corinthians 5:7)).

(iii) Firstfruits; "But now is Christ risen from the dead, and become the firstfruits of them that slept" (1 Corinthians15:20).

(iv) Weeks - harvesting season - is countered by the church beginning the harvesting of souls on the day of Pentecost: "the same day there were added unto them about three thousand souls." (Acts 2:41).

(v) Trumpet: - the church now awaits the trumpet of the rapture: "For the Lord himself shall descend from heaven with a shout, with the voice of the archangel, and with the trump of God: and the dead in Christ shall rise first: Then we which are alive *and* remain shall be caught up together with them in the clouds, to meet the Lord in the air: and so shall we ever be with the Lord" (1 Thessalonians 4:16-17).

(vi) Atonement: after the rapture comes the great tribulation: "Alas! for that day is great, so that none is like it: it is even the time of Jacob's trouble, but he shall be saved out of it" (Jeremiah 30:7).

(vii) Tabernacles: - will be fulfilled in the millennium,

following the great tribulation: "¹⁶ And it shall come to pass, that every one that is left of all the nations which came against Jerusalem shall even go up from year to year to worship the King, the Lord of hosts, and to keep the feast of tabernacles" (Zechariah 14:16).

The Rapture is going to happen before the Great Tribulation; and the Millennium is going to take place after the Great Tribulation.

And so we see that after the feast of the weeks of harvesting is followed by the trumpet of the rapture. From the resurrection of the Lord Jesus Christ and the coming of the Holy Spirit on the day of Pentecost, we have been living in the time of the feast of the harvest of souls. No change has taken place in God's overall program until this day. Change will come when we hear the trumpet of the angel of the Lord: "Behold, I shew you a mystery; We shall not all sleep, but we shall all be changed, In a moment, in the twinkling of an eye, at the last trump: for the trumpet shall sound, and the dead shall be raised incorruptible, and we shall be changed" (1 Corinthians 15:51-52). "Wherefore comfort one another with these words" (1 Thessalonians 4:18). It is very important for believers to know that they will not pass through the great tribulation; and that there is no wrath from God upon his children, as the Lord Jesus comforts us saying: "Verily, verily, I say unto you, He that heareth my word, and believeth on him that sent me, hath everlasting life, and shall not come into condemnation; but is passed from death unto life" (John 5:24).

Study the two concepts of "the fullness of the Gentiles" and "the Times of the Gentiles" in the Bible, and you will conclude that it is impossible for the church to pass through the great tribulation. They are two synonymous concepts in the Bible:

(i) "Times of the Gentiles"
(ii) "Fullness of the Gentiles", also called,

"Fullness of Times"

Both are related to the seventieth week of Daniel, and are interwoven with each other.

The Times of the Gentiles refers to the time period in which Gentile powers have dominion over the city of Jerusalem. The Times of the Gentiles began in 586 BC and will end at the end of the great tribulation when the Lord Jesus will rescue Jerusalem and establish his kingdom. The different ages of the Gentiles can be seen in the massive statue which Nebuchadnezzar saw and was interpreted by Daniel: "As for thee, O king, thy thoughts came into thy mind upon thy bed, what should come to pass hereafter: and he that revealeth secrets maketh known to thee what shall come to pass"; "And he shall confirm the covenant with many for one week: and in the midst of the week he shall cause the sacrifice and the oblation to cease, and for the overspreading of abominations he shall make it desolate, even until the consummation, and that determined shall be poured upon the desolate" (Daniel 2:29; 9:27).

The Times of the Gentiles began in 586 BC; when Jerusalem was trodden down by the Gentiles; until the end of the tribulation when the Jews: "shall fall by the edge of the sword, and shall be led away captive into all nations: and Jerusalem shall be trodden down of the Gentiles, until the Times of the Gentiles be fulfilled" (Luke 21:24).

The Times of the Gentiles consist of four successive powers represented by the four metals of the statue of Nebuchadnezzar:

(i) Gold: Babylonian (or Chaldean) kingdom (present day Iraq).

(ii) Silver: Medes and Persians kingdom (present day Iran).

(iii) Brass: Greek kingdom (present day Greece).

(iv) Iron/Clay: Roman Empire, which will be revived in the last days in the form of the European Union; Eastern Europe and Western Europe being represented in the two legs of the statue. The statue's ten toes indicate that the European Union will be composed of ten alliances.

The Roman Empire is the only world power which was not overthrown; rather, it disintegrated and faded away. Since that time, the greatest power in the world has been a European civilization. At the end of times,

the Roman Empire will be revived and will be the greatest power in the world; and will be the seat of the Antichrist. From the rise of the first Roman Empire until this day, we continue to live in the age of the fourth power of the Times of the Gentiles, which will conclude after the seven years of the great tribulation in the Battle of Armageddon. At the end of this battle, the Lord Jesus, the stone cut out of the mountain, will destroy the forth power, the Revived Roman Empire: "And in the days of these kings shall the God of heaven set up a kingdom, which shall never be destroyed: and the kingdom shall not be left to other people, but it shall break in pieces and consume all these kingdoms, and it shall stand for ever. Forasmuch as thou sawest that the stone was cut out of the mountain without hands, and that it brake in pieces the iron, the brass, the clay, the silver, and the gold; the great God hath made known to the king what shall come to pass hereafter: and the dream is certain, and the interpretation thereof sure" (Daniel 2:44-45). Jesus will destroy the Roman power and establish his kingdom, which will endure forever. "I saw in the night visions, and, behold, one like the Son of man came with the clouds of heaven, and came to the Ancient of days, and they brought him near before him. And there was given him dominion, and glory, and a kingdom, that all people, nations, and languages, should serve him: his dominion is an everlasting dominion, which shall not pass away, and his kingdom that which shall not be destroyed ... I beheld, and the same horn made war with the saints, and prevailed against them; Until the Ancient of days came, and judgment was given to the saints of the most High; and the time came that the saints possessed the kingdom ... And the kingdom and dominion, and the greatness of the kingdom under the whole heaven, shall be given to the people of the saints of the most High, whose kingdom is an everlasting kingdom, and all dominions shall serve and obey him" (Daniel 7:13-14, 21-22, 27). "And I saw the beast, and the kings of the earth, and their armies, gathered together to make war against him that sat on the horse, and against his army. And the beast was taken, and with him the False prophet that wrought miracles before him, with which he deceived them that had received the mark of the beast, and them that worshiped his image. These both were cast alive into a lake of fire burning with brimstone. And the remnant were slain with the sword of him that sat upon the horse, which sword proceeded out of his mouth: and all the fowls were filled with their flesh" (Revelation 19:19-21). The purpose of the Times of the Gentiles is to punish Israel for its apostasy from the Lord Jesus.

The phrase "the Times of the Gentiles" is negative, and in contrast, the phrase "the fullness of the Gentiles" is positive. In the "fullness of the Gentiles" the Lord God suspends his dealings with the nation of Israel; between the sixty-ninth week and the seventieth one, he creates a new institution, namely the church, consisting of both Jews and Gentiles. The Old Testament ended with the ministry of John the Baptist: "He that hath the bride is the bridegroom: but the friend of the bridegroom, which standeth and heareth him, rejoiceth greatly because of the bridegroom's voice: this my joy therefore is fulfilled" (John 3:29); and the Church age began with the calling of the twelve disciples: "from the days of John the Baptist until now the kingdom of heaven suffereth violence, and the violent take it by force" (Matthew 11:12). Yet the dispensation of Grace, also known as the Fullness of Times, and the Fullness of the

Gentiles, did not begin until the day of Pentecost, when the church received the power and the blessing of the Holy Spirit. So the Fullness of the Gentiles will end when the Lord Jesus raptures his church and the Holy Spirit is lifted up: "For I would not, brethren, that ye should be ignorant of this mystery, lest ye should be wise in your own conceits; that blindness in part is happened to Israel, until the fullness of the Gentiles be come in" (Romans 11:25). At that time, the wicked one, the son of perdition, the Antichrist will be revealed: "For the mystery of iniquity doth already work: only he who now letteth will let, until he be taken out of the way. And then shall that Wicked be revealed, whom the Lord shall consume with the spirit of his mouth and shall destroy with the brightness of his coming" (2 Thessalonians 2:7-8). This particular point blows a big hole in the theories of those who do not believe in the pretribulational rapture of the church. The Holy Spirit, who descended upon the church on the day of Pentecost and commenced its full ministry, will lift her up with him when he ascends back to heaven. The church will not be on the earth when the Antichrist is revealed.

The purpose of the "Fullness of the Gentiles" is to create a heavenly people who are the church, which is the body of Christ: "And hath put all things under his feet, and gave him to be the head over all things to the church, Which is his body, the fullness of him that filleth all in all ... For this cause shall a man leave his father and mother, and shall be joined unto his wife, and they two shall be one flesh. This is a great mystery: but I speak concerning Christ and the church" (Ephesians 1:22-23; 5:31-32). "And he is the head of the body, the church: who is the beginning, the firstborn from the dead; that in all things he might have the preeminence" (Colossians 1:18).

In these two periods termed "the Times of the Gentiles" and "the Fullness of the Gentiles", God fulfills his promise to Abraham by giving him two seeds: "I will multiply thy seed as the stars of the heaven, and as the sand which is upon the sea shore" (Genesis 22:17). So God has blessed Abraham two seeds:

(i) The Heavenly seed is fulfilled in Isaac: "And I will make thy seed to multiply as the stars of heaven" (Genesis 26:4).

(ii) The Earthly seed is fulfilled in Jacob: "And thy seed shall be as the dust of the earth" (Genesis 28:14).

Prophetically and futuristically these two seeds are:

(i) Earthly or physical seed, which is Israel, for Abraham, Isaac, and Jacob, are the fathers of Israel: "Go, and gather the elders of Israel together, and say unto them, The Lord God of your fathers, the God of Abraham, of Isaac, and of Jacob, appeared unto me" (Exodus 3:16);

(ii) Heavenly or spiritual seed, which is the church, and Abraham and Sarah are the father and mother of the believers: "Abraham our father" (James 2:21), and "Even as Sara....whose daughters ye are" (1 Peter 3:6).

Israel and the Church are interrelated for they have the same parents but are different in spirituality for Israel is the harlot woman of God while the Church is the virgin bride of Christ. The Church has the blessing of the Fulness of the Gentiles; while Israel gets the tribulation of the Times the Gentiles.

Additional evidence that the church does not go through the great tribulation is found in the four gospels; for the synoptic gospels of, Matthew, Mark, and Luke, addressed "Israel" where Jesus came and preached the kingdom of heaven on earth. He came to earth to go to the cross to redeem his people and then rise to establish his kingdom. But the Jews rejected him; so the Gospel of John, which is addressed to the church, starts by saying: "He came unto his own, and his own received him not. But as many as received him, to them gave he power to become the sons of God, even to them that believe on his name: Which were born, not of blood, nor of the will of the flesh, nor of the will of man, but of God." (John 1:11-13). Therefore from the onset of the

Gospel of John, Christ addresses his church and elaborately declares his deity that he is Jesus Christ the Son of God. Therefore in a comparison between the Gospels of Matthew, Mark, and Luke on one hand and the Gospel of John on the other, we find:

(i) The Gospel of John mentions 8 miracles, of which 6 are not recorded in the synoptic gospels.

(ii) Two discourses on soul winning mentioned only in the Gospel of John:

(a) Nicodemus

(b) Samaritan woman

(iii) Only in the Gospel of John are there teachings that the Lord Jesus is:

(a) The bread that came down from heaven,

(b) The light of the world,

(c) The good shepherd who sacrifices his life for the whole world,

(d) The door to heaven, and

(e) The vine whose fruit is eternal life.

(iv) The Gospels of Matthew, Mark, and Luke speak in parables, while the Gospel of John speaks in discourses.

(v) The Gospels of Matthew, Mark, and Luke record the deeds of Christ, while the Gospel of John brings us the words and sayings of Christ.

(vi) Matthew, Mark, and Luke emphasize the human nature of Christ. John emphasizes his deity, and thus does not mention:

(a) Birth of Jesus

(b) Baptism of Jesus

(c) Temptations of Jesus

(d) Transfiguration of Jesus

(e) Visit of Jesus to the garden of Gethsemane

(vii) Matthew 24, Mark 13, and Luke 21 speak of the great tribulation, but there is no mention of tribulation in John. This is a clear indication that the Church does not pass through it, for the synoptic gospels are addressed to Israel while the gospel of John is addressed to the church.

At the end of the Times of the Gentiles, the church will be raptured, and the great tribulation will begin. Then, the Lord will resume his dealings with Israel, completing the seventieth week, sometimes referred to as Jacob's week or Rachel's week: "Fulfil her week, and we will give thee this also for the service which thou shalt serve with me yet seven other years" (Genesis 29:27); "Seventy weeks are determined upon thy people and upon thy holy city, to finish the transgression, and to make an end of sins, and to make reconciliation for iniquity, and to bring in everlasting righteousness, and to seal up the vision and prophecy, and to anoint the most Holy"" (Daniel 9:24). It is also known as Jacob's trouble and the sea of affliction: "Alas! for that day is great, so that none is like it: it is even the time of Jacob's trouble, but he shall be saved out of it" (Jeremiah 30:7); "And he shall pass through the sea with affliction, and shall smite the waves in the sea, and all the deeps of the river shall dry up: and the pride of Assyria shall be brought down, and the scepter of Egypt shall depart away" (Zechariah 10:11). The Times of the Gentles end at the return of Christ.

Another proof that the church will not pass through the great tribulation are the two times that heaven opens up in the book of Revelation; between these two openings there is church no mention of it:

(i) The first time it opens is when the Lord Jesus raptures the church to heaven: "After this I looked, and, behold, a door was opened in heaven: and the first voice which I heard was as it were of a trumpet talking with me; which said, Come up hither, and I will shew thee things which must be hereafter. And immediately I was in the spirit: and, behold, a throne was set in heaven, and one sat on the throne" (Revelation 4:1-2). The church is removed from the earth and the great tribulation begins; during which time, she, the church, the Bride of Christ, prepares herself in heaven so that she will be wedded to Christ, the Bridegroom, when she returns to earth to reign with him: "Let us be glad and rejoice, and give honour to him: for the marriage of the Lamb is come, and his wife hath made herself ready" (Revelation 19:7).

(ii) The second time is when the Lord Jesus returns with the church at end of the tribulation: "And the Lord my God shall come, and all the saints with thee" (Zechariah 14:5). This marks the end of the Times of the Gentiles and the destruction of the Antichrist and the False prophet; and their kingdom. Jesus establishes his millennial kingdom which he spoke about in the sermon on the mount in the Gospel of Matthew chapters 5-7. Also, the Book of Revelation speaks about the events of this second opening: "And I saw thrones, and they sat upon them, and judgment was given unto them: and I saw the souls of them that were beheaded for the witness of Jesus, and for the word of God, and which had not worshiped the beast, neither his image, neither had received his mark upon their foreheads, or in their hands; and they lived and reigned with Christ a thousand years. But the rest of the dead lived not again until the thousand years were finished. This is the first resurrection. Blessed and holy is he that hath part in the first resurrection: on such the second death hath no power, but they shall be priests of God and of Christ, and shall reign with him a thousand years." (Revelation 20:4-6).

Additional proof is that from Revelation 4 forward, there is no mention of the word church on the earth. The familiar phrase: "He that hath an ear, let him hear what the Spirit saith unto the churches", which appears seven times in chapters 2 and 3,; is mentioned in part in chapter 13: "If any man have an ear, let him hear" but the statement does not conclude with: "what the Spirit saith unto the churches" After the ascension of the church (Revelation 4:1), the phrase "What the Spirit saith unto the churches" is no longer used.

One of the foundations of solid sound Bible doctrine is finding relevant Bible verses and connecting them. Some theologians teach that the church will pass through the great tribulation, and they all rely on a misunderstanding of half a verse, namely)2 Thessalonians 2:2(. They need an understanding of the meaning of "the day of Christ" in its two aspects of the first and the second which are; "the appearing" or "rapture" and "coming the second return to earth" or "the kingdom": "I charge thee therefore before God, and the Lord Jesus Christ, who shall judge the quick and the dead at his appearing and his kingdom" (2 Timothy 4:1). If it were true that the church will pass through the tribulation, we would have seen several verses clearly expressing this idea; but there are none. Also Paul the Apostle could not have contradicted himself when he had addressed the same group, the Thessalonian believers, when in comforting their hearts, he said: "Jesus, which delivered us from the wrath to come" (1 Thessalonians 1:10); Paul says "from wrath"; not "in" it: "For God hath not appointed us to wrath, but to obtain salvation by our Lord Jesus Christ" (1 Thessalonians 5:9).

The sudden and unanticipated passing of the church into heaven is a teaching which is very comforting and very important because, otherwise, the doctrine of the imminent return of Christ must be discarded. There are many signs which point to the great tribulation. If the church must pass through the great tribulation, then the return of the Lord Jesus Christ to earth will no longer be imminent, as all the signs in question must occur first. This is would be heresy as it destroys the lively spirit of hope that we are going to be redeemed in the rapture. It would be heresy because it would leave us waiting for the great tribulation to descend on an evil world. But we are: "Looking for that blessed hope, and the glorious appearing of the great God and our Saviour Jesus Christ" (Titus 2:13). This our comfort; in proper teaching we await the return of the Lord Jesus for us, anticipating that it might take place at any moment. This being the case, we should labor and persevere in living a life of righteousness, piety, and holiness unto the Lord, constantly waiting for his return. As the Holy Spirit says: "Then we which are alive and remain shall be caught up together with them in the clouds, to meet the Lord in the air: and so shall we ever be with the Lord. Wherefore comfort one another with these words" (1 Thessalonians 4:17-18).

(2) "And immediately I was in the spirit: and, behold, a throne was set in heaven, and one sat on the throne."

We, the church, shall be raptured into heaven, and with our eyes, we shall see God's blessed throne, and the shining bright glory of God sitting on the throne. Who can imagine let alone envision or conceive of such a blessed scene; like Paul said to the Corinthian believers: "Eye hath not seen, nor ear heard, neither have entered into the heart of man" (1 Corinthians 2:9).

(3) "And he that sat was to look upon like a jasper and a sardine stone: and there was a rainbow round about the throne, in sight like unto an emerald."

This is an appearance of the glory of God, for God is "invisible" (1 Timothy 1:17). "God is spirit" (John 4:24). "God is light" (1 John 1:5). He is omnipresent: "by him all things consist" (Colossians 1:17). God cannot be restricted or bounded by a throne; and the scene is a manifestation of his glory!

Jasper points to the purity of holiness, Red sardine is a symbol of the blood of redemption, the rainbow stands for peace, and the green emerald speaks of love and life, for: "God is love" (1 John 4:8,16). He is the "**I AM**", the one who exists and lives forever: "And Moses said unto God, Behold, when I come unto the children of Israel, and shall say unto them, The God of your fathers hath sent me unto you; and they shall say to me, What is his name? what shall I say unto them? And God said unto Moses, **I Am** That **I Am**: and he said, Thus shalt thou say unto the children of Israel, **I Am** hath sent me unto you"

(Exodus 3:13-14); "Jesus said unto them, Verily, verily, I say unto you, Before Abraham was, **I AM**" (John 8:58); "As soon then as he had said unto them, **I AM HE**, they went backward, and fell to the ground (for had disclosed his deity)". Of course, these verses are not sufficient to describe God's eternal **I AM** , nevertheless these scenes are very beautiful.

(4) "And round about the throne were four and twenty seats: and upon the seats I saw four and twenty elders sitting, clothed in white raiment; and they had on their heads crowns of gold."

Around the throne, we see twenty-four elders. Who are these elders? A logical analysis says that they are:

(i) The twelve tribes of Israel, on behalf of the nation of Israel.

(ii) The twelve apostles of Christ representing the church. Note that these elders are human beings, since they are redeemed by the blood of the Lord Jesus: ⁸And when he had taken the book, the four beasts and four and twenty elders fell down before the Lamb, having every one of them harps, and golden vials full of odours, which are the prayers of saints. ⁹And they sung a new thereof: for thou wast slain, and hast redeemed us to God by thy blood out of every kindred, and tongue, and people, and nation; ¹⁰And hast made us unto our God kings and priests: and we shall reign on the earth" (Revelation 5:8-10).

God has a joint plan for Israel and the church as we can tell from the description of the foundations of the gates of the New Jerusalem: "And he carried me away in the spirit to a great and high mountain, and shewed me that great city, the holy Jerusalem, descending out of heaven from God, Having the glory of God: and her light was like unto a stone most precious, even like a jasper stone, clear as crystal; And had a wall great and high, and had twelve gates, and at the gates twelve angels, and names written thereon, which are the names of the twelve tribes of the children of Israel: On the east three gates; on the north three gates; on the south three gates; and on the west three gates. And the wall of the city had twelve foundations, and in them the names of the twelve apostles of the Lamb" (Revelation 21:10-14). It is, therefore, not difficult to say that the twenty four elders of chapter 4 represent the twelve apostles of the Lord Jesus and the twelve tribes of Israel. All they each will have crowns and will reign with Christ by virtue of their faithfulness to the Lord Jesus.

(5) "And out of the throne proceeded lightnings and thunderings and voices: and there were seven lamps of fire burning before the throne, which are the seven Spirits of God."

- And out of the throne proceeded lightnings and thunderings and voices - This is a description of the greatness and almighty power of God's presence. It is also an indication of the awesomeness of the proclamations of God's eternal purpose: "And it came to pass on the third day in the morning, that there were thunders and lightnings, and a thick cloud upon the mount, and the voice of the trumpet exceeding loud; so that all the people that was in the camp trembled. And Moses brought forth the people out of the camp to meet with God; and they stood at the nether part of the mount. And mount Sinai was altogether on a smoke, because the Lord descended upon it in fire: and the smoke thereof ascended as the smoke of a furnace, and the whole mount quaked greatly. And when the voice of the trumpet sounded long, and waxed louder and louder" (Exodus 19:16-19).

- And there were seven lamps of fire burning before the throne, which are the seven Spirits of God - Before the throne, we see the presence of the Holy Spirit, who illuminates, for all of creation, God's works of righteousness, making this heavenly scene even more brilliant and magnificent.

(6) "And before the throne there was a sea of glass like unto crystal: and in the midst of the throne, and round about the throne, were four beasts full of eyes before and behind."

- And before the throne there was a sea of glass like unto

crystal - "Before the throne" implies in the direct presence of God's presence, whereas "the midst of the throne" implies surrounding in close proximity to the throne. The sea speaks of the vastness of the throne of God and the crystal reflects the transparency of God's nature; so the sea of crystal speaks of the stillness quiet repose and tranquility of God's presence.

- And in the midst of the throne, and round about the throne, were four beasts full of eyes before and behind - These are the four cherubims who are the seat of the throne of God: "Thou that dwellest between the cherubimss, shine forth" (Psalm 80:1). "He sitteth between the cherubimss" (Psalm 99:1).

(7) "And the first beast was like a lion, and the second beast like a calf, and the third beast had a face as a man, and the fourth beast was like a flying eagle."

These are the cheburims, who are also described by Ezekiel. "And I looked, and, behold, a whirlwind came out of the north, a great cloud, and a fire unfolding itself, and a brightness was about it, and out of the midst thereof as the colour of amber, out of the midst of the fire. Also out of the midst thereof came the likeness of four living creatures. And this was their appearance; they had the likeness of a man. And every one had four faces, and every one had four wings. And their feet were straight feet; and the sole of their feet was like the sole of a calf's foot: and they sparkled like the colour of burnished brass. And they had the hands of a man under their wings on their four sides; and they four had their faces and their wings. Their wings were joined one to another; they turned not when they went; they went every one straight forward. As for the likeness of their faces, they four had the face of a man, and the face of a lion, on the right side: and they four had the face of an ox on the left side; they four also had the face of an eagle. Thus were their faces: and their wings were stretched upward; two wings of every one were joined one to another, and two covered their bodies. And they went every one straight forward: whither the spirit was to go, they went; and they turned not when they went. As for the likeness of the living creatures, their appearance was like burning coals of fire, and like the appearance of lamps: it went up and down among the living creatures; and the fire was bright, and out of the fire went forth lightning. And the living creatures ran and returned as the appearance of a flash of lightning. Now as I beheld the living creatures, behold one wheel upon the earth by the living creatures, with his four faces. The appearance of the wheels and their work was like unto the colour of a beryl: and they four had one likeness: and their appearance and their work was as it were a wheel in the middle of a wheel. When they went, they went upon their four sides: and they turned not when they went. As for their rings, they were so high that they were dreadful; and their rings were full of eyes round about them four. And when the living creatures went, the wheels went by them: and when the living creatures were lifted up from the earth, the wheels were lifted up. Whithersoever the spirit was to go, they went, thither was their spirit to go; and the wheels were lifted up over against them: for the spirit of the living creature was in the wheels. When those went, these went; and when those stood, these stood; and when those were lifted up from the earth, the wheels were lifted up over against them: for the spirit of the living creature was in the wheels. And the likeness of the firmament upon the heads of the living creature was as the colour of the terrible crystal, stretched forth over their heads above. And under the firmament were their wings straight, the one toward the other: every one had two, which covered on this side, and every one had two, which covered on that side, their bodies. And when they went, I heard the noise of their wings, like the noise of great waters, as the voice of the Almighty, the voice of speech, as the noise of an host: when they stood, they let down their wings. And there was a voice from the firmament that was over their heads, when they stood, and had let down their wings. And above the firmament that was over their heads was the likeness of a throne, as the appearance of a sapphire stone: and upon the likeness of the throne was the likeness as the appearance of a man above upon it. And I saw as the colour of amber, as the appearance of fire round about within it, from the appearance of his loins even upward, and from the appearance of his loins even downward, I saw as it were the appearance of fire, and it had brightness round about. As the appearance of the bow that is in the cloud in the day of rain, so was the appearance of the brightness round about. This was the appearance of the likeness of the glory of the Lord." "And when I looked, behold the four wheels by the cherubims, one wheel by one cherub, and another wheel by another cherub: and the appearance of the wheels was as the colour of a beryl stone. And as for their appearances, they four had one likeness, as if a wheel had been in the midst of a wheel. When they went, they went upon their four sides; they turned not as they went, but to the place whither the head looked they followed it; they turned not as they went. And their whole body, and their backs, and their hands, and their wings, and the wheels, were full of eyes round about, even the wheels that they four hA.D. As for the wheels, it was cried unto them in my hearing, O wheel. And every one had four faces: the first face was the face of a cherub, and the second face was the face of a man, and the third the face of a lion, and the fourth the face of an eagle. And the cherubimss were lifted up. This is the living creature that I saw by the river of Chebar. And when the cherubimss went, the wheels went by them: and when the cherubimss lifted up their wings to mount up from the earth, the same wheels also turned not from beside them. When they stood, these stood; and when they were lifted up, these lifted up themselves also: for the spirit of the living creature was in them"; "This is the living creature that I saw under the God of Israel by the river of Chebar; and I knew that they were the cherubimss" (Ezekiel 1:4-28; 10:9-17,20).

In this description, we see the following symbols: "lion" is a symbol of God's power, "calf" is a symbol of God's untiring and unfailing perseverance, "the face of a man" is a symbol of God's wisdom and understanding, and a "flying eagle" is a symbol of God's swiftness.

(8) "And the four beasts had each of them six wings about him; and they were full of eyes within: and they rest not day and night, saying, Holy, holy, holy, Lord God Almighty, which was, and is, and is to come."

The many eyes symbolize the comprehensiveness of God's vision, that he sees all and nothing is hidden from him. Saying "Holy" three times speaks of the Triune God, and of his complete holiness!

Every cherub is independent of the other cherubims. "And he rode upon a cherub, and did fly: and he was seen upon the wings of the wind" (2 Samuel 22:11). "And he rode upon a cherub, and did fly: yea, he did fly upon the wings of the wind" (Psalm 18:10).

The four cherubims form the throne of God the Father, God the Son, and God the Holy Spirit. Elohim dwells between the cherubims: "O Lord God of Israel, which dwellest between the cherubimss" (2 Kings 19:15). "The Lord reigneth; let the people tremble: he sitteth between the cherubimss" (Psalms 99:1). "Then did the cherubimss lift up their wings, and the wheels beside them; and the glory of the God of Israel was over them above" (Ezekiel 11:22).

(9) "And when those beasts give glory and honour and thanks to him that sat on the throne, who liveth for ever and ever."

There is organization and hierarchy in the realm of angels:

(i) First are, the cherubims are the highest ranking angels: "And the sound of the cherubimss wings was heard even to the outer court, as the voice of the Almighty God when he speaketh" (Ezekiel 10:5).

(ii) Second, after them in position are the seraphim: "In the year that king Uzziah died I saw also the Lord sitting upon a throne, high and lifted up, and his train filled the temple. Above it stood the seraphims" (Isaiah 6:1-2).

(iii) Third, are the chief princes, the archangels. There are two of them mentioned by name in Scripture: Michael and Gabriel. A third is mentioned in the apocrypha: Raphael; and a fourth one, Ariel, mentioned in Jewish tradition. Here are the Biblical two: "But the prince of the kingdom of Persia withstood me one and twenty days: but, lo, Michael, one of the chief princes, came to help me; and I remained there with the kings of Persia" (Daniel 10:13); "And the angel answering said unto him, I am Gabriel, that stand in the presence of God; and am sent to speak unto thee, and to shew thee these glad tidings" (Luke 1:19); "For the Lord himself shall descend from heaven with a shout, with the voice of the archangel" (1 Thessalonians 4:16).

(iv) Fourth are the elect angles: "When the Son of man shall come in his glory, and all the holy angels with him, then shall he sit upon the throne of his glory" (Matthew 25:31).

The whole world of righteous angels stand in the presence of God in his temple where they:

(i) Continuously praise him: "And in his temple doth every one speak of his glory" (Psalms 29:9); "I saw also the Lord sitting upon a throne, high and lifted up, and his train filled the temple. Above it stood the seraphims: each one had six wings; with twain he covered his face, and with twain he covered his feet, and with twain he did fly. And one cried unto another, and said, Holy, holy, holy, is the Lord of hosts: the whole earth is full of his glory. And the posts of the door moved at the voice of him that cried, and the house was filled with smoke" (Isaiah 6:1-4).

(ii) And serve him: "I saw the Lord sitting on his throne, and all the host of heaven standing by him on his right hand and on his left" (1 Kings 22:19).

(10) "The four and twenty elders fall down before him that sat on the throne, and worship him that liveth for ever and ever, and cast their crowns before the throne, saying,"

The twenty-four elders also worship the Lord Jesus Christ; casting their crowns to give him recognition and proclaim before all that these crowns that they possess were received through the grace of Christ: "I am the vine, ye are the branches: He that abideth in me, and I in him, the same bringeth forth much fruit: for without me ye can do nothing" (John 15:5). Thus, all worship and adoration belong to the Lord Jesus Christ.

(11) "Thou art worthy, O Lord, to receive glory and honour and power: for thou hast created all things, and for thy pleasure they are and were created."

Indeed, all honour and glory and power and blessing and greatness belong to the Lord Jesus Christ; for of him, through him, and to him are all things. He is the creator and: "in him we live, and move, and have our being" (Acts 17:28). Jesus is the creator of the universe and: "Upholding all things by the word of his power"; "And, Thou, Lord, in the beginning hast laid the foundation of the earth; and the heavens are the works of thine hands" (Hebrews 1:10). Today, the world is subject to vanity, but it will be liberated; it will be delivered unto the liberty of the glory of God. "For the earnest expectation of the creature waiteth for the manifestation of the sons of God. For the creature was made subject to vanity, not willingly, but by reason of him who hath subjected the same in hope, Because the creature itself also shall be delivered from the bondage of corruption into the glorious liberty of the children of God" (Romans 8:19-21).

The cherubims are intelligent, and so are the smart elders, for they bring all glory to its rightful place, to the feet of the Lord Jesus. This would be the behavior of every intelligent person among us, because: "at the name of Jesus every knee should bow, of things in heaven, and things in earth, and things under the earth; And that every tongue should confess that Jesus Christ is Lord, to the glory of God the Father." (Philippians 2:10-11). Acknowledge him now as your Lord and Saviour, or later, as your judge. Repent of your sins and open your heart to Jesus so that you will be saved!

5
THE EARTH'S DEED OF OWNERSHIP

(1) "And I saw in the right hand of him that sat on the throne a book written within and on the backside, sealed with seven seals."

At the right hand of Majesty, that is at the right hand of God the Father, we see the earth's title deed of ownership. It is sealed with God's judgment which consists of seven seals; where the seventh seal opens up seven trumpets, and the seventh trumpet pours out seven vials completing the wrath of God.

The judgement of God begins with the first seal: "And I saw when the Lamb opened one of the seals, and I heard, as it were the noise of thunder, one of the four beasts saying, Come and see" (Revelation 6:1); and ends with the last vial: "And the seventh angel poured out his vial into the air; and there came a great voice out of the temple of heaven, from the throne, saying, It is done" (Revelation 16:17); which will have brought about the end of Babylon: "And the light of a candle shall shine no more at all in thee; and the voice of the bridegroom and of the bride shall be heard no more at all in thee: for thy merchants were the great men of the earth; for by thy sorceries were all nations deceived. And in her was found the blood of prophets, and of saints, and of all that were slain upon the earth." (Revelation 18:23-24).

And so the great tribulation extends from (Revelation 6:1) to (Revelation 18:24), and Revelation 19 ushers in Christ's reign on the earth: "And a voice came out of the throne, saying, Praise our God, all ye his servants, and ye that fear him, both small and great. And I heard as it were the voice of a great multitude, and as the voice of many waters, and as the voice of mighty thunderings, saying, Alleluia: for the Lord God omnipotent reigneth" (Revelation 19:5-6).

(2) "And I saw a strong angel proclaiming with a loud voice, Who is worthy to open the book, and to loose the seals thereof?"

We saw in Revelation 4:6 that the One sitting upon the throne is, in fact, sitting upon four cherubims. In studying Scripture, we understand that God had created five cherubims to serve as his throne. In one of these five cherubims, the anointed covering cherub, iniquity was found for he was lifted with pride. This was Lucifer himself: "How art thou fallen from heaven, O Lucifer, son of the morning! how art thou cut down to the ground, which didst weaken the nations! For thou hast said in thine heart, I will ascend into heaven, I will exalt my throne above the stars of God: I will sit also upon the mount of the congregation, in the sides of the north: I will ascend above the heights of the clouds; I will be like the most High" (Isaiah 14:12-14); "Thou art the anointed cherub that covereth; and I have set thee so: thou wast upon the holy mountain of God; thou hast walked up and down in the midst of the stones of fire. Thou wast perfect in thy ways from the day that thou wast created, till iniquity was found in thee" (Ezekiel 28:14-15).

In the Bible there is an enigma called "the mystery of iniquity" (2 Thessalonians 2:7) that we do not understand, but the Lord Jesus will reveal it to us when we are with him for then we will be like him: "Beloved, now are we the sons of God, and it doth not yet appear what we shall be: but we know that, when he shall appear, we shall be like him; for we shall see him as he is" (1 John 3:2). What happened to the cherub in whom iniquity was found, namely Lucifer? God expelled him from heaven, and threw him to earth and he assumed its ownership. This is clear from what the Bible says when he records one of the temptations of Jesus when Satan tried Christ: "And the devil said unto him, All this power will I give thee, and the glory of them: for that is delivered unto me; and to whomsoever I will I give it" (Luke 4:6). Satan the accursed held dominion over this earthly globe and brought to both man and animal, death, diseases, disabilities, sadness, crying, tears, thorns, ruin, and destruction, accompanied with hatred, envy, murder, malice, fornication, theft, and lying for he is the father of lies and a murderer from the beginning).

The world became sold under sin, enslaved to Satan; the human race and all creation groans, travails, and suffers: "Because the creature itself also shall be delivered from the bondage of corruption into the glorious liberty of the children of God. For we know that the whole creation groaneth and travaileth in pain together until now" (Romans 8:21-22). So all seek salvation: "Of which salvation the prophets have enquired and searched diligently, who prophesied of the grace that should come unto you: Searching what, or what manner of time the Spirit of Christ which was in them did signify, when it testified beforehand the sufferings of Christ, and the glory that should follow" (1 Peter 1:10-11). Thank God, for Jesus, completed salvation for us on the cross when he announced to the Father; and to us: "It is finished" (John 19:30).

(3) "And no man in heaven, nor in earth, neither under the earth, was able to open the book, neither to look thereon."

It seemed as if the state of man was without hope, without redemption, and without salvation, for it looked as if there was no one capable or worthy to provide a remedy for man's calamity.

(4) "And I wept much, because no man was found worthy to open and to read the book, neither to look thereon."

John cried and even heaven cried over man and his state because there was no one worthy to redeem man and buy him back and regain the title deed of ownership of the earth to God.

(5) "And one of the elders saith unto me, Weep not: behold, the Lion of the tribe of Judah, the Root of David, hath prevailed to open the book, and to loose the seven seals thereof."

One of the twenty four elders comforted John and encouraged him that the Lord Jesus is the Almighty one who won, on the cross, and is therefore able to open the seven seals of the book and claim ownership of the book.

We do not know why God, in his wisdom, gave Satan dominion over planet earth, but we know that there is a spiritual war raging today in the heavenly places as God uses the four cherubims to reclaim the title deed of ownership of the earth from Satan, the fallen cherub. So it is with us believers as we are engaged in a war against Satan for the souls of people in our communities, with the purpose of winning these souls to Jesus Christ: "For we wrestle not against flesh and blood, but against principalities, against powers, against the rulers of the darkness of this world, against spiritual wickedness in high places" (Ephesians 6:12); "Now thanks be unto God, which always causeth us to triumph in Christ, and maketh manifest the savour of his knowledge by us in every place" (2 Corinthians 2:14); "Blessed be the God and Father of our Lord Jesus Christ, who hath blessed us with all spiritual blessings in heavenly places in Christ" (Ephesians 1:3).

The joy of our hearts is that God in his holy love has sent his beloved Son, Jesus Christ, to purchase the earth and redeem the human race. So we thank God that our comfort and our salvation are in Jesus. But who is Jesus? He is God incarnate the flesh; the one with both a divine nature and a human nature. "And without controversy great is the mystery of godliness: God was manifest in the flesh" (1 Timothy 3:16). God put on the robe of humanity and was incarnated of the seed of Abraham, to whom the Lord God had said: "And in thy seed shall all the kindreds of the earth be blessed" (Acts 3:25); and Isaac gave birth to Jacob who is Israel: "Thy name shall be called no more Jacob, but Israel: for as a prince hast thou power with God and with men, and hast prevailed" (Genesis 32:28). The seed of Jacob is: "Israelites; to whom pertaineth the adoption, and the glory, and the covenants, and the giving of the law, and the service of God, and the promises; Whose are the fathers, and of whom as concerning the flesh Christ came" (Romans 9:4-5). Jesus came of the seed of Israel, and in particular, from the tribe of Judah: "For Judah prevailed above his brethren, and of him came the chief ruler" (1 Chronicles 5:2). "And thou Bethlehem, in the land of Juda, art not the least among the princes of Juda: for out of thee shall come a Governor, that shall rule my people Israel" (Matthew 2:6). This was prophesied by Zechariah, the father of John the Baptist when he said: "Blessed be the Lord God of Israel; for he hath visited and redeemed his people, And hath raised up an horn of salvation for us in the house of his servant David" (Luke 1:68-69).

God was incarnated in the person of Jesus Christ; and because Christ was born of a virgin, he was without sin, and so was capable or eligible to purchase us with his own blood, the blood of God: "The church of God, which he hath purchased with his own blood" (Acts 20:28). The virgin birth was necessary because a man inherits the characteristics of the blood of his father. So the blood of Jesus was undefiled because of God the Holy Spirit not of man was therefore able to atone for the sins of the world. The Christian religion is the only religion in the world that excels in that it has the distinctive of providing a solution for the problem of sin: "For the wages of sin is death; but the gift of God is eternal life through Jesus Christ our Lord" (Romans 6:23). "And without shedding of blood is no remission"

(Hebrews 9:22). "The blood of Jesus Christ his Son cleanseth us from all sin" (1 John 1:7).

This is why the Lord Jesus testifies that the prophets that came before him were robbers and thieves; for they did offer forgiveness of sins and salvation to man. Likewise those that come after him are false prophets for there is no need for them because Jesus has already provided the solution for the sins of mankind, his precious blood.

(6) "And I beheld, and, lo, in the midst of the throne and of the four beasts, and in the midst of the elders, stood a Lamb as it had been slain, having seven horns and seven eyes, which are the seven Spirits of God sent forth into all the earth."

This lion is at the same time, the Lamb of God who was slain so that our sins may be forgiven: "The next day John seeth Jesus coming unto him, and saith, Behold the Lamb of God, which taketh away the sin of the world" (John 1:29). This is Christ the Son of God who has all the power of God, as symbolized in the seven horns: and possesses all the perfect holiness of God, represented in the seven Holy Spirits of God. He is the Son of God who was sent down to the earth, and is standing now before the Father to commence his judgment on earth. It is about to begin with opening of the first seal in Revelation 6:1.

(7) "And he came and took the book out of the right hand of him that sat upon the throne."

Jesus went to the cross, where he overcame and triumphed and returned to heaven with the victory of his resurrection and purchased us with his own blood. So it became his legitimate right to take the book from the right hand of the presence of God and to open its seals, because it became his by the power of his cross.

The Lord Jesus came for our redemption, finished his work, and returned to heaven after giving us the great commission, in asking people to surrender the title deeds of their lives to the Lord Jesus, so that he will forgive their sins and thus be saved from the fires of hell and bringing them to eternal life in paradise, in the third heaven, the presence of the throne of God: "Such an one caught up to the third heaven ... caught up into paradise, and heard unspeakable words, which it is not lawful for a man to utter" (2 Corinthians 12:2-4).

Get the message and take the lesson oh man for what is the average lifespan of a man? "The days of our years are threescore years and ten; and if by reason of strength they be fourscore years, yet is their strength labour and sorrow" (Psalm 90:10); that is to say, there is nothing in this life worth living for except the love of the Lord Jesus and the opportunity to serve him: "Behold, I stand at the door, and knock: if any man hear my voice, and open the door, I will come in to him, and will sup with him, and he with me. To him that overcometh will I grant to sit with me in my throne, even as I also overcame, and am set down with my Father in his throne" (Revelation 3:20-21).

(8) "And when he had taken the book, the four beasts and four and twenty elders fell down before the Lamb, having every one of them harps, and golden vials full of odours, which are the prayers of saints."

The four cherubims and the twelve tribes with the twelve apostles and all the great heaven and earth and creation willl bow down and offer prayers of thanksgiving and worship to the Lord Jesus!

(9) "And they sung a new song, saying, Thou art worthy to take the book, and to open the seals thereof: for thou wast slain, and hast redeemed us to God by thy blood out of every kindred, and tongue, and people, and nation."

Jesus is worthy to be praised with songs from the heart because he deserves all adoration and worship and exaltation. For he left his glory in heaven and took upon himself the form of a servant and went to the cross and purchased us with his shed blood and died and arose from the dead, securing our redemption: "What? know ye not that your body is the temple of the Holy Ghost which is in you, which ye have of God, and ye are not your own? For ye are bought with a price: therefore glorify God in your body, and in your spirit, which are God's"; "Ye are bought with a price; be not ye the servants of men" (1 Corinthians 6:19-20; 7:23).

(10) "And hast made us unto our God kings and priests: and we shall reign on the earth."

He paid his blood as the price for our purchase; and when we became his own, we became heirs of the kingdom with him: "Heirs of the kingdom which he hath promised to them that love him" (James 2:5), and so he made us kings and priests with him in his millennial reign on the earth.

(11) "And I beheld, and I heard the voice of many angels round about the throne and the beasts and the elders: and the number of them was ten thousand times ten thousand, and thousands of thousands."

All of heaven, including thousands and millions of holy angels and righteous saints, participate in adoration and worship of the Lord Jesus Christ, the Son of the living God: "And let all the angels of God worship him" (Hebrews 1:6); "That at the name of Jesus every knee should bow, of things in heaven, and things in earth, and things under the earth; And that every tongue should confess that Jesus Christ is Lord, to the glory of God the Father" (Ephesians 2:10-11).

(12) "Saying with a loud voice, Worthy is the Lamb that was slain to receive power, and riches, and wisdom, and strength, and honour, and glory, and blessing."

One word sums up all: "worthy". The Lord Jesus deserves all the fullness of praise that is comprised of:

(i) Power,
(ii) Riches,
(iii) Wisdom,
(iv) Strength,
(v) Honour,

(vi) Glory,

(vii) Blessing!

(13) "And every creature which is in heaven, and on the earth, and under the earth, and such as are in the sea, and all that are in them, heard I saying, Blessing, and honour, and glory, and power, be unto him that sitteth upon the throne, and unto the Lamb for ever and ever."

All creation: "In the beginning God created the heaven and the earth" (Genesis 1:1); "I have made the earth, the man and the beast that are upon the ground, by my great power and by my outstretched arm" (Jeremiah 27:5). They all are going to worship and exalt God the father and the Lord Jesus Christ.

(14) "And the four beasts said, Amen. And the four and twenty elders fell down and worshipped him that liveth for ever and ever."

Heaven asserts this declaration and affirmedly absolutely executes worship and exaltation and praise, non-stop for-ever.

6
THE SIX SEALS – BEGINNING OF JUDGMENTS ON EARTH –

(1) "And I saw when the Lamb opened one of the seals, and I heard, as it were the noise of thunder, one of the four beasts saying, Come and see."

In Revelation 4 the scene changed from the Earth to Heaven, and here in Revelation 6 the focus goes back from Heaven to Earth, where God continues the Daniel great week described as "Jacob's trouble". At that point, God is going to pour out his wrath on the people of Israel for crucifying Jesus Christ: "Wrath upon this people" (Luke 21:23); as they themselves ruled when they said: "His blood be on us, and on our children" (Matthew 27:25).

What is important about this scene is that the one who pours out the wrath is the Lord Jesus himself for the Bible says: "the Father judgeth no man, but hath committed all judgment unto the Son: That all men should honour the Son, even as they honour the Father. He that honoureth not the Son honoureth not the Father which hath sent him" (John 5:22-23). The one who commences the pouring out of God's wrath is Jesus: "the righteous judge" (2 Timothy 4:8).

We return to the subject of the seventy weeks whose particular features are:

(I) A double implementation of the seventy weeks of years:

(i) The first fulfilment is a historical implementation of Jeremiah's prophecy in which he states that God has appointed seventy years of punishment on Israel for defiling the Lord's Sabbaths. This began in 607 B.C. with the first Babylonian captivity of Judah; and lasted 70 years ending with the call of Cyrus king of Persia for the Jews to return to the land and rebuild the temple: "[11]And this whole land shall be a desolation, and an astonishment; and these nations shall serve the king of Babylon seventy years.[12] And it shall come to pass, when seventy years are accomplished, that I will punish the king of Babylon"; "[7]And all nations shall serve him, and his son, and his son's son"; "[10]For thus saith the Lord, That after seventy years be accomplished at Babylon I will visit you, and perform my good word toward you, in causing you to return to this place" (Jeremiah 25:11-12; 27:7; 29:10) ; "[2]In the first year of his reign I Daniel understood by books the number of the years, whereof the word of the Lord came to Jeremiah the prophet, that he would accomplish seventy years in the desolations of Jerusalem", "[23]At the beginning of thy supplications the commandment came forth, and I am come to shew thee; for thou art greatly beloved: therefore understand the matter, and consider the vision. [24]Seventy weeks are determined upon thy people and upon thy holy city, to finish the transgression, and to make an end of sins, and to make reconciliation for iniquity, and to bring in everlasting righteousness, and to seal up the vision and prophecy, and to anoint the most Holy" (Daniel 9:2, 23-24) ; "[1]Now in the first year of Cyrus king of Persia, that the word of the Lord by the mouth of Jeremiah might be fulfilled, the Lord stirred up the spirit of Cyrus king of Persia, that he made a proclamation throughout all his kingdom, and put it also in writing, saying, [2]Thus saith Cyrus king of Persia, The

Lord God of heaven hath given me all the kingdoms of the earth; and he hath charged me to build him an house at Jerusalem, which is in Judah" (Ezra 1:1-2).

(ii) The second fulfilment is prophetic and is current today:

(a) It began with the decree of Artaxerxes in 449 B.C. to Nehemiah to rebuild the walls of the city of Jerusalem: "⁷Moreover I said unto the king, If it please the king, let letters be given me to the governors beyond the river, that they may convey me over till I come into Judah; ⁸And a letter unto Asaph the keeper of the king's forest, that he may give me timber to make beams for the gates of the palace which appertained to the house, and for the wall of the city, and for the house that I shall enter into. And the king granted me, according to the good hand of my God upon me. ⁹Then I came to the governors beyond the river, and gave them the king's letters. Now the king had sent captains of the army and horsemen with me" (Nehemiah 2:7-9).

(b) The 69 weeks continued and lasted until 34 A.D. $(7 + 62 = 69 \times 7) = 483$ B.C. $-$ 449 B.C., the year of Artaxerxes decree, take us to 34 A.D. the year in which Christ was crucified, risen and ascended to heaven.

(c) We now are in the state of suspension awaiting the culmination of the Church age for resuming and finishing off the seventieth week: "²⁵Know therefore and understand, that from the going forth of the commandment to restore and to build Jerusalem unto the Messiah the Prince shall be seven weeks, and threescore and two weeks: the street shall be built again, and the wall, even in troublous times. ²⁶And after threescore and two weeks shall Messiah be cut off, but not for himself: and the people of the prince that shall come shall destroy the city and the sanctuary; and the end thereof shall be with a flood, and unto the end of the war desolations are determined" (Daniel 9:25-26).

Then will be completed God's dealing with the nation of Israel in the last week of chastisement over Jerusalem before bringing in the everlasting righteousness and bliss: ²⁷And he shall confirm the covenant with many for one week: and in the midst of the week he shall cause the sacrifice and the oblation to cease, and for the overspreading of abominations he shall make it desolate, even until the consummation, and that determined shall be poured upon the desolate."(Daniel 9:27).

(II) The entire prophecy revolves around the "people" of Daniel and the "holy city" of Daniel; that is the people of Israel and the city of Jerusalem.

(III) The seventy weeks in the prophecy are weeks of years: "Fulfil her week, and we will give thee this also for the service which thou shalt serve with me yet seven other years" (Gen 29:27).

(IV) There are two princes mentioned in these weeks:

(i) The first is "Messiah the Prince" who is the Lord Jesus Christ in the time of his incarnation; that is, in his first coming;

(ii) The second is the "prince that shall come" who is the Antichrist, the last little horn in Daniel's prophecy: "I considered the horns, and, behold, there came up among them another little horn, before whom there were three of the first horns plucked up by the roots: and, behold, in this horn were eyes like the eyes of man, and a mouth speaking great things" (Daniel 7:8). It is he whose people or his army are going to lay siege to Jerusalem and destroy it a third time: "And when ye shall see

Jerusalem compassed with armies, then know that the desolation thereof is nigh" (Luke 21:20); before the second coming of the Lord Jesus "the Messiah the Prince" (Daniel 9:25).

(V) Historically, the destruction Jerusalem occurs three times:

(i) The first time at hands of Nebuchadnezzar in 586 B.C.;

(ii) The second time at the hands of Titus the Roman general in 70 A.D.;

(iii) The third will be at the hands of the Antichrist and his armies at the end of the seventieth week. When the Lord Jesus returns he is going to deliver Jerusalem from the Gentiles who had trodden her for a third time: "And they shall fall by the edge of the sword, and shall be led away captive into all nations: and Jerusalem shall be trodden down of the Gentiles, until the Times of the Gentiles be fulfilled" (Luke 21:24).

(VI) The last week, the seven year period, is divided into two halves, three and a half years each: "And he shall confirm the covenant with many for one week: and in the midst of the week he shall cause the sacrifice and the oblation to cease, and for the overspreading of abominations he shall make it desolate, even until the consummation, and that determined shall be poured upon the desolate" (Daniel 9:27). The first half is called the Tribulation and is characterized by a false peace. The second is called the Great Tribulation and is referred to in several ways throughout the Bible:

(i) "A time and times and the dividing of time": "And he shall speak great words against the most High, and shall wear out the saints of the most High, and think to change times and laws: and they shall be given into his hand until a time and times and the dividing of time" (Daniel 7:25). "And to the woman were given two wings of a great eagle, that she might fly into the wilderness, into her place, where she is nourished for a time, and times, and half a time, from the face of the serpent" (Revelation 12:14).

(ii) "Forty and two months": "But the court which is without the temple leave out, and measure it not; for it is given unto the Gentiles: and the holy city shall they tread under foot forty and two months" (Revelation 11:2). "And there was given unto him a mouth speaking great things and blasphemies; and power was given unto him to continue forty and two months" (Revelation 13:5).

(iii) One thousand two hundred and sixty days": "But the court which is without the temple leave out, and measure it not; for it is given unto the Gentiles: and the holy city shall they tread under foot forty and two months. And I will give power unto my two witnesses, and they shall prophesy a thousand two hundred and threescore days, clothed in sackcloth" (Revelation 11:2-3). "And the woman fled into the wilderness, where she hath a place prepared of God, that they should feed her there a thousand two hundred and threescore days" (Revelation 12:6).

(VII) The Times of the Gentiles, Jeremiah's seventy years, and Daniel's seventy weeks, all center around the captivity of Judah and the fall of Jerusalem. The number "seven" is important in Jewish numerology and a seven year span is important in Jewish time-reckoning. The Jews violated the commandment to keep the seventh or "sabbatical" year. So when God

brought upon them the judgment of the Babylonian captivity, he determined its length by the number of years in which they violated the sabbatical years. That was from the days of King Saul until the time of

captivity, around four hundred and ninety years equivalent to seventy sabbatical years: "^{3}Ye shall

fear every man his mother, and his father, and keep my sabbaths: I am the Lord your God"; "^{4}But in the seventh year shall be a sabbath of rest unto the land, a sabbath for the Lord: thou shalt neither sow thy field, nor prune thy vineyard"; "^{43}The land also shall be left of them, and shall enjoy her sabbaths, while she lieth desolate without them: and they shall accept of the punishment of their iniquity: because, even because they despised my judgments, and because their soul abhorred my statutes" (Leviticus 19:3; 25:4; 26:43); "²⁰And them that had escaped from the sword carried he away to Babylon.... for as long as she lay desolate she kept sabbath, to fulfil threescore and ten years" (2 Chronicles 36:20...21).

(VIII) The captivity was in 3 phases:

(i) The first captivity, the captivity of Manasseh, occurred in 607 B.C.: "³³Wherefore the LORD brought upon them the captains of the host of the king of Assyria, which took Manasseh among the thorns, and bound him with fetters, and carried him to Babylon" (2 Chronicles 33:11).

(ii) The second captivity, the captivity of Jehoiachin, occurred in 597 B.C. "⁹Jehoiachin was eight years old when he began to reign, and he reigned three months and ten days in Jerusalem: and he did that which was evil in the sight of the LORD. ¹⁰And when the year was expired, king Nebuchadnezzar sent, and brought him to Babylon, with the goodly vessels of the house of the LORD, and made Zedekiah his brother king over Judah and Jerusalem" (2 Chronicles 36:9-10).

(iii) The third and final captivity, the captivity of Zedekiah, occurred in 586 B.C.: "⁵but the Babylonian army pursued the king and overtook him in the plains of Jericho. All his soldiers were separated from him and scattered, ⁶and he was captured. He was taken to the king of Babylon at Riblah, where sentence was pronounced on him. ⁷They killed the sons of Zedekiah before his eyes. Then they put out his eyes, bound him with bronze shackles and took him to Babylon. ⁸On the seventh day of the fifth month, in the nineteenth year of Nebuchadnezzar king of Babylon, Nebuzaradan commander of the imperial guard, an official of the king of Babylon, came to Jerusalem. ⁹He set fire to the temple of the Lord, the royal palace and all the houses of Jerusalem. Every important building he burned down. ¹⁰The whole Babylonian army under the commander of the imperial guard broke down the walks around Jerusalem. (2 Kings 25:5-10).

Jerusalem did not fall until the third stage of the captivity and the Temple and walls were destroyed.

(IX) The main events of the final "week" are that at the beginning of the wee, the Antichrist will make a peace treaty with all the factions of the world especially with the Jews and Arabs; and in the middle of that week he will suddenly breach the treaty with the Jews and desecrate the Temple that will have been rebuilt then: "²⁷And he shall confirm the covenant with many for one

week: and in the midst of the week he shall cause the sacrifice and the oblation to cease, and for the overspreading of abominations he shall make it desolate, even until the consummation, and that determined shall be poured upon the desolate" (Daniel 9:27).

(X) The intervening period between the sixty-ninth week and the seventieth week is the period of the Fullness of the Gentiles, also known as the dispensation of the church: "¹¹Blindness in part is happened to Israel, until the fullness of the Gentiles be come in" (Romans 11:25).

At the end of the seventieth week, judgment comes on the one who has ruined and destroyed the world, who is the Antichrist. And then comes the "everlasting righteousness" of the true Christ the Lord Jesus the Son of the living God is brought in, with all the blessings of the kingdom of the true real Christ: "I saw in the night visions, and, behold, one like the Son of man came with the clouds of heaven, and came to the Ancient of days, and they brought him near before him. And there was given him dominion, and glory, and a kingdom, that all people, nations, and languages, should serve him: his dominion [is] an everlasting dominion, which shall not pass away, and his kingdom that which shall not be destroyed … And the kingdom and dominion, and the greatness of the kingdom under the whole heaven, shall be given to the people of the saints of the most High, whose kingdom is an everlasting kingdom, and all dominions shall serve and obey him. Hitherto is the end of the matter. As for me Daniel, my cogitations much troubled me, and my countenance changed in me: but I kept the matter in my heart" (Daniel 7:13-14, 27-28).

This final week has not yet come. This is established by the fact that Christ clearly associates many of its main events with his second coming. "And ye shall hear of wars and rumours of wars: see that ye be not troubled: for all these things must come to pass, but the end is not yet ... When ye therefore shall see the abomination of desolation, spoken of by Daniel the prophet, stand in the holy place, (whoso readeth, let him understand)" (Matthew 24:6,15).

We return now to exposition of verse 1. In (Revelation 4:1) the church age has ended. It was: "The dispensation of the grace of God", "the mystery of Christ", "That the Gentiles should be fellowheirs, and of the same body, and partakers of his promise in Christ by the gospel", "to make all men see what is the fellowship of the mystery, which from the beginning of the world hath been hid in God, who created all things by Jesus Christ" (Ephesians 3:2,4,6,9). Now in (Revelation 6:1) the church age has ended, and God is now finishing off his chastisement of the nation of Israel.

The great tribulation begins with the opening of the first of the seven seals; the seals which kept the title deed to the earth closed (as mentioned in chapter five). Here, one of the four cherubims speaks with John and calls him to watch the great tribulation from heaven; and to see is going to happen upon the earth. In like manner, we, the believers, the church of Christ, will watch from heaven and see what will be happening on the earth during the great tribulation!

(2) "And I saw, and behold a white horse: and he that sat on

him had a bow; and a crown was given unto him: and he went forth conquering, and to conquer."

The first event that occurs after the rapture of the Church is the revealing of the Antichrist: "For the mystery of iniquity doth already work: only he who now letteth will let, until he be taken out of the way. And then shall that Wicked be revealed" (2 Thessalonians 2:7-8). This cannot be a description of the person of the Lord Jesus Christ, the Lord of glory. "And I saw heaven opened, and behold a white horse; and he that sat upon him was called Faithful and True, and in righteousness he doth judge and make war. His eyes were as a flame of fire, and on his head were many crowns; and he had a name written, that no man knew, but he himself. And he was clothed with a vesture dipped in blood: and his name is called The Word of God. And the armies which were in heaven followed him upon white horses, clothed in fine linen, white and clean. And out of his mouth goeth a sharp sword, that with it he should smite the nations: and he shall rule them with a rod of iron: and he treadeth the winepress of the fierceness and wrath of Almighty God. And he hath on his vesture and on his thigh a name written, King Of Kings, And Lord Of Lords" (Revelation 19:11-16).

Some of the comparisons between Christ and the Antichrist are:

(1) Antichrist: Son of Perdition
Christ: Son of God
(2) Antichrist: Carries a bow with arrows hidden for deception
Christ: Carries a sword for justice
(3) Antichrist: Wears a single crown because he is king over Europe only
Christ: Wears many crowns for he is King over all kingdoms of earth
(4) Antichrist: Rides a white horse with no mention of the colour of his attire for his coming is

with a pretense only of peace

Christ: Attire is red because the blood of Jesus brings true lasting peace

(5) Antichrist: Brings famine, plagues, wars, and death

Christ: Brings peace, love, life, joy, and gladness

(6) Antichrist: No one knows where he come from

Christ: Heavens opens up and Christ descends

(7) Antichrist: Liar

Christ: Truthful

(8) Antichrist: Idol Shepherd

Christ: Good Shepherd

(9) Antichrist: Comes to do his own will

Christ: Came to do the Father's will

(10) Antichrist: Beast from the bottomless pit

Christ: Lamb of God

(11) Antichrist: Seed of the Serpent

Christ: Seed of the woman

(12) Antichrist: Murderer

Christ: Gives Life

So here begins the first of God's judgments with a false peace that the Antichrist will make with many nations in the world once he sits upon the throne of Europe, the throne of the Antichrist. The European Union will be the center of the Antichrist's authority and from there he will have influence over the whole world. The Roman Empire was the great ruling power in the world (including the Middle East) at the time of the first coming of Christ; similarly, the European Union will have great influence in the Middle East at that end of days, at the time of the second coming of Christ. The boundaries of European influence and authority will be the same as the borders of the Roman Empire in the days of Christ. There, the beast who will be revived will rule: "And I saw one of his heads as it were wounded to death; and his deadly wound was healed: and all the world wondered after the beast" (Revelation 13:3).

Daniel says that the Antichrist will come as a tax collector: "Then shall stand up in his estate a raiser of taxes in the glory of the kingdom" (Daniel 11:20). On the world stage today, we can already see how taxation in European countries has increased dramatically.

Another characteristic of the Antichrist, mentioned in the book of Daniel, is that he will be a man of deceit: "And in the latter time of their kingdom, when the transgressors are come to the full, a king of fierce countenance, and understanding dark sentences, shall stand up" (Daniel 8:23). He will be wily as a fox in the implementation of his plans.

The beginning of the Antichrist's administration will involve the spreading of a false peace which is seen in the image of a rider having a bow but without any arrows. He will appear on the world stage as a man who can solve all the problems facing humanity, and so begins the great tribulation: "For when they shall say, Peace and safety; then sudden destruction cometh upon them, as travail upon a woman with child; and they shall not escape" (1 Thessalonians 5:3).

A horse is a symbol of strength and success in the Bible. The implication is that the Antichrist will succeed in forging a false peace between the Jews and the Arabs. Establishing peace between Jews and Arabs will be an amazing, historic achievement. However, once we become aware of the identity of the Antichrist, the amazement fades, since it be obvious how he created this false peace, one that will only last for three and a half years: "And he shall confirm the covenant with many for one week" (Daniel 9:27). It is his identity that is going to help achieve his goals. It is going to be as such: In Acts chapter 8, 9, and 10, three specific individuals are saved, namely the Ethiopian eunuch who is of the line of Ham; Saul of Tarsus who is of the line of Shem; and the Roman centurion, Cornelius, who is of the line of Japheth. This means that the salvation of God reaching all the human race thru Shem, Ham, Japheth, Noah, and Adam. On the opposite end of the spectrum, the entire human race will be guilty of the Antichrist, who will have some lineal connection with each of Shem, Ham, and Japheth:

(i) With regard to the line of Ham, the Antichrist will have blood of the line of Ishmael. The Bible says of Ishmael: "And he grew, and dwelt in the wilderness, and became an archer" (Genesis 21:20). This is prophecy fulfilled when the Antichrist appears on the world scene as an archer.

(ii) With regard to Shem, the Bible prophecy says that: "Dan shall be a serpent by the way, an adder in the path, that biteth the horse heels, so that his rider shall fall backward" (Genesis 49:17). The serpent is a symbol of Satan and also of the Antichrist. For this reason, the tribe of Dan is not mentioned in the 144,000, who are given the special ministry of testifying to the Real Christ during the great tribulation (Revelation 7:4-8). The tribes of Israel are thirteen not twelve because Joseph gets two shares - Ephraim and Manasseh: "And now thy two sons, Ephraim and Manasseh, which were born unto thee in the land of Egypt before I came unto thee into Egypt, are mine; as Reuben and Simeon, they shall be mine" (Genesis 48:5). Only every time they are listed in the Bible they are listed as twelve; each time, one of them is excluded for some reason, depending on the matter in hand. For instance, in the book of Joshua, at the distribution of the land to the twelve tribes, the tribe of Levi had no portion of the land. Here, because of the connection between the tribe of Dan and the Antichrist, Dan is excluded (Revelation 7:4-8) from witnessing for the Lord Jesus during the great tribulation.

(iii) The Antichrist will be a European figure of the Revived Roman Empire in Europe, which is the land of Japheth; therefore, he will be a descendant of Japheth.

So the Antichrist will be a European person with a Jewish

father and a Moslem mother, or a Moslem father and a Jewish mother; he will have ties to Ham, Sam, and Japheth. For this reason, both sides with trust him, and he will be the one who will make the false peace between the Jews and the Arabs. That is why today we see a sudden great migration of Arabs and Moslems to Europe where many Jews live and are become lax on inter racial marriage. This has created an environment where marriage between a Moslem Arab and a Jew is not uncommon, which paves the way for the emergence of a person like this. These matters are hard for the human mind to accept, but they are written in the Bible for our learning and admonition. We should be vigilant and faithful to the Lord, as these matters unfold before us.

(3) "And when he had opened the second seal, I heard the second beast say, Come and see."

A second cherub calls on John to witness the second great judgment upon the human race.

(4) "And there went out another horse that was red: and power was given to him that sat thereon to take peace from the earth, and that they should kill one another: and there was given unto him a great sword."

The red horse is the symbol of wars. There will be great wars and nation shall rise against nation, and kingdom against kingdom. There will be no liberty nor peace but a revolution against the Antichrist on account of his oppression, and that we are seeing glimpses of in the world today. Portents of these troubles are becoming more visible in Europe and the world today: "And the fourth kingdom shall be strong as iron: forasmuch as iron breaketh in pieces and subdueth all things: and as iron that breaketh all these, shall it break in pieces and bruise" (Daniel 2:40). "For when they shall say, Peace and safety; then sudden destruction cometh upon them" (1 Thessalonians 5:3). "And ye shall hear of wars and rumours of wars" (Matthew 24:6). Great wars will cover the face of the earth, with far worse consequences than the evils of World War I & II.

We praise God that our peace is in Jesus Christ, the Prince of peace. We will not be passing through these woes, but simply watching them from heaven!

(5) "And when he had opened the third seal, I heard the third beast say, Come and see. And I beheld, and lo a black horse; and he that sat on him had a pair of balances in his hand."

The colour black represents famine: "Our skin was black like an oven because of the terrible famine" (Lamentations 5:10). Starvation darkens the skin.

So then, the third powerful judgment is famines upon the earth: "For nation shall rise against nation, and kingdom against kingdom: and there shall be earthquakes in divers places, and there shall be famines and troubles: these are the beginnings of sorrows" (Mark 13:8).

(6) "And I heard a voice in the midst of the four beasts say, A measure of wheat for a penny, and three measures of barley for a penny; and see thou hurt not the oil and the wine."

- And I heard a voice in the midst of the four beasts say, A measure of wheat for a penny, and three measures of barley for a penny - One of the woes of the great tribulation is that the average individual will have around one meal per day because of hyperinflation. One dinar, which used to buy one measure of wheat, now can only purchase one-eighth of a measure; it used to purchase one measure of barley, but now it can only purchase three-eighths of a measure. The message is that high cost of living is going to be unbearable and the economical distress even worse in light of the taxes that the Antichrist will levy, as he is described in the Bible as: "A raiser of taxes" (Daniel 11:20).

- And see thou hurt not the oil and the wine - In spite of all the famines, there will still be a class of rich people of the velvet societies that will not be affected by what will unfold. The gap between the rich and the poor will not be limited to certain civilizations but worldwide, and will reach unprecedented levels that will be the worst in history.

(7) "And when he had opened the fourth seal, I heard the voice of the fourth beast say, Come and see."

Now the fourth and last cherub calls on John to watch, from heaven, the fourth judgment upon the ungodly world for refusing to bow to the Lord Jesus.

(8) "And I looked, and behold a pale horse: and his name that sat on him was Death, and Hell followed with him. And power was given unto them over the fourth part of the earth, to kill with sword, and with hunger, and with death, and with the beasts of the earth."

The pale horse is the horse of death for vast multitudes of people will die in this phase. One fourth of the inhabitants of the earth will die by means of wars, diseases, and earthquakes. All these calamities will befall the human race because of the wickedness of the Antichrist, the false Christ. But thanks be to the Lord Jesus the righteous Judge, who will remove from the world, the vile influences of the rule of the Antichrist when he casts him into the lake of fire: "And I saw the beast, and the kings of the earth, and their armies, gathered together to make war against him that sat on the horse, and against his army. And the beast was taken, and with him the False prophet that wrought miracles before him, with which he deceived them that had received the mark of the beast, and them that worshipped his image. These both were cast alive into a lake of fire burning with brimstone" (Revelation 19:19-20). At this point in time, the Lord Jesus Christ will establish the kingdom of heaven on earth. We shall reign with him for one thousand years: "And I saw thrones, and they sat upon them, and judgment was given unto them: and I saw the souls of them that were beheaded for the witness of Jesus, and for the word of God, and which had not worshipped the beast, neither his image, neither had received his mark upon their foreheads, or in their hands; and they lived and reigned with Christ a thousand years" (Revelation 20:4).

Then there will be a short war with the forces of the North: "⁷And when the thousand years are expired, Satan shall be loosed out of his prison, ⁸And shall go out to deceive the nations which are in the four quarters of the earth, Gog, and Magog, to gather them together to battle: the number of whom is as the sand of the sea. ⁹And they went up on the breadth of the earth, and compassed the camp of the saints about, and the beloved city: and fire came down from God out of heaven, and devoured them. ¹⁰And the devil that deceived them was cast into the lake of fire and brimstone, where the beast and the False prophet are, and shall be tormented day and night for ever and ever" (Revelation 20:7-10).

Finally we the believers shall reign with Christ forever and ever: "And the ten horns out of this kingdom are ten kings that shall arise: and another shall rise after them; and he shall be diverse from the first, and he shall subdue three kings. And he shall speak great words against the most High, and shall wear out the saints of the most High, and think to change times and laws: and they shall be given into his hand until a time and times and the dividing of time. But the judgment shall sit, and they shall take away his dominion, to consume and to destroy it unto the end. And the kingdom and dominion, and the greatness of the kingdom under the whole heaven, shall be given to the people of the saints of the most High, whose kingdom is an everlasting kingdom" (Daniel 7:24-25).

(9) "And when he had opened the fifth seal, I saw under the altar the souls of them that were slain for the word of God, and for the testimony which they held."

- And when he had opened the fifth seal - Each of the first four seals were opened by one of the four cherubims; and their judgments were directed at all the inhabitants of the earth. John does not tell us who opens this fifth seal but tells us that its judgment is directed against the particular inhabitants of the earth, those who participated in killing the followers the Lord Jesus Christ who took a stand of loyalty to him during the great tribulation.

- I saw under the altar - The martyrs of the tribulation are close to the lamb that was slain, the Lord Jesus.

- The souls - Here we see the "souls" of the martyrs; but later on we are going to see these souls united with their glorified "bodies" at the resurrection of the end of the great tribulation: "And I saw thrones, and they sat upon them, and judgment was given unto them: and I saw the souls of them that were beheaded for the witness of Jesus, and for the word of God ... and they lived and reigned with Christ a thousand years" (Revelation 20:4). Souls and bodies will be united according to the Bible: "I pray God your whole spirit and soul and body be preserved blameless unto the coming of our Lord Jesus Christ" (1 Thessalonians 5:23).

- Of them that were slain for the word of God, and for the testimony which they held - The age of grace is over and now this is the tribulation period. Everyone who believes from then on that Jesus Christ is the Son of the Living God, will have to suffer his bloodshed for his salvation, for he will be killed. We see a large crowd, a multitude, of martyrs for Jesus in the great tribulation. After the rapture takes place then as we read in Matthew 24, Mark 13, and Luke 21; all those who will believe on Jesus shall be persecuted by the wicked of the earth, who will kill every person who testifies to Jesus. Keep in mind that the righteous of the church age will not be present then because they will have gone up in the rapture. Therefore, if you do not know Jesus as a personal saviour yet: "Acquaint now thyself with him, and be at peace: thereby good shall come unto thee" (Job 22:21).

All those that get killed in the judgment of this fifth seal are specifically people who have killed the believers of the tribulation: "For he that toucheth you toucheth the apple of his eye" (Zechariah 2:8).

(10) "And they cried with a loud voice, saying, How long, O Lord, holy and true, dost thou not judge and avenge our blood on them that dwell on the earth?"

Here the elect martyrs ask Christ to do them justice and to do so quickly, liberating the earth of the wicked men who inhabit it. And this is what the Lord Jesus does at the opening of this sixth seal.

(11) "And white robes were given unto every one of them; and it was said unto them, that they should rest yet for a little season, until their fellowservants also and their brethren, that should be killed as they were, should be fulfilled."

The "white robes" are the robes of the righteousness of Christ. The angel tells those who were slain for the name of Jesus to rest for a little while, for only a short time remains of the great tribulation. Persecution from the Antichrist is ongoing and the killing continues, and there are elect who have not yet been martyred but will soon become martyrs of Christ. When their number is completed, the Lord Jesus, the Righteous Judge, shall return to earth. He then will eradicate the evil of the Antichrist, the False prophet, and all their followers.

(12) "And I beheld when he had opened the sixth seal, and, lo, there was a great earthquake; and the sun became black as sackcloth of hair, and the moon became as blood;"

This is the judgment of the sixth seal and as in the case of the fifth seal, we do not know who opened it. The entire world will be dark. It is worth noticing that this judgment will be repeated and amplified later on in the fifth vial: "And the fifth angel poured out his vial upon the seat of the beast; and his kingdom was full of darkness; and they gnawed their tongues for pain" (Revelation 16:10).

(13) "And the stars of heaven fell unto the earth, even as a fig

tree casteth her untimely figs, when she is shaken of a mighty wind."

The stars of heaven fall to the earth exactly as we read in Mark's gospel: "And the stars of heaven shall fall, and the powers that are in heaven shall be shaken" (Mark 13:25). The Lord has comforting words for the righteous and the heroes of the faith of the great tribulation when he says: "And when these things begin to come to pass, then look up, and lift up your heads; for your redemption draweth nigh" (Luke 21:28).

(14) "And the heaven departed as a scroll when it is rolled together; and every mountain and island were moved out of their places."

Heaven opened up in the beginning of chapter four to receive the church and now it opens up again in anticipation of the emergence of Christ from heaven and his descent to earth. The first time he came down to earth as a gentle meek baby born in a stable, but as he promised, this time he comes back as a victorious king to establish his kingdom which he has promised us.

(15) "And the kings of the earth, and the great men, and the rich men, and the chief captains, and the mighty men, and every bondman, and every free man, hid themselves in the dens and in the rocks of the mountains;"

Jesus is coming back to the earth to avenge the blood of his servants; and so all who participated in killing them are struck with terror at the wrath of the Lord Jesus, the righteously avenging Judge.

(16) "And said to the mountains and rocks, Fall on us, and hide us from the face of him that sitteth on the throne, and from the wrath of the Lamb."

- And said to the mountains and rocks, "Fall on us, and hide us from the face of him that sitteth on the throne" - This expresses the magnitude of the hatred of the wicked for the Lord Jesus. They prefer that the mountains and rocks fall upon them and kill them rather than that they lead lives of holiness. The Lord is filled with indignation against those who have plumbed the depths of sin, those who have killed his servants and witnesses. Nahum's wondering question is befitting here: "Who can stand before his indignation?" (Nahum 1:6).

- And from the wrath of the Lamb - It is common for people to be afraid of a lion or tiger or wolf, but who fears a lamb?! The whole world fears this Lamb who was slain, for he is Jesus Christ the crucified, he is the King of kings and the Lord of lords, the righteous holy Son of God!

(17) "For the great day of his wrath is come; and who shall be able to stand?"

The tribulation is about to end and the Judge of all the earth, the Lord Jesus Christ, is returning to the earth with great wrath upon every nation in the world. He will gather them to the war of Armageddon. He will exterminate all the wicked; and will establish the kingdom of his true peace.

Notice that it is the killing of his believers which inflamed the anger of the Lord. "Sing praises to the LORD, which dwelleth in Zion: declare among the people his doings. When he maketh inquisition for blood, he remembereth them: he forgetteth not the cry of the humble" (Psalm 9:11-12). "For he that toucheth you toucheth the apple of his eye" (Zechariah 2:8).

7
SELECTING 144,000 SERVANTS OF THE GOSPEL

(1) "And after these things I saw four angels standing on the four corners of the earth, holding the four winds of the earth, that the wind should not blow on the earth, nor on the sea, nor on any tree."

After the last verse of the previous chapter: "For the great day of his wrath is come; and who shall be able to stand?", it stands to reason to expect the opening of the seventh seal at this point! But we see a pause in the sequence of events; the succession of seal-openings stops. Why? For the grace of Christ is forever alive and abundant to any who will turn to him for salvation even in the middle of the wrath of God. The Lord Jesus is so long suffering that he temporarily holds the winds from pouring out his wrath, so that he could appoint 144,000 witnesses to carry the glad tidings of his hope and saving grace to the entire world. This is before his wrath inundates the whole world, before his anger falls upon every part of land and sea where the four winds blow.

(2) "And I saw another angel ascending from the east, having the seal of the living God: and he cried with a loud voice to the four angels, to whom it was given to hurt the earth and the sea."

- And I saw another angel ascending from the east - God sends his angel from the rising of the sun which represents the light of God: "God is light" (1 John 1:5). God sends his angel with the right hand of his power: "Thy right hand, O Lord, is become glorious in power" (Exodus 15:6). He sends his angel to hold his judgement in order to seal his servants.

- Having the seal of the living God - The seal represents ownership. Many people have their own private seals, while many others use their signatures. Kings always use a seal to affirm their words and their authority. Thus those who are sealed by the angel of God belong to Christ and enjoy active divine protection forever and ever.

- And he cried with a loud voice to the four angels, to whom it was given to hurt the earth and the sea - So this angel postpones the execution of God's trembling wrath.

(3) "Saying, Hurt not the earth, neither the sea, nor the trees, till we have sealed the servants of our God in their foreheads."

At the rapture of the church, which occurs at the end of the age of grace, all the righteous upon the earth are raised up to heaven. No saved Christians remain on earth. So now heaven chooses servants for the Lord Jesus Christ out of the Israelites, who are going to come to faith in Jesus during the tribulation. These believing Israelites are given the privilege of service, specifically of witnessing for Jesus Christ in the great tribulation.

Teaching prophecy is so important even though now many may hear apathetically. However, when they remain on the earth after the rapture, the Holy Spirit will remind them of these sayings, and they will believe and become witnesses for Jesus in the great tribulation.

(4) "And I heard the number of them which were sealed: and there were sealed an hundred and forty and four thousand of all the tribes of the children of Israel."

There are twelve thousand drawn from each of the twelve

tribes of Israel. We have already seen that the tribes of Israel are actually thirteen in number. Here, the sealed are chosen from twelve tribes only. The missing tribe is Dan because like we said previously, the tribe of Dan will be guilty of some connection to the Antichrist. Thus, the tribe of Dan will not have a prominent role in witnessing for Jesus Christ during the great tribulation.

Jesus came down from heaven and offered himself as a sacrifice for our sins. He then ascended into heaven, but before his ascension, he told his disciples to win souls, which was the purpose of his coming. The Lord asks us now to win souls for him. This is always the burden of his heart, even now and at the climax of the great tribulation, we see him concerned for the salvation of souls. Jesus' mercy, tenderness, and love shine through, even during wrath.

(5) "Of the tribe of Juda were sealed twelve thousand. Of the tribe of Reuben were sealed twelve thousand. Of the tribe of Gad were sealed twelve thousand."

There is a spiritual and logical consideration in which the twelve tribes are collected into four groups.

Judah was Jacob's fourth son from Leah, but he became chief: "For Judah prevailed above his brethren, and of him came the chief ruler" (1 Chronicles 5:2). Judah earned great honour because he delivered all of Jacob's seed during the days of famine, and he guaranteed the safety of his brother Benjamin: "And Judah said unto Israel his father, Send the lad with me, and we will arise and go; that we may live, and not die, both we, and thou, and also our little ones. I will be surety for him; of my hand shalt thou require him: if I bring him not unto thee, and set him before thee, then let me bear the blame for ever..... Judah, thou art he whom thy brethren shall praise: thy hand shall be in the neck of thine enemies; thy father's children shall bow down before thee" (Genesis 43:8-9; 49:8). Today, all the descendants of Jacob are called Jewish after the name of Judah. More importantly, Jesus came into this world as a descendant of

Judah: "The sceptre shall not depart from Judah, nor a lawgiver from between his feet, until Shiloh come; and unto him shall the gathering of the people be" (Genesis 49:10); and "Behold, the Lion of the tribe of Judah" (Revelation 5:5).

Reuben was Jacob's firstborn from his first official wife Leah, but he defiled his father's bed and lost his birthright and his being chief ruler: "Unstable as water, thou shalt not excel; because thou wentest up to thy father's bed; then defilest thou it: he went up to my couch" (Genesis 49:4). The eldest son normally receives the birthright; however, the father has the prerogative to bestow these privileges on someone else. Jacob gave the birthright to Joseph.

Gad was Jacob's first son from Zilpah, the maid of Leah: "And Zilpah Leah's maid bare Jacob a son. And Leah said, A troop cometh: and she called his name Gad" (Genesis 30:10-11).

So we see the common connection of these three tribes in that they are all the children of Leah and her maid.

(6) "Of the tribe of Aser were sealed twelve thousand. Of the tribe of Nepthalim were sealed twelve thousand. Of the tribe of Manasses were sealed twelve thousand."

Asher was the second son of Zilpah, the maid of Leah: "And Zilpah Leah's maid bare Jacob a second son. And Leah said, Happy am I, for the daughters will call me blessed: and she called his name Asher" (Genesis 30:12-13).

Naphtali was the second son of Bilhah, the maid of Rachel (Genesis 30:8). The first son of Bilhah was Dan, who is excluded from this list.

Manasseh was the firstborn of Joseph who was the firstborn of Rachel and Jacob: "And God remembered Rachel, and God hearkened to her, and opened her womb. And she conceived, and bare a son; and said, God hath taken away my reproach: And she called his name Joseph; and said, The Lord shall add to me another son" (Genesis 30:22-24). Joseph had two sons: Manasseh and Ephraim: "And Joseph called the name of the firstborn Manasseh: For God, said he, hath made me forget all my toil, and all my father's house. And the name of the second called he Ephraim: For God hath caused me to be fruitful in the land of my affliction" (Genesis 41:51-52). Manasseh with his brother Ephraim were counted as Jacob's when, on his deathbed, Jacob said to his son Joseph, "And now thy two sons, Ephraim and Manasseh, which were born unto thee in the land of Egypt before I came unto thee into Egypt, are mine; as Reuben and Simeon, they shall be mine" (Genesis 48:5).

Asher and Naphtali were the sons of handmaids and Manasseh was a grandson through Jacob's second wife (born of a strange woman in a foreign land). As such, these three tribes had the common connection that none of them was completely a legitimate heir of Jacob: "The sons of Rachel Jacob's wife; Joseph, and Benjamin. And unto Joseph in the land of Egypt were born Manasseh and Ephraim, which Asenath the daughter of Potipherah priest of On bare unto him" (Genesis 46:19-20).

(7) "Of the tribe of Simeon were sealed twelve thousand. Of the tribe of Levi were sealed twelve thousand. Of the tribe of Issachar were sealed twelve thousand."

Simeon was Jacob's second son from Leah: "And she conceived again, and bare a son; and said, Because the Lord hath heard I was hated, he hath therefore given me this son also: and she called his name Simeon" (Genesis 29:33).

Levi was Jacob's third son from Leah: "And she conceived again, and bare a son; and said, Now this time will my husband be joined unto me, because I have born him three sons: therefore was his name called Levi" (Genesis 29:34).

Issachar was Jacob's fifth son from Leah after she hired Jacob from Rachel: "And Jacob came out of the field in the evening, and Leah went out to meet him, and said, Thou must come in unto me; for surely I have hired thee with my son's mandrakes. And he lay with her that night. And God hearkened unto Leah, and she conceived, and bare Jacob the fifth son. And Leah said,

God hath given me my hire, because I have given my maiden to my husband: and she called his name Issachar" (Genesis 30:16-18). These three have a common factor in that they are sons of Jacob by Leah.

(8) "Of the tribe of Zabulon were sealed twelve thousand. Of the tribe of Joseph were sealed twelve thousand. Of the tribe of Benjamin were sealed twelve thousand."

Zebulon was Jacob's sixth son from Leah. "And Leah said, God hath endued me with a good dowry; now will my husband dwell with me, because I have born him six sons: and she called his name Zebulun" (Genesis 30:20).

As we mentioned in the previous verse, Joseph was Jacob's first son from Rachel. Joseph's two sons received portion in his place, as he was considered the firstborn: "But the birthright was Joseph's" (1 Chronicles 5:2). But the name of Ephraim was associated with idols: "Ephraim is joined to idols: let him alone" (Hosea 4:17). "And Jeroboam the son of Nebat, an Ephrathite of Zereda, Solomon's servant.... And the man Jeroboam was a mighty man of valour: and Solomon seeing the young man that he was industrious, he made him ruler over all the charge of the house of Joseph" (1 Kings 11:26-28). Jeroboam: "lifted up his hand against the king", King Solomon; he split the tribes of Israel and led ten of the tribes away from the Lord and into idolatry: "Whereupon the king took counsel, and made two calves of gold, and said unto them, It is too much for you to go up to Jerusalem: behold thy gods, O Israel, which brought thee up out of the land of Egypt ... And he shall give Israel up because of the sins of Jeroboam, who did sin, and who made Israel to sin" (1 Kings 12:28; 14:16). Ephraim led Israel away from the worship of the Lord. So the Lord deprives him of the mention of his name. His brother's name, Manasseh, is mentioned. Ephraim's name is hidden, as it were, under the name of his father Joseph. As we mentioned earlier, he was the second son of Joseph who, in turn, was the son of Rachel.

Benjamin, the brother of Joseph, was Jacob's second son from Rachel. He was the twelfth and last of the sons of Jacob: "And they journeyed from Bethel; and there was but a little way to come to Ephrath: and Rachel travailed, and she had hard labour .... And it came to pass, as her soul was in departing, (for she died) that she called his name Benoni: but his father called him Benjamin" (Genesis 35:16,18). Ephraim and Benjamin were descendants of Rachel. Zebulon was the sixth son of Leah, however, he was the second from her after she hired Jacob from Rachel: "And Leah conceived again, and bare Jacob the sixth son. And Leah said, God hath endued me with a good dowry; now will my husband dwell with me, because I have born him six sons: and she called his name Zebulun" (Genesis 30:19-20).

So these three sons have a common connection to Rachel.

(9) "After this I beheld, and, lo, a great multitude, which no man could number, of all nations, and kindreds, and people, and tongues, stood before the throne, and before the Lamb, clothed with white robes, and palms in their hands;"

The work of the 144,000 sealed of these tribes produces fruit winning countless souls to the Lord Jesus Christ from every nation, kindred, people, including both Jews and Gentiles. Many people are going to get saved in the great tribulation and will be martyred for Jesus' name's sake. They are going to go up to heaven justified by the blood of Jesus Christ. They shall be dressed in white robes, a symbol of righteousness. They are going to be victorious holding palm branches, which are a symbol of victory for these branches lift and stretch upwards.

(10) "And cried with a loud voice, saying, Salvation to our God which sitteth upon the throne, and unto the Lamb."

The shouts of joy emanate from the mouths of the saved, the redeemed as they praise both God who is seated on his throne in heaven and the Lord Jesus, the Saviour who is sitting at the right of the throne glory; for: "When he had by himself purged our sins, sat down on the right hand of the Majesty on high" (Hebrews 3:1).

(11) "And all the angels stood round about the throne, and about the elders and the four beasts, and fell before the throne on their faces, and worshipped God,"

All the angels of heaven, the apostles of the Lamb, the tribes of Israel, the four cherubims, all of heaven in its entirety bows down in submission and worship to the Lord God, the Lord of Glory Jesus Christ.

(12) "Saying, Amen: Blessing, and glory, and wisdom, and thanksgiving, and honour, and power, and might, be unto our God for ever and ever. Amen."

Once again, after: "And I beheld, and I heard the voice of many angels round about the throne and the beasts and the elders: and the number of them was ten thousand times ten thousand, and thousands of thousands; Saying with a loud voice, Worthy is the Lamb that was slain to receive power, and riches, and wisdom, and strength, and honour, and glory, and blessing", we hear seven noble and sublime attributes which are ascribed to the Lord Jesus Christ, the Lord of glory:

(i) Blessing: Greatness and glamour and happiness

(ii) Glory: Magnificence and gladness

(iii) Wisdom: Sound knowledge

(iv) Thanksgiving: Expressions of gratitude

(v) Honour: Dignity ascribed to a person as a result of his exalted character

(vi) Power: Intrinsic and natural ability to do and to say

(vii) Might: Associated with power, great ability to

utilize power

(13) "And one of the elders answered, saying unto me, What are these which are arrayed in white robes? and whence came they?"

One of the twenty four elders asks John who are these redeemed people, and from where have they come? He is examining his ability to discern and understand what is going on before him.

(14) "And I said unto him, Sir, thou knowest. And he said to me, These are they which came out of great tribulation, and have washed their robes, and made them white in the blood of the Lamb."

John addresses the elder courteously, calling him "sir". The elder affirms that these are the martyrs of true Christianity who were martyred, killed in the tribulation by the Antichrist and the False prophet and their followers. From heaven's point of view, these are they who won the battle; these are the true and righteous heroes of Christ.

(15) "Therefore are they before the throne of God, and serve him day and night in his temple: and he that sitteth on the throne shall dwell among them."

All of these redeemed will live and dwell in heaven in the presence God and the Lamb and without ceasing they will be in continuous fellowship with the Lord Jesus in his glory: "And in his temple doth every one speak of his glory" (Psalms 29:9).

(16) "They shall hunger no more, neither thirst any more; neither shall the sun light on them, nor any heat."

In the great tribulation, the Antichrist will have persecuted the true believers and had warred against them and prevented them from buying food and selling. They will have wandered hungry and thirsty in the wilderness with no shade to keep them from the heat of the sun. But now and forever we see them in a state of joy and glory and comfort and rest with Jesus in perpetual paradise in everlasting bliss: "But as it is written, Eye hath not seen, nor ear heard, neither have entered into the heart of man, the things which God hath prepared for them that love him. But God hath revealed them unto us by his Spirit" (1 Corinthians 2:9-10); "I knew a man in Christ above fourteen years ago, (whether in the body, I cannot tell; or whether out of the body, I cannot tell: God knoweth;) such an one caught up to the third heaven. And I knew such a man, (whether in the body, or out of the body, I cannot tell: God knoweth;) How that he was caught up into paradise, and heard unspeakable words, which it is not lawful for a man to utter" (2 Corinthians 12:2-4).

(17) "For the Lamb which is in the midst of the throne shall feed them, and shall lead them unto living fountains of waters: and God shall wipe away all tears from their eyes."

The Lord Jesus who is the focal point and in the midst of the throne of God in heaven, will wipe away every tear from their eyes, will lead them to springs of living fountains of water in heaven, where there is joy, comfort, victory, and triumph forever and ever.

8
THE JUDGMENT OF THE FIRST FOUR TRUMPETS

(1) "And when he had opened the seventh seal, there was silence in heaven about the space of half an hour."

We saw in chapter 6 how that God began to pour his wrath upon the world by the opening of the six seals. In chapter 7 we saw a parenthetical period in which God's servants were sealed on their foreheads. Now in chapter 8 we shall see the opening of the seventh and final seal.

When this seal is opened up by the angel, seven trumpets appear; where the seventh one consists of seven vials: "And the seventh angel sounded; and there were great voices in heaven, saying, The kingdoms of this world are become the kingdoms of our Lord, and of his Christ; and he shall reign for ever and ever ... And the seven angels came out of the temple, having the seven plagues, clothed in pure and white linen, and having their breasts girded with golden girdles. And one of the four beasts gave unto the seven angels seven golden vials full of the wrath of God, who liveth for ever and ever" (Revelation 11:15; 15:6-7).

Notice that in the book of Revelation there is a sequence of seven seals followed by seven trumpets and then seven vials.

Thus, there are three groups of seven through which the wrath of God pours down upon the earth in the great tribulation.

The seventh angel now blows the trumpet, and its formidable power of this judgment produces a pervading silence in the midst of the cacophony of judgments. Astonishment fills the universe at the unleashing of the fearful, awesome judgment of the seven trumpets. A silence of half an hour is nothing from the perspective of eternity. But time has great value during an interval of waiting; for instance, the waiting period in a trial before the judge issues his verdict might be short, but from the perspective of those who are waiting, it appears very long. In like manner, a half of an hour wait for God's decision is a very short interval, but it feels very long. In a time of gladness, the opposite applies and time flies by swiftly, and this was the experience of Jacob when he loved Rachel: "And Jacob served seven years for Rachel; and they seemed unto him but a few days, for the love he had to her" (Genesis 29:20).

(2) "And I saw the seven angels which stood before God; and to them were given seven trumpets."

Think of the presence of a great king, how much more is the presence of the King of kings and Lord of lords, the Lord Jesus Christ, Son of the living God. In his presence stand seven angels having seven trumpets, which are the judgments of Jesus Christ on the Antichrist and his kingdom.

(3) "And another angel came and stood at the altar, having a golden censer; and there was given unto him much incense, that he should offer it with the prayers of all saints upon the golden altar which was before the throne."

The seven new judgments, the judgments of the seven trumpets, are mixed with the prayers of saints, who are crying out demanding heavenly justice: "And they cried with a loud voice, saying, How long, O Lord, holy and true, dost thou not judge and avenge our blood on them that dwell on the earth?" (Revelation 6:10).

(4) "And the smoke of the incense, which came with the prayers of the saints, ascended up before God out of the angel's hand."

The most beautiful thing from heaven's perspective is the prayers of the saints. When the church meets together and prays, heaven rejoices and strongly answers their prayers. Incense is a symbol of the prayers of the believers, like David puts it: "Let my prayer be set forth before thee as incense" (Psalms 141:2). This is similar to the case with us when we offer our prayers to heaven: "And golden vials full of odours, which are the prayers of saints" (Revelation 5:8). These prayers bring joy to the heart of God, and he values them greatly as we shall see in the next verse.

(5) "And the angel took the censer, and filled it with fire of the altar, and cast it into the earth: and there were voices, and thunderings, and lightnings, and an earthquake."

Here we see the angel taking the censer and filling it with fire from the altar, and casting on the earth, causing its foundations to shake. This causes tremendous voices, thundering and lightning with an earthquake to happen on the earth, in preparation for the fearful things to come as we shall see in the next verse.

The cries of the righteous have been remembered before the throne of God, and now his just judgment is being executed; like the fire from the altar that purified the lips of Isaiah: "Then said I, Woe is me! for I am undone; because I am a man of unclean lips, and I dwell in the midst of a people of unclean lips: for mine eyes have seen the King, the Lord of hosts. Then flew one of the seraphims unto me, having a live coal in his hand, which he had taken with the tongs from off the altar: And he laid it upon my mouth, and said, Lo, this hath touched thy lips; and thine iniquity is taken away, and thy sin purged" (Isaiah 6:5-7). In like manner, God's wrath, poured out with fire from the altar, will purify the earth from the wicked and from the wickedness of their sin.

(6) "And the seven angels which had the seven trumpets prepared themselves to sound."

All is ready for the sequence of God's judgments upon the earth to continue with the seven trumpets.

(7) "The first angel sounded, and there followed hail and fire mingled with blood, and they were cast upon the earth: and the third part of trees was burnt up, and all green grass was burnt up."

When the first trumpet sounds, the scene shifts back from heaven to earth, where we see the Lord of glory, the Judge, the Lord Jesus Christ, continuing what he had begun in chapter 6. God's wrath is now manifest in the form of hail and fire, which calls to mind the wrath of the Lord on Egypt and her gods. Hail and fire rain down on every kind of plant and grass. It is strange that man can be so overly concerned about nature without ever thinking of the one who gave this natural world and made all the bountiful plant life. We see man caring for nature and making long term plans for nature, as if it is an idol in his life. For this reason, we see God pour out his wrath on nature, smiting the trees and every green grass. Europe, the kingdom of the coming Antichrist, has already appeared on the world scene and has become a formidable power. Also Europe has grown colder and colder in its love for God so that it has become a spiritual iceberg. One can hardly find a true church worshiping the Lord Jesus in the cities of Europe today. Its capitals and cities are devoid of the fear of God; their focus is only on self, on the "me", and on nature. They have forgotten God, the creator of all these, so we see God's anger on each and every one.

(8) "And the second angel sounded, and as it were a great mountain burning with fire was cast into the sea: and the third part of the sea became blood;"

The second trumpet sounds, and we plunge into a world of symbolism. A mountain represents a strong kingdom, which is here the Babylonian kingdom: "And I will render unto Babylon and to all the inhabitants of Chaldea all their evil that they have done in Zion in your sight, saith the LORD. Behold, I am against thee, O destroying mountain, saith the LORD, which destroyest all the earth: and I will stretch out mine hand upon thee, and roll thee down from the rocks, and will make thee a burnt mountain" (Jeremiah 51:24-25).

The sea stands for the world of peoples and nations: "Which stilleth the noise of the seas, the noise of their waves, and the tumult of the people"; "For, lo, thine enemies make a tumult: and they that hate thee have lifted up the head" (Psalms 65:7; 83:2). The prophecy here concerns military Babylon, the European Union military alliance, which is boiling over with rioting and ethnic conflicts. These problems will explode and burst out upon all the peoples of the world. Many from Africa, Middle East, and Far East are immigrating to Europe seeking political asylum or economic relief. But these immigrants to Europe come from many different ethnicities that find great difficulty integrating into European society like Daniel says: "And whereas thou sawest iron mixed with miry clay, they shall mingle themselves with the seed of men: but they shall not cleave one to another, even as iron is not mixed with clay" (Daniel 2:43). Even though Europeans today are following their leaders who are forcing them to accept many refugees and immigrants, the day will come when nationalistic emotions will erupt and inflame civil wars and even world wars between the larger nations. These wars will be driven by the desire to control and dominate the world, as was the case in the days of Genghis Khan, Alexander the Great, Julius Caesar, Napoleon Bonaparte, and Hitler; but this time under the Antichrist, the blood of a third of the human race will be spilled.

Note that there are four Babylon's which are going to be destroyed in the book of Revelation:

(i) Political Babylon: "And I saw, and behold a white horse: and he that sat on him had a bow; and a crown was given unto him: and he went forth conquering, and to conquer" (Revelation 6:2).

(ii) Military Babylon: "And the second angel sounded, and as it were a great mountain burning with fire was cast into the sea: and the third part of the sea became blood" (Revelation 8:8).

(iii) Religious Babylon: "[15]And he saith unto me, The waters which thou sawest, where the whore sitteth, are peoples, and multitudes, and nations, and tongues [16] And the ten horns which thou sawest upon the beast, these shall hate the whore, and shall make her desolate and naked, and shall eat her flesh, and burn her with fire" (Revelation 17:15-16).

(iv) Commercial Babylon: "[2]And he cried mightily with a strong voice, saying, Babylon the great is fallen, is fallen, and is become the habitation of devils, and the hold of every foul spirit, and a cage of every unclean and hateful bird", "[17]or in one hour so great riches is come to nought. And every shipmaster, and all the company in ships, and sailors, and as many as trade by sea, stood afar off" (Revelation 18:2,17).

(9) "And the third part of the creatures which were in the sea, and had life, died; and the third part of the ships were destroyed."

One third of the inhabitants of the earth die; and world trade is disrupted, as ships are a symbol of trade.

(10) "And the third angel sounded, and there fell a great star from heaven, burning as it were a lamp, and it fell upon the third part of the rivers, and upon the fountains of waters;"

A star is a person, an individual in a position of leadership, as we saw in chapter one: "[20]The mystery of the seven stars which thou sawest in my right hand, and the seven golden candlesticks. The seven stars are the angels of the seven churches: and the seven candlesticks which thou sawest are the seven churches" (Revelation 1:20). The third angel sounds his trumpet, and a figure of world renown and of global importance begins his mission, which is to poison the thoughts of men.

These verses may very well have a literal interpretation, like a mountain falling into the sea. However, it is more important to dwell on the spiritual symbolism that the Lord Jesus emphasized from the beginning of this book when he spoke of candlesticks and stars as symbols of churches and pastors. This is why it is important to study these verses with an open mind, knowing that many of these verses have dual meanings, a literal and a symbolic one.

(11) "And the name of the star is called Wormwood: and the third part of the waters became wormwood; and many men died of the waters, because they were made bitter."

Wormwood is bitter like quinine and is fatal in its bitterness and devoid of life. Since this person's teachings are bitter as a toxic acid; he will infect the world and their thoughts with his corrupt teachings. This person is the Antichrist himself and here the world will discover his true identity which is a far cry from the title "man of peace" under which he first achieved prominence: "And I saw, and behold a white horse: and he that sat on him had a bow; and a crown was given unto him: and he went forth conquering, and to conquer" (Revelation 6:2).

(12) "And the fourth angel sounded, and the third part of the sun was smitten, and the third part of the moon, and the third part of the stars; so as the third part of them was darkened, and the day shone not for a third part of it, and the night likewise."

After the exposure of the true nature of the Antichrist and his ambition to dominate the world, the fourth angel sounds his trumpet which shows that a third of the sun, moon, and stars, symbolizing third of the powers and authorities of the world, will be swallowed up by the Antichrist and fall under his control.

(13) "And I beheld, and heard an angel flying through the midst of heaven, saying with a loud voice, Woe, woe, woe, to the inhabiters of the earth by reason of the other voices of the trumpet of the three angels, which are yet to sound!"

Now, in the second half of the tribulation, the woes of the oppression of the Antichrist begin to fall upon men and upon the whole globe. The seven years of the tribulation are divided into two equal halves:

(i) First half, 1260 days; or a time, times, and an half; or three and a half years is called "the tribulation";

(ii) Second half of equal length of 42 months is called "the great tribulation". The entirety of the seven years are commonly interchangeably referred to as "the Tribulation" or "the Great Tribulation".

9

THE JUDGMENTS OF THE FIFTH AND SIXTH TRUMPETS

(1) "And the fifth angel sounded, and I saw a star fall from heaven unto the earth: and to him was given the key of the bottomless pit."

The first four trumpets fall in the first half of the great tribulation; now the fifth and sixth trumpets fall in the second half of it, the "Great Tribulation". In chapter 8, we saw the Lord's judgments upon the world of nature, now in chapter 9, we see the Lord's judgment upon the spiritual factors of the world. Satan, the prince of this world: "[31]Now shall the prince of this world be cast out"; "[30]for the prince of this world cometh, and hath nothing in me"; "[11]because the prince of this world is judged" (John 12:31; 14:30; 16:11), will increase his satanic activities in the tribulation period since the Holy Spirit, which came down on the day of Pentecost, will have ascended back to heaven on the day of the rapture. People left behind on this earth will be in the later stages of complete spiritual collapse and ruin and destruction into hell with Satan and his evil satanic angels.

After the threefold woe at in the last verse of the previous chapter, matters now are solemn dark and extremely fearful.

A star is a symbol of a prominent person or a person in a

position of leadership like we saw in chapter 1 where a star represented the pastor of a church: "[20]The mystery of the seven stars which thou sawest in my right hand, and the seven golden candlesticks. The seven stars are the angels of the seven churches: and the seven candlesticks which thou sawest are the seven churches" (Revelation 1:20). We will see this again in chapter 12 where the twelve stars represent the twelve sons of Jacob: "And there appeared a great wonder in heaven; a woman clothed with the sun, and the moon under her feet, and upon her head a crown of twelve stars" (Revelation 12:1). This is clearly seen in the explanation of Joseph's dream in the book of Genesis: "I have dreamed a dream more; and, behold, the sun and the moon and the eleven stars made obeisance to me. And he told it to his father, and to his brethren: and his father rebuked him, and said unto him, What is this dream that thou hast dreamed? Shall I and thy mother and thy brethren indeed come to bow down ourselves to thee to the earth?" (Genesis 37:9-10).

This star refers to a great leader, namely the devil, Satan, Lucifer the covering cherub who fell and who is now being cast out of heaven: "[12]Therefore rejoice, ye heavens, and ye that dwell in them. Woe to the inhabiters of the earth and of the sea! for the devil is come down unto you, having great wrath, because he knoweth that he hath but a short time" (Revelation 12:12). Therefore, using all his powers he will open a deep pit in the heart of the earth that burns with fire. Into this deep fiery pit do the souls of the wicked descend; like the soul of the rich man in the story of Lazarus: "[22]The rich man also died, and was buried; [23]And in hell he lift up his eyes, being in torments" (Luke 16:22-23). There they will suffer until the day of judgment, when they shall stand before the great white throne of God and reach their final destination, namely hell: "And the devil that deceived them was cast into the lake of fire and brimstone, where the beast and the False prophet are, and shall be tormented day and night for ever and ever … And whosoever was not found written in the book of life was cast into the lake of fire" (Revelation 20:10,15).

When the pit is opened, the fallen angels, also known as devils and evil spirits, will emerge. These are the angels that aligned themselves with Satan when he fell from before the throne of God: "And the angels which kept not their first estate, but left their own habitation, he hath reserved in everlasting chains under darkness unto the judgment of the great day" (Jude 6). They will emerge and spread on the face of the entire earth.

This fifth trumpet is very frightful for when Satan falls and the gates of hell are opened up, satanic movements will spread energetically over the whole world, for they will know their days are numbered. Today we hear of the church of Satan, Satanic music, and Satan-worshipers under the leadership of Satan. Their movements seem to be ever-increasing now, but when the age of grace ends and the Holy Spirit is lifted up at the rapture of the church, these demonic forces are going to become tyrannical. The farther away from the Lord Jesus a person is, the more he is subject to satanic influence. In contrast, those who seek refuge in the Lord Jesus are liberated from such influences: "⁷The angel of the Lord encampeth round about them that fear him, and delivereth them" (Psalm 34:7).

In our days, we are kept from this evil, but woe is to the one who, in the days of tribulation, meets up with these satanic activities. Run now to Jesus and ask for the power of his blood of the cross so that your sins will be forgiven and you can be saved from what is to come.

(2) "And he opened the bottomless pit; and there arose a smoke out of the pit, as the smoke of a great furnace; and the sun and the air were darkened by reason of the smoke of the pit."

We cannot deny that these events might be literally true, as is the case with the first four trumpets in the previous chapter. As we have seen before, here again the book of Revelation speaks both literally and figuratively:

(i) Sometimes it speaks literally as seen in: "And the heaven departed as a scroll when it is rolled together; and every mountain and island were moved out of their places. And the kings of the earth, and the great men, and the rich men, and the chief captains, and the mighty men, and every bondman, and every free man, hid themselves in the dens and in the rocks of the mountains; And said to the mountains and rocks, Fall on us, and hide us from the face of him that sitteth on the throne, and from the wrath of the Lamb: For the great day of his wrath is come; and who shall be able to stand?" (Revelation 6:14-17).

(ii) Sometimes it speaks figuratively as when it refers to the stars, the sword out of the Lord Jesus Christ's mouth, and the woman clothed with the sun and moon. And so we say that the smoke represents the satanic teachings and wicked thoughts which will fill the world and will confuse and muddle the thoughts of men. Recall that Satan will open the door of the pit in the inner earth, from which will emerge demons and evil spirits, and their task will be to torment men. Some day, in the great tribulation, these spirits will be seen with the naked eye and people will feel their presence and the pressure which they exert.

(3) "And there came out of the smoke locusts upon the earth: and unto them was given power, as the scorpions of the earth have power."

These locusts are symbols of average sinful human beings who will be instruments in the hand of Satan. Their personality is described in verses 7- 10 of this chapter.

As we consider the spirit of the text, it seems that the torment in question is more of the soul and mind more than of the body. Locusts eat everything living, green thing. In like manner, these wicked soldiers of Satan will destroy every good

Christian teaching and sound doctrine and will afflict men with poisonous soul-destroying thoughts and ideas and teachings.

(4) "And it was commanded them that they should not hurt the grass of the earth, neither any green thing, neither any tree; but only those men which have not the seal of God in their foreheads."

But they will not be able to poison the thinking of any child in the faith (the grass of the earth), of any who are mature spiritually (green thing), or of any of the mature or mainstays of the Christian faith (tree), as each and every one of them is protected, being protected under the blood of Jesus. They also bear the mark of Christ on their foreheads. Satan and his foot-soldiers will only be able to poison the minds of unbelievers, those who reject the authority of the Lord Jesus over their lives and so have no defenses of heavenly privileges of spiritual immunity. Satan will posses their minds and torment them will confusing, hellish thoughts.

(5) "And to them it was given that they should not kill them, but that they should be tormented five months: and their torment was as the torment of a scorpion, when he striketh a man."

A snake bite kills, and a scorpion bite torments in pain. Satan will torment men with scorpions which bring mental, moral, personal, and especially spiritual affliction. The pain involved will be very strong, but not to the extent of driving men to suicide.

(6) "And in those days shall men seek death, and shall not find it; and shall desire to die, and death shall flee from them."

People will desire suicide and death to rid themselves of the conviction of their consciences. But God allows an iota of his fear to remain in them so they abstain from killing themselves. Among them are some who will repent and believe on the Lord Jesus Christ. There will still be hope of deliverance in the great tribulation because the mercy of God never fails nor waivers.

God will save some of them as Scripture testifies: "And I saw another angel fly in the midst of heaven, having the everlasting gospel to preach unto them that dwell on the earth, and to every nation, and kindred, and tongue, and people, Saying with a loud voice, Fear God, and give glory to him; for the hour of his judgment is come: and worship him that made heaven, and earth, and the sea, and the fountains of waters" (Revelation 14:6-7).

(7) "And the shapes of the locusts were like unto horses prepared unto battle; and on their heads were as it were crowns like gold, and their faces were as the faces of men."

- And the shapes of the locusts were like unto - These are human soldiers as we explained in our description of verse 3.

- Horses prepared unto battle - They aggressively attack the thoughts and minds of men.

- And on their heads were as it were crowns like gold - This is evidence of their deceptive nature. They delude men into thinking that they are right and that their sayings are correct.

- And their faces were as the faces of men - They will be normal human beings but allow themselves to be instruments in the hands of the devil. They will appear to others as men of dignity and independent mindedness and desirous of the welfare of society.

(8) "And they had hair as the hair of women, and their teeth were as the teeth of lions."

- And they had hair as the hair of women - In reality, these people will be weak of mind and prisoners of Satan's evil power and his dark oppression.

- And their teeth were as the teeth of lions - They are going to devour people and will use violence to make men captive and control the minds and bodies of the masses of people

(9) "And they had breastplates, as it were breastplates of iron; and the sound of their wings was as the sound of chariots of many horses running to battle."

- And they had breastplates, as it were breastplates of iron -

It will be difficult to pierce their intellectual defenses; to break through to them with the truth.

- And the sound of their wings was as the sound of chariots of many horses running to battle - That is they are going to terrorize the hearts of all human beings.

(10) "And they had tails like unto scorpions, and there were stings in their tails: and their power was to hurt men five months."

A tail represents weakness implying that their evil is so strong that even the weak part of that evil is more powerful than the strength of men; too powerful for men's resistance.

(11) "And they had a king over them, which is the angel of the bottomless pit, whose name in the Hebrew tongue is Abaddon, but in the Greek tongue hath his name Apollyon."

The name of the angel "Abaddon" or "Apollyon" means "destroyer" who is Satan. His goal is to devastate, destroy, and annihilate all people, both Jews and Gentiles for his goal is to kill every member of the human race: "Ye are of your father the devil, and the lusts of your father ye will do. He was a murderer from the beginning, and abode not in the truth, because there is no truth in him. When he speaketh a lie, he speaketh of his own: for he is a liar, and the father of it" (John 8:44).

(12) "One woe is past; and, behold, there come two woes more hereafter."

This is only one woe. Two great woes remain, which are of the same scale and even greater.

(13) "And the sixth angel sounded, and I heard a voice from the four horns of the golden altar which is before God,"

Remember that the seven year tribulation is in two stages:

(i) In the first three and a half years, the Antichrist, with the help of the False prophet, will establish false peace over the entire world.

(ii) At the end of the first half begins the second half or Great Tribulation, the Antichrist will breach his treaty with the Jews, go to the temple and place his image in the temple as if he is a god, and demand to be worshiped by the world as a whole: "²⁷And he shall confirm the covenant with many for one week: and in the midst of the week he shall cause the sacrifice and the oblation to cease, and for the overspreading of abominations he shall make it desolate, even until the consummation, and that determined shall be poured upon the desolate" (Daniel 9:27).

There are several verses in the Bible that indicate that the temple will be rebuilt after the rapture of the church of Christ. These passages also prophesy of God's renewed dealings with the nation of Israel which will lead to the fulfillment of biblical prophecies: "¹And the Lord, whom ye seek, shall suddenly come to his temple" (Malachi 3:1); "¹⁵When ye therefore shall see the abomination of desolation, spoken of by Daniel the prophet, stand in the holy place, (whoso readeth, let him understand:)" (Matthew 24:15); "¹⁴But when ye shall see the abomination of desolation, spoken of by Daniel the prophet, standing where it ought not, let him that readeth understand" (Mark 13:14).

The great abomination is that the Antichrist will defile the alter of sacrifices in the temple in the middle of the great tribulation, and that is why we see in the verse that we are studying, why one of the horns of the altar cries out against the Antichrist and his kingdom. This great woe is from the Lord Jesus who is always zealous for the house of the Lord: "¹⁷And his disciples remembered that it was written, The zeal of thine house hath eaten me up" (John 2:17). This woe is also serves as an answer to the prayers of the saints: "¹⁰And they cried with a loud voice, saying, How long, O Lord, holy and true, dost thou not judge and avenge our blood on them that dwell on the earth? ... ³And another angel came and stood at the altar, having a golden censer; and there was given unto him much incense, that he should offer it with the prayers of all saints upon the golden altar which was before the throne" (Revelation 6:10; 8:3).

The angel here blows the trumpet in the service of the Lord

Jesus, who is seated at the right hand of Majesty; and the angelic hosts serving him. Each angel has his rank and his station in the service of the Lord Jesus as we have noted earlier, and they are: Cherubims, Seraphims, Archangels, and elect angles.

Here we remember an important lesson in Scripture; that wars are appointed of God. Many wars have occurred in history and they either were a punishment upon peoples for their iniquity, or as a means of chastisement being an instrument used of the Lord to bring his people and his individual children back in repentance to him.

God allows wars and he uses human instrumentality and moves it by spiritual heavenly influence. When a man lives a life of righteousness the Lord is pleased. As a result, he sees goodness, blessing, and peace, and he lives a victorious, Christian life. But when a man is swept into a life of sin, there is no favor from the Lord upon his life. He lives a life of defeat, devoid of blessing, and tribulation and wars come upon him. You may ask where is the mercy of the Lord? The mercy is that he does not wipe you out but leads to repentance: "the goodness of God leadeth thee to repentance" (Romans 2:4).

(14) "Saying to the sixth angel which had the trumpet, Loose the four angels which are bound in the great river Euphrates."

There are four angels because, in the garden of Eden, there were four rivers: "And a river went out of Eden to water the garden; and from thence it was parted, and became into four heads. The name of the first is Pison: that is it which compasseth the whole land of Havilah, where there is gold; And the gold of that land is good: there is bdellium and the onyx stone. And the name of the second river is Gihon: the same is it that compasseth the whole land of Ethiopia. And the name of the third river is Hiddekel: that is it which goeth toward the east of Assyria. And the fourth river is Euphrates" (Genesis 2:10-14); and each angel, by the authority of the Lord Jesus Christ, was responsible for a river.

The fourth was the Euphrates and the source of the other three as we understand from this verse that we are expounding. The Euphrates is the gate to the East. Historically it was the eastern boundary of the Roman Empire. It was also the eastern boundary of the authority of the kingdom of Israel, which encompassed the Fertile Crescent, from the Euphrates to the Nile, in the days of Kings David and Solomon: "And David smote Hadarezer king of Zobah unto Hamath, as he went to stablish his dominion by the river Euphrates" (1 Chronicles 18:3).

The Lord Jesus is holding back his judgement today in the age of grace, but the day will come when he will allow the awakening of the "yellow giant", which represents the forces of the orient, the nations of the rising sun. They will invade the world: "And the sixth angel poured out his vial upon the great river Euphrates; and the water thereof was dried up, that the way of the kings of the east might be prepared. And I saw three unclean spirits like frogs come out of the mouth of the dragon, and out of the mouth of the beast, and out of the mouth of the False prophet. For they are the spirits of devils, working miracles, which go forth unto the kings of the earth and of the whole world, to gather them to the battle of that great day of God Almighty" (Revelation 16:12-14). Napoleon said "Woe to the world when the yellow giant awakes;" and what he spoke of will come to pass towards the end of the great tribulation. Now the angel of the Lord prepares the armies of the Asian people to cross the Euphrates and attack the kingdom of the Antichrist. And the first front will be Israel.

(15) "And the four angels were loosed, which were prepared for an hour, and a day, and a month, and a year, for to slay the third part of men."

All things happen at the time appointed by God for every event has its timing appointed by God. Examples are: "In the six hundredth year of Noah's life, in the second month, the seventeenth day of the month, the same day were all the fountains of the great deep broken up, and the windows of heaven were opened" (Genesis 7:11); "And it came to pass at the end of the four hundred and thirty years, even the selfsame day it came to pass, that all the hosts of the LORD went out from the land of Egypt" (Exodus 12:41); "But of that day and hour knoweth no man, no, not the angels of heaven, but my Father only" (Matthew 24:36).

One third of the inhabitants of the earth is going to die in the battle of Armageddon. That is, if the world population then is 9 billion people; then 3,000,000,000 are going to die in it.

(16) "And the number of the army of the horsemen were two hundred thousand thousand: and I heard the number of them."

An army of two hundred million soldiers is terrifying and the number is hard to imagine. So, John the Beloved confirms that this is the true literal figure. In the eighties, a Chinese military leader boasted that, if it becomes necessary, China can call up and deploy two hundred million soldiers. This number is not a coincidence but rather an affirmation of John's prophecy. We already had a taste of that in 2019 when China sent hundreds of millions of the Corona viruses into the world.

(17) "And thus I saw the horses in the vision, and them that sat on them, having breastplates of fire, and of jacinth, and brimstone: and the heads of the horses were as the heads of lions; and out of their mouths issued fire and smoke and brimstone."

Here, the situation is completely different than that of the fifth trumpet where to maintain correct theology, we had to interpret the text figuratively in harmony with the preceding and following verses. Arbitration leads to logical flaws, opening the door to interpretations which can easily be considered unbiblical. In our previous passage, we saw a symbol of evil spirits; but here, we have a literal description of a military scene. It is a description which speaks of nuclear war, nuclear tanks, and weapons of destruction which are quite like what we have in our day and time. This is what we see in this verse.

(18) "By these three was the third part of men killed, by the fire, and by the smoke, and by the brimstone, which issued out of their mouths."

A third of the inhabitants of the earth will be killed by the various weapons of destruction, which include nuclear missiles and other nuclear radiation devices.

(19) "For their power is in their mouth, and in their tails: for their tails were like unto serpents, and had heads, and with them they do hurt."

This is a description of a nuclear tank, which kills, disfigures, and maims.

(20) "And the rest of the men which were not killed by these plagues yet repented not of the works of their hands, that they should not worship devils, and idols of gold, and silver, and brass, and stone, and of wood: which neither can see, nor hear, nor walk:"

With all that this woe brings of spiritual torment and nuclear death, the living remnant do not repent of their evils; do not turn to worship the Lord Jesus. Rather, they continue to seek after devils as they continue to worship material things and money.

(21) "Neither repented they of their murders, nor of their sorceries, nor of their fornication, nor of their thefts."

All the various facets of this scene speak of a refusal to return to the Lord Jesus. People will not repent because of four things which they cling to and which they practice: murders, sorceries, fornication, and thefts.

Day by day crime is on the rise in the world. The same is true of sorcery for people follow after horoscopes, conjure up spirits, enjoy watching magic shows on television, and worship Satan. Through such things, they provoke the Lord Jesus, the only true God, to anger for he is a jealous God who desires to protect his name, and to protect us from evil: "thou shalt worship no other god: for the Lord, whose name is Jealous, is a jealous God" (Exodus 34:14).

In addition, we see in these last days the proliferation of divorce. We see people embracing fornication and living together without marriage, making it easier for them to go on to their next partners. This behavior culminates in sexual deviancy and homosexuality which is that final stage before God's rejection: "And even as they did not like to retain God in their knowledge, God gave them over to a reprobate mind, to do those things which are not convenient" (Romans 1:28).

Theft is very widespread today. This includes all forms of technological fraud and deception, as well as theft of homes, warehouses, and companies. No one thinks of repentance and returning to the Lord Jesus. The living word of God is clear, and is being fulfilled today: "This know also, that in the last days perilous times shall come. For men shall be lovers of their own selves, covetous, boasters, proud, blasphemers, disobedient to parents, unthankful, unholy, Without natural affection, trucebreakers, false accusers, incontinent, fierce, despisers of those that are good, Traitors, heady, highminded, lovers of pleasures more than lovers of God" (2 Timothy 3:1-4).

10
THE LITTLE OPEN BOOK

(1) "And I saw another mighty angel come down from heaven, clothed with a cloud: and a rainbow was upon his head, and his face was as it were the sun, and his feet as pillars of fire:"

Between the sixth seal and the seventh seal, we saw a gap in which the scene translated from earth to heaven (Revelation 6:12- 7:17). We now see, in similar fashion, a gap between the sixth trumpet and the seventh trumpet, which again takes us up to a scene in heaven (Revelation 9:13- 11:15).

In these gaps, or rests from witnessing the wrath on earth, the scene shifts to heaven to show us that while the woes are raining down on the dark kingdom of the Antichrist on earth, preparations are already underway in heaven for the coming light of the kingdom of Christ on the earth, when the peace of Jesus will spread to every corner of the globe.

How beautiful it is to see the divine correlation between what is happening in heaven and what is happening on earth and the race to fulfil God's program for the redemption of man and his deliverance from Satan and his influences.

Now we see a very powerful angel, blessed and brilliant in radiance, descend from heaven. The angel is clothed with a cloud which represents a riddle or a mystery about his identity and his purpose. The rainbow as we have seen in the throne scene, symbolizes peace and gladness: "And he that sat was to look upon like a jasper and a sardine stone: and there was a rainbow round about the throne, in sight like unto an emerald" (Revelation 4:3). In the description of the angel's face as the sun and his feet as pillars of fire, we see that the angel's master, the Lord Jesus (verse 6) is the one who sent this angel. He is the one who shines with righteousness and joy in heaven and treads the earth underfoot with his judgment.

(2) "And he had in his hand a little book open: and he set his right foot upon the sea, and his left foot on the earth"

- And he had in his hand a little book open - We cannot foretell what is in this book, but it contains imminent prophecies as we can glean from the next two verses 3 & 4, which seem to indicate that this is the case. The fact that it is a small book points to the possibility it does not involve a long or wide range of prophecies of things to come.

- and he set his right foot upon the sea, and his left foot on the earth - John's wonder regarding the greatness of the angel should also be noted. As a towering colossus, the angel sets his right foot upon the sea, and his left foot on the earth.

(3) "And cried with a loud voice, as when a lion roareth: and when he had cried, seven thunders uttered their voices."

This mighty angel cried and a judgment of seven thunders were proclaimed, and their utterances came from the Lord Jesus.

(4) "And when the seven thunders had uttered their voices, I was about to write: and I heard a voice from heaven saying unto me, Seal up those things which the seven thunders uttered, and write them not."

The Lord saw fit to keep these sayings hidden from John; but only for a short while as explained in verse seven: "But in the days of the voice of the seventh angel, when he shall begin to sound, the mystery of God should be finished, as he hath declared to his servants the prophets" (Revelation 10:7). We do not know what were the words that were spoken by the seven thunders; but we will know them when we go up to be with the Lord Jesus and dwell with him. We do not know the voice that spoke to John, but it could have been the voice of the Lord Jesus himself, as was the case in: "I was in the Spirit on the Lord's day, and heard behind me a great voice, as of a trumpet, Saying, I am Alpha and Omega, the first and the last" (Revelation 1:10-11).

(5) "And the angel which I saw stand upon the sea and upon the earth lifted up his hand to heaven,"

The lifting of the hand to heaven indicates the serious and solemn nature of what is about to be spoken, as was the case with:

(i) Abraham: "And Abram said to the king of Sodom, I have lift up mine hand unto the Lord, the most high God, the possessor of heaven and earth, That I will not take from a thread even to a shoe latchet, and that I will not take any thing that is thine, lest thou shouldest say, I have made Abram rich" (Genesis 14:22-23).

(ii) The Lord Jesus, when he said to Moses: "And I will bring you in unto the land, concerning the which I did swear to give it to Abraham, to Isaac, and to Jacob; and I will give it you for an heritage: I am the Lord" (Exodus 6:8). Note that the statement "I did swear" indicates the raising of one's hand.

(iii) And nature in praising the Jesus, the Creator: "The mountains saw thee, and they trembled: the overflowing of the water passed by: the deep uttered his voice, and lifted up his hands on high" (Habakkuk 3:10).

(6) "And sware by him that liveth for ever and ever, who created heaven, and the things that therein are, and the earth, and the things that therein are, and the sea, and the things which are therein, that there should be time no longer:"

Let's address the issue of swearing an oath by looking at it from all sides:

(i) The Lord Jesus performed it: "And said, By myself have I sworn, saith the Lord, for because thou hast done this thing, and hast not withheld thy son, thine only son" (Genesis 22:16). "I have sworn by myself, the word is gone out of my mouth in righteousness, and shall not return, That unto me every knee shall bow, every tongue shall swear" (Isaiah 45:23).

(ii) The Lord Jesus endorsed it: "And ye shall not swear by my name falsely, neither shalt thou profane the name of thy God: I am the Lord" (Leviticus 19:12). "Thou shalt fear the Lord thy God, and serve him, and shalt swear by his name ... Thou shalt fear the Lord thy God; him shalt thou serve, and to him shalt thou cleave, and swear by his name. He is thy praise, and he is thy God" (Deuteronomy 6:13; 10:20-21).

(iii) The Lord Jesus prohibited it: "But I say unto you, Swear not at all ... But let your communication be, Yea, yea; Nay, nay: for whatsoever is more than these cometh of evil" (Matthew 5:34,37). "But above all things, my brethren, swear not, neither by heaven, neither by the earth, neither by any other oath: but let your yea be yea; and your nay, nay; lest ye fall into condemnation" (James 5:12).

(iv) It was practiced by believers:

(a) Abraham: "²²And Abram said to the king of Sodom, I have lift up mine hand unto the LORD, the most high God, the possessor of heaven and earth, ²³That I will not *take* from a thread even to a shoelatchet, and that I will not take any thing that *is* thine, lest thou shouldest say, I have made Abram rich: " (Genesis 14:22-23);

(b) David: "As the Lord liveth, that hath redeemed my soul out of all distress, Even as I sware unto thee by the Lord God of

Israel, saying, Assuredly Solomon thy son shall reign after me, and he shall sit upon my throne in my stead; even so will I certainly do this day" (1 Kings 1:29-30);
(c) Paul, "I say the truth in Christ, I lie not, my conscience also bearing me witness in the Holy Ghost" (Romans 9:1).

(v) God sanctioned its usage between people: "For men verily swear by the greater: and an oath for confirmation is to them an end of all strife. Wherein God, willing more abundantly to shew unto the heirs of promise the immutability of his counsel, confirmed it by an oath" (Hebrews 6:16-17).

Since the entire Bible is inspired by God and the Word of God is living or alive today, then when you want to build a doctrine or a teaching, gather all the verses that address that subject and reach a sound proper decision. In the case of swearing, it should not be used lightly or in every other sentence that we utter in our daily lives. Rather we should only swear to confirm a serious matter. Also when a person swears an oath, he is responsible to keep his word. The Devil will try to get you to breach your oath so as to sully the name of the Lord. This is a trap and a snare and a test, so read the verses listed above again as it is better not to swear and oath in the first place if you are not determined to keep your oath. We read advice on this matter from the wise king Solomon who says: "When thou vowest a vow unto God, defer not to pay it; for he hath no pleasure in fools: pay that which thou hast vowed. Better is it that thou shouldest not vow, than that thou shouldest vow and not pay. Suffer not thy mouth to cause thy flesh to sin; neither say thou before the angel, that it was an error: wherefore should God be angry at thy voice, and destroy the work of thine hands?" (Ecclesiastes 5:4-6).

The angel swore by the Lord Jesus, meaning that his authority was from the Lord Jesus Christ, the living Son of God, who sits at the right hand of Majesty on high. Jesus who: "When he had by himself purged our sins, sat down on the right hand of the Majesty on high" (Hebrews 1:3).

The angel swore by the Lord Jesus that the time of human rule has definitely come to an end. The time has come for the beginning of the kingdom of Christ.

(7) "But in the days of the voice of the seventh angel, when he shall begin to sound, the mystery of God should be finished, as he hath declared to his servants the prophets."

- But in the days of the voice of the seventh angel, when he shall begin to sound,

- When the seventh trumpet shall sound, following the fifth and sixth trumpets, the world will come to an end. So then reaches the end of the world; and the wrath which is already descending upon the earth will now be greater and more terrifying than what it has already been.

- The mystery of God should be finished, as he hath declared to his servants the prophets - In the midst of wrath, as we hear seven mighty thunders speaking, the Lord, as always, is full of consolation, so he reminds us in this verse that what he is doing is not hidden from his servants, but he had already revealed it to the believers as is the case with the book of Revelation. We remember Sodom and Gomorrah and what the Lord said: "Shall I hide from Abraham that thing which I do?" (Genesis 18:17). This distinction is for every faithful servant of the Lord Jesus, as the Bible says: "Surely the Lord God will do nothing, but he revealeth his secret unto his servants the prophets" (Amos 3:7). The Lord always gives his children an unveiling of things to come, and an understanding of events spiritually ambiguous. The believer never encounters the difficulty which the unsaved person faces in reading and understanding the word of life, the Bible; and in particular, the book of Revelation.

With regard to the unbeliever, the future is a riddle, incomprehensible and unknown. He has no understanding of what will unfold in the end times, of the judgment which is coming on the entirety of this evil world. We thank the Lord for his Holy Spirit who indwells us, illuminates our hearts and minds, and shines his brilliant, glorious light on the pages of the Bible, and gives us the ability to understand the book of Revelation so beautifully and delightfully.

We, the believers, will see these events transpire on earth from our heavenly vantage point, where bliss and peace will be our portion. All these blessings are bestowed upon each one of us who, with a repentant heart, has received the Lord Jesus as his personal Lord and Saviour. If you have not done so yet, accept him now and expect a happy joyful blessed eternity in heaven.

(8) "And the voice which I heard from heaven spake unto me again, and said, Go and take the little book which is open in the hand of the angel which standeth upon the sea and upon the earth."

This great voice speaking directly to John again asks him to go to the mighty angel and take the little book from his hand. This is the angel we discussed in verse one. John must have gone in the spirit because he was witnessing futuristic events to come of the book of Revelation.

(9) "And I went unto the angel, and said unto him, Give me the little book. And he said unto me, Take it, and eat it up; and it shall make thy belly bitter, but it shall be in thy mouth sweet as honey."

John immediately did what he was commanded to do. Would that each believer in the Lord Jesus obey and implement this verse's order of reading the words of the Bible, and meditate on it so that he could grow and vibrant be in his spiritual life.

(10) "And I took the little book out of the angel's hand, and ate it up; and it was in my mouth sweet as honey: and as soon as I had eaten it, my belly was bitter."

The Bible speaks of a similar experience in three other passages:

(i) "How sweet are thy words unto my taste! yea, sweeter than honey to my mouth! Through thy precepts I get understanding: therefore I hate every false way" (Psalm 119:103-104). The Word of the Lord brings joy and refreshment; and when we apply it to our lives, we face persecution because the world is dominated by the wicked.

(ii) "Thy words were found, and I did eat them; and thy word was unto me the joy and rejoicing of mine heart: for I am called by thy name, O LORD God of hosts. I sat not in the assembly of the mockers, nor rejoiced; I sat alone because of thy hand: for thou hast filled me with indignation. Why is my pain perpetual, and my wound incurable, which refuseth to be healed? wilt thou be altogether unto me as a liar, and as waters that fail?" (Jeremiah 15:16-18). Jeremiah took God's word and ate it and enjoyed it in its entirety, and when he put it into practice, great persecution came upon him, and he sat alone.

(iii) "And when I looked, behold, an hand was sent unto me; and, lo, a roll of a book was therein; And he spread it before me; and it was written within and without: and there was written therein lamentations, and mourning, and woe. Moreover he said unto me, Son of man, eat that thou findest; eat this roll, and go speak unto the house of Israel. So I opened my mouth, and he caused me to eat that roll. And he said unto me, Son of man, cause thy belly to eat, and fill thy bowels with this roll that I give thee. Then did I eat it; and it was in my mouth as honey for sweetness. And he said unto me, Son of man, go, get thee unto the house of Israel, and speak with my words unto them ... So the spirit lifted me up, and took me away, and I went in bitterness, in the heat of my spirit; but the hand of the Lord was strong upon me" (Ezekiel 2:9-11; 3:4,14).

Reading the Bible is interesting and enjoyable; applying it is burdensome. The word of the Lord Jesus is sweet, beautiful, and delightful, and imparts spiritual warmth and growth as we put it into practice. This is the portion of every believer who wants to live for the Lord according to his word. The word of God challenges us to take a righteous stand for the Lord Jesus. There are many who wish to live for the Lord, but they are defeated. Satan wars against them and defeats them, making them fruitless in this world. These are saved born again believers but they have one eye on the Lord and the other on the world. What does the Bible say: "And Jesus said unto him, No man, having put his hand to the plough, and looking back, is fit for the kingdom of God" (Luke 9:62). Focus both your eyes on the Lord Jesus, and you will be fit for the service of the kingdom of God.

(11) "And he said unto me, Thou must prophesy again before many peoples, and nations, and tongues, and kings."

The Bible gives the ability and the right to anticipate, according to Biblical principals, to be instruments of encouragement, exhortation, and guidance; or of chastisement, rebuke, and reproof in a spirit of love.

11
THE SEVENTH TRUMPET THE TWO WITNESSES

(1) "And there was given me a reed like unto a rod: and the angel stood, saying, Rise, and measure the temple of God, and the altar, and them that worship therein."

It is difficult to interpret this chapter figuratively, but if we stick to the literal interpretation then the picture is simple and very beautiful and delightful and quite logical.

We are still in a transitional stage between the sixth and seven trumpets. After John has heard what the seven thunders had to say, and after he has eaten the little book, the angel asks him to measure the temple of Jerusalem. John is asked to measure the details of the temple and Holy of Holies and altar which are the refuge and shelter for the faithful believing Jews.

(2) "But the court which is without the temple leave out, and measure it not; for it is given unto the Gentiles: and the holy city shall they tread under foot forty and two months."

The outer courtyard will be overtaken by the Gentiles who will tread it down underfoot for forty two months or three and a half years, the second half of the great tribulation.

We recall once again that the Antichrist will establish false peace between the Jews and the nations, especially the Arab ones, for three and a half years. Then he will suddenly reveal his true colours and usurp authority over the whole world, breaking his covenant with the Jews, afflicting, and oppressing the whole human race. He will come to go to Jerusalem and sit in the temple as a god, and force all men worship him: "And that man of sin be revealed, the son of perdition; Who opposeth and exalteth himself above all that is called God, or that is worshipped; so that he as God sitteth in the temple of God, shewing himself that he is God" (2 Thessalonians 2:3-4). He will make everyone bear a mark, probably a laser seal, making all become his property: "And he causeth all, both small and great, rich and poor, free and bond, to receive a mark in their right hand, or in their foreheads" (Revelation 13:16).

For these prophecies to be fulfilled, it is inevitable that the temple will be rebuilt for in the middle of the great tribulation the Antichrist will enter and sit in the temple.

Also, the Lord Jesus Christ will also return to this same temple, at the end of the great tribulation: "And the Lord, whom ye seek, shall suddenly come to his temple, even the messenger of the covenant, whom ye delight in: behold, he shall come, saith the Lord of hosts. But who may abide the day of his coming?" (Malachi 3:1-2).

We will not see these things happen now because we are in the age of grace, the age of Christ's church. But as soon as the rapture happens and we the followers of Christ taken up with the Holy Spirit who came down on the day of Pentecost, then the Antichrist will emerge and the temple will be rebuilt to continue God's dealing with Jerusalem according to Daniel's seventieth week. It must be that the Antichrist is already born and alive in the world today; however, no one will know who he is until after the rapture of the church: "Remember ye not, that, when I was yet with you, I told you these things? And now ye know what withholdeth that he might be revealed in his time. For the mystery of iniquity doth already work: only he who now letteth will let, until he be taken out of the way. And then shall that Wicked be revealed, whom the Lord shall consume with the spirit of his mouth, and shall destroy with the brightness of his coming: Even him, whose coming is after the working of Satan with all power and signs and lying wonders, And with all deceivableness of unrighteousness in them that perish; because they received not the love of the truth, that they might be saved. And for this cause God shall send them strong delusion, that they should believe a lie: That they all might be damned who believed not the truth, but had pleasure in unrighteousness" (2 Thessalonians 2:5-12).

According to orthodox Jewish media statements, all the materials needed to build the temple have been prepared, including clothing for priests and all functional items for worship. With today's level of technology, it would take only one week to rebuild the temple and begin offering sacrifices on it.

These are signs that the coming of the Lord Jesus is imminent: "So ye in like manner, when ye shall see these things come to pass, know that it is nigh, even at the doors ... For the Son of Man is as a man taking a far journey, who left his house, and gave authority to his servants, and to every man his work, and commanded the porter to watch. Watch ye therefore: for ye know not when the master of the house cometh, at even, or at midnight, or at the cockcrowing, or in the morning: Lest coming suddenly he find you sleeping. And what I say unto you I say unto all, Watch" (Mark 13:29, 34-37). The Lord Jesus wants us to be vigilant when it comes to the spiritual condition of our lives, our children's lives, and our churches!

(3) "And I will give power unto my two witnesses, and they shall prophesy a thousand two hundred and threescore days, clothed in sackcloth."

Even in the darkest days of the Antichrist's oppression, the Lord Jesus does not leave himself without a witness on earth:

"Nevertheless he left not himself without witness" (Acts 14:17); even two witnesses for: "At the mouth of two witnesses, or at the mouth of three witnesses, shall the matter be established" (Deuteronomy 19:15); "In the mouth of two or three witnesses shall every word be established" (2 Corinthians 13:1). These two witnesses will appear suddenly on the world scene, specifically in the city of Jerusalem. They shall withhold and stand against the Antichrist, and humbly wearing sackcloth, the two are going to testify throughout the second half of the tribulation and proclaim the salvation in the Lord Jesus Christ. They are going to invite people to get saved in Jesus Christ.

The dilemma is ascertaining the identity of these two witnesses! Who will they be? It is possible that they will be Moses and Elijah, for the two witnesses' ministries are similar to the roles played by each of Moses and Elijah during their ministry on the earth as described in verses five and six of fire descending from heaven by Elijah and water turned into blood by Moses. Also, Moses and Elijah are the ones who appeared with the Lord Jesus on the mount of transfiguration and spoke with him of his coming glory: "And it came to pass about an eight days after these sayings, he took Peter and John and James, and went up into a mountain to pray. And as he prayed, the fashion of his countenance was altered, and his raiment was white and glistering. And, behold, there talked with him two men, which were Moses and Elias: Who appeared in glory, and spake of his decease which he should accomplish at Jerusalem" (Luke 9:28-31).

But logic of the Bible is that God cannot be constrained. It could be that these two witnesses will be two new persons, who will be born into the world and will have a mighty ministry of witnessing to the light of Christ in the darkest days which man will ever know upon the earth, at the apex of the Antichrist's oppressive rule over the sinful souls of men upon the earth. Their role will be to declare that Jesus is alive and is sitting on his throne in heaven, and he is the one overseeing all that is happening on earth in the outpouring of God's wrath on all evil-doers. Even in the worst time in history, the Lord is able to allow to be born two new heroes of the faith, as was true when the Jews returned from the Babylonian captivity and the Lord raised up two olive trees and two new candlesticks, namely Zerubbabel the son of Shealtiel, governor of Judah and Joshua the son of Josedech, the high priest: "And the LORD stirred up the spirit of Zerubbabel the son of Shealtiel, governor of Judah, and the spirit of Joshua the son of Josedech, the high priest" (Haggai 1:14).

(4) "These are the two olive trees, and the two candlesticks standing before the God of the earth."

This verse gives strong credence to the idea that the two witnesses will be two new persons, serving the Lord upon the earth for the first time, as Joshua and Zerubbabal did in the Old Testament: "And he answered me and said, Knowest thou not what these be? And I said, No, my lord. Then said he, These are the two anointed ones, that stand by the Lord of the whole earth" (Zechariah 4:13-14).

Additionally, when Moses and Elijah appeared on the mount of transfiguration, the Bible says that they appeared in glory: "^{30}And, behold, there talked with him two men, which were Moses and Elias: ^{31}Who appeared in glory" (Luke 9:30-31)! The possibility that a person can transition back from a glorified body to mortal human form has no precedence in God's word; and it is in conflict with the logic of birth and death and salvation once and forever that the Bible teaches.

(5) "And if any man will hurt them, fire proceedeth out of their mouth, and devoureth their enemies: and if any man will hurt them, he must in this manner be killed."

This reminds us of what happened with Elijah: "And Elijah answered and said to the captain of fifty, If I be a man of God, then let fire come down from heaven, and consume thee and thy fifty. And there came down fire from heaven, and consumed him and his fifty" (2 Kings 1:10). The ministry of the two witnesses will be that of divine judgment on the wicked.

(6) "These have power to shut heaven, that it rain not in the days of their prophecy: and have power over waters to turn them to blood, and to smite the earth with all plagues, as often as they will."

- These have power to shut heaven, that it rain not in the days of their prophecy - This reminds us of what happened with Elijah: "Elias was a man subject to like passions as we are, and he prayed earnestly that it might not rain: and it rained not on the earth by the space of three years and six months" (James 5:17). Then, there was divine wrath on Israel in the days of King Ahab who sold himself to do evil in the eyes of the Lord Jesus: "And it came to pass, when Ahab saw Elijah, that Ahab said unto him, Art thou he that troubleth Israel? And he answered, I have not troubled Israel; but thou, and thy father's house, in that ye have forsaken the commandments of the Lord, and thou hast followed Baalim ... But there was none like unto Ahab, which did sell himself to work wickedness in the sight of the Lord, whom Jezebel his wife stirred up" (1 Kings 18:17-18; 21:25). Here again, this is a description of the ministry of these two witnesses that focuses on chastising and punishing the evildoers and wicked people of the great tribulation.

And so, because of God's wrath on these wicked people who will sell their souls to the worship of the Antichrist, the two witnesses will prevent rain from falling, which will result in worldwide drought and hunger.

- And have power over waters to turn them to blood, and to smite the earth with all plagues, as often as they will - This is reminiscent of what occurred with Moses: "And Moses and Aaron did so, as the LORD commanded; and he lifted up the rod, and smote the waters that were in the river, in the sight of Pharaoh, and in the sight of his servants; and all the waters that were in the river were turned to blood. And the fish that was in the river died; and the river stank, and the Egyptians could not drink of the water of the river; and there was blood throughout all the land of Egypt" (Exodus 7:20-21). In the previous verse God's wrath was directed at people, but here it is directed at nature.

(7) "And when they shall have finished their testimony, the beast that ascendeth out of the bottomless pit shall make war against them, and shall overcome them, and kill them."

It has been 7 years since the great tribulation has begun, and the second half of the tribulation will be about to end. So it will be time for Christ to return to the earth, and therefore there is going to be manifestation the last deed of abuse, injustice, and malevolence from Satan who is described as:

(i) He is Lucifer, the star that fell from heaven to earth: "How art thou fallen from heaven, O Lucifer, son of the morning! how art thou cut down to the ground, which didst weaken the nations!" (Isaiah 14:12).

(ii) He is the one out of the bottomless pit, "And the fifth angel sounded, and I saw a star fall from heaven unto the earth: and to him was given the key of the bottomless pit" (Revelation 9:1).

(iii) He is the one who is destined for perdition: "The beast that thou sawest was, and is not; and shall ascend out of the bottomless pit, and go into perdition" (Revelation 17:8).

In this verse, the beast described is Satan who will ascend out of the bottomless pit and kill the two heroic witnesses of Christ. He will only do so when they have completed their ministry. This will be the darkest day before the breaking of dawn, before the coming up on the earth, the reign of Christ Jesus, King of kings and Lord of lords.

This is one additional proof that heaven is sovereign. No one can experience any adversity without the Lord Jesus allowing it first. Job suffered the same: "And the Lord said unto Satan,

Behold, all that he hath is in thy power; only upon himself put not forth thine hand ...And the Lord said unto Satan, Behold, he is in thine hand; but save his life. So went Satan forth from the presence of the Lord, and smote Job with sore boils from the sole of his foot unto his crown" (Job 1:12; 2:6-7). Nothing happens in the entire universe without permission or commandment from the Lord Jesus Christ: "I form the light, and create darkness: I make peace, and create evil: I the Lord do all these things" (Isaiah 45:7); "Who is he that saith, and it cometh to pass, when the Lord commandeth it not? Out of the mouth of the most High proceedeth not evil and good?" (Lamentations 3:37-38); "And he doeth according to his will in the army of heaven, and among the inhabitants of the earth: and none can stay his hand, or say unto him, What doest thou?" (Daniel 4:35); "Shall there be evil in a city, and the Lord hath not done it?" (Amos 3:6). He is God, the almighty ruler of whom the Bible says: "Far be it from God, that he should do wickedness; and from the Almighty, that he should commit iniquity. For the work of a man shall he render unto him, and cause every man to find according to his ways. Yea, surely God will not do wickedly, neither will the Almighty pervert judgment ... Touching the Almighty, we cannot find him out: he is excellent in power, and in judgment, and in plenty of justice: he will not afflict" (Job 34:10-12; 37:23).

(8) "And their dead bodies shall lie in the street of the great city, which spiritually is called Sodom and Egypt, where also our Lord was crucified."

This city is Jerusalem, where the Lord Jesus was crucified at a time of great spiritual darkness as we can tell from the number of lame and sick and lepers and blind and deaf and demon possessed people in those days. Likewise, at the time of Jesus' second coming, Jerusalem will spiritually be like Sodom, a city filled with physical fornication and sexual perversion. Today, these sins are becoming widespread in Israel; Tel Aviv is now the world capital and number one travel destination of the sexually perverse. Egypt is a symbol of enslavement to the material world. The spiritual condition of Jerusalem at that time will be very poor and the materialism of its people will be the worst it has ever been; the love of money among the people in Jerusalem will be worse than in the days of Jesus. The Gentiles will be in control of the city. Fornication, immoral filthiness, and the pursuit of money will be rampant. The people of the city will be very far removed from a spirit of repentance to Jesus Christ, whose coming will then be imminent. Therefore the Lord Jesus poses the question: "When the Son of man cometh, shall he find faith on the earth?" (Luke 18:8). Faith will be nonexistent but for the grace of Jesus!

(9) "And they of the people and kindreds and tongues and nations shall see their dead bodies three days and an half, and shall not suffer their dead bodies to be put in graves."

All the people of the world, Jews or Gentiles, are the sons of darkness. They are sinners who mock when any harm comes the way of the children of Christ, the children of light. Their hatred and lack of respect for the dead will reach an epic when they will not allow the burial of the bodies of these two witnesses of heaven.

(10) "And they that dwell upon the earth shall rejoice over them, and make merry, and shall send gifts one to another; because these two prophets tormented them that dwelt on the earth."

Worse than that, they will be sending gifts to each other in the outflow of their great joy at being delivered from the chastisement of these two witnesses of the righteousness of Christ.

(11) "And after three days and an half the Spirit of life from God entered into them, and they stood upon their feet; and great fear fell upon them which saw them."

But suddenly, the Lord Jesus is going to intervene and raise the two witnesses from the dead, even as he rose from the dead in victory over his enemies. As the adversaries of Christ were vanquished then, so also the Saviour will turn the tables on those who will mock his two prophets. From the dawn of history, Satan thinks that he will win in the end, but the opposite is always the case! The devil's loss is so very big that his end is going to be in hell's fire forever: "And the devil that deceived them was cast into the lake of fire and brimstone, where the beast and the False prophet are, and shall be tormented day and night for ever and ever" (Revelation 20:10). Thanks and praise be to the Lord Jesus!

In every occasion, we see the greatness of our Lord and his victory over Satan, for Jesus is always triumphant! So is the lot of everyone who takes sides with Jesus! The rejoicing of the wicked will hardly be complete, for while still sending gifts to each other, after the passing of three and half days, divine victory over Satan will be manifested visibly. This is always the case that after the believer lays down his life for Jesus, he experiences a following glorious resurrection.

(12) "And they heard a great voice from heaven saying unto them, Come up hither. And they ascended up to heaven in a cloud; and their enemies beheld them."

Just like the Lord Jesus ascended into heaven after his glorious resurrection, so in like manner Jesus calls up these two faithful witnesses to ascend to heavenly glory. What an illustrious honour for these two, who completed their course faithfully, sealed their ministry with their own blood, and experienced a blessed resurrection to life everlasting! They will obtain rewards and prized and crowns and radiate light forever in the firmament of the heavens.

The rapture of these two prophets will be a very visible public event seen by many people, similar to how Elijah ascended into heaven: "And it came to pass, as they still went on, and talked, that, behold, there appeared a chariot of fire, and horses of fire, and parted them both asunder; and Elijah went up by a whirlwind into heaven. And Elisha saw it, and he cried, My father, my father, the chariot of Israel, and the horsemen thereof" (2 Kings 2:11-12). People will see them rise from the dead and ascend into heaven before their very eyes.

In contrast to the rapture of these two prophets, the rapture of the church will take place in an instant, and no one will be aware of it except for those who believe in Christ. This is like the experience of Enoch: "And Enoch walked with God: and he was not; for God took him" (Genesis 5: 24). It is also similar to the rapture of the righteous at the end of the great tribulation: "I tell you, in that night there shall be two men in one bed; the one shall be taken, and the other shall be left. Two women shall be grinding together; the one shall be taken, and the other left. Two men shall be in the field; the one shall be taken, and the other left" (Luke 17:34-36). We thank the Lord for we will be watching from heaven with all the redeemed and righteous believers who are sanctified in Christ Jesus.

(13) "And the same hour was there a great earthquake, and the tenth part of the city fell, and in the earthquake were slain of men seven thousand: and the remnant were affrighted, and gave glory to the God of heaven."

- And the same hour was there a great earthquake, and the tenth part of the city fell, and in the earthquake were slain of men seven thousand – So then at that moment, the wrath of the Lord will descend heavily on the city of Jerusalem, causing an earthquake that will kill seven thousand people. This figure represents one tenth of the population of the city of Jerusalem, which shows that the number of the inhabitants of the earth has dwindled very markedly. Most of the inhabitants of the earth will have been killed by the numerous judgments of the great tribulation.

- And the remnant were affrighted, and gave glory to the God of heaven - Those who are not killed in the earthquake are filled with fear at the might and magnificence of our God; they give him glory and admit that he has power over all things: "All things were made by him; and without him was not any thing made that was made" (John 1:3); "And he is before all things, and by him all things consist" (Colossians 1:17); "Upholding all things by the word of his power" (Hebrews 1:3). Unfortunately, they will not repent; therefore, more of God's wrath will come their way.

(14) "The second woe is past; and, behold, the third woe cometh quickly."

In our study of chapter eight, we heard the voice of an angel flying through the midst of heaven, saying with a loud voice: "Woe, woe, woe, to the inhabiters of the earth by reason of the other voices of the trumpet of the three angels, which are yet to sound!" (Revelation 8:13). The first woe was the fifth trumpet (Revelation 9:1-12). The second woe was the sixth trumpet (Revelation 9:13-21). Now comes the third woe.

(15) "And the seventh angel sounded; and there were great voices in heaven, saying, The kingdoms of this world are become the kingdoms of our Lord, and of his Christ; and he shall reign for ever and ever."

Now the time has come for the seventh trumpet, which is the third woe. This trumpet concludes with the return of the Lord Jesus Christ to the earth to reign forever.

Time-wise, here we are at the end of the great tribulation, just before the return of the Lord Jesus. We are at the end of the second narrative of the return of the Lord Jesus. This narrative started in chapter eight, and followed the first narrative which ended in chapter six.

Just like there are 4 narratives of the first advent of Christ in Matthew Mark Luke and John, so there are four narratives of the second advent of Christ:

(i) The first narrative describes the general worldwide depression and the conflicts between different peoples (Chapters 5-6).

(ii) The second narrative describes the heavenly judgments that fall upon nature and humanity (Chapters 7-11).

(iii) Third narrative describes the spiritual warfare in heaven and on earth during the great tribulation (Chapter 12).

(iv) The fourth and final narrative, is the longest one and describes the coming out of all the forces of evil represented by Satan, the Antichrist, and the False prophet. That will terminate the great tribulation, when the Lord Jesus will return to the earth and cast the Antichrist and the False prophet into the lake of fire (Chapters 13-19). Satan, however, will be cast into hell after one thousand years: "And I saw an angel come down from heaven, having the key of the bottomless pit and a great chain in his hand. And he laid hold on the dragon, that old serpent, which is the Devil, and Satan, and bound him a thousand years ...And the devil that deceived them was cast into the lake of fire and brimstone, where the beast and the False prophet are, and shall be tormented day and night for ever and ever" (Revelation 20:1-2,10).

(16) "And the four and twenty elders, which sat before God on their seats, fell upon their faces, and worshipped God,"

These are the elders whom we considered in chapter four: "And round about the throne were four and twenty seats: and upon the seats I saw four and twenty elders sitting, clothed in white raiment; and they had on their heads crowns of gold" (Revelation 4:4). Here they are worshiping the Lord Jesus and giving him the glory.

(17) "Saying, We give thee thanks, O Lord God Almighty, which art, and wast, and art to come; because thou hast taken to thee thy great power, and hast reigned."

- Saying, We give thee thanks, O Lord God Almighty - When the Lord Jesus first introduced himself to the human race, he presented himself as "God Almighty" (Exodus 6:3). He is the one who upholds "All things by the word of his power" (Hebrews 1:3). He is God: "But unto the Son he saith, Thy throne, O God, is for ever and ever" (Hebrews 1:8). In him: "we live, and move, and have our being" (Acts 17:28). Amen.

- Which art, and wast, and art to come - "Jesus Christ the same yesterday, and to day, and for ever" (Hebrews 13:8). He is the eternal **I AM**: 1- From eternity past, having no beginning; 2- Unto eternity future, having no end; 3- Everlasting, always existing.

- Because thou hast taken to thee thy great power, and hast reigned - The Lord Jesus went to the cross and died and rose again, and thus triumphed over Satan and his crowd. He triumphed over 1- Satan, 2- the Antichrist, 3- the False prophet, and 4- the wicked angels. Now the time has come for Jesus' kingdom to usher in, and he will reign for one thousand years.

(18) "And the nations were angry, and thy wrath is come, and the time of the dead, that they should be judged, and that thou shouldest give reward unto thy servants the prophets, and to the saints, and them that fear thy name, small and great; and shouldest destroy them which destroy the earth."

The wicked were angry with God because they did not want to live for righteousness. Now it is the Lord Jesus who is angry with them and is going to kill them: "And I saw the beast, and the kings of the earth, and their armies, gathered together to make war against him that sat on the horse, and against his army. And the beast was taken, and with him the False prophet that wrought miracles before him, with which he deceived them that had received the mark of the beast, and them that worshipped his image. These both were cast alive into a lake of fire burning with brimstone. And the remnant were slain with the sword of him that sat upon the horse, which sword proceeded out of his mouth: and all the fowls were filled with their flesh" (Revelation 19:19-21).

It is Jesus Christ's servants to reign with him: "And I saw thrones, and they sat upon them, and judgment was given unto them: and I saw the souls of them that were beheaded for the witness of Jesus, and for the word of God, and which had not worshipped the beast, neither his image, neither had received his mark upon their foreheads, or in their hands; and they lived and reigned with Christ a thousand years" (Revelation 20:4).

Then he will punish the wicked with everlasting perdition: "But the rest of the dead lived not again until the thousand years were finished. This is the first resurrection. And I saw a great white throne, and him that sat on it, from whose face the earth and the heaven fled away; and there was found no place for them. And I saw the dead, small and great, stand before God; and the books were opened: and another book was opened, which is the book of life: and the dead were judged out of those things which were written in the books, according to their works. And the sea gave up the dead which were in it; and death and hell delivered up the dead which were in them: and they were judged every man according to their works. And death and hell were cast into the lake of fire. This is the second death. And whosoever was not found written in the book of life was cast into the lake of fire" (Revelation 20:5,11-15). The time has come for the rule of heaven upon the earth!

(19) "And the temple of God was opened in heaven, and there was seen in his temple the ark of his testament: and there were lightnings, and voices, and thunderings, and an earthquake, and great hail."

- And the temple of God was opened in heaven, and there was seen in his temple the ark of his testament - The temple of God was opened in heaven, and there was seen in his temple the ark of his covenant. The temple of God is open in heaven, and we see the ark of the covenant, whose cover is overspread by the wings of two cherubims. The ark resides in the Holy of Holies into which the high priest enters once a year: "And after the second veil, the tabernacle which is called the Holiest of all; Which had the golden censer, and the ark of the covenant overlaid round about with gold, wherein was the golden pot that had manna, and Aaron's rod that budded, and the tables of the covenant; And over it the cherubims of glory shadowing the mercyseat; of which we cannot now speak particularly. Now when these things were thus ordained, the priests went always into the first tabernacle, accomplishing the service of God. But into the second went the high priest alone once every year" (Hebrews 9:3-7). But the Lord Jesus did away with the veil which separated the Holy place from the Holy of Holies, when he went to the cross and brought eternal redemption and everlasting righteousness to man: "Jesus, when he had cried again with a loud voice, yielded up the ghost. And, behold, the veil of the temple was rent in twain from the top to the bottom; and the earth did quake, and the rocks rent; And the graves were opened; and many bodies of the saints which slept arose" (Matthew 27:50-52). There is no more need for the veil as we now have the right and the ability to enter directly into the presence of the Lord in heaven by virtue of the blood of the cross. Jesus rent the veil and abolished the O.T. sacrifices when he fulfilled them himself and gave us free presence before the throne of grace through his atoning work for us.

- And there were lightnings, and voices, and thunderings, and an earthquake, and great hail - This supernatural intervention accompanies and seals the account which we are given, emphasizing that it is indeed a great heavenly scene.

12
SATAN PERSECUTES ISRAEL

(1) "And there appeared a great wonder in heaven; a woman clothed with the sun, and the moon under her feet, and upon her head a crown of twelve stars:"

We return to symbolism in understanding the book of Revelation, for the woman is the nation of Israel according to the dream of Joseph, who said: "Behold, I have dreamed a dream more; and, behold, the sun and the moon and the eleven stars made obeisance to me. And he told it to his father, and to his brethren: and his father rebuked him, and said unto him, What is this dream that thou hast dreamed? Shall I and thy mother and thy brethren indeed come to bow down ourselves to thee to the earth? And his brethren envied him; but his father observed the saying" (Genesis 37:9-11). The sun and the moon were Jacob and Leah, while the twelve stars are the twelve tribes of Israel. This description is in harmony with the picture which we are now considering, for we are speaking of the people of Israel as they face the calamity of the last and darkest days of the great tribulation. The end of the world is nigh; the Battle of Armageddon is at the door. This is the time of Jacob's trouble, and Jacob is Israel.

(2) "And she being with child cried, travailing in birth, and pained to be delivered."

Israel endured much suffering and hardship throughout its history, starting in the days of Egypt, and continuing in the days of Babylon, Haman, and the Romans. Israel was waiting for the coming of the messiah, Jesus. It bore the harsh bondage of Rome before the first coming of Christ. However, when Christ came, he was rejected and crucified; therefore, Israel will suffer again at the hands of the revived Roman Empire: "After this I saw in the night visions, and behold a fourth beast, dreadful and terrible, and strong exceedingly; and it had great iron teeth: it devoured and brake in pieces, and stamped the residue with the feet of it: and it was diverse from all the beasts that were before it; and it had ten horns" (Daniel 7:7); "And I saw one of his heads as it were wounded to death; and his deadly wound was healed: and all the world wondered after the beast" (Revelation 13:3). Rome will rise again and its empire will be revived in the last days, and it will persecute Israel again. Israel is still waiting for the messiah who will return again; it will believe in him upon his second coming, and he will deliver and save it: "And one shall say unto him, What are these wounds in thine hands? Then he shall answer, Those with which I was wounded in the house of my friends" (Zachariah 13:6). "The desire of all nations shall come: and I will fill this house with glory, saith the Lord of hosts" (Haggai 2:7); "And then shall appear the sign of the Son of man in heaven: and then shall all the tribes of the earth mourn, and they shall see the Son of man coming in the clouds of heaven with power and great glory" (Matthew 24:30).

(3) "And there appeared another wonder in heaven; and behold a great red dragon, having seven heads and ten horns, and seven crowns upon his heads."

Just like in verse one we see a great wonder in the heaven which signifies the deliverance of the human race, so now Satan in opposing God's work, will attempt to counter with a sign of his own in heaven.

The dragon is Satan, who will use the Antichrist: "The dragon which gave power unto the beast" (Revelation 13:4). He is the embodiment of the union of European countries, which will constitute the renewed Roman Empire in these end times. They will be the kingdom of the Antichrist, the despicable ruler of the world during the great tribulation. He will play a principal role in the events of the last days. Satan will give the Antichrist "His power, and his seat, and great authority" (Revelation 13:2). The Bible says that people will worship both the Antichrist and Satan:

(i) "they worshipped the dragon which gave power unto the beast",

(ii) "and they worshipped the beast, saying, Who is like unto the beast? who is able to make war with him?" (Revelation 13:4).

The False prophet will help the Antichrist and will be his spokesman: "And I beheld another beast coming up out of the earth; and he had two horns like a lamb, and he spake as a dragon" (Revelation 13:11).

Demonic spirits are going to go forth from each of the dragon, the Antichrist, and the False prophet; calling the kingdoms of the world to the battle of Armageddon: "And I saw three unclean spirits like frogs come out of the mouth of the dragon, and out of the mouth of the beast, and out of the mouth of the False prophet. For they are the spirits of devils, working miracles, which go forth unto the kings of the earth and of the whole world, to gather them to the battle of that great day of God Almighty" (Revelation 16:13-14). From this point on, the evil of Satan will grow stronger and stronger, especially after he is cast down to the earth in verse 9 which says: "And the great dragon was cast out, that old serpent, called the Devil, and Satan, which deceiveth the whole world: he was cast out into the earth, and his angels were cast out with him."

The heads, horns, and crowns have to do with the history of the great Roman Empire which is the red dragon- the dragon of war, bloodshed, and destruction. "And there went out another horse that was red: and power was given to him that sat thereon to take peace from the earth, and that they should kill one another: and there was given unto him a great sword" (Revelation 6:4).

(4) "And his tail drew the third part of the stars of heaven, and did cast them to the earth: and the dragon stood before the woman which was ready to be delivered, for to devour her child as soon as it was born."

This verse confirms that the dragon is Satan himself who fell from heaven from his position as covering cherub: "How art thou fallen from heaven, O Lucifer, son of the morning! how art thou cut down to the ground, which didst weaken the nations! For thou hast said in thine heart, I will ascend into heaven, I will exalt my throne above the stars of God: I will sit also upon the mount of the congregation, in the sides of the north: I will ascend above the heights of the clouds; I will be like the most High. Yet thou shalt be brought down to hell, to the sides of the pit" (Isaiah 14:12-15); "Thou art the anointed cherub that covereth; and I have set thee so: thou wast upon the holy mountain of God; thou hast walked up and down in the midst of the stones of fire. Thou wast perfect in thy ways from the day that thou wast created, till iniquity was found in thee" (Ezekiel 28:14-15). "And the angels which kept not their first estate, but left their own habitation, he hath reserved in everlasting chains under darkness unto the judgment of the great day" (Jude 6). When Satan fell, a third of the angels of heaven fell with him, as the current verse declares: "His tail drew the third part of the stars of heaven". These wicked fallen angels will serve Satan in his persecution of Israel:

(i) As what happened in Egypt when pharaoh ordered: "And he said, When ye do the office of a midwife to the Hebrew women, and see them upon the stools; if it be a son, then ye shall kill him" (Exodus 1:16).

(ii) At the first coming of Jesus when Herod "Sent forth, and slew all the children that were in Bethlehem, and in all the coasts thereof, from two years old and under, according to the time which he had diligently inquired of the wise men" (Matthew 2:16).

(iii) As did Pontius Pilate: "And so Pilate, willing to content the people, released Barabbas unto them, and delivered Jesus, when he had scourged him, to be crucified" (Mark 15:15).

(iv) As did the nations: "For of a truth against thy holy child Jesus, whom thou hast anointed, both Herod, and Pontius Pilate, with the Gentiles" (Acts 4:27).

(v) Even, as the people of Israel did once where: "^{26}The kings of the earth stood up, and the rulers were gathered together against the Lord, and against his Christ. ^{27}For of a truth against thy holy child Jesus, whom thou hast anointed, both Herod, and Pontius Pilate, with the Gentiles, and the people of Israel, were gathered together" (Acts 4:26-27).

All have gathered and will gather yet together again against Jesus because he is the only salvation for this world from the oppression of Satan.

(5) "And she brought forth a man child, who was to rule all nations with a rod of iron: and her child was caught up unto God, and to his throne."

- And she brought forth a man child, who was to rule all nations with a rod of iron - Jesus Christ in his humanity, with regard to his human flesh, was of the seed of Israel: "Of whom as concerning the flesh Christ came, who is over all, God blessed for ever. Amen" (Romans 9:5). More specifically, Jesus is of the tribe of Judah: "And one of the elders saith unto me, Weep not: behold, the Lion of the tribe of Judah, the Root of David, hath prevailed to open the book, and to loose the seven seals thereof" (Revelation 5:5).

In the millennium, Jesus will rule along with all those who have been faithful to him, including the Jews who believe in Jesus during the great tribulation and people from all nations: "And I saw thrones, and they sat upon them, and judgment was given unto them: and I saw the souls of them that were beheaded for the witness of Jesus, and for the word of God, and which had not worshipped the beast, neither his image, neither had received his mark upon their foreheads, or in their hands; and they lived and reigned with Christ a thousand years" (Revelation 20:4).

The Lord Jesus will rule the nations with a rod of iron: "Ask of me, and I shall give thee the heathen for thine inheritance, and the uttermost parts of the earth for thy possession. Thou shalt break them with a rod of iron; thou shalt dash them in pieces like a potter's vessel" (Psalm 2:8-9); "And the armies which were in heaven followed him upon white horses, clothed in fine linen, white and clean. And out of his mouth goeth a sharp sword, that with it he should smite the nations: and he shall rule them with a rod of iron: and he treadeth the winepress of the fierceness and wrath of Almighty God. And he hath on his vesture and on his thigh a name written, King Of Kings, And Lord Of Lords" (Revelation 19:14-16).

Jesus went up to heaven and will return to rule on earth forever: "And the kingdom and dominion, and the greatness of the kingdom under the whole heaven, shall be given to the people of the saints of the most High, whose kingdom is an everlasting kingdom, and all dominions shall serve and obey him" (Daniel 7:27).

- And her child was caught up unto God, and to his throne. Christ came, died, was buried, rose from the dead, and returned to heaven: "Wherefore he saith, When he ascended up on high, he led captivity captive, and gave gifts unto men. (Now that he ascended, what is it but that he also descended first into the lower parts of the earth? He that descended is the same also that ascended up far above all heavens, that he might fill all things.)" (Ephesians 4:8-10). Then concept of being raptured or caught up from the earth to heaven appears in Bible ten times in different forms:

(i) Enoch: "And Enoch walked with God: and he was not; for God took him" (Genesis 5:24).

(ii) Elijah: "And it came to pass, as they still went on, and talked, that, behold, there appeared a chariot of fire, and horses of fire, and parted them both asunder; and Elijah went up by a whirlwind into heaven" (2 Kings 2:11).

(iii) Ezekiel: "So the spirit lifted me up, and took me away, and I went in bitterness, in the heat of my spirit; but the hand of the Lord was strong upon me" (Ezekiel 3:14).

(iv) Jesus: "He was taken up; and a cloud received him out of their sight" (Acts 1:9).

(v) Philip: "And when they were come up out of the water, the Spirit of the Lord caught away Philip, that the eunuch saw him no more: and he went on his way rejoicing" (Acts 8:39).

(vi) Paul: "I knew a man in Christ above fourteen years ago, (whether in the body, I cannot tell; or whether out of the body, I cannot tell: God knoweth;) such an one caught up to the third heaven" (2 Corinthians 12:2).

(vii) John the beloved: "Come up hither, and I will shew thee things which must be hereafter. And immediately I was in the spirit" (Revelation 4:1-2).

(viii) Christ's church: "For the Lord himself shall descend from heaven with a shout, with the voice of the archangel, and with the trump of God: and the dead in Christ shall rise first: Then we which are alive and remain shall be caught up together with them in the clouds, to meet the Lord in the air" (1 Thessalonians 4:16-17).

(ix) The two witnesses of the great tribulation: "And after three days and an half the spirit of life from God entered into them, and they stood upon their feet; and great fear fell upon them which saw them. And they heard a great voice from heaven saying unto them, Come up hither. And they ascended up to heaven in a cloud; and their enemies beheld them" (Revelation 11:11-12).

(x) The righteous of the great tribulation: "For as in the days that were before the flood they were eating and drinking, marrying and giving in marriage, until the day that Noe entered into the ark, And knew not until the flood came, and took them all away; so shall also the coming of the Son of man be. Then shall two be in the field; the one shall be taken, and the other left. Two women shall be grinding at the mill; the one shall be taken, and the other left" (Matthew 24:38-41).

These ten incidents together form a clearer beautiful picture of what we the believers in Christ will experience the moment we are raptured and lifted up by the power of the Holy Spirit. For example, the human body does not have the capability to fly; but the might of the Holy Spirit will lift us up as he did Ezekiel, and we will rise up in our clothes, as was the case for Elijah and others.

(6) "And the woman fled into the wilderness, where she hath a place prepared of God, that they should feed her there a thousand two hundred and threescore days."

Between verse five and verse six there is a time-gap which is the age of grace, also known as the mystery of the fullness of the Gentiles and as the age of the church that Paul spoke about: "The mystery which hath been hid from ages and from generations, but now is made manifest to his saints" (Colossians 1:26).

The nation of Israel will be persecuted and taken captive again by Satan: "For these be the days of vengeance, that all things which are written may be fulfilled. But woe unto them that are with child, and to them that give suck, in those days! for there shall be great distress in the land, and wrath upon this people. And they shall fall by the edge of the sword, and shall be led away captive into all nations: and Jerusalem shall be trodden down of the Gentiles, until the Times of the Gentiles be fulfilled" (Luke 21:22-24). In the middle of the great tribulation, the Israelites will go into captivity into all the nations of the world for a period of three and a half years because of the oppression of the beast who is the Antichrist and his kingdom the European Union, all by the instigation of Satan.

Satan persecuting the nation of Israel is no new thing. In the days of Abraham, Satan attempted to prevent the birth of Isaac, the son of promise: "Now we, brethren, as Isaac was, are the children of promise" (Galatians 4:28). Through the generations, Satan has tried to exterminate the nation of Israel, as in the days of Esther and Mordecai. He has attempted to do so because the male child born of Israel is the Saviour of mankind. Satan tried to kill the infant Jesus because he is the redeemer of the human race.

(7) "And there was war in heaven: Michael and his angels fought against the dragon; and the dragon fought and his angels,"

As this persecution is taking place on earth, there is a corresponding spiritual war taking place in heaven.

Satan is: "the prince of the power of the air" (Ephesians 2:2). Our war against him is a spiritual war: "For we wrestle not against flesh and blood, but against principalities, against powers, against the rulers of the darkness of this world, against spiritual wickedness in high places" (Ephesians 6:12). This is what will happen on earth and in heaven.

There are four important persons in this chapter:

(i) The woman, who represents Israel.

(ii) The dragon, who is Satan, the head of the Antichrist and the rejuvenated Roman Empire.

(iii) The male child, who is Jesus Christ.

(iv) Michael, the archangel.

Michael is the only archangel in the Bible who is mentioned by his title, even though he is not the only one in heaven. The book of Daniel gives the impression that there are several archangels: "But, lo, Michael, one of the chief princes, came to help me" (Daniel 10:13). Gabriel, who visited Zachariah, was also an archangel: "I am Gabriel, that stand in the presence of God; and am sent to speak unto thee, and to shew thee these glad tidings" (Luke 1:19). This is not the first time other than this verse that Michael is involved in a confrontation with the devil: "Yet Michael the archangel, when contending with the devil he disputed about the body of Moses" (Jude 9).

(8) "And prevailed not; neither was their place found any more in heaven."

Only this time, Satan is going to be expelled from heaven. Michael the archangel and the good angels at his command, will protect the Jews especially those who will believe on the Lord Jesus and accept him as their Lord and Saviour: "And at that time shall Michael stand up, the great prince which standeth for the children of thy people: and there shall be a time of trouble, such as never was since there was a nation even to that same time: and at that time thy people shall be delivered, every one that shall be found written in the book" (Daniel 12:1).

(9) "And the great dragon was cast out, that old serpent, called the Devil, and Satan, which deceiveth the whole world: he was cast out into the earth, and his angels were cast out with him."

The Lord Jesus describes Satan as: "He was a murderer from the beginning, and abode not in the truth, because there is no truth in him. When he speaketh a lie, he speaketh of his own: for he is a liar, and the father of it" (John 8: 44). To do so cunningly, Satan appears in several forms:

(a) Satan enters into the serpent;
(b) Satan appears as a lion;
(c) Satan appears as a wolf in sheep's clothing;
(d) Satan appears as an angel of light;
(e) Satan appears as a dragon.

Satan deceives and lies and kills. Now, the time has come for the Lord Jesus to give Satan what is due him; so Satan and his bad angels will be cast from the heavenly places down to earth, and on their way eventually to hell.

(10) "And I heard a loud voice saying in heaven, Now is come salvation, and strength, and the kingdom of our God, and the power of his Christ: for the accuser of our brethren is cast down, which accused them before our God day and night."

Heaven will now and forever after be free. Heaven will be delivered from the wickedness and spitefulness of Satan, who accuses the brethren, taking advantage of their shortcomings, lapses, and mistakes.

(11) "And they overcame him by the blood of the Lamb, and by the word of their testimony; and they loved not their lives unto the death."

But these believers who are justified by the blood of the Lamb, have washed their robes and made them white in the blood of the Lord Jesus. That is why the Father looks upon them and us through the blood of Christ that has covered our sins and iniquities, and so sees no flaws in them and us. These believers are truly righteous, as they have remained faithful to Jesus and to the truths of the Bible even in the darkest days of the history of mankind. They remained faithful until they were martyred for the Lord Jesus, who redeemed them and who covered all their sins.

(12) "Therefore rejoice, ye heavens, and ye that dwell in them. Woe to the inhabiters of the earth and of the sea! for the devil is come down unto you, having great wrath, because he knoweth that he hath but a short time."

Defeated and cast out of heaven, Satan is burning with rage, knowing that soon he will be cast into hell, his eternal prison and abode: "And the devil that deceived them was cast into the lake of fire and brimstone, where the beast and the False prophet are, and shall be tormented day and night for ever and ever" (Revelation 20:10).

(13) "And when the dragon saw that he was cast unto the earth, he persecuted the woman which brought forth the man child."

Satan will persecute Israel with horrible afflictions in his last days, because out of her came Jesus who defeated him. Also, Jesus is going to bind him and cast him into darkness in the fire of hell. This is the place prepared for Satan, the Antichrist, the False prophet, the fallen angels, and all sinful wicked people. It is a place of eternal torment, of flaming fire and brimstone, infested with worms, bound in chains and darkness; and echoing with the sounds of screams, wails, and the gnashing of teeth.

Jesus is the firstborn male who is the redeemer of the righteous and the judge of the wicked. He is the saviour of men: "Whosoever believeth that Jesus is the Christ is born of God ... For whatsoever is born of God overcometh the world: and this is the victory that overcometh the world, even our faith. Who is he that overcometh the world, but he that believeth that Jesus is the Son of God?" (1 John 5:1,4-5).

Are you redeemed? Are you saved? Does the Father look at you and sees no sin in you because you have been washed in the blood of Jesus?! This is the most important question in your entire life; is your eternity secure in Jesus in heaven? If the answer is no, kneel down and surrender the title deed of your life to him that you might live! If your answer is yes, then blessed and happy are you!

(14) "And to the woman were given two wings of a great eagle, that she might fly into the wilderness, into her place, where she is nourished for a time, and times, and half a time, from the face of the serpent."

This description is reminiscent of the exodus of Israel from the bondage of Egypt: "Ye have seen what I did unto the Egyptians, and how I bare you on eagles' wings, and brought you unto myself" (Exodus 19:4). The people of Israel wandered in the wilderness, where the Lord helped them and sustained them for forty years until they entered the promised land.

The phrase "two wings of a great eagle" leads us to understand that the flight will be great, mighty, and quick. The Israelites will escape from the face of Satan, the Antichrist, and the False prophet. This escape will last three and a half years until the Lord returns to the earth to deliver them: "And ye shall flee to the valley of the mountains; for the valley of the mountains shall reach unto Azal: yea, ye shall flee, like as ye fled from before the earthquake in the days of Uzziah king of Judah: and the Lord my God shall come, and all the saints with thee" (Zechariah 14:5); "And they shall fall by the edge of the sword, and shall be led away captive into all nations: and Jerusalem shall be trodden down of the Gentiles, until the Times of the Gentiles be fulfilled. And there shall be signs in the sun, and in the moon, and in the stars; and upon the earth distress of nations, with perplexity; the sea and the waves roaring; Men's hearts failing them for fear, and for looking after those things which are coming on the earth: for the powers of heaven shall be shaken. And then shall they see the Son of man coming in a cloud with power and great glory. And when these things begin to come to pass, then look up, and lift up your heads; for your redemption draweth nigh" (Luke 21:24-28); "Behold, he cometh with clouds; and every eye shall see him, and they also which pierced him: and all kindreds of the earth shall wail because of him. Even so, Amen" (Revelation 1:7).

The big marked difference between the captivity of Jerusalem and its destruction at the hands of Nebuchadnezzar destroyed 586 BC, and again by the Roman general in 70 A.D., is that this time Jerusalem will not fall for Christ will intervene through his coming, and deliver her: "As birds flying, so will the LORD of hosts defend Jerusalem; defending also he will deliver it; and passing over he will preserve it" (Isaiah 31:5); "For I will gather all nations against Jerusalem to battle; and the city shall be taken, and the houses rifled, and the women ravished; and half of the city shall go forth into captivity, and the residue of the people shall not be cut off from the city. Then shall the Lord go forth, and fight against those nations, as when he fought in the day of battle. And his feet shall stand in that day upon the mount of Olives, which is before Jerusalem on the east, and the mount of Olives shall cleave in the midst thereof toward the east and toward the west, and there shall be a very great valley; and half of the mountain shall remove toward the north, and half of it toward the south. And ye shall flee to the valley of the mountains; for the valley of the mountains shall reach unto Azal: yea, ye shall flee, like as ye fled from before the earthquake in the days of Uzziah king of Judah: and the Lord my God shall come, and all the saints with thee" (Zechariah 14:2-5).

Just as Satan used the snake to deceive Eve in the beginning of creation so, similarly in the last days, he will use cunning and deceit in an attempt to destroy the nation of Israel.

(15) "And the serpent cast out of his mouth water as a flood after the woman, that he might cause her to be carried away of the flood."

History repeats itself as do Satan's schemes. Just like the Pharaoh of Egypt used the river Nile to kill the male newborns of Israel in an attempt to eliminate baby Moses, so in similar fashion, Satan and the Antichrist will wage a spiritual river in media and propaganda and misinformation like a river flowing from the mouths of the Antichrist and the False prophet. This is reminiscent of what Adolf Hitler, and his head of intelligence Heinrich Himmler, did with their evil misinformation propaganda campaigns that were designed to eradicate the Jews during the second world war.

(16) "And the earth helped the woman, and the earth opened

her mouth, and swallowed up the flood which the dragon cast out of his mouth."

As was the case with Europe and America who reached out to deliver the Jews during World War II, likewise, the nations of the world will then help the Jews, receiving them and protecting them from Satan and the Antichrist. Satan will fail.

(17) "And the dragon was wroth with the woman, and went to make war with the remnant of her seed, which keep the commandments of God, and have the testimony of Jesus Christ."

This will anger Satan, who will gather his armies and come with the Antichrist to fight Israel in the Battle of Armageddon. Satan will gather all the nations of the world to Armageddon, and will focus his attack on the Jews who put their faith in Jesus during the great tribulation, especially those who keep their beautiful testimony of faithfulness to the Lord Jesus Christ and to his word, the Bible.

Here we arrive at the end of the third narrative of the second coming of the Lord Jesus Christ. We are for a third time now at the end of the seven years of the great tribulation. This narrative provides a description of the spiritual wars in heaven and on the earth during the seven years of tribulation.

13
THE ANTICHRIST AND THE FALSE PROPHET

(1) "And I stood upon the sand of the sea, and saw a beast rise up out of the sea, having seven heads and ten horns, and upon his horns ten crowns, and upon his heads the name of blasphemy."

At first, our reading seems hard to understand, but actually it is very simple. The beast that rises from the sea symbolizes a beastly character who appears in the midst of the sea of nations, the sea of the perplexity of nations: "Upon the earth distress of nations, with perplexity; the sea and the waves roaring" (Luke 21:25). The world will be perplexed, lost, and in utter confusion; it will be in dire need of someone to rescue it. Then enters a character who is a master of deception and deceit, the Antichrist: "And with all deceivableness of unrighteousness in them that perish; because they received not the love of the truth, that they might be saved" (2 Thessalonians 2:10). The Antichrist initially appeared as a person who has solutions to all the problems in the world.

This chapter really compliments the previous one in describing the unleashing of all the evil forces in the second half of the great tribulation. In the first half of it we see how the Antichrist will appear on the European scene as the so-called man of peace, an honest person with solutions to all the problems of the world. He shows up on a white horse: "And I saw, and behold a white horse: and he that sat on him had a bow; and a crown was given unto him: and he went forth conquering, and to conquer" (Revelation 6:2). Now he appears as his true self, a dictator who presides over the revived Roman Empire. This empire arises out of the framework of the European Union, which is represented by the legs of the statue of Nebuchadnezzar: "His legs of iron, his feet part of iron and part of clay" (Daniel 2:37-43).

This is the beast who rises up out of the sea. He is the Antichrist seated on the throne of the nations in the Times of the Gentiles. The heads, horns, and crowns represent the combination of the sequence of the four world empires comprising the Times of the Gentiles; and the Antichrist leads them as the embodiment of all the forces of evil now ruling over the forth empire: "After this I saw in the night visions, and behold a fourth beast, dreadful and terrible, and strong exceedingly; and it had great iron teeth: it devoured and brake in pieces, and stamped the residue with the feet of it: and it was diverse from all the beasts that were before it; and it had ten horns. I considered the horns, and, behold, there came up among them another little horn, before whom there were three of the first horns plucked up by the roots: and, behold, in this horn were eyes like the eyes of man, and a mouth speaking great things" (Daniel 7:7-8).

All of these powers are, in the final analysis, the powers of the Times of the Gentiles, which are headed by Satan, who specializes in blasphemy against God. From his very beginning, Satan has always been filled with enmity and insults against the Lord: "I will ascend above the heights of the clouds; I will be like the most High" (Isaiah 14:14). He will control and direct the Antichrist.

(2) "And the beast which I saw was like unto a leopard, and

his feet were as the feet of a bear, and his mouth as the mouth of a lion: and the dragon gave him his power, and his seat, and great authority."

This beast rules over the fourth world power, the revived Roman Empire which rises anew in the form of a European alliance. The power which preceded it was the kingdom of the Greeks, which Daniel likened to a leopard. Before that was Media and Persia, which Daniel referred to as a bear. Before that was the first and initial power, the Chaldean kingdom of Nebuchadnezzar, compared by Daniel to a lion: "In the first year of Belshazzar king of Babylon Daniel had a dream and visions of his head upon his bed: then he wrote the dream, and told the sum of the matters. Daniel spake and said, I saw in my vision by night, and, behold, the four winds of the heaven strove upon the great sea. And four great beasts came up from the sea, diverse one from another. The first was like a lion, and had eagle's wings: I beheld till the wings thereof were plucked, and it was lifted up from the earth, and made stand upon the feet as a man, and a man's heart was given to it. And behold another beast, a second, like to a bear, and it raised up itself on one side, and it had three ribs in the mouth of it between the teeth of it: and they said thus unto it, Arise, devour much flesh. After this I beheld, and lo another, like a leopard, which had upon the back of it four wings of a fowl; the beast had also four heads; and dominion was given to it" (Daniel 7:1-6).

This European alliance is a mixture, in terms of its characteristics, of the four world powers of the Times of the Gentiles. All of these world powers are, in the final analysis, the kingdom of the Times of the Gentiles, the kingdom of darkness, the kingdom of Satan. To put things simply, verse one speaks of a man, a head, a leader who is the Antichrist. Verse two speaks of a kingdom, the kingdom of Antichrist.

(3) "And I saw one of his heads as it were wounded to death;

and his deadly wound was healed: and all the world wondered after the beast."

The Antichrist, the son of perdition, the wicked one, will not be known to the world at first. Then some sort of an accident occurs, possibly involving a blow to the head such as an assassination attempt and he will approach death. But suddenly he will revive with great satanic power, astounding the world.

The world has rejected the Lord Jesus through the ages. Now, the Lord rejects them and delivers them to the work of delusion and deception which will persuade them to worship Satan himself. People will wonder at his recovery and bow down to him, and worship Satan who healed him.

The revived Roman empire is currently latent; it is not manifest to the world at present. The world will be astonished when it will re-emerge again publicly with the spirit of Rome, and with such tremendous power that will crush all who stand in its way. The Antichrist will be its leader; he will guide it to destruction and everlasting perdition.

(4) "And they worshipped the dragon which gave power unto the beast: and they worshipped the beast, saying, Who is like unto the beast? who is able to make war with him?"

The world of unbelievers whose are not sealed for the Lord Jesus, and: "Which have not the seal of God in their foreheads" (Revelation 9:4), will be amazed at the Antichrist and will worship him. All the nations of the world will flock to his banner.

(5) "And there was given unto him a mouth speaking great things and blasphemies; and power was given unto him to continue forty and two months."

The Antichrist will speak great swelling words of vanity, as Peter the Apostle prophesied: "For when they speak great swelling words of vanity, they allure through the lusts of the flesh, through much wantonness, those that were clean escaped from them who live in error. While they promise them liberty, they themselves are the servants of corruption: for of whom a man is overcome, of the same is he brought in bondage" (2 Peter 2:18-19).

The Antichrist will take immense power from Satan and will do many deeds of wickedness throughout the great tribulation. He will delude people, enslave them, and lead them in the way of perdition, the way of Satan.

(6) "And he opened his mouth in blasphemy against God, to blaspheme his name, and his tabernacle, and them that dwell in heaven."

From the dawn of history, Satan has been attempting to usurp upon God and upon his throne: "How art thou fallen from heaven, O Lucifer, son of the morning! how art thou cut down to the ground, which didst weaken the nations! For thou hast said in thine heart, I will ascend into heaven, I will exalt my throne above the stars of God: I will sit also upon the mount of the congregation, in the sides of the north: I will ascend above the heights of the clouds; I will be like the most High" (Isaiah 14:12-14). This is what the Antichrist will do openly and publicly in the great tribulation. He will blaspheme against God, his throne, and those who dwell in heaven; including us, the believers who will have passed into glory.

At this time, Satan will do the following:

(a) He will blaspheme against God.

(b) He will blaspheme against God's name.

(c) He will blaspheme against the tabernacle of God.

(d) He will blaspheme against the believers who are in heaven in the presence of God.

(e) He will wage war against those who believe in Jesus and are still on this earth.

All these doings will grow to full maturity of wickedness in the great tribulation, but we can already see signs and glimpses of their presence in the world todayl so blessed are be those who will remain faithful to the end!

(7) "And it was given unto him to make war with the saints, and to overcome them: and power was given him over all kindreds, and tongues, and nations."

The believing Jews and Gentiles upon the earth will be killed by the Antichrist and his assassins. Today, the children of light and the children of darkness co-exist with each other. But then there will be no co-existence of any kind, but a fury of hatred and enmity from those who bear the seal of the Antichrist against each and every individual who bears the seal of the Lamb who was slain.

(8) "And all that dwell upon the earth shall worship him, whose names are not written in the book of life of the Lamb slain from the foundation of the world."

All who do not bear the seal of Christ lack protection, immunity, and strength. They will submit to the Antichrist and perish with him.

(9) "If any man have an ear, let him hear."

The Lord Jesus said on the Mount of Olives: "For there shall arise false Christs, and false prophets, and shall shew great signs and wonders; insomuch that, if it were possible, they shall deceive the very elect" (Matthew 24:24).

Here, the Lord Jesus repeats the warning which appeared seven times in Revelation chapters 2 and 3. Not everyone who will hear and listen, will heed the warning; but only those who bear the seal of the Father on their foreheads will heed the admonition.

(10) "He that leadeth into captivity shall go into captivity: he that killeth with the sword must be killed with the sword. Here is the patience and the faith of the saints."

Many of the believers of the great tribulation will be uprooted and displaced in a great captivity. Many will be scattered in various places. Many will be martyred for their testimony and faithfulness to:

(i) The name of the Lord Jesus;

(ii) The Bible: "And one of the elders answered, saying unto me, What are these which are arrayed in white robes? and whence came they? And I said unto him, Sir, thou knowest. And he said to me, These are they which came out of great tribulation, and have washed their robes, and made them white in the blood of the Lamb" (Revelation 7:13-14); "And they overcame him by the blood of the Lamb, and by the word of their testimony; and they loved not their lives unto the death" (Revelation 12:11); "And I saw the woman drunken with the blood of the saints, and with the blood of the martyrs of Jesus: and when I saw her, I wondered with great admiration" (Revelation 17:6).

The great challenge facing the believers of the great tribulation is to maintain their Christian testimony.

(11) "And I beheld another beast coming up out of the earth; and he had two horns like a lamb, and he spake as a dragon."

This beast is the False prophet who looks like a lamb with two horns and has the logic and the tongue of Satan.

Satan imitates heaven as much as he can. In heaven, there is a holy trinity of the Father, the Son, and the Holy Spirit. Here, we see Satan and his evil trinity, which consists of:

(i) The beast that rises from the bottomless pit, who is the dragon, Satan.

(ii) The beast that rises from the sea, the Antichrist.

(iii) The beast that rises from the earth, the False prophet.

The three of them are unclean evil wicked spirits; they constitute an unholy trinity: "And I saw three unclean spirits like frogs come out of the mouth of the dragon, and out of the mouth of the beast, and out of the mouth of the False prophet" (Revelation 16:13).

(12) "And he exerciseth all the power of the first beast before

him, and causeth the earth and them which dwell therein to worship the first beast, whose deadly wound was healed."

The Antichrist, with the help of the culprit, the False prophet, will unite all denominations and religions of the world in one religion that worships the devil himself. This False prophet will fulfil and complete the ecumenical movement which has already started in our time.

Most of the people who seek to unite denominations and religions are guilty of a great evil, as they are preparing the world for the days of the great tribulation, which is soon to come upon the earth. They are attempting to destroy the holy purity of worship to the Lord Jesus alone only. They are covering it up intentionally under the guise of false peaceful coexistence. The Lord Jesus came to create a divide between the righteous and the unrighteous: "Think not that I am come to send peace on earth: I came not to send peace, but a sword. For I am come to set a man at variance against his father, and the daughter against her mother, and the daughter in law against her mother in law. And a man's foes shall be they of his own household" (Matthew 10:34-36). Again and again, the Lord Jesus Christ teaches us to separate from the world and to be consecrated and dedicated to him. But people insistently determine to attempt to remain in their traditional churches and reform them, in spite of the clear commandment of the Lord Jesus. "Wherefore come out from among them, and be ye separate, saith the Lord, and touch not the unclean thing; and I will receive you" (2 Corinthians 6:17).

There are also two developments underway and are even more dangerous:

(i) First, some 2,000 years ago, John the beloved said that the spirit of the Antichrist was already in the world. He specifically described it as the spirit of denying the humanity of Christ: "³And every spirit that confesseth not that Jesus Christ is come in the flesh is not of God: and this is that spirit of antichrist, whereof ye have heard that it should come; and even now already is it in the world".

The subject of the Christology and the 2 natures of Christ, both his divinity and his humanity, had been the center of theological strife for 600 years.

Historically, one result of that was the Moslem religion which clearly denies the human crucifixion of Jesus.

Based on this fact, the Moslem religion is a continuation of the same spirit of the Antichrist. So in the last days the Moslem religion is going to spread further across the world; as the time approaches for the Antichrist to appear on the world scene.

(ii) Second, the globe's ecumenical movement I mentioned above, will open up to the Moslem religion, and the False prophet in his cunning is going to amalgamate all the religions under a one world religion.

All this is already in the making now.

All these evil trends will take their final form in the great tribulation. But they have assumed prominence in our day since we are in the age of the church of Laodicea. We are at the doorsteps of the rapture.

We see in all these matters an imitation of Jesus Christ, for the devil tries to imitate Christ in order to delude the world away from receiving the truth. Jesus Christ said of himself: "I am the light of the world: he that followeth me shall not walk in darkness, but shall have the light of life" (John 8:12). "Jesus saith unto him, I am the way, the truth, and the life: no man cometh unto the Father, but by me" (John 14:6).

Satan resists the righteousness of Jesus: "For there shall arise false Christs, and false prophets, and shall shew great signs and wonders; insomuch that, if it were possible, they shall deceive the very elect" (Matthew 24:24); "And no marvel; for Satan himself is transformed into an angel of light" (2 Corinthians 11:14).

Jesus is the Lamb of God who was slain for our sins and died and arose again. Opposing that imitation, the Antichrist attempts to present himself in the same fashion in a state of death; but returns to life surprising the world with his personality and his kingdom. The devil is a loser who is evil, liar, and murderer whose purpose is to imitate Christ. This is done with the goal of deceiving many people and leading them to the eternal fires of hell. Likewise the people of the world imitate believers in what they say, but without the Christian spirit of repentance or life. We thank the Lord Jesus who freed us: "If the Son therefore shall make you free, ye shall be free indeed" (John 8:36).

(13) "And he doeth great wonders, so that he maketh fire come down from heaven on the earth in the sight of men,"

This False prophet will imitate the prophets of the Lord Jesus. He will make fire come down upon the earth as did the Lord Jesus, and Elijah: "Then the Lord rained upon Sodom and upon Gomorrah brimstone and fire from the Lord out of heaven" (Genesis 19:24); "Hear me, O Lord, hear me, that this people may know that thou art the Lord God, and that thou hast turned their heart back again. Then the fire of the Lord fell, and consumed the burnt sacrifice, and the wood, and the stones, and the dust, and licked up the water that was in the trench. And when all the people saw it, they fell on their faces: and they said, The Lord, he is the God; the Lord, he is the God" (1 Kings 18:37-39). For this reason Paul is not surprised and says: "And no marvel".

(14) "And deceiveth them that dwell on the earth by the means of those miracles which he had power to do in the sight of the beast; saying to them that dwell on the earth, that they should make an image to the beast, which had the wound by a sword, and did live."

Based on this verse, it seems that the Antichrist will be the target of a very dangerous assassination attempt; however, he survives and manifests his Satanic power, as we noted in verses 3 and 12 above.

In our day and time, we continue to hear of apparitions of alleged appearance of Virgin Mary and of the saints. Many cling to such matters not just because of the shallowness of their minds but also because of the depth of their wickedness. The devil does the impossible to draw people away from Christ. He hates the church, the Lord Jesus, and his people. He does that especially at Easter which reminds us of the cross of Jesus and the Resurrection. Always at that time, the miracles of Mary abound as Satan seeks to draw people's attention away from Christ and his sacrifice on the cross. Neither Mary nor the saints can save the souls of the sons of men. The devil tries to blind their spiritual eyes, so that they may not see and return to the Lord Jesus and get saved. The true Christian faith built on the foundation of the saving power of the blood of Jesus, can provide salvation, healing, and life: "^{23}For all have sinned, and come short of the glory of God; ^{24}Being justified freely by his grace through the redemption that is in Christ Jesus: ^{25}Whom God hath set forth to be a propitiation through faith in his blood, to declare his righteousness for the remission of sins that are past, through the forbearance of God" (Romans 3:23-25); "In whom we have redemption through his blood, the forgiveness of sins, according to the riches of his grace" (Ephesians 1:7).

(15) "And he had power to give life unto the image of the beast, that the image of the beast should both speak, and cause that as many as would not worship the image of the beast should be killed."

Today we hear about paintings or statues of saints that amazingly start to drip oil. People with weak minds embrace these hoaxes and shams because of their evil nature. They do not respect the ten commandments of the Lord Jesus, the first and the second of which say: "Thou shalt have no other gods before me. Thou shalt not make unto thee any graven image, or any likeness of any thing that is in heaven above, or that is in the earth beneath, or that is in the water under the earth" (Exodus 20:3-4). Therefore the Lord will give them up to darkness: "Their sorrows shall be multiplied that hasten after another god: their drink offerings of blood will I not offer, nor take up their names into my lips" (Psalms 16:4). "For, lo, they that are far from thee shall perish: thou hast destroyed all them that go a whoring from thee" (Psalms 73:27); "Who changed the truth of God into a lie, and worshipped and served the creature more than the Creator, who is blessed for ever. Amen. For this cause God gave them up unto vile affections" (Romans 1:25-26).

Every miracle which does not glorify the Lord Jesus is a satanic work. During the great tribulation, Satan will have the ability to make an image speak. In those days, the Jewish people will be oppressed and downtrodden. The False prophet will bring the image of the Antichrist into the temple and will make it speak.

But this will just be a first step. The Antichrist will enter the temple and demand to be worshipped: "Let no man deceive you by any means: for that day shall not come, except there come a falling away first, and that man of sin be revealed, the son of perdition; Who opposeth and exalteth himself above all that is called God, or that is worshipped; so that he as God sitteth in the temple of God, shewing himself that he is God" (2 Thessalonians 2:3-4). People will be forced to worship the Antichrist and to bow down to his image. All who refuse to do so will be killed.

(16) "And he causeth all, both small and great, rich and poor, free and bond, to receive a mark in their right hand, or in their foreheads:"

The Antichrist will enslave all men, imprinting them with something like a laser seal or a computer micro chip grafted on their foreheads and on their right hands.

All who live upon the face of the earth will bear either the seal of Christ, if they are children of light, or the mark of Antichrist and Satan, if they are the children of darkness.

(17) "And that no man might buy or sell, save he that had the mark, or the name of the beast, or the number of his name."

The human race has always been divided spiritually into two sections even though this division is invisible: "There were giants in the earth in those days; and also after that, when the sons of God came in unto the daughters of men, and they bare children to them, the same became mighty men which were of old, men of renown" (Genesis 6:4); "Be ye not unequally yoked together with unbelievers: for what fellowship hath righteousness with unrighteousness? and what communion hath light with darkness?" (2 Corinthians 6:14); "For ye were sometimes darkness, but now are ye light in the Lord: walk as children of light" (Ephesians 5:8).

The day will come when the whole world will use a substitute for cash and credit cards. An idea currently being studied and developed involves the replacement of a credit card with a seal imprinted by laser on a person's hand and forehead. This process will be completed in the great tribulation, and it will provide Satan with the opportunity to control and subjugate men. Technology, in the end, will result in the subjugation and destruction of the human race. We, the children of the Lord, should be armed with wisdom, understanding, and spiritual insight; we should keep a healthy distance from social media platforms. The governments of the world spend billions to gather information about people. Today, social media platforms provide such information free of charge to the governments of the world, on a platter of gold, so to speak. In general, people are spiritually blind because of their love of the world and worldly things. They do not realize what they are doing. They are losing their privacy and the privacy of their children. Confidential information is openly displayed to the world. The biggest winner will be the government of the Antichrist.

(18) "Here is wisdom. Let him that hath understanding count the number of the beast: for it is the number of a man; and his number is Six hundred threescore and six."

The Antichrist is experienced, shrewd, and wise. He is like Satan, who is wise to do evil: "Thou sealest up the sum, full of wisdom, and perfect in beauty" (Ezekiel 28:12). With his wisdom, he deceives men but we have the mind of Christ: "For who hath known the mind of the Lord, that he may instruct him? But we have the mind of Christ" (1 Corinthians 2:16). So beware and do not give the devil a chance.

Six is the number of man and 3 is the number of completion. The Antichrist will not say to people "I am a false Christ", rather, he will manifest himself as a man, having every perfect human trait. He will appear to be excellent in his person, presence, understanding, charm, beauty, charisma, and leadership, as well as in his ability to solve economic, social, and geographic problems. At that time, the wise and prudent and discerning person will then beware and flee, even as the Lord Jesus commanded: "When ye therefore shall see the abomination of desolation, spoken of by Daniel the prophet, stand in the holy place, whoso readeth, let him understand: Then let them which be in Judaea flee into the mountains: Let him which is on the housetop not come down to take any thing out of his house" (Matthew 24:15-17).

The exhortation throughout history for every believer in the Lord Jesus is run away from the defilements and sins of this world, and practice godly living and contentment in whatever state the Lord Jesus puts you in, knowing that his deliverance is certainly sure to come.

14
THE PURE 144,000 THE BEGINNING OF THE END OF THE

(1) "And I looked, and, lo, a Lamb stood on the mount Sion, and with him an hundred forty and four thousand, having his Father's name written in their foreheads."

- And I looked, and, lo, a Lamb stood on the mount Sion – After chapter 13 and the scene of the Antichrist and his kingdom and his accomplices, now the scene shifts to heaven, where we see the Lord Jesus Christ and his kingdom on the heavenly mount Zion, God's mountain: "Mount Zion, on the sides of the north, the city of the great King" (Psalms 48:2). With him we see his entourage, a crowd of pure 144,000 men. We know that this scene is in heaven because of the presence of the cherubims in verse three.

- And with him an hundred forty and four thousand, having his Father's name written in their foreheads - These one hundred and forty-four thousand are different from the ones mentioned in chapter seven. Those were of Israel and these are of the church of Jesus Christ.

The number, one hundred and forty-four thousand, is a literal number; similar to the seven churches, the one thousand two hundred and sixty days, and the twelve thousand from each of the twelve tribes of Israel. We say that because of the basic principles of Biblical hermeneutics, the science of interpretation, dictates that if the literal sense makes sense, seek no other sense. Therefore, we hold to what the verse says that these are actually literally one hundred and forty four thousand men.

(2) "And I heard a voice from heaven, as the voice of many waters, and as the voice of a great thunder: and I heard the voice of harpers harping with their harps:"

This multitude of one hundred and forty-four thousand is in a state of joyful celebration and joyful song, for they are the courtiers of the Lord Jesus, and they are always in his presence.

(3) "And they sung as it were a new song before the throne, and before the four beasts, and the elders: and no man could learn that song but the hundred and forty and four thousand, which were redeemed from the earth."

They sing a special hymn which is peculiar to them, a hymn which no one else knows. It is special and unique to them, just as every believer has special and unique characteristics with the Lord Jesus in heaven, such as the special and unique name we read about in chapter two: "And will give him a white stone, and in the stone a new name written, which no man knoweth saving he that receiveth it" (Revelation 2:17).

(4) "These are they which were not defiled with women; for they are virgins. These are they which follow the Lamb whithersoever he goeth. These were redeemed from among men, being the firstfruits unto God and to the Lamb."

- These are they which were not defiled with women; for they are virgins. These are they which follow the Lamb whithersoever he goeth - Again from a hermeneutical principle if the content of a text makes sense from a literal perspective, there is no need to interpret it figuratively. So, does the phrase "not defiled" mean that they have not known women literally, or does it have a spiritual connotation that they have not worshipped any god except the Lord Jesus Christ? The figurative interpretation is far-fetched and not needful as there are cases in the Bible that teach this literal principal of holiness. So these men mentioned above were never married and who had devoted their lives completely to the service of the Lord Jesus. Examples are seen in both the Old and the New Testaments: "And Moses went down from the mount unto the people, and sanctified the people; and they washed their clothes. And he said unto the people, Be ready against the third day: come not at your wives" (Exodus 19:14-15). In this passage, Moses did not ask the people to avoid adultery, rather he asked them to abstain from sexual relations with their wives as part of observing and respecting a holy spiritual occasion. In the new testament, sex between legitimate husband and wife is forbidden during a time of fasting: "Defraud ye not one the other, except it be with consent for a time, that ye may give yourselves to fasting and prayer; and come together again, that Satan tempt you not for your incontinency" (1 Corinthians 7:5). Sexual relations in the framework of marriage are sanctioned and legitimate, but sex can be considered physically defiling when a time is set apart as holy unto the Lord.

Let us look at the issue from another viewpoint. The Son of Man came to this our earth and lived, in his humanity, a life of holy abstention. And so he chose unto himself a particular group from among the human race, one hundred and forty-four thousand men, to whom he gave special and divine election and special privilege of being his entourage wherever he goes.

This does not mean that we are going to be distant from him for: "For the Lamb which is in the midst of the throne shall feed them, and shall lead them unto living fountains of waters: and God shall wipe away all tears from their eyes" (Revelation 7:17). The distinction is that with Jesus there are ranks or offices or positions. When Jesus Christ sits on his throne neither you nor I will sit on thrones with him, but rather the twelve apostles: "And Jesus said unto them, Verily I say unto you, That ye which have followed me, in the regeneration when the Son of man shall sit in the throne of his glory, ye also shall sit upon twelve thrones, judging the twelve tribes of Israel" (Matthew 19:28). This is a principle that is taught in the Bible, such like that Peter, James, and John were closer to Jesus than the other nine disciples. Similarly, these one hundred and forty-four thousand are very close to Jesus. We too shall be extremely close, for Jesus is omnipresent, however "Every man in his own order" (1 Corinthians 15:23).

- These were redeemed from among men, being the firstfruits unto God and to the Lamb. This is echoed in: "But ye are come unto mount Sion, and unto the city of the living God, the heavenly Jerusalem, and to an innumerable company of angels, To the general assembly and church of the firstborn, which are written in heaven, and to God the Judge of all, and to the spirits of just men made perfect")Hebrews 12:22-23). This passage confirms that the one hundred and forty-four thousand are New Testament believers.

(5) "And in their mouth was found no guile: for they are without fault before the throne of God."

They have lived sincere lives of honesty and truthfulness to the Lord Jesus, like all the righteous of the Bible: "LORD, who shall abide in thy tabernacle? who shall dwell in thy holy hill? He that walketh uprightly, and worketh righteousness, and speaketh the truth in his heart. He that backbiteth not with his tongue, nor doeth evil to his neighbour, nor taketh up a reproach against his neighbour" (Psalm 15:1-3); "That he might present it to himself a glorious church, not having spot, or wrinkle, or any such thing; but that it should be holy and without blemish" (Ephesians 5:27); "That ye may be blameless and harmless, the sons of God, without rebuke, in the midst of a crooked and perverse nation, among whom ye shine as lights in the world ... Concerning zeal, persecuting the church; touching the righteousness which is in the law, blameless"

(Philippians 2:15; 3:6); "A bishop then must be blameless" (1 Timothy 3:2).

(6) "And I saw another angel fly in the midst of heaven, having the everlasting gospel to preach unto them that dwell on the earth, and to every nation, and kindred, and tongue, and people,"

Now we see another blessed angel soar in the midst of earth's skies, proclaiming the "everlasting gospel" which comprises:

(i) The gospel of the grace of God, which is gospel of the salvation of Jesus Christ: "And the ministry, which I have received of the Lord Jesus, to testify the gospel of the grace of God" (Acts 20:24);

(ii) The gospel of the Kingdom of God, which is gospel of the lordship of Christ: "And Jesus went about all the cities and villages, teaching in their synagogues, and preaching the gospel of the kingdom, and healing every sickness and every disease among the people" (Matthew 9:35); "Now after that John was put in prison, Jesus came into Galilee, preaching the gospel of the kingdom of God" (Mark 1:14).

To put it simply, the everlasting gospel is the "the gospel of the grace of God" plus "the gospel of the kingdom of God", just as Jesus is Lord and Saviour.

(7) "Saying with a loud voice, Fear God, and give glory to him; for the hour of his judgment is come: and worship him that made heaven, and earth, and the sea, and the fountains of waters."

This angel warns the inhabitants of the earth, like he warns them in the last verse of this chapter, to repent because the hour of God's fearful wrath has come; and that he is capable of judging because he is the Creator.

(8) "And there followed another angel, saying, Babylon is fallen, is fallen, that great city, because she made all nations drink of the wine of the wrath of her fornication."

The second angel came to make a proclamation as well. This proclamation has to do with the fall of the kingdom of the Antichrist, whose first foundation was laid in the tower of Babel and the kingdom of Nimrod, as recorded in the book of Genesis. Nimrod's kingdom became the foundation of the kingdom of Nebuchadnezzar and the Chaldeans, whose capital, Babylon, is the capital of the Times of Gentiles' power. It was the first capital and the foundation of all the capitals of the four kingdoms of the Times of the Gentiles.

This Babylon is:
(a) Political
(b) Religious
(c) Economic
(d) Military

Babylon is the foundation of the wickedness of the world's kingdoms beginning with the table of nations in Genesis 10, when following Noah's flood, the human race spread out over the face of the earth: "And Cush begat Nimrod: he began to be a mighty one in the earth. He was a mighty hunter before the LORD: wherefore it is said, Even as Nimrod the mighty hunter before the LORD. And the beginning of his kingdom was Babel, and Erech, and Accad, and Calneh, in the land of Shinar" (Genesis 10:8-10); "And they said, Go to, let us build us a city and a tower, whose top may reach unto heaven; and let us make us a name, lest we be scattered abroad upon the face of the whole earth. And the LORD came down to see the city and the tower, which the children of men builded. And the LORD said, Behold, the people is one, and they have all one language; and this they begin to do: and now nothing will be restrained from them, which they have imagined to do. Go to, let us go down, and there confound their language, that they may not understand one another's speech. So the LORD scattered them abroad from thence upon the face of all the earth: and they left off to build the city. Therefore is the name of it called Babel; because the

LORD did there confound the language of all the earth: and from thence did the LORD scatter them abroad upon the face of all the earth" (Genesis 11:4-9).

From the onset of the beginning of civilization, the Lord separated the peoples of this earth and defined their borders so that they could better worship him and see his goodness: "When the Most High divided to the nations their inheritance, when he separated the sons of Adam, he set the bounds of the people" (Deuteronomy 32:8); "And hath made of one blood all nations of men for to dwell on all the face of the earth, and hath determined the times before appointed, and the bounds of their habitation; That they should seek the Lord, if haply they might feel after him, and find him" (Acts 17:26-27); "And whosoever will not receive you, when ye go out of that city, shake off the very dust from your feet for a testimony against them" (Luke 9:5); "Wherefore come out from among them, and be ye separate, saith the Lord, and touch not the unclean thing; and I will receive you. And will be a Father unto you, and ye shall be my sons and daughters, saith the Lord Almighty" (2 Corinthians 6:17-18); The Lord asks us to be separate, and has diversified our languages to bring about this separation. However, the world is constantly trying to unify against the Lord Jesus.

The Antichrist and his kingdom, spiritual Babylon, will attempt to unite the economy and currency of the world, the religions of the world, and the military powers of the world. He will seek to unify all under his control so that they worship Satan who, under the banner of unification, will purpose to distort all truth. But the Lord Jesus will smite Babylon with a great judgment that spans the globe: "Babylon hath been a golden cup in the LORD'S hand, that made all the earth drunken: the nations have drunken of her wine; therefore the nations are mad" (Jeremiah 51:7). We will study the details of this eternal punishment in Revelation 17 and 18.

(9) "And the third angel followed them, saying with a loud

voice, If any man worship the beast and his image, and receive his mark in his forehead, or in his hand,"

The first angel proclaims the salvation of Christ. The second angel declares the fall of the kingdom of the Antichrist. Therefore, the third angel warns of the trap of submitting to the authority of the Antichrist. All who accept his mark will have their portion in eternal perdition.

(10) "The same shall drink of the wine of the wrath of God, which is poured out without mixture into the cup of his indignation; and he shall be tormented with fire and brimstone in the presence of the holy angels, and in the presence of the Lamb:"

God's wrath will fall upon all who submit to the Antichrist and their portion will be hellfire forever.

(11) "And the smoke of their torment ascendeth up for ever and ever: and they have no rest day nor night, who worship the beast and his image, and whosoever receiveth the mark of his name."

Eternal torment without rest forever as was the fate of the rich man in the story of Lazarus: "The rich man also died, and was buried; And in hell he lift up his eyes, being in torments ... And beside all this, between us and you there is a great gulf fixed: so that they which would pass from hence to you cannot; neither can they pass to us, that would come from thence" (Luke 16:22-23, 26). This place of torment will be the eternal abode of all who accept the mark of the Antichrist.

(12) "Here is the patience of the saints: here are they that keep the commandments of God, and the faith of Jesus."

It is important to be patient in your faithfulness to the Lord Jesus. There are two examples of patience mentioned in the Bible, namely the patience of Job and the patience of the Christ. What is the difference between the two? The patience of Job leads to riches and honour; "So the LORD blessed the latter end of Job more than his beginning" (Job 42:12); "Behold, we count them happy which endure. Ye have heard of the patience of Job, and have seen the end of the Lord" (James 5:11). The patience of Christ leads to the cross, the resurrection, the ascension to eternal, heavenly glory; "And the Lord direct your hearts into the love of God, and into the patient waiting for Christ" (2 Thessalonians 3:5).

We thank the Lord that there are always men faithful to the Lord Jesus in every kindred and tongue and people and nation. We must worship the Lord Jesus and not be afraid of man. It behoves us to be like Daniel and Shadrach and Meshach and Abednego who refused to bow down to the statue of Nebuchadnezzar, which is a symbol of the Antichrist and his kingdom. Here in is excellence. All who love the Lord Jesus will patiently endure, even to martyrdom and death, for the sake of his name and his word. Sufficient consolation it is for us to quote some precious verses that speak about loyalty and faithfulness in testifying of Jesus: "And hast borne, and hast patience, and for my name's sake hast laboured, and hast not fainted" (Revelation 2:3). "And thou holdest fast my name, and hast not denied my faith" (Revelation 2:13). "And hast kept my word, and hast not denied my name" (Revelation 3:8). "Thou hast kept the word of my patience" (Revelation 3:10); "Him that overcometh will I make a pillar in the temple of my God" (Revelation 3:12). "I saw under the altar the souls of them that were slain for the word of God, and for the testimony which they held" (Revelation 6:9). "And they overcame him by the blood of the Lamb, and by the word of their testimony; and they loved not their lives unto the death" (Revelation 12:11); "And I saw thrones, and they sat upon them, and judgment was given unto them: and I saw the souls of them that were beheaded for the witness of Jesus, and for the word of God, and which had not worshipped the beast, neither his image, neither had received his mark upon their foreheads, or in their hands; and they lived and reigned with Christ a thousand years" (Revelation 20:4). Amen.

(13) "And I heard a voice from heaven saying unto me, Write,

Blessed are the dead which die in the Lord from henceforth: Yea, saith the Spirit, that they may rest from their labours; and their works do follow them."

- And I heard a voice from heaven saying unto me - This is the voice of the Lord Jesus himself, as we see in some other passages: "I was in the Spirit on the Lord's day, and heard behind me a great voice, as of a trumpet, Saying, I am Alpha and Omega, the first and the last" (Revelation 1:10-11); "And when the seven thunders had uttered their voices, I was about to write: and I heard a voice from heaven saying unto me, Seal up those things which the seven thunders uttered, and write them not" (Revelation 10:4); "And they heard a great voice from heaven saying unto them, Come up hither. And they ascended up to heaven in a cloud; and their enemies beheld them" (Revelation 11:12); "And I heard another voice from heaven, saying, Come out of her, my people, that ye be not partakers of her sins, and that ye receive not of her plagues" (Revelation 18:4); the phrase "my people" shows that the speaker is Jesus.

- Write, Blessed are the dead which die in the Lord from henceforth - "Blessed" means "fortunate" or "lucky"! Here, the Lord Jesus says that he is fortunate who remains faithful to the end, as those who can kill the body can do no more than that. But after martyrdom and death comes going to heaven, where there is eternal joy with eternal reward. This is soul salvation that Jesus spoke about repeatedly, and implemented it himself: "and I lay down my life for the sheep"; "He that loveth his life shall lose it; and he that hateth his life in this world shall keep it unto life eternal" (John 10:15; 12:25).

It is important to notice that there is a big difference between the salvation of the soul and the salvation of the spirit. Man was created in the image and likeness of God; that is, he was created in the image of JESUS and in the likeness of the triune God of Father, Son, and Holy Ghost in one entity. Man is made up of spirit, soul, and Body in one triune person:

I- Body is our material being by which we interact through our five senses with life and nature, be it man or animal or vegetation.

II- Soul is our immaterial being that constitutes our feelings and our thinking. It is who we are, our self, our life. It is our person, our personality, the seat of our emotions. It is our being that is related to decisions and deeds; that is, it is the achievements and accomplishments of our entire life span.

III- Spirit is our spirit within us which is related to life, worship, communion, and divine influence: "God is a Spirit: and they that worship him must worship him in spirit and in truth" (John 4:24); "I was in the Spirit on the Lord's day" (Revelation 1:10).

There is a definite divide between spirit & soul & Body: "For the word of God is quick, and powerful, and sharper than any two edged sword, piercing even to the dividing asunder of soul and spirit, and of the joints and marrow, and is a discerner of the thoughts and intents of the heart" (Hebrews 4:12). They are independent yet interwoven and interact with each other although soul and spirit are sometimes addressed interchangeably in scripture. Compare: "Now is my soul troubled; and what shall I say? Father, save me from this hour: but for this cause came I unto this hour." (John 12:27) with: "When Jesus had thus said, he was troubled in spirit, and testified, and said, Verily, verily, I say unto you, that one of you shall betray me" (John 13:21). Also compare "Therefore we were comforted in your comfort: yea, and exceedingly the more joyed we for the joy of Titus, because his spirit was refreshed by you all" (2 Corinthians 7:13) with: "Take my yoke upon you, and learn of me; for I am meek and lowly in heart: and ye shall find rest unto your souls" (Matthew 11:29).

When man fell in sin, his entire being fell. Since we are born in the likeness of God and God is Love, he sent his only begotten son Jesus Christ in order to redeem our entire triune being: "And the very God of peace sanctify you wholly; and I pray God your whole spirit and soul and body be preserved blameless unto the coming of our Lord Jesus Christ" (1 Thessalonians 5:23).

The salvation of our entire being was not instant or complete at the moment of conversion even though it was far reaching to all three of spirit, soul and body: "let us cleanse ourselves from all filthiness of the flesh and spirit" (2 Corinthians 7:1); "abstain from fleshly lusts, which war against the soul" (1 Peter 2:11).

I- Body salvation is yet future in enjoying a glorified Body like that of the Lord Jesus Christ at the moment of the resurrection: " In a moment, in the twinkling of an eye, at the last trump: for the trumpet shall sound, and the dead shall be raised incorruptible, and we shall be changed" (1 Corinthians 15:52); " Beloved, now are we the sons of God, and it doth not yet appear what we shall be: but we know that, when he shall appear, we shall be like him; for we shall see him as he is" (1 John 3:2).

II- Spirit salvation happened in an instant at the moment of putting our trust and faith in Jesus Christ: "Sirs, what must I do to be saved? And they said, Believe on the Lord Jesus Christ, and thou shalt be saved, and thy house" (Acts 4:30-31). Spirit salvation is enjoying eternal life in Heaven with the Lord JESUS CHRIST, regardless of your works of consecration: "⁴In the name of our Lord Jesus Christ, when ye are gathered together, and my spirit, with the power of our Lord Jesus Christ, ⁵To deliver such an one unto Satan for the destruction of the flesh, that the spirit may be saved in the day of the Lord Jesus" (1 Cor 5:4-5).

III- Soul salvation is difficult to understand. In it, Jesus admonishes us to heed the well being of our lives or souls: "For what is a man profited, if he shall gain the whole world, and lose his own soul? or what shall a man give in exchange for his soul?"

(Matthew 16:16). The soul is synonyms with life's accomplishments, and consequently the heavenly rewards: "But God said unto him Thou fool this night thy soul shall be required of thee: then whose shall those things be, which thou hast provided?" (Luke 12:20). That is why Jesus admonishes us saying: "In your patience possess ye your souls" (Luke 21:19).

So soul salvation does not happen automatically whenever a person gets saved, but it is the commencement of the journey in that direction and the progression towards that goal: "[1]I beseech you therefore, brethren, by the mercies of God, that ye present your bodies a living sacrifice, holy, acceptable unto God, which is your reasonable service. [2]And be not conformed to this world: but be ye transformed by the renewing of your mind, that ye may prove what is that good, and acceptable, and perfect, will of God" (Romans 12:1-2).

At the moment of conversion, spirit salvation is instantaneous but soul salvation is a life time journey: "Wherefore lay apart all filthiness and superfluity of naughtiness, and receive with meekness the engrafted word, which is able to save your souls" (James 1:21). The difference between spirit salvation and soul salvation is similar to the difference between grace and works. The spirit is saved by faith in Jesus Christ, while the soul is saved by faithfulness to Jesus Christ. Spirit salvation is when you come to Jesus. Soul salvation is following Jesus. Spirit salvation determines that a person enters heaven. Soul salvation determines the rewards you get in heaven.

Jesus explains the requirement for soul salvation: "[34]And when he had called the people unto him with his disciples also, he said unto them, Whosoever will come after me, let him deny himself, and take up his cross, and follow me. [35]For whosoever will save his life shall lose it; but whosoever shall lose his life for my sake and the gospel's, the same shall save it. [36]For what shall it profit a man, if he shall gain the whole world, and lose his own soul? [37]Or what shall a man give in exchange for his soul?

³⁸Whosoever therefore shall be ashamed of me and of my words in this adulterous and sinful generation; of him also shall the Son of man be ashamed, when he cometh in the glory of his Father with the holy angels" (Mark 8:34-38).

Soul salvation is denying self, denying career, and denying personal ambitions. Some Christians will enter heaven with a lost soul or a with lost reward because of unfaithfulness to Jesus while on earth: "If any man's work shall be burned, he shall suffer loss: but he himself shall be saved; yet so as by fire" (1 Corinthians 3: 15).

Soul salvation is the result of works: "⁷That the trial of your faith, being much more precious than of gold that perisheth, though it be tried with fire, might be found unto praise and honour and glory at the appearing of Jesus Christ: ⁸Whom having not seen, ye love; in whom, though now ye see him not, yet believing, ye rejoice with joy unspeakable and full of glory: ⁹Receiving the end of your faith, even the salvation of your souls" (1 Pet 1:7-9).

The salvation of the soul lies in sacrificial living in the service of the King of Kings the Lord Jesus Christ. It is living a life of spreading His Kingdom; and therefore, the Christian who lives a life of faithful spiritual Christian service will receive a reward, even rewards, at the Reward Seat of Christ: "For we must all appear before the judgment seat of Christ; that every one may receive the things done in his Body, according to that he hath done, whether it be good or bad" (2 Corinthians 5:10). "And they that be wise shall shine as the brightness of the firmament; and they that turn many to righteousness as the stars for ever and ever." (Daniel 12:3). This is the savlation of the soul!

Even though many rewards await all the believers in heaven, these martyrs of Christ shall receive special privileged rewards in appreciation of the bitter trials which they shall endure in the great tribulation. During that period, the persecution of believers will be so intense, unlike any seen before or after. It will not be a matter of getting saved and living a life of consecration, rather it will be a matter of cleaving to Christ all the way till martyrdom. Every person converted in the great tribulation will pay his blood as the price for his salvation, becoming a martyr for the Lord Jesus: "For in those days shall be affliction, such as was not from the beginning of the creation which God created unto this time, neither shall be" (Mark 13:19). Heroism will reside in holding firmly to the name of Jesus and to the Bible, even as the church of Philadelphia did: "And hast kept my word, and hast not denied my name" (Revelation 3:8). There shall be no escape and nor deliverance from the hand of the Antichrist, except through true Christian martyrdom in those dark days of the horror of worshiping the Antichrist and his image. Those will be the days of the tyranny of Babylon, the mother of harlots. Those faithful Christians shall receive great recognition and appreciation: "And they overcame him by the blood of the Lamb, and by the word of their testimony; and they loved not their lives unto the death" (Revelation 12:11); "And I saw thrones, and they sat upon them, and judgment was given unto them: and I saw the souls of them that were beheaded for the witness of Jesus, and for the word of God, and which had not worshipped the beast, neither his image, neither had received his mark upon their foreheads, or in their hands; and they lived and reigned with Christ a thousand years" (Revelation 20:4).

- Yea, saith the Spirit - This blessing bestowed by the Lord Jesus is seconded by the Holy Spirit. It is only by the grace imparted by the Holy Spirit that any man can remain faithful to the point of martyrdom.

- That they may rest from their labors; and their works do follow them - In the end, those faithful to the Lord will receive their rewards that include reigning with Christ: "If we suffer, we shall also reign with him: if we deny him, he also will deny us" (2 Timothy 2:12); "I have fought a good fight, I have finished my course, I have kept the faith: Henceforth there is laid up for me a crown of righteousness, which the Lord, the righteous judge, shall give me at that day: and not to me only, but unto all them also that love his appearing" (2 Timothy 4:7-8); "And hast made us unto our God kings and priests: and we shall reign on the earth" (Revelation 5:10).

(14) "And I looked, and behold a white cloud, and upon the cloud one sat like unto the Son of man, having on his head a golden crown, and in his hand a sharp sickle."

- And I looked, and behold a white cloud, and upon the cloud one sat like unto the Son of man - When the end comes, the Lord Jesus will return to earth. He returns riding upon a cloud, even as a cloud took him up to heaven: "And when he had spoken these things, while they beheld, he was taken up; and a cloud received him out of their sight" (Acts 1:9). In the same manner he will return: "And then shall they see the Son of man coming in a cloud with power and great glory" (Luke 21:27). The Lord Jesus uses clouds for transportation: "Who maketh the clouds his chariot" (Psalm 104:3); "I saw in the night visions, and, behold, one like the Son of man came with the clouds of heaven, and came to the Ancient of days" (Daniel 7:13); "Then we which are alive and remain shall be caught up together with them in the clouds, to meet the Lord in the air" (1 Thessalonians 4:17).

- Having on his head a golden crown - Jesus will be returning in regal splendour with a crown of pure gold on his head.

- And in his hand a sharp sickle - From the parable of the wheat and the tares, we know that the sickle refers to the angels of the Lord Jesus serving his purpose in uprooting all the unsaved sinners from the earth in order to begin his millennial reign: "And then shall he send his angels, and shall gather together his elect from the four winds, from the uttermost part of the earth to the uttermost part of heaven" (Mark 13:27).

(15) "And another angel came out of the temple, crying with a loud voice to him that sat on the cloud, Thrust in thy sickle, and reap: for the time is come for thee to reap; for the harvest of the earth is ripe."

- And another angel came out of the temple, crying with a loud voice to him that sat on the cloud - The great tribulation will then come to an end when the commandment goes forth from the temple of God, from heaven's palace of justice. The angels will now carry out the royal divine orders to gather the elect into the kingdom of Christ. For when Christ returns to earth, he will first deliver the righteous of the great tribulation. There are two sickles mentioned in this passage, the first in this verse and the second in verse 17.

- Thrust in thy sickle, and reap: for the time is come for thee to reap; for the harvest of the earth is ripe - This first sickle represents the second rapture:

(i) The first rapture is that of the church at the end of the church age: "And to wait for his Son from heaven, whom he raised from the dead, even Jesus, which delivered us from the wrath to come"; "For the Lord himself shall descend from heaven with a shout, with the voice of the archangel, and with the trump of God: and the dead in Christ shall rise first: Then we which are alive and remain shall be caught up together with them in the clouds, to meet the Lord in the air: and so shall we ever be with the Lord" (1 Thessalonians 1:10; 4:16-17).

(ii) The second rapture takes place at the end of the great tribulation when the "King of kings and Lord of lords" (Revelation 19:16) returns to the earth to establish his kingdom: "So shall also the coming of the Son of man be. Then shall two be in the field; the one shall be taken, and the other left. Two women shall be grinding at the mill; the one shall be taken, and the other left" (Matthew 24:39-41); "But in those days, after that tribulation, the sun shall be darkened, and the moon shall not give her light, And the stars of heaven shall fall, and the powers that are in heaven shall be shaken. And then shall they see the Son of man coming in the clouds with great power and glory. And then shall he send his angels, and shall gather together his elect from the four winds, from the uttermost part of the earth to the uttermost part of heaven" (Mark 13:24-27).

The first and second raptures are for the righteous saints of the Church age and the Great Tribulation period.

(iii) The third rapture is not exactly a rapture in the true sense of the word. Its purpose will be to gather the

tares, that is, the wicked, from the kingdom so that they will be burned in the fires of hell. This so-called third rapture will occur one thousand years after the second rapture as it will take place at the end of the millennium. The Lord will send forth his angels, who will gather from his kingdom all who are wicked and unbelieving: "The harvest is the end of the world; and the reapers are the angels. As therefore the tares are gathered and burned in the fire; so shall it be in the end of this world. The Son of man shall send forth his angels, and they shall gather out of his kingdom all things that offend, and them which do iniquity; And shall cast them into a furnace of fire: there shall be wailing and gnashing of teeth. Then shall the righteous shine forth as the sun in the kingdom of their Father" (Matthew 13:39-43).

Then we shall enter eternity.

(16) "And he that sat on the cloud thrust in his sickle on the earth; and the earth was reaped."

The Lord Jesus will gather all the righteous from the earth: "There shall be two men in one bed; the one shall be taken, and the other shall be left. Two women shall be grinding together; the one shall be taken, and the other left. Two men shall be in the field; the one shall be taken, and the other left" (Luke 17:34-36).

(17) "And another angel came out of the temple which is in heaven, he also having a sharp sickle."

This is the second sickle. The first sickle, mentioned in verse 15 was for gathering the righteous into the kingdom of heaven on earth. This second sickle gathers the wicked to the Battle of Armageddon of verse 20. For here we are at the doorsteps of entering the millennial Kingdom of Christ at the point of his return to earth. So each of the 2 sickles is doing its duty according to the command of King Lord Jesus Christ: "^{31}When the Son of man shall come in his glory, and all the holy angels with him, then shall he sit upon the throne of his glory: ^{32}And before him shall be gathered all nations: and he shall separate them one from another, as a shepherd divideth his sheep from the goats: ^{33}And he shall set the sheep on his right hand, but the goats on the left. ^{34}Then shall the King say unto them on his right hand, Come, ye blessed of my Father, inherit the kingdom prepared for you from the foundation of the world:", "46 And these shall go away into everlasting punishment: but the righteous into life eternal." (Matthew 25:31-34, 46).

(18) "And another angel came out from the altar, which had power over fire; and cried with a loud cry to him that had the sharp sickle, saying, Thrust in thy sharp sickle, and gather the clusters of the vine of the earth; for her grapes are fully ripe."

We remember that here it is time to answer the crying out of the souls under the altar: "And when he had opened the fifth seal, I saw under the altar the souls of them that were slain for the word of God, and for the testimony which they held: And they cried with a loud voice, saying, How long, O Lord, holy and true, dost thou not judge and avenge our blood on them that dwell on the earth? And white robes were given unto every one of them; and it was said unto them, that they should rest yet for a little season, until their fellowservants also and their brethren, that should be killed as they were, should be fulfilled" (Revelation 6:9-11).

From that same altar went forth the angel of fire, having power over fire, including the fires of hell, whence the wicked of the earth shall be cast. This second, sharp sickle gathers the wicked, whose abominations have filled the cup of Lord's wrath.

(19) "And the angel thrust in his sickle into the earth, and gathered the vine of the earth, and cast it into the great winepress of the wrath of God."

The angels of the Lord will gather the wicked of the whole world to the war which ends the world, as Joel prophesied: "Alas for the day! for the day of the LORD is at hand, and as a destruction from the Almighty shall it come" (Joel 1:15). "For, behold, in those days, and in that time, when I shall bring again the captivity of Judah and Jerusalem, I will also gather all nations, and will bring them down into the valley of Jehoshaphat, and will plead with them there" (Joel 3:1-2); "Assemble yourselves, and come, all ye heathen, and gather yourselves together round about: thither cause thy mighty ones to come down, O LORD. Let the heathen be wakened, and come up to the valley of Jehoshaphat: for there will I sit to judge all the heathen round about. Put ye in the sickle, for the harvest is ripe: come, get you down; for the press is full, the fats overflow; for their wickedness is great. Multitudes, multitudes in the valley of decision: for the day of the LORD is near in the valley of decision" (Joel 3:11-14). Zephaniah also prophesied in like manner: "Therefore wait ye upon me, saith the Lord, until the day that I rise up to the prey: for my determination is to gather the nations, that I may assemble the kingdoms, to pour upon them mine indignation, even all my fierce anger: for all the earth shall be devoured with the fire of my jealousy" (Zephaniah 3:8). This is the Battle of Armageddon: "In that day shall there be a great mourning in Jerusalem, as the mourning of Hadadrimmon in the valley of Megiddon" (Zechariah 12:11); "And they had a king over them, which is the angel of the bottomless pit, whose name in the Hebrew tongue is Abaddon, but in the Greek tongue hath his name Apollyon" (Revelation

9:11); "And he gathered them together into a place called in the Hebrew tongue Armageddon" (Revelation 16:16); "And he treadeth the winepress of the fierceness and wrath of Almighty God" (Revelation 19:15).

(20) "And the winepress was trodden without the city, and blood came out of the winepress, even unto the horse bridles, by the space of a thousand and six hundred furlongs."

- And the winepress was trodden without the city, and blood came out of the winepress, even unto the horse bridles - Outside of the city walls of Jerusalem will gather all the armies of the world. Their number will be so immense that the blood will rise and reach even to the bridle of a horse. This is the blood of the slain of the wicked of the earth.

- By the space of a thousand and six hundred furlongs. The distance mentioned here is equivalent to 220 miles, that is from Armageddon, passing through Jerusalem, and reaching to Bozrah in the land of Edom: "The sword of the LORD is filled with blood, it is made fat with fatness, and with the blood of lambs and goats, with the fat of the kidneys of rams: for the LORD hath a sacrifice in Bozrah, and a great slaughter in the land of Idumea" (Isaiah 34:6) "Who is this that cometh from Edom, with dyed garments from Bozrah? this that is glorious in his apparel, travelling in the greatness of his strength? I that speak in righteousness, mighty to save" (Isaiah 63:1).

The slaughter is going to be so hideous and appalling then. God's wrath upon the wicked will be beyond measure. Indeed, the angel spoke the truth in verse seven when he said: "Fear God, and give glory to him."

15
THE PROCEEDINGS OF THE LAST SEVEN JUDGMENTS

(1) "And I saw another sign in heaven, great and marvellous, seven angels having the seven last plagues; for in them is filled up the wrath of God."

Chapters 12, 13, and 14 were like three clarifying windows to shed light on what was going on in heaven and upon the earth.

After the sign of the woman clothed with the sun the moon and the twelve stars in (Revelation 12:1), and the sign of the dragon rising from the sea in (Revelation 12:3), we return to a narrative which records the continuing judgments of the great tribulation.

The sum total of the judgment of God consisted of seven seals, followed by seven trumpets, and seven vials. The seventh seal consisted of the seven trumpets, and the seventh trumpet consisted of the seven vials.

The Bible talks about the principle of seven chastisements: "And I, even I, will chastise you seven times" (Leviticus 26:28). However, these are not chastisements but judgements. Here the three sevens of judgements complete the wrath of God.

Now, seven angels go forth from the presence of the throne

of God in the midst of heaven. They carry out the awesome seven vial judgments, which are difficult for us to comprehend, yet they are about to pour out the completion of the wrath of the Lord Jesus on the kingdom of the Antichrist.

(2) "And I saw as it were a sea of glass mingled with fire: and them that had gotten the victory over the beast, and over his image, and over his mark, and over the number of his name, stand on the sea of glass, having the harps of God."

This crystal court represents the glory of God which consists of water and blood. He is worthy to stand thereupon whoever has received the redemption of the blood of Christ and has followed Jesus in consecration by obeying the first step of water baptism. As at all other times, so also in the great tribulation, all who receive Jesus as Lord and Saviour have the privilege and honour to stand in the presence of the throne of God in a state of jubilation in music and with singing hymns of praise.

(3) "And they sing the song of Moses the servant of God, and the song of the Lamb, saying, Great and marvellous are thy works, Lord God Almighty; just and true are thy ways, thou King of saints."

- And they sing the song of Moses the servant of God, and the song of the Lamb. The song of Moses and the song of the Lamb represent the fact that the salvation of the Old Testament and the salvation of the New Testament are both in Jesus Christ. The two songs complement each other, such as:

(i) The song of Moses points to triumph over Egypt, and the song of the Lamb points to triumph over Babylon, the spiritual Egypt.

(ii) The song of Moses is a symbol of leaving the world, while the song of the Lamb is a symbol of entering heaven.

(iii) The song of Moses is the first hymn in the Bible, while the song of the Lamb is the last hymn in the Bible.

(iv) Both the song of Moses and the song of the Lamb speaks of:

(a) Destruction of the wicked,

(b) Anticipation of the honouring of the righteous,

(c) Exaltation of the Lord Jesus!

- Saying, Great and marvellous are thy works, Lord God Almighty; just and true are thy ways, thou King of saints - Whether in the Old Testament or in the New Testament, divine justice and heavenly holiness meet in the King of kings and Lord of lords, the Son of God Jesus Christ.

(4) "Who shall not fear thee, O Lord, and glorify thy name? for thou only art holy: for all nations shall come and worship before thee; for thy judgments are made manifest."

To appreciate this verse, it is good to remember the witness of heaven to the greatness and glory of Jesus from everlasting to everlasting: "In the year that king Uzziah died I saw also the Lord sitting upon a throne, high and lifted up, and his train filled the temple. Above it stood the seraphims: each one had six wings; with twain he covered his face, and with twain he covered his feet, and with twain he did fly. And one cried unto another, and said, Holy, holy, holy, is the LORD of hosts: the whole earth is full of his glory. And the posts of the door moved at the voice of him that cried, and the house was filled with smoke" (Isaiah 6:1-4).

(5) "And after that I looked, and, behold, the temple of the tabernacle of the testimony in heaven was opened:"

The source of all the judgments which come upon the earth in the great tribulation is the divine palace of justice, the throne of God, and specifically the Holy of Holies in God's heavenly temple, wherein is the ark of the covenant and the ten commandments.

The Holy of Holies is the jewel and the essence of the tabernacle of testimony:

(i) "Tabernacle of witness" (Numbers 18:2);

(ii) "Ark of the testimony" (Exodus 30:26);

(iii) "Tabernacle of testimony" (Exodus 38:21).

The execution of divine justice stems from the ten commandments that the Lord Jesus gave, and which the human race did not obey: "For the wrath of God is revealed from heaven" (Romans 1:18); "For which things' sake the wrath of God cometh on the children of disobedience" (Colossians 3:6); "Because the law worketh wrath" (Romans 4:15).

(6) "And the seven angels came out of the temple, having the seven plagues, clothed in pure and white linen, and having their breasts girded with golden girdles."

- And the seven angels came out of the temple, having the seven plagues – Notice that, at this point, the angels do not have the seven vials. They will receive them in verse seven from one of the cherubims. Yet they do have a clear mission to pour out the plagues of God's judgment upon the earth. The fact that they come out of the temple reminds us that they are obeying heavenly orders which come from the throne of God and of Christ. This is what we also saw in the previous chapter: "And another angel came out of the temple, crying with a loud voice to him that sat on the cloud, Thrust in thy sickle, and reap: for the time is come for thee to reap; for the harvest of the earth is ripe ... And another angel came out of the temple which is in heaven" (Revelation 14:15, 17). This is also seen in the next chapter: "And the seventh angel poured out his vial into the air; and there came a great voice out of the temple of heaven, from the throne, saying, It is done" (Revelation 16:17).

- Clothed in pure and white linen, and having their breasts girded with golden girdles - Linen is a symbol of holiness: "Thus shall Aaron come into the holy place: with a young bullock for a sin offering, and a ram for a burnt offering. He shall put on the holy linen coat, and he shall have the linen breeches upon his flesh, and shall be girded with a linen girdle, and with the linen mitre shall he be attired: these are holy garments" (Leviticus 16:3-4). The word "pure" speaks of "bright clean" or "shining"; it reminds us of God's radiance and magnificence: "Glory and honour are in his presence" (1 Chronicles 16:27); "Deck thyself now with majesty and excellency; and array thyself with glory and beauty" (Job 40:10). Girdles or sashes around the chest speak of unbiased and solemn judgement: "And in the midst of the seven candlesticks one like unto the Son of man, clothed with a garment down to the foot, and girt about the paps with a golden girdle" (Revelation 1:13). There we are also told of his feet: "And his feet like unto fine brass" (Revelation 1:15). In the Bible, brass is a symbol of judgment. The mission of these angels is to carry out the sentence of the Lord's justice.

(7) "And one of the four beasts gave unto the seven angels seven golden vials full of the wrath of God, who liveth for ever and ever."

The cherubims are the highest ranking in the world of angelology and some of their offices are:

(i) Cherubims are the seat of the throne of God: "He sitteth between the cherubims" (Psalm 99:1); "And before the throne there was a sea of glass like unto crystal: and in the midst of the throne, and round about the throne, were four beasts full of eyes before and behind" (Revelation 4:6);

(ii) Cherubims are an integral part of the formation of the mercy seat they are witnesses of the mercy of God: "And the cherubims shall stretch forth their wings on high, covering the mercy seat with their wings, and their faces shall look one to another; toward the mercy seat shall the faces of the cherubims be" (Exodus 25:20);

(iii) Cherubims are also the executors and witnesses of divine justice and judgment, as was case in the book of Genesis: "So he drove out the man; and he placed at the east of the garden of Eden Cherubims, and a flaming sword which turned every way, to keep the way of the tree of life" (Genesis 3:24).

Therefore this wrath of God comes from anywhere closer, for from the throne of God and from the seat of that throne comes the punishment of God upon Satan and his kingdom and his world.

(8) "And the temple was filled with smoke from the glory of God, and from his power; and no man was able to enter into the temple, till the seven plagues of the seven angels were fulfilled."

- And the temple was filled with smoke from the glory of God and from his power. This description speaks of the presence of God, the seriousness of the matter at hand, and God's favour upon what is unfolding. Remember what happened when the tabernacle was completed and erected in the wilderness: "Then a cloud covered the tent of the congregation, and the glory of the LORD filled the tabernacle. And Moses was not able to enter into the tent of the congregation, because the cloud abode thereon, and the glory of the LORD filled the tabernacle" (Exodus 40:34-35). This is similar to what happened when King Solomon first dedicated the temple in Jerusalem: "And it came to pass, when the priests were come out of the holy place, that the cloud filled the house of the LORD, So that the priests could not stand to minister because of the cloud: for the glory of the LORD had filled the house of the LORD" (1 Kings 8:10-11). Remember, again, that when the time came for the Lord to rebuke Israel for their apostasy from him, he revealed himself to Isaiah: "Also I heard the voice of the Lord, saying, Whom shall I send, and who will go for us? Then said I, Here am I; send me. And he said, Go, and tell this people, Hear ye indeed, but understand not; and see ye indeed, but perceive not. Make the heart of this people fat, and make their ears heavy, and shut their eyes; lest they see with their eyes, and hear with their ears, and understand with their heart, and convert, and be healed" (Isaiah 6:8-10).

- And no man was able to enter into the temple, till the seven plagues of the seven angels were fulfilled - As we just read, the overwhelming fearful majesty of the Lord prevented Moses from entering the tabernacle and the priests from entering the temple. It is as if the Lord's long-suffering has reached its limit. The moment has come for his wrath to be poured out. Even if the righteous desired the postponement of his indignation and fury, they would not be able to approach him at this time to request a delay. Here we recall a comparable situation when God poured out his wrath and judgement on Judah before their captivity: "Then said the Lord unto me, Though Moses and Samuel stood before me, yet my mind could not be toward this people: cast them out of my sight, and let them go forth" (Jeremiah 15:1).

Therefore, if you have not experienced the salvation of the Lord, do not procrastinate or postpone for the Bible says: "How shall we escape, if we neglect so great salvation; which at the first began to be spoken by the Lord, and was confirmed unto us by them that heard him?" (Hebrews 2:3). Also do not harden your heart: "While it is said, To day if ye will hear his voice, harden not your hearts, as in the provocation" (Hebrews 3:15). Today is the day of salvation: "For he saith, I have heard thee in a time accepted, and in the day of salvation have I succoured thee: behold, now is the accepted time; behold, now is the day of salvation" (2 Corinthians 6:2).

Come to the Lord Jesus and open your heart to him: "For the wages of sin is death; but the gift of God is eternal life through Jesus Christ our Lord" (Romans 6:23). Come! "And the Spirit and the bride say, Come. And let him that heareth say, Come. And let him that is athirst come. And whosoever will, let him take the water of life freely" (Revelation 22:17). Amen.

16

THE SEVEN VIALS AND THE WAR OF ARMAGEDDON

(1) "And I heard a great voice out of the temple saying to the seven angels, Go your ways, and pour out the vials of the wrath of God upon the earth."

In this chapter, the word "great" is repeated eight times:

(i) Great Voice
(ii) Great Heat
(iii) Great Day
(iv) Great Earthquake
(v) Great City Babylon
(vi) Great Hail
(vii) Great Plague
(viii) Great River Euphrates.

Therefore this chapter is great in the Bible, but what specifically is great about it? It is that in this chapter we see the completion of the final sequence of the judgments which God brings upon the world of wickedness. These judgments began with the seven seals, which were followed by the seven trumpets, and which were succeeded by the seven vials. The great tribulation began with the first seal in chapter 6 and ends in this chapter, with the seventh vial. We are now in the middle of the fourth narrative of the return of Jesus to the earth! The first narrative was in Revelation 6, the second in Revelation 8-11, the third in Revelation 12, and the fourth in Revelation 13-19. In this verse, the command is given to pour out the seven vials and bring the whole of God's judgment to its conclusion.

(2) "And the first went, and poured out his vial upon the earth; and there fell a noisome and grievous sore upon the men which had the mark of the beast, and upon them which worshipped his image."

According to proper Bible interpretation, this is a literal judgment. It is quite similar to the sixth plague in the ten plagues with which Moses and Aaron smote Egypt: "And they took ashes of the furnace, and stood before Pharaoh; and Moses sprinkled it up toward heaven; and it became a boil breaking forth with blains upon man, and upon beast" (Exodus 9:10).

The first angel poured his vial upon the land only, not upon the rivers and seas. The result was very painful sores which came upon all the kingdom of the Antichrist and all those bearing his mark.

(3) "And the second angel poured out his vial upon the sea; and it became as the blood of a dead man: and every living soul died in the sea."

This judgment is directed to the seas of the world, which will be transformed into real blood. All the creatures of the sea will die.

(4) "And the third angel poured out his vial upon the rivers and fountains of waters; and they became blood."

Springs and rivers will also be transformed into real blood, and all the creatures that live in the rivers will die.

(5) "And I heard the angel of the waters say, Thou art righteous, O Lord, which art, and wast, and shalt be, because thou hast judged thus."

Eating blood is repugnant in God's sight: "And whatsoever man there be of the children of Israel, or of the strangers that sojourn among you, which hunteth and catcheth any beast or fowl that may be eaten; he shall even pour out the blood thereof, and cover it with dust. For it is the life of all flesh; the blood of it is for the life thereof: therefore I said unto the children of Israel, Ye shall eat the blood of no manner of flesh: for the life of all flesh is the blood thereof: whosoever eateth it shall be cut off" (Leviticus 17:13-14). "Only ye shall not eat the blood; ye shall pour it upon the earth as water ... Only be sure that thou eat not the blood: for the blood is the life; and thou mayest not eat the life with the flesh. Thou shalt not eat it; thou shalt pour it upon the earth as water. Thou shalt not eat it; that it may go well with thee, and with thy children after thee" (Deuteronomy 12:16, 23-25). This is also true for people in the New Testament(Acts 15:20).

We see in this verse and in the next a testimony to divine righteousness and justice: "Which art, and wast, and shalt be" which points to the fact that divine justice and righteousness are everlasting!

(6) "For they have shed the blood of saints and prophets, and thou hast given them blood to drink; for they are worthy."

This is an answer to the prayers of the martyred souls under the altar, mentioned in the fifth seal: "And when he had opened the fifth seal, I saw under the altar the souls of them that were slain for the word of God, and for the testimony which they held: And they cried with a loud voice, saying, How long, O Lord, holy and true, dost thou not judge and avenge our blood on them that dwell on the earth?" (Revelation 6:9-10). At the same time, it is a fulfilment of divine justice and righteousness.

It is an innate human instinct for man to know that Jesus is just. Even barbarians, who do not know God, have learned from their experiences that there is justice in this world. Remember what they said when Paul the Apostle was bitten by a snake: "And when the barbarians saw the venomous beast hang on his hand, they said among themselves, No doubt this man is a murderer, whom, though he hath escaped the sea, yet vengeance suffereth not to live" (Acts 28:4). The Lord Jesus is just and loves justice and executes justice: "For the righteous Lord loveth righteousness; his countenance doth behold the upright" (Psalms 11:7); "To do justice and judgment is more acceptable to the Lord than sacrifice" (Proverbs 21:3); "And the times of this ignorance God winked at; but now commandeth all men every where to repent: Because he hath appointed a day, in the which he will judge the world in righteousness by that man whom he hath ordained; whereof he hath given assurance unto all men, in that he hath raised him from the dead" (Acts 17:30-31). Our God is just and faithful, as Abraham acknowledged with amazement when he said: "Shall not the Judge of all the earth do right?" (Genesis 18:25).

(7) "And I heard another out of the altar say, Even so, Lord God Almighty, true and righteous are thy judgments."

The Lord has so ordained that whosoever touches his children, touches the apple of his eye: "For he that toucheth you toucheth the apple of his eye" (Zechariah 2:8). How much more will the Lord do with those who delight in killing his children, as happens in the world today and will happen, to a much greater extent, in the great tribulation? The Lord Jesus will punish evil and avenge his children swiftly.

(8) "And the fourth angel poured out his vial upon the sun; and power was given unto him to scorch men with fire."

With the depletion of the ozone layer, the phenomenon of heat retention (also known as global warming) has become a general concern. The minds of the world's leaders are perturbed regarding possible increases in skin cancer and other diseases. They also have grave concerns regarding a gloomy future for the earth's environment. How insignificant will these concerns be when compared to a work of our God's power! In his burning wrath, God will multiply the power of the sun, and men's skins will be scorched as a result.

This judgment is opposite to that of the fourth trumpet and does not involve the moon and the stars, as the judgment of the fourth trumpet does: "And the fourth angel sounded, and the third part of the sun was smitten, and the third part of the moon, and the third part of the stars; so as the third part of them was darkened, and the day shone not for a third part of it, and the night likewise" (Revelation 8:12). These things will surely happen, and when they do they will confirm to the world of atheists that the book of Genesis is literally true. God is indeed the Creator who made the heavens and the earth and all that is in them in six literal days and nights: "In the beginning God created the heaven and the earth" (Genesis 1:1); "For in six days the LORD made heaven and earth, the sea, and all that in them is" (Exodus 20:11). That was when God made Adam and Eve: "But from the beginning of the creation God made them male and female" (Mark 10:6). Of course, this is contrary to what the world that does not know God believes. They teach theories of evolution that required development over millions of years. In reality, all of creation was brought about in an instant when Jesus spoke, and it was and is today, for he is "upholding all things by the word of his power" (Hebrews 1:3). Here he will then pour out his wrath on these wicked men, confirming the truth of what he says in Luke: "And there shall be signs in the sun, and in the moon, and in the stars; and upon the earth distress of nations, with perplexity" (Luke 21:25).

The Lord Jesus controls the sun as he pleases. He can hold it in place in the sky as he did with Joshua: "Then spake Joshua to the Lord in the day when the Lord delivered up the Amorites before the children of Israel, and he said in the sight of Israel, Sun, stand thou still upon Gibeon; and thou, Moon, in the valley of Ajalon. And the sun stood still, and the moon stayed, until the people had avenged themselves upon their enemies. Is not this written in the book of Jasher? So the sun stood still in the midst of heaven, and hasted not to go down about a whole day. And there was no day like that before it or after it, that the Lord hearkened unto the voice of a man: for the Lord fought for Israel" (Joshua 10:12-14). Jesus made the sun move backwards as he did for Hezekiah at the command of the prophet Isaiah: "And this shall be a sign unto thee from the Lord, that the Lord will do this thing that he hath spoken; Behold, I will bring again the shadow of the degrees, which is gone down in the sun dial of Ahaz, ten degrees backward. So the sun returned ten degrees, by which degrees it was gone down" (Isaiah 38:7-8).

As we saw in the previous verse, Jesus can both extinguish the sun and can increase its temperature to the point where it burns the flesh of evil people. He is God. He is the creator. He is omnipotent, all powerful!

Jesus is light and his light shines brighter than the light of the sun. Saul of Tarsus experienced that on the road to Damascus: "And his brightness was as the light; he had horns coming out of his hand: and there was the hiding of his power" (Habakkuk 3:4); "And after six days Jesus taketh Peter, James, and John his brother, and bringeth them up into an high mountain apart, And was transfigured before them: and his face did shine as the sun, and his raiment was white as the light" (Matthew 17:1-2); "Whereupon as I went to Damascus with authority and commission from the chief priests, ^{13}At midday, O king, I saw in the way a light from heaven, above the brightness of the sun, shining round about me and them which journeyed with me" (Acts 26:12-13).

The sun derives its light from the light of Jesus, for he is light! The light of Jesus was and is present when: "God said, Let there be light: and there was light. ^{4}And God saw the light, that it was good: and God divided the light from the darkness. ^{5}And God called the light Day, and the darkness he called Night. And the evening and the morning were the first day" (Genesis 1:3-5). That was before the creation of the sun and the moon on the fourth day: "And God said, Let there be lights in the firmament of the heaven to divide the day from the night; and let them be for signs, and for seasons, and for days, and years: ^{15}And let them be for lights in the firmament of the heaven to give light upon the earth: and it was so. ^{16}And God made two great lights; the greater light to rule the day, and the lesser light to rule the night: he made the stars also. ^{17}And God set them in the firmament of the heaven to give light upon the earth, ^{18}And to rule over the day and over the night, and to divide the light from the darkness: and God saw that it was good. ^{19}And the evening and the morning were the fourth day" (Genesis 1:14-19). The light of the Sun and the world come from Jesus. God is light. Jesus is the light of the world. Jesus shines his light on the entire universe!

(9) "And men were scorched with great heat, and blasphemed the name of God, which hath power over these plagues: and they repented not to give him glory."

- And men were scorched with great heat - They will be scorched severely, as Isaiah, the great prophet, saw and described: "Therefore hath the curse devoured the earth, and they that dwell therein are desolate: therefore the inhabitants of the earth are burned, and few men left" (Isaiah 24:6).

Indeed, most of the inhabitants of the earth will have died by this point as a result of the successive judgments throughout the seven years of the great tribulation. Sadly, man's intents are so evil in their rejection of the Lord Jesus, that they remain non repentant; rather, they will gather for a world slaughter at the battle of Armageddon.

We observe that the judgments of the trumpets and the judgments of the vials are similar, only the latter are wider in scope, and more comprehensive in total mass destruction.

- And blasphemed the name of God, which hath power over these plagues: and they repented not to give him glory - It is sufficient here to cite the wisdom of King Solomon: "Though thou shouldest bray a fool in a mortar among wheat with a pestle, yet will not his foolishness depart from him" (Proverbs 27:22).

Man is evil and does not want to repent. Many times, we preach the gospel to people who then understand the message of salvation, however, they do not want to repent: "For the spirit of whoredoms hath caused them to err, and they have gone a whoring from under their God ... They will not frame their doings to turn unto their God: for the spirit of whoredoms is in the midst of them, and they have not known the Lord" (Hosea 4:12; 5:4).

(10) "And the fifth angel poured out his vial upon the seat of the beast; and his kingdom was full of darkness; and they gnawed their tongues for pain,"

Like the first vial, this judgment is directed to the very heart of the kingdom of the Antichrist. This judgment is similar to the ninth plague with which Egypt was smitten: "And the LORD said unto Moses, Stretch out thine hand toward heaven, that there may be darkness over the land of Egypt, even darkness which may be felt. And Moses stretched forth his hand toward heaven; and there was a thick darkness in all the land of Egypt three days: They saw not one another, neither rose any from his place for three days: but all the children of Israel had light in their dwellings" (Exodus 10:21-23).

Man is a combination of spirit, soul, and body. The spirit of man fears the fires of hell. The soul of man fears the unknown future. The body of man experiences frightful pain when it is constricted or placed in total darkness. One of the torments that will experienced by those who will go to hell is eternal darkness without the hope of ever seeing light again: "They shall never see light" (Psalms 49:19). Therefore, let the sinner repent and follow Jesus, who will lead him to eternal light in Heaven: "And there shall be no night there; and they need no candle, neither light of the sun; for the Lord God giveth them light: and they shall reign for ever and ever" (Revelation 22:5).

(11) "And blasphemed the God of heaven because of their pains and their sores, and repented not of their deeds."

The wicked respond to God by clinging to their wickedness; they refuse to repent and, instead, blaspheme against God. Repentance is very difficult for the proud person, for he refuses to humble himself and confess that he is a sinner in need of Jesus.

The basis of the gospel of Jesus Christ is repentance, which is clearly stated by him in the Bible: "Now after that John was put in prison, Jesus came into Galilee, preaching the gospel of the kingdom of God, And saying, The time is fulfilled, and the kingdom of God is at hand: repent ye, and believe the gospel" (Mark 1:14-15); "And they went out, and preached that men should repent" (Mark 6:12).

(12) "And the sixth angel poured out his vial upon the great river Euphrates; and the water thereof was dried up, that the way of the kings of the east might be prepared."

The sixth angel will pour God's wrath from his vial, and the springs of the river will cease gushing forth, drying up its course. This judgment is similar to, and complements, the judgment of the sixth trumpet found in chapter 9: "And the sixth angel sounded, and I heard a voice from the four horns of the golden altar which is before God, Saying to the sixth angel which had the trumpet, Loose the four angels which are bound in the great river Euphrates. And the four angels were loosed, which were prepared for an hour, and a day, and a month, and a year, for to slay the third part of men. And the number of the army of the horsemen were two hundred thousand thousand: and I heard the number of them" (Revelation 9:13-16).

The Euphrates River is closely associated with the historical city of Babylon. The city of Babylon was built upon this river and it was taken by the Persians when they diverted the course of the Euphrates and passed in its old course under the city walls and took the city. The Persians were Eastern people who worship the sun. The title of the shah of Iran was "Shahanshah Aryamehr," that is "king of kings, son of the sun." History repeats itself and when the Eastern powers will come to war against spiritual-military Babylon of the European Union. The great Euphrates River will be emptied of its waters. Its bed will dry up, allowing easy passage for the armies of the eastern lands.

At the first coming of Christ, wise men from the East came to worship the Lord Jesus: "Now when Jesus was born in Bethlehem of Judaea in the days of Herod the king, behold, there came wise men from the east to Jerusalem, Saying, Where is he that is born King of the Jews? for we have seen his star in the east, and are come to worship him" (Matthew 2:1-2). At the second coming of Christ, the kings of the East will come to wage war against the Antichrist and on the mountain of the Lord Jesus: "But tidings out of the east and out of the north shall trouble him: therefore he shall go forth with great fury to destroy, and utterly to make away many. And he shall plant the tabernacles of his palace between the seas in the glorious holy mountain; yet he shall come to his end, and none shall help him" (Daniel 11:44-45).

(13) "And I saw three unclean spirits like frogs come out of the mouth of the dragon, and out of the mouth of the beast, and out of the mouth of the False prophet."

- And I saw three unclean spirits ... out of the mouth - The mouth is the organ from which words emerge, expressing desire, giving orders, and manifesting a desire to hold sway over others.

- Out of the mouth of the dragon, and out of the mouth of the beast, and out of the mouth of the False prophet – They are the unholy trinity.

There are three beasts mentioned in the book of Revelation; and they form an unholy trinity. They are:

(i) The first beast, is the one mentioned here, the beast that ascends out of the bottomless pit, Satan himself: "The beast that ascendeth out of the bottomless pit" (Revelation 11:7).

(ii) The second beast is the one comes out from the sea, the Antichrist: "And I stood upon the sand of the sea, and saw a beast rise up out of the sea" (Revelation 13:1).

(iii) The third beast is the one that comes out from the earth, the False prophet: "And I beheld another beast coming up out of the earth" (Revelation 13:11).

- Like frogs - Frogs are unclean animals according to the law, and they are some of the ugliest animals one can ever set eye upon. Their appearance inspires thoughts of grumbling and dissatisfaction, and their voices are coarse and grating. It is a wonder of wonders that many people in the world today decorate their houses and their children's rooms with frogs, not being able to discern that these creatures are associated with wickedness and with a curse. Also, in ancient days, frogs were symbols of witchcraft and sorcery. Wicked philosophers were described as frogs. Frogs are amphibious animals who live in swamps. They subsist on flies, mosquitoes, and filth. This is a symbol of those who reject the Lord and live in the mud of sin. Frogs inflate their neck to show their prowess. In like manner, pride is foundation upon which men stand when they reject the Lord Jesus; it is also the foundation of many disputes between people: "Only by pride cometh contention: but with the well advised is wisdom" (Proverbs 13:10). Do you have an ongoing dispute with anyone? Go to them and discuss your concerns honestly, for Jesus says, "Moreover if thy brother shall trespass against thee, go and tell him his fault between thee and him alone" (Matthew 18:15). If you do not go, then the reason is pride, and pride is from the devil who exalted himself above God.

(14) "For they are the spirits of devils, working miracles, which go forth unto the kings of the earth and of the whole

world, to gather them to the battle of that great day of God Almighty."

The evil trinity deceives the kings, presidents, and armies of all this earth into going to war at Armageddon. This should not be surprising, as Satan was a deceiver, a liar, and a murderer from the beginning: "Ye are of your father the devil, and the lusts of your father ye will do. He was a murderer from the beginning, and abode not in the truth, because there is no truth in him. When he speaketh a lie, he speaketh of his own: for he is a liar, and the father of it" (John 8:44).

The activity of evil spirits will increase immensely in the great tribulation, as the age of the church will be over and the Holy Spirit will be lifted out of the world. These things have begun to manifest themselves on the world's stage today. We are at the end of the church age, and the Bible warns us: "Now the Spirit speaketh expressly, that in the latter times some shall depart from the faith, giving heed to seducing spirits, and doctrines of devils; Speaking lies in hypocrisy; having their conscience seared with a hot iron" (1 Timothy 4:1-2).

(15) "Behold, I come as a thief. Blessed is he that watcheth, and keepeth his garments, lest he walk naked, and they see his shame."

Here we see heavenly intervention in the midst of world encompassing spiritual darkness as we see the Lord Jesus encouraging the believers of the great tribulation to maintain their faithfulness to him. He admonishes them not to faint,

nor grow tired, or else they would lose their reward of their testimony for Christ. The jewel of our faith is our faithful testimony to the Lord Jesus and to his Word, the Bible.

Satan will try to deceive, if possible, even the elect, as the Lord Jesus warns: "For there shall arise false Christs, and false prophets, and shall shew great signs and wonders; insomuch that, if it were possible, they shall deceive the very elect. Behold, I have told you before" (Matthew 24:24-25). The Holy Spirit also warns of the Antichrist: "Even him, whose coming is after the working of Satan with all power and signs and lying wonders, And with all deceivableness of unrighteousness in them that perish" (2 Thessalonians 2:9-10). Thanks be to the Lord Jesus, who is victorious: "And the beast was taken, and with him the False prophet that wrought miracles before him, with which he deceived them that had received the mark of the beast, and them that worshipped his image. These both were cast alive into a lake of fire burning with brimstone" (Revelation 19:20).

(16) "And he gathered them together into a place called in the Hebrew tongue Armageddon."

- And he gathered them together. Before the seventh angel pours out his vial, Satan will gather all men of the world to the battle of Armageddon. Satan, the enemy of souls, the head of the evil trinity, assembles all the kingdoms of the world to participate in the greatest battle in the history of mankind. For 2,000 years the world has been hearing about the battle of Armageddon, which will be the worst of all wars. Wars and death come from Satan who in the end days will assemble all the kingdoms of the world to battle to slaughter each other, and die, and go down with him into the eternal fire of hell "prepared for the devil and his angels" (Matthew 25:41).

- Into a place called in the Hebrew tongue Armageddon - Armageddon lies in the plain of Megiddo, which constitutes the northern part of the plain and the valley of Jezreel, located to the southeast of the coastal city of Haifa in northern Israel. The word "Armageddon" means "the mountain of sorrows". Historically, this plain was associated with much sorrow due to the large number of armies which gathered there to fight their battles. Its oldest name in the Bible is "Harosheth of the Gentiles": "But Barak pursued after the chariots, and after the host, unto Harosheth of the Gentiles: and all the host of Sisera fell upon the edge of the sword; and there was not a man left"

(Judges 4:16). In this same place, Jehu, king of Israel, killed Ahaziah, king of Judah: "But when Ahaziah the king of Judah saw this, he fled by the way of the garden house. And Jehu followed after him, and said, Smite him also in the chariot. And they did so at the going up to Gur, which is by Ibleam. And he fled to Megiddo, and died there" (2 Kings 9:27). This was also the field where Nechoh, pharaoh of Egypt, fought and killed Josiah, king of Judah: "In his days Pharaoh nechoh king of Egypt went up against the king of Assyria to the river Euphrates: and king Josiah went against him; and he slew him at Megiddo, when he had seen him" (2 Kings 23:29).

When Napoleon conquered Akko, he came down to Haifa and saw the landscape the plains of Megiddo, surrounded by hills of varying sizes. He said, "This is the best location in the world for military manoeuvres". The Lord will use this place for the last war with this wicked world. Armies will come from Europe, the lands of the eastern sunrise, Africa, Russia, and faraway isles, marching under the banner of the Antichrist against Israel. It is the target because the Lord Jesus Christ came from Israel, from the tribe of Judah, to save all people.

Finally the summary of the end of Babylon is going to be seen as such:

(i) In chapter 16, destruction of military Babylon;
(ii) In chapter 17, destruction of religious Babylon;
(iii) In chapter 18, destruction of economical Babylon;
(iv) In chapter 19, destruction of political Babylon.

(17) "And the seventh angel poured out his vial into the air; and there came a great voice out of the temple of heaven, from the throne, saying, It is done."

This is the last judgment in the sequence of the three sets of judgments: of the seals, the trumpets, and the vials. It will be the final judgment which will engulf all the dominion of Satan's power, namely the air: "The prince of the power of the air, the spirit that now worketh in the children of disobedience" (Ephesians 2:2); "For we wrestle not against flesh and blood, but against principalities, against powers, against the rulers of the darkness of this world, against spiritual wickedness in high places" (Ephesians 6:12).

These forces of evil had recently fallen to the earth: "And the great dragon was cast out, that old serpent, called the Devil, and Satan, which deceiveth the whole world: he was cast out into the earth, and his angels were cast out with him" (Revelation 12:9). They retained control over the earth's air, a temporary power which comes to an end in this verse when the statement "It is done!" echoes from God's throne in the heavens.

The first time Jesus uttered these words "It is finished" as in "It is done", he was hanging upon the cross to complete the redemption of man. Now seated at the right hand of majesty and having completed the task of executing divine judgment that precedes the establishment of his kingdom; Jesus says once again: It is done, it is finished.

(18) "And there were voices, and thunders, and lightnings; and there was a great earthquake, such as was not since men were upon the earth, so mighty an earthquake, and so great."

- And there were voices, and thunders, and lightnings - This is the same description of the greatness of God's presence which we saw in chapter 6: "And the angel took the censer, and filled it with fire of the altar, and cast it into the earth: and there were voices, and thunderings, and lightnings, and an earthquake" (Revelation 8:5).

- And there was a great earthquake, such as was not since men were upon the earth, so mighty an earthquake, and so great - This will be the most powerful, most violent earthquake which the globe has ever known since the creation of the earth and of man. Haggai and Zechariah prophesied of this earthquake: "For thus saith the LORD of hosts; Yet once, it is a little while, and I will shake the heavens, and the earth, and the sea, and the dry land; And I will shake all nations, and the desire of all nations shall come: and I will fill this house with glory, saith the LORD of hosts" (Haggai 2:6-7). "Then shall the LORD go forth, and fight against those nations, as when he fought in the day of battle. And his feet shall stand in that day upon the mount of Olives, which is before Jerusalem on the east, and the mount of Olives shall cleave in the midst thereof toward the east and toward the west, and there shall be a very great valley; and half of the mountain shall remove toward the north, and half of it toward the south. And ye shall flee to the valley of the mountains; for the valley of the mountains shall reach unto Azal: yea, ye shall flee, like as ye fled from before the earthquake in the days of Uzziah king of Judah: and the LORD my God shall come, and all the saints with thee" (Zechariah 14:3-5).

(19) "And the great city was divided into three parts, and the cities of the nations fell: and great Babylon came in remembrance before God, to give unto her the cup of the wine of the fierceness of his wrath."

- And the great city was divided into three parts, and the cities of the nations fell - The great city is Babylon: "And there followed another angel, saying, Babylon is fallen, is fallen, that great city" (Revelation 14:8).

- And great Babylon came in remembrance before God, to give unto her the cup of the wine of the fierceness of his wrath – Babylon is the capital of Nimrod and of the Antichrist and of Satan, and so her destiny is hell. So also of anyone who does not accept Jesus as Lord and Master over his life: "Babylon the great is fallen, is fallen, and is become the habitation of devils, and the hold of every foul spirit, and a cage of every unclean and hateful bird" (Revelation 18:2).

(20) "And every island fled away, and the mountains were not found."

We have already seen that at the opening of the sixth seal: "Every mountain and island were moved out of their places" (Revelation 6:14). Here, they dol not just move out of their place, but rather they flee away completely. The geography of planet earth will change in its entirety. Such geographical changes will sweep away millions of people. Few will remain, and that in accord with the description given by Jeremiah the prophet: "I beheld the earth, and, lo, it was without form, and void; and the heavens, and they had no light. I beheld the mountains, and, lo, they trembled, and all the hills moved lightly. I beheld, and, lo, there was no man, and all the birds of the heavens were fled. I beheld, and, lo, the fruitful place was a wilderness, and all the cities thereof were broken down at the presence of the LORD, and by his fierce anger" (Jeremiah 4:23-26).

In those last days of the great tribulation, Psalm 46 will be, in a very literal way, the tongue of the righteous: "God is our refuge and strength, a very present help in trouble. Therefore will not we fear, though the earth be removed, and though the mountains be carried into the midst of the sea; Though the waters thereof roar and be troubled, though the mountains shake with the swelling thereof. Selah ... The heathen raged, the kingdoms were moved: he uttered his voice, the earth melted. The LORD of hosts is with us; the God of Jacob is our refuge. Selah" (Psalm 46:1-3, 6-7).

(21) "And there fell upon men a great hail out of heaven, every stone about the weight of a talent: and men blasphemed God because of the plague of the hail; for the plague thereof was exceeding great."

A judgment involving hail is mentioned more than once in the Bible, beginning with the plagues with which the Lord Jesus smote the land of Egypt: "And Moses stretched forth his rod toward heaven: and the LORD sent thunder and hail, and the fire ran along upon the ground; and the LORD rained hail upon the land of Egypt. So there was hail, and fire mingled with the hail, very grievous, such as there was none like it in all the land of Egypt since it became a nation. And the hail smote throughout all the land of Egypt all that was in the field, both man and beast; and the hail smote every herb of the field, and brake every tree of the field. Only in the land of Goshen, where the children of Israel were, was there no hail" (Exodus 9:23-26). The Lord smote the Amorites with hail when Joshua fought against them on the longest day in history, a day which lasted 36 hours: "And it came to pass, as they fled from before Israel, and were in the going down to Bethhoron, that the LORD cast down great stones from heaven upon them unto Azekah, and they died: they were more which died with hailstones than they whom the children of Israel slew with the sword" (Joshua 10:11). The Lord will use hail to smite the alliance of Russian powers at the end of the millennium: "And it shall come to pass at the same time when Gog shall come against the land of Israel, saith the Lord GOD, that my fury shall come up in my face ... And I will plead against him with pestilence and with blood; and I will rain upon him, and upon his bands, and upon the many people that are with him, an overflowing rain, and great hailstones, fire, and brimstone. Thus will I magnify myself, and sanctify myself; and I will be known in the eyes of many nations, and they shall know that I am the LORD" (Ezekiel 38:18; 22-23).

Job saw that the Lord Jesus has the treasures of snow: "Hast thou entered into the treasures of the snow? or hast thou seen the treasures of the hail?" (Job 38:22). The Lord uses the treasures of the snow to punish the wicked; but instead of repenting, they will grow more insistent and intransigent. Huge, fearful hailstones, weighing between thirty and forty kilograms, will come down upon their heads; however, they do not repent and come to relief and salvation. They prefer to proceed even further into heresy, to wallow all the more in sin, and to sink so deeply into iniquity that only hellfire can be their portion, where, side by side with the devil and his angels, they will be tormented forever and ever. This is the portion of all that reject the sovereignty of the Lord Jesus in their lives.

Repent of your sinful ways and surrender your life to Jesus. Taste and see that the Lord is good! Blessed are they that rely on the Lord Jesus, the son of the living God!

17
THE WOMAN AND THE BEAST – THE DESTRUCTION OF ECCLESIASTICAL BABYLON –

(1) "And there came one of the seven angels which had the seven vials, and talked with me, saying unto me, Come hither; I will shew unto thee the judgment of the great whore that sitteth upon many waters:"

- And there came one of the seven angels which had the seven vials, and talked with me, saying unto me - When the seventh angel proclaimed, "It is done" in (Revelation 16:17), it meant that God's judgments of the seals and the trumpets and the vials reached their conclusion. Now, one of these angels invites John to view a detailed explanation, in chapters 17 - 19 of that conclusion. John is given the opportunity to see more details about the end of the False prophet, the Antichrist, and their kingdom the great revived Roman Empire, which the spiritual Babylon. Once again, we saw in chapter 16 the destruction of military Babylon. In this chapter, we get to see the destruction of religious Babylon, in chapter 18 economic Babylon, and in chapter 19 the details of the destruction of political Babylon.

- Come hither; I will shew unto thee - The angel presents to John a lengthy description of the end of the kingdom of the Antichrist.

- The judgment of the great whore - The Bible describes "Religious Babylon" as a great whore that has turned away from the Lord Jesus Christ. It is the Vatican in Rome, the center of worldwide Catholicism and traditional Christianity, that has encouraged people to worship individuals and objects in the name of Jesus but kept them away from worshiping Jesus only. The Catholic Church, the Orthodox Church, and all other traditional religions have filled the world with their spiritual adultery, away from the Lord Jesus: "Which did corrupt the earth with her fornication" (Revelation 19:2). They have killed the true followers of the Lord Jesus: "Drunken with the blood of the saints, and with the blood of the martyrs of Jesus" (Revelation 17:6).

- That sitteth upon many waters - The Vatican sits upon many waters, which means that it has authority over the peoples of the world. The word "sitteth" indicates being in a state of rest and ease. The Vatican has a dominating influence and a powerful sway over the minds of the peoples and presidents of the world. They in turn, seek its favor, the favor of the pope of Rome and the Vatican. Millions and millions of human souls are lost, going astray from salvation and heaven and destined to perish forever solely because they cling to traditional churches, which refuse to depend exclusively on the intercession of the blood of Christ and salvation by grace alone, without works.

In his letter to the Galatians, Paul the Apostle addresses the topic of salvation by faith alone. In Galatians chapters three and four he points out that salvation is by faith alone without works. Those who think that salvation is by faith and works are foolish: "O foolish Galatians, who hath bewitched you, that ye should not obey the truth, before whose eyes Jesus Christ hath been evidently set forth, crucified among you? This only would I learn of you, Received ye the Spirit by the works of the law, or by the hearing of faith? Are ye so foolish? having begun in the Spirit, are ye now made perfect by the flesh?" (Galatians

3:1-3). It is madness and insanity and evil for anyone to believe that salvation is by works or by faith plus works, yet, this is exactly what the Vatican in Rome teaches. She is the mother of spiritual adultery and abomination throughout the entire globe.

(2) "With whom the kings of the earth have committed fornication, and the inhabitants of the earth have been made drunk with the wine of her fornication."

The fornication here is spiritual, for any worship directed toward a creature, object, or person other than the Lord Jesus is spiritual fornication: "Thou hast destroyed all them that go a whoring from thee" (Psalm 73:27); "For thou hast gone a whoring from thy God" (Hosea 9:1); "And they transgressed against the God of their fathers, and went a whoring after the gods of the people of the land" (1 Chronicles 5:25).

After the rapture of God's children, the Vatican will strengthen its ascendency over the whole world under the leadership of the False prophet; it will steer the world towards spiritual adultery and away from the worship of the Lord Jesus Christ. The Vatican will lead the world powers in a worldwide persecution of all those who "keep the commandments of God, and have the testimony of Jesus Christ" (Revelation 12:17), a persecution culminates in mass martyrdom: "I saw the souls of them that were beheaded for the witness of Jesus, and for the word of God, and which had not worshipped the beast, neither his image, neither had received his mark upon their foreheads, or in their hands; and they lived and reigned with Christ a thousand years" (Revelation 20:4).

Satan has direct influence over the False prophet and over the Antichrist and his kingdom. They all drink his devilish poisons. They are all under his influence. They are all drunk with the influence of his evil hosts, which rise from hell (see Revelation 9:1-12).

(3) "So he carried me away in the spirit into the wilderness:

and I saw a woman sit upon a scarlet coloured beast, full of names of blasphemy, having seven heads and ten horns."

- So he carried me away in the spirit into the wilderness: and I saw a woman sit upon a scarlet coloured beast, full of names of blasphemy - The wilderness is the world of the nations: "the wilderness of the people" (Ezekiel 20:35). The woman is sitting upon the beast, which rises from the earth: "And I beheld another beast coming up out of the earth" (Revelation 13:11). The woman represents the Vatican and the scarlet beast is the kingdom of the Antichrist, the beast that rises from the sea (Revelation 13:1).

Purple garb is one of the features of highly-ranked religious leaders, such as the cardinals of the Catholic church. Such individuals constitute religious Rome, which is, spiritually speaking, religious Babylon. We see the woman, the Vatican, in complete concord with the scarlet beast, the kingdom of the Antichrist.

In chapter 13, we saw how the dragon gave the beast his power. The kingdom of the Antichrist and the work of the False prophet are driven by Satanic power whose source is the dragon, Satan, the enemy of souls, who rises from the pit.

They are each filled with blasphemy against the name of God, against the name of his Son, Jesus, and against his flock. They each open their mouths with blasphemy against the throne of heaven: "And they worshipped the dragon which gave power unto the beast: and they worshipped the beast, saying, Who is like unto the beast? who is able to make war with him? And there was given unto him a mouth speaking great things and blasphemies; and power was given unto him to continue forty and two months. And he opened his mouth in blasphemy against God, to blaspheme his name, and his tabernacle, and them that dwell in heaven" (Revelation 13:4-6).

- Having seven heads and ten horns. This description matches with what we have covered earlier: "And behold a great red dragon, having seven heads and ten horns, and seven crowns upon his heads" (Revelation 12:3). This confirms that the scarlet beast mentioned in this verse is the kingdom of the Antichrist. The seven horns are seven powers or seven lines of Roman lineage, seven lines from Roman history which are difficult to determine exactly. But the seventh power will take the form of an alliance of ten kings, or ten powers. Some of these powers will be strong and others will be weak. These two types of powers are represented in Daniel by iron and clay: "And as the toes of the feet were part of iron, and part of clay, so the kingdom shall be partly strong, and partly broken" (Daniel 2:42). This alliance of these ten powers under the banner of the Antichrist will constitute the revived Roman empire, which will be in place at the return of the Lord Jesus to earth: "And in the days of these kings shall the God of heaven set up a kingdom, which shall never be destroyed" (Daniel 2:44).

Today, the European Union is made up of some nations and others that are not as powerful: "And whereas thou sawest iron mixed with miry clay, they shall mingle themselves with the seed of men: but they shall not cleave one to another, even as iron is not mixed with clay" (Daniel 2:43). Immigration to Europe has brought many poor people into European society who do not integrate into it. They hold strong to their false religions that do not recognize the Lord Jesus Christ as the son of the living God.

(4) "And the woman was arrayed in purple and scarlet colour, and decked with gold and precious stones and pearls, having a golden cup in her hand full of abominations and filthiness of her fornication:"

This clear description of the papacy of Rome exposes the true nature of the Vatican see. It is bright in its colours, and its external decorations are pleasing to the eye. But inwardly, it is filled with filthy doctrines and immersed in the sordidness of lustful, sexual practices, having departed adulterously form the Lord Jesus. On the outside, gold, diamonds, and precious stones; on the inside, abominations, impurity, and adultery away from Jesus.

(5) "And upon her forehead was a name written, MYSTERY, BABYLON THE GREAT, THE MOTHER OF HARLOTS AND ABOMINATIONS OF THE EARTH."

The shame of its adultery is explicitly visible on its forehead. But yet its true nature remains a mystery hidden from the eyes of men, who follow it and who do not desire to see the truth. Adultery robs the heart: "Whoredom and wine and new wine take away the heart" (Hosea 4:11). The description in this verse matches the reality of historical Babylon for before it disappeared from the annals of history, Babylon had a shocking, appalling religious role, filled with adultery, fornication, promiscuity, and sexual and moral degeneracy.

(6) "And I saw the woman drunken with the blood of the saints, and with the blood of the martyrs of Jesus: and when I saw her, I wondered with great admiration."

Rome or religious Babylon, will shed the blood of Christians far more than any other city on the face of the earth throughout history. Thus, it will be drunk with the blood of the saints.

Rome has killed Christians in numbers which cannot be reckoned in the first, second, and third centuries A.D. The middle ages were famous for being called the dark ages because in them Rome shed spiritual darkness and killed fifty million Christians. It slaughtered believers in the Lord Jesus and the Bible because they would not accept the baptism of infants, the intercession of Mary and the saints, and transubstantiation (the miraculous transformation of bread and grape juice into the actual body and real blood of the Lord Jesus Christ). The Bible teaches that communion is symbolic, not literal, with respect to the body and blood of Christ: "He that eateth my flesh, and drinketh my blood, dwelleth in me, and I in him … It is the spirit that quickeneth; the flesh profiteth nothing: the words that I speak unto you, they are spirit, and they are life" (John

6:56, 63). The Lord forbids the drinking of blood completely: "No soul of you shall eat blood, neither shall any stranger that sojourneth among you eat blood ... for the life of all flesh is the blood thereof: whosoever eateth it shall be cut off" (Leviticus 17:12, 14); "That ye abstain from meats offered to idols, and from blood" (Acts 15:29).

The evils of Roman Emperors and Vatican Popes will result in an intoxicated Rome having drunk deeply and plentifully of the blood of its victims, the martyr Christians who believe in the Lord Jesus and the Bible.

Today, heads of states seek the pope's face and the Vatican's favor. Rome controls the minds of unthinking men, whose preoccupation is spiritual adultery.

And the worst part is that millions and millions of people are lost and on their way to eternal destruction because they cling to traditional churches which teach everything and anything except the teachings of the Bible. They reject salvation through the blood of Jesus Christ, who says of them: "Let them alone: they be blind leaders of the blind. And if the blind lead the blind, both shall fall into the ditch ... Woe unto you, scribes and Pharisees, hypocrites! for ye are like unto whited sepulchres, which indeed appear beautiful outward, but are within full of dead men's bones, and of all uncleanness. Even so ye also outwardly appear righteous unto men, but within ye are full of hypocrisy and iniquity. Woe unto you, scribes and Pharisees, hypocrites! because ye build the tombs of the prophets, and garnish the sepulchres of the righteous, And say, If we had been in the days of our fathers, we would not have been partakers with them in the blood of the prophets. Wherefore ye be witnesses unto yourselves, that ye are the children of them which killed the prophets. Fill ye up then the measure of your fathers. Ye serpents, ye generation of vipers, how can ye escape the damnation of hell?" (Matthew 15:14; 23:27-33).

After the rapture of the true church which consists of all

those who believe and practice the gospel, then nominal and traditional Christianity, headed by the Vatican, will go even farther in their spiritual idolatry. It will plunge even deeper into new, fearful harlotries, following the Antichrist and the False prophet, who together will unite the religions of the world in a worship of the Antichrist: "And he had power to give life unto the image of the beast, that the image of the beast should both speak, and cause that as many as would not worship the image of the beast should be killed" (Revelation 13:15). Thus, the False prophet will fill the world with adulteries against the true Christ, persecuting all those who follow the Lord Jesus Christ.

(7) "And the angel said unto me, Wherefore didst thou marvel? I will tell thee the mystery of the woman, and of the beast that carrieth her, which hath the seven heads and ten horns."

John marveled at the greatness of this enigma, at the thought that the Vatican will support the Antichrist and ally itself with him and with his kingdom against the children of the Lord Jesus. John is taken aback by the greatness of the paradox of the Vatican's material wealth and by the degree of its spiritual depravity. John is also surprised by the scope of the authority of the apostolic see, historically and geographically. And so the angel volunteers to explain this mystery in that the woman in verse 18 is the False prophet. As for the mysterious heads and horns, they represent the kingdom of the Antichrist, as we shall see in verses 8- 12. In fact, the rest of this chapter is dedicated to explaining the identity of the woman and the beast.

(8) "The beast that thou sawest was, and is not; and shall ascend out of the bottomless pit, and go into perdition: and they that dwell on the earth shall wonder, whose names were not written in the book of life from the foundation of the world, when they behold the beast that was, and is not, and yet is."

The word "beast" refers to both a king and a kingdom at the same time:

(i) Firstly, it refers to a kingdom, to the revived Roman empire as described in Daniel: "After this I saw in the night visions, and behold a fourth beast, dreadful and terrible, and strong exceedingly; and it had great iron teeth: it devoured and brake in pieces, and stamped the residue with the feet of it: and it was diverse from all the beasts that were before it; and it had ten horns" (Daniel 7:7).

(ii) Secondly, it refers to a person: "I beheld then because of the voice of the great words which the horn spake: I beheld even till the beast was slain, and his body destroyed, and given to the burning flame" (Daniel 7:11).

Rome as an empire faded away at the end of the fifth century A.D.. For hundreds of years thereafter, Rome remained a powerful state but continued in declining strength until the end of the sixth century when it became an average power.

In recent times, Rome has experienced a revival, beginning with the Treaty of Rome, signed on March 25, 1957, with the founding of the European Common Market.

On March 6, 2014, the newly elected prime minister of Italy, announced in his inaugural speech that he wanted to make Rome once again the leading world power. This attitude is woven into the mindset of the Roman people today.

After the rapture of the church, the old Roman empire will be revived during the tribulation by the power of Satan, the fallen angel of the fifth trumpet: "And the fifth angel sounded, and I saw a star fall from heaven unto the earth: and to him was given the key of the bottomless pit. And he opened the bottomless pit; and there arose a smoke out of the pit, as the smoke of a great furnace; and the sun and the air were darkened by reason of the smoke of the pit. And there came out of the smoke locusts upon the earth: and unto them was given power, as the scorpions of the earth have power" (Revelation 9:1-3). He is described by the Bible as the destroyer. "And they had a king over them, which is the angel of the bottomless pit, whose name in the Hebrew tongue is Abaddon, but in the Greek tongue hath his name Apollyon" (Revelation 9:11).

The source of this kingdom is the pit, and its destiny is destruction.

This revival will be astounding to the human race, but only to those who do not known the Lord Jesus as Master of their lives and minds.

(9) "And here is the mind which hath wisdom. The seven heads are seven mountains, on which the woman sitteth."

- And here is the mind which hath wisdom - The seven heads are seven mountains. Although the city of Rome is built on seven hills, we should understand from verses one through six that heavenly wisdom is needed to discern the identity of the seven heads and the seven mountains. The seven heads are seven kings, and the seven mountains are the kingdoms of the seven kings, as we explained in considering the previous verse.

- On which the woman sitteth - The False prophet will derive his support from the kingdom of the Antichrist, which, at the same time, he will control. The authority which he will exercise will be filled with corruption and spiritual and moral degeneracy. The woman is religious Babylon, and the beast is political Babylon.

(10) "And there are seven kings: five are fallen, and one is, and the other is not yet come; and when he cometh, he must continue a short space."

These seven kings are seven kingdoms in history which had an impact both on the nations and on Israel:

(i) The first kingdom was Babylon, inasmuch as the concept of an elect, believing seed, chosen from the human race, began to appear when the Lord confused the languages of the world.

(ii) The second kingdom was Assyria, which took the ten tribes captive to Nineveh, Halah, and Habor, by the river of Gozan.

(iii) The third was the Chaldean kingdom, which took the two remaining tribes captive to Babylon.

(iv) The fourth was the kingdom of the Medes and Persians.

(v) The fifth kingdom was Greece.

(vi) When John received this vision, the time of five of these kings had past. They had already disappeared; they had already vanished. The king of the time was the Caesar of Rome.

(vii) The seventh kingdom will be the new Roman empire, revived in the form of an eastern and western European Union, which are represented symbolically by the two legs of the statue of Daniel ("His legs of iron" (Daniel 2:33)) and by the statue's ten toes (Daniel 2:42). Out of this seventh kingdom will come the kingdom of the Antichrist, which will be the eight and final kingdom.

The concept of world unification was first conceived with Babylon: "And they said, Go to, let us build us a city and a tower, whose top may reach unto heaven; and let us make us a name, lest we be scattered abroad upon the face of the whole earth. And the Lord came down to see the city and the tower, which the children of men builded. And the Lord said, Behold, the people is one, and they have all one language" (Genesis 11:4-6).

The concept of world unification has been championed by great military leaders throughout history; it is the message of spiritual Babylon since the dawn of history. On this foundation, the fourth and final empire of the Times of the Gentiles will prosper, as it unifies all the governments of the world. For this reason, there has been much talk recently of world unity. For the same reason, there is much talk today of unifying Christian denominations and also of unifying the world religions; such efforts will lead ultimately to the worship of the Antichrist. The devil will: "cause that as many as would not worship the image of the beast should be killed" (Revelation 13:15). But thanks be to the triumphant Lord Jesus: "And the beast was taken, and with him the False prophet that wrought miracles before him, with which he deceived them that had received the mark of the beast, and them that worshipped his image. These both were cast alive into a lake of fire burning with brimstone" (Revelation 19:20).

The Antichrist's role will be satanic work to unify all men and to drive them to the devil and to hell. This is in contrast to the Lord's will who desires that every nation live within the borders that he has placed for her, hence avoiding spiritual corruption and providing the space needed to live for the Lord Jesus. This leads to a better life in Christ as we noted in our study of Revelation 14:8. From the beginning, the Lord separated the nations and established their borders so that they may worship him and experience his blessing: "When the Most High divided to the nations their inheritance, when he separated the sons of Adam, he set the bounds of the people" (Deuteronomy 32:8); "And hath determined the times before appointed, and the bounds of their habitation; That they should seek the Lord, if haply they might feel after him, and find him" (Acts 17:26-27). The Lord confused our communications to force us to disperse over the face of the earth; however, the world continually strives to unite and reach heaven in a fashion that is antagonistic to the Lord Jesus.

(11) "And the beast that was, and is not, even he is the eighth, and is of the seven, and goeth into perdition."

The beast, also known as the Antichrist, will be the eighth king. He will rule and reign over the seventh kingdom, empowered and controlled by the power of Satan: "Even him, whose coming is after the working of Satan with all power and signs and lying wonders, And with all deceivableness of unrighteousness in them that perish; because they received not the love of the truth, that they might be saved" (2 Thessalonians 2:9-10). Satan is present in the spirit of each of these seven kingdoms, from Babylon to the kingdom of the Antichrist, who is the eighth king and is of the seven and shares their spirit and their agenda.

(12) "And the ten horns which thou sawest are ten kings, which have received no kingdom as yet; but receive power as kings one hour with the beast."

- And the ten horns which thou sawest are ten kings, which have received no kingdom as yet - In the last days, the Roman empire will be revived. Geographically, it will hold sway over both eastern and western Europe (represented by the statue's two legs). Politically, this empire will include ten alliances, heads, or kingdoms (represented by the ten toes). The extent of its dominion will be similar to that of the old Roman empire that existed in the days of Christ ministry on this earth. The preeminent power on earth after the rapture of the church will not be China or Russia, it will be the European Union.

- But receive power as kings one hour with the beast. These ten alliances, powers, or nations are headed by ten kings, who govern in the shadow of one authority, namely the Antichrist. The Antichrist will appear as the head of a new coalition of these ten European alliances: "And of the ten horns that were in his head, and of the other which came up, and before whom three fell" (Daniel 7:20). All these developments are beginning to be apparent on the world's stage today and will reach their zenith under the Antichrist during the great tribulation. We now see a European Union which includes both east and west. We see an alliance of European Union nations which have elected a president of the European Union. This is the seat of the Antichrist. This position was created on January 19, 2009. Its first occupant was Herman Van Rompuy, a former Belgian minister of finance and of the national budget. What an amazing coincidence that the first person to fill this position believed in raising taxes. Daniel describes the Antichrist as a gatherer of taxes: "Then shall stand up in his estate a raiser of taxes in the glory of the kingdom" (Daniel 11:20). All these things have begun to unfold one the world's stage today! We are at the doorstep of the end of this Christ-rejecting world. The King of kings shall soon return to slay the wicked, destroy their kingdoms, and establish his kingdom which will last forever and ever.

(13) "These have one mind, and shall give their power and strength unto the beast."

The leaders and the rulers of the European Union will govern as subordinates of the Antichrist. They will be under his authority.

(14) "These shall make war with the Lamb, and the Lamb shall overcome them: for he is Lord of lords, and King of kings: and they that are with him are called, and chosen, and faithful."

All these rulers, along with the Antichrist, will be controlled by Satan. They will be of one mind and give their authority to the devil, who controls them completely. Satan's mind set is to oppose the Lord Jesus the Saviour of the world. The whole world will war against the Lord Jesus, the Holy Son of God, because them of their sins. The kingdoms of the world will fight against the Lamb, but he will overcome them, for he is King of kings and Lord of lords!

(15) "And he saith unto me, The waters which thou sawest, where the whore sitteth, are peoples, and multitudes, and nations, and tongues."

After explaining the identity of the seven heads and the ten horns, the angel goes on to explain the identity of the harlot, which represents Vatican Rome, as we understand from the verses 1-6 and verse 18. This verse explains the domain of the woman's influence on the minds of all the rulers and nations of the world.

(16) "And the ten horns which thou sawest upon the beast, these shall hate the whore, and shall make her desolate and naked, and shall eat her flesh, and burn her with fire."

As we said earlier, the dominance of the Roman Catholic

church will again become very strong after the rapture of the true church of Christ. But this time, the church's tyranny will not be long lived because as soon as the Antichrist, the heir of Satan and his representative on the earth, will consolidate his power on the world scene, he will do away with the authority and the prerogatives of the False prophet. The ten powers who will be serving the Antichrist will turn on the False prophet, the pope of Rome and his Vatican, also known as religious Babylon, the mother of the spiritual harlotries and the enemy of the Lord Jesus.

The Bible does not tell us why the Antichrist will turn on the False prophet. For some reason, he will hate the harlot, destroy her, and strip her of her ornaments (verse 4) and power. He will take away all her privileges and make her fate like that of Jezebel: "Wherefore they came again, and told him. And he said, This is the word of the LORD, which he spake by his servant Elijah the Tishbite, saying, In the portion of Jezreel shall dogs eat the flesh of Jezebel: And the carcase of Jezebel shall be as dung upon the face of the field in the portion of Jezreel; so that they shall not say, This is Jezebel" (2 Kings 9:36-37). The fact that she will be burned with fire is an example of just punishment; since she burned with fire the servants of the Lord Jesus, the true Christians of the second and third centuries and throughout the dark ages. We see here a complete, comprehensive, and eternal annihilation of all the darkness of Rome, the spiritual Babylon.

It is appropriate here to quote a prophecy from Jeremiah which addresses the same subject which we are speaking of: "And when thou art spoiled, what wilt thou do? Though thou clothest thyself with crimson, though thou deckest thee with ornaments of gold, though thou rentest thy face with painting, in vain shalt thou make thyself fair; thy lovers will despise thee, they will seek thy life" (Jeremiah 4:30).

Note that, although the False prophet will be stripped of his prerogatives and his privileges, he will nevertheless remain an instrument in the hand of the Antichrist until the day when the Lord brings judgment on the two of them together: "And the beast was taken, and with him the False prophet that wrought miracles before him, with which he deceived them that had received the mark of the beast, and them that worshipped his image. These both were cast alive into a lake of fire burning with brimstone" (Revelation 19:20).

(17) "For God hath put in their hearts to fulfil his will, and to agree, and give their kingdom unto the beast, until the words of God shall be fulfilled."

The Lord Jesus is sovereign in the universe and in the kingdom of men, whether they be good or evil. The Lord Jesus is the one who governs all things including all the events of the book of Revelation. He does that even starting with the first rise to prominence of the Antichrist at the beginning of the tribulation: "And I saw, and behold a white horse: and he that sat on him had a bow; and a crown was given unto him: and he went forth conquering, and to conquer" (Revelation 6:2); continuing through in forty-two months: "And there was given unto him a mouth speaking great things and blasphemies; and power was given unto him to continue forty and two months" (Revelation 13:5), and finally culminating with his destruction in the lake of fire and brimstone: "And the beast was taken, and with him the False prophet that wrought miracles before him, with which he deceived them that had received the mark of the beast, and them that worshipped his image. These both were cast alive into a lake of fire burning with brimstone" (Revelation 19:20).

The goal of the Lord Jesus will be to bring about divine righteousness and justice: "For true and righteous are his judgments: for he hath judged the great whore, which did corrupt the earth with her fornication, and hath avenged the blood of his servants at her hand" (Revelation 19:2).

As we explained above, these ten horns are kings, powers, or

European alliances which are subordinate to the Antichrist's political and military leadership. They will be subservient to him and will agree with his decision to eliminate the False prophet so that the Antichrist would be the sole leader. This will be by God's disposing. The consolidation of authority in the Antichrist's hands will allow Satan to strengthen his powerful grip on this world. This deepest hour of spiritual darkness in the history of the human race will come before the break of the dawn of the Lord Jesus: "the bright and morning star" (Revelation 22:16).

(18) "And the woman which thou sawest is that great city, which reigneth over the kings of the earth."

Again this is the same city which for long periods of time, held sway over the minds of the world's rulers and interfered in their affairs, both internal and external. It is the papacy of Rome, the spiritual Babylon, the mother of all adulterous departures from the worship of the Lord Jesus, the Lord of glory, blessed is his name: "Babylon is fallen, is fallen, that great city, because she made all nations drink of the wine of the wrath of her fornication... And the kings of the earth, who have committed fornication and lived deliciously with her, shall bewail her, and lament for her... Alas, alas that great city, that was clothed in fine linen, and purple, and scarlet, and decked with gold, and precious stones, and pearls! ...Rejoice over her, thou heaven, and ye holy apostles and prophets; for God hath avenged you on her. And a mighty angel took up a stone like a great millstone, and cast it into the sea, saying, Thus with violence shall that great city Babylon be thrown down, and shall be found no more at all ... for by thy sorceries were all nations deceived. And in her was found the blood of prophets, and of saints, and of all that were slain upon the earth" (Revelation 14:8; 18:9, 16, 20-21, 23-24).

This is the spiritual Babylon whose curse first starts spreads out in the last days out of Shinar, Iran today, onto the face of the whole earth: "And, behold, there was lifted up a talent of lead: and this is a woman that sitteth in the midst of the ephah. And he said, This is wickedness. And he cast it into the midst of the ephah; and he cast the weight of lead upon the mouth thereof. Then lifted I up mine eyes, and looked, and, behold, there came out two women, and the wind was in their wings; for they had wings like the wings of a stork: and they lifted up the ephah between the earth and the heaven. Then said I to the angel that talked with me, Whither do these bear the ephah? And he said unto me, To build it an house in the land of Shinar: and it shall be established, and set there upon her own base" (Zechariah 5:7-11). In our present day the curse of terrorism started with Iran and has plagued the whole world today.

Babylon, the city of man, is first mentioned in the book of Genesis: "And Cush begat Nimrod: he began to be a mighty one in the earth. He was a mighty hunter before the LORD: wherefore it is said, Even as Nimrod the mighty hunter before the LORD. And the beginning of his kingdom was Babel, and Erech, and Accad, and Calneh, in the land of Shinar" (Genesis 10:8-10); "And the LORD said, Behold, the people is one, and they have all one language; and this they begin to do: and now nothing will be restrained from them, which they have imagined to do. Go to, let us go down, and there confound their language, that they may not understand one another's speech. So the LORD scattered them abroad from thence upon the face of all the earth: and they left off to build the city. Therefore is the name of it called Babel; because the LORD did there confound the language of all the earth: and from thence did the LORD scatter them abroad upon the face of all the earth" (Genesis 11:6-9). Babylon will be once and forever annihilated in the book of Revelation, to be replaced by the city of God, the new Jerusalem, which will come down from heaven and which will be the abode of all the righteous forever.

Notice some beautiful contrasts between the city of man and the city of God:

(i) City of Man: Babylon
City of God: New Jerusalem
(ii) City of Man: Great city (Revelation 17:1)
City of God: Great city (Revelation 21:10)
(iii) City of Man: Built by Man (Genesis 10:10; 11:4)
City of God: Built by God (Revelation 21:2,10)
(iv) City of Man: Seated in the wilderness (Revelation 17:3)
City of God: Sits on a high mountain (Revelation 21:10)
(v) City of Man: Pointed to by an angel (Revelation 17:1)
City of God: Pointed to by an angel (Revelation 21:9)
(vi) City of Man: Defiled (Revelation 17:4)
City of God: Holy (Revelation 21:2)
(vii) City of Man: Harlot (Ezekiel 16:35)
City of God: Virgin (Revelation 21:2,9)
(viii) City of Man: Decorated with precious stones (Revelation 17:4)
City of God: Decorated with precious stones (Revelation 21:18-20)
(ix) City of Man: Decorated with pearls (Revelation 17:4)
City of God: Decorated with pearls (Revelation 21:21)
(x) City of Man: Clothed with purple and scarlet (Revelation 18:16)
City of God: Clothed with light (Revelation 21:11, 23-24)
(xi) City of Man: Filled with the blood of the saints (Revelation 17:6; 18:24)

City of God: Filled with the saints (Revelation 21:24, 27)

(xii) City of Man: Filled with demons (Revelation 18:2)
City of God: Filled with the redeemed (Revelation 21:24)

(xiii) City of Man: Founded on names of blasphemy (Revelation 17:3)
City of God: Founded on the names of the Lamb's apostles (Revelation 21:14)

(xiv) City of Man: Filled with abominations and filthiness (Revelation 17:4)
City of God: Not entered by any abomination (Revelation 21:27)

(xv) City of Man: Commits fornication with kings (Revelation 17:2; 18:3)
City of God: Has the glory of the Kings of kings (Revelation 21:10-11)

(xvi) City of Man: Deserted forever (Revelation 18:21)
City of God: Inhabited vibrant forever (Revelation 22:5)

18

THE DESTRUCTION OF ECONOMIC BABYLON – THE DESTRUCTION OF THE ECONOMY OF

(1) "And after these things I saw another angel come down from heaven, having great power; and the earth was lightened with his glory."

This angel is different than the one we saw in chapter 17 who was: "one of the seven angels which had the seven vials" (Revelation 17:1). This angel is great might, and is resplendent in brilliant light and acts with great authority and strength given to him by the Lord Jesus.

(2) "And he cried mightily with a strong voice, saying, Babylon the great is fallen, is fallen, and is become the habitation of devils, and the hold of every foul spirit, and a cage of every unclean and hateful bird."

Europe's economic greatness is now collapsed and scattered and gone. The worldwide influence of the European Common Market is now destroyed. Its goal was to control the economy of the world, instigated by the satanic motive of the love of money. The person who sets his eyes on money loses his joy and suffers the pain of abhorrent evil influences of evil spirits: "For the love of money is the root of all evil: which while some coveted after, they have erred from the faith, and pierced themselves through with many sorrows" (1 Timothy 6:10).

(3) "For all nations have drunk of the wine of the wrath of her fornication, and the kings of the earth have committed fornication with her, and the merchants of the earth are waxed rich through the abundance of her delicacies."

All people and nations will deviate from the Lord God because of their adulterous pursuit after money. The love of money blinds the eyes, makes the wise man foolish, and makes the straight crooked: "And thou shalt take no gift: for the gift blindeth the wise, and perverteth the words of the righteous" (Exodus 23:8); "A gift doth blind the eyes of the wise, and pervert the words of the righteous" (Deuteronomy 16:19). All these kings and leaders will care for is money; and they shall lose their minds as though they are drunk in their mad run after money; all instead of loving the Lord Jesus, who teaches us that: "No man can serve two masters: for either he will hate the one, and love the other; or else he will hold to the one, and despise the other. Ye cannot serve God and mammon" (Matthew 6:24).

These kings and leaders will choose to pursue money and wealth and social status and fleshly enjoyment, after the vanities of life, and hate the Lord Jesus. They are going to hate Christ and will not care for their own souls to seek after Christ, so they are going to lose all: "For what shall it profit a man, if he shall gain the whole world, and lose his own soul?" (Mark 8:36).

(4) "And I heard another voice from heaven, saying, Come out of her, my people, that ye be not partakers of her sins, and that ye receive not of her plagues."

The Lord reminds his people who are alive upon the earth during the great tribulation not to run after material gain, but rather to maintain their separation and consecration. This call reminds us of Lot's call, and teaches us to heed it of it: "And the men said unto Lot, Hast thou here any besides? son in law, and thy sons, and thy daughters, and whatsoever thou hast in the city, bring them out of this place: For we will destroy this place, because the cry of them is waxen great before the face of the Lord; and the Lord hath sent us to destroy it. And Lot went out, and spake unto his sons in law, which married his daughters, and said, Up, get you out of this place; for the Lord will destroy this city. But he seemed as one that mocked unto his sons in law" (Genesis 19:12-14).

(5) "For her sins have reached unto heaven, and God hath remembered her iniquities."

Be it religious, or economic, or military, or political Babylon, God's cup of wrath will be then overflown because of the city's continual rebellion against the Lord Jesus. Its sins will reach their peak rising up to heaven. The Lord's cup of judgment is spilling over, and so the time of reckoning is come. Here he will expose publicly her sins and reveal the record of all her sins, past and present.

(6) "Reward her even as she rewarded you, and double unto her double according to her works: in the cup which she hath filled fill to her double."

Babylon has always been evil towards believers, desiring to bring harm and damage their way, whether spiritually or socially or in any other manner. Now and then the time will come for its punishment. God's children should not be sorry over Babylon when they see the Lord judging her and smiting her double for all that it will have done. All shall see then the strength of the Lord and of the heaviness of the retribution he visits upon her.

(7) "How much she hath glorified herself, and lived deliciously, so much torment and sorrow give her: for she saith in her heart, I sit a queen, and am no widow, and shall see no sorrow."

The conceit and arrogance and pride of Europe economically will necessitate the Lord's judgment. Its heart will be smitten with blindness; it will not see or know the fear of the

Lord, neither be aware of the fearful condition into which she will fall.

(8) "Therefore shall her plagues come in one day, death, and mourning, and famine; and she shall be utterly burned with fire: for strong is the Lord God who judgeth her."

That is why Babylon will deserve the full punishment that the Lord God, the just and mighty Judge sentences her with, be it woes, famine, sadness, death, and eternal hell fire.

(9) "And the kings of the earth, who have committed fornication and lived deliciously with her, shall bewail her, and lament for her, when they shall see the smoke of her burning,"

Who will mourn Babylon? Who will pity it and cry over it? Only the wicked who will have partaken in its sins and descended to the depths of spiritual harlotry with her. Wicked kings and rulers cry, for their time has come as well. They shall receive the same punishment as Babylon. They shall suffer the same fate.

(10) "Standing afar off for the fear of her torment, saying, Alas, alas, that great city Babylon, that mighty city! for in one hour is thy judgment come."

The whole world will cry at the fall of the European economic empire, the kingdom of the Antichrist, whose demise will come in a single moment. All this greatness will pass away and be annihilated forever. What will be the portion of all those who will have had dealings with Babylon and benefited from it?

(11) "And the merchants of the earth shall weep and mourn over her; for no man buyeth their merchandise any more:"

They will weep and wail and mourn, not over Babylon's wickedness that will have come to an end, but rather over their inability to benefit from her anymore. Their hearts will be so much filled with spiritual blindness because of their love for money. Instead of repenting and turning to the Redeemer of souls, the Lord Jesus Christ, we see they will search new markets for their wares. Their judgement will soon follow and their end will in the fire of hell forever, Amen.

(12) "The merchandise of gold, and silver, and precious stones, and of pearls, and fine linen, and purple, and silk, and scarlet, and all thyine wood, and all manner vessels of ivory, and all manner vessels of most precious wood, and of brass, and iron, and marble,"

The benefits which Babylon will provide to the world will be material and earthly riches and prideful, bodily lust, devoid of the spirit of the Lord Jesus: "For all that is in the world, the lust of the flesh, and the lust of the eyes, and the pride of life, is not of the Father, but is of the world. And the world passeth away, and the lust thereof: but he that doeth the will of God abideth for ever. Little children, it is the last time: and as ye have heard that antichrist shall come, even now are there many antichrists; whereby we know that it is the last time" (1 John 2:16-18).

(13) "And cinnamon, and odours, and ointments, and frankincense, and wine, and oil, and fine flour, and wheat, and beasts, and sheep, and horses, and chariots, and slaves, and souls of men."

Europe is rich in perfumes. It has many companies which specialize in fashionable clothing, fine cuisine, and refined drinks. It exploits poor countries and enslaves their people to live in the shadow of fearful spiritual coldness. Europe today is a spiritual iceberg. It knows no fear of God, having rejected all its historical Christian values.

(14) "And the fruits that thy soul lusted after are departed from thee, and all things which were dainty and goodly are departed from thee, and thou shalt find them no more at all."

But the time has come for the Lord's punishment, and she has lost all things. She will then receive the penalty of her life of lust and love of money and of the world. All that will remain for her is God's eternal punishment.

(15) "The merchants of these things, which were made rich

by her, shall stand afar off for the fear of her torment, weeping and wailing,"

All its partner nations who benefited from trade with it and enjoyed associating with it, have now forsaken it. They stand afar, out of fear for their own interests and out of know the fact that her punishment is soon coming upon them as well.

(16) "And saying, Alas, alas, that great city, that was clothed in fine linen, and purple, and scarlet, and decked with gold, and precious stones, and pearls!"

Babylon, the kingdom of the Antichrist, the revived Roman Empire, the fourth kingdom in the Times of the Gentiles, will be the tinkling beauty and the richest of all nations on earth, noted for its fine clothes, high standards of living, refinement, societal progress, advanced civilization, and material wealth; but destitute of the fear of God. All the large sums of capital in the world today are deposited in European banks, especially in Britain and Switzerland.

(17) "For in one hour so great riches is come to nought. And every shipmaster, and all the company in ships, and sailors, and as many as trade by sea, stood afar off,"

For all these sins God's wrath will come upon Babylon, In one moment, it will be judged with a persecution: "and none hindereth" (Isaiah 14:6). The persecution will extend to all those who deal with it and trade with it. Its richness will pass away, and all her partners will flee away from her.

(18) "And cried when they saw the smoke of her burning, saying, What city is like unto this great city!"

This is a cry of pain over their own souls, for they shall lose what they shall think is an opportunity to profit. They shall suffer a double loss, a material, and a spiritual loss. They shall find out that the time is come for them to reap what they have sown, and soon will they be judged by God. They will sow for the flesh, and so will reap eternal destruction: "For he that soweth to his flesh shall of the flesh reap corruption; but he that soweth to the Spirit shall of the Spirit reap life everlasting" (Galatians 6:8).

(19) "And they cast dust on their heads, and cried, weeping and wailing, saying, Alas, alas, that great city, wherein were made rich all that had ships in the sea by reason of her costliness! for in one hour is she made desolate."

Kings and leaders and seasoned traders will be brought low by the Lord. God's punishment is great because he will destroy all that adulterously departed from Jesus. They will mourn over themselves and over their trade, which will end with shocking and devastating losses, in spite of the greatness of Babylon and the size of its commercial fleet.

(20) "Rejoice over her, thou heaven, and ye holy apostles and prophets; for God hath avenged you on her."

Heaven will rejoice at the casting out of Satan from the heaven to earth: "And the great dragon was cast out, that old serpent, called the Devil, and Satan, which deceiveth the whole world: he was cast out into the earth, and his angels were cast out with him ... And they overcame him by the blood of the Lamb, and by the word of their testimony; and they loved not their lives unto the death. Therefore rejoice, ye heavens, and ye that dwell in them. Woe to the inhabiters of the earth and of the sea! for the devil is come down unto you, having great wrath, because he knoweth that he hath but a short time" (Revelation 12:9, 11-12). In like manner, heaven will rejoice at the fall of the city of Babylon: "Therefore, behold, the days come, that I will do judgment upon the graven images of Babylon: and her whole land shall be confounded, and all her slain shall fall in the midst of her. Then the heaven and the earth, and all that is therein, shall sing for Babylon" (Jeremiah 51:47-48).

The righteous will rejoice when they see that the Lord Jesus has judged Babylon, as they ask him to: "And when he had opened the fifth seal, I saw under the altar the souls of them that were slain for the word of God, and for the testimony which they held: And they cried with a loud voice, saying, How long, O Lord, holy and true, dost thou not judge and avenge our blood on them that dwell on the earth?" (Revelation 6:9-10).

The beginning of chapter 19 is filled with praises in heaven on the occasion of the fall of Babylon (Revelation 19:1-5).

(21) "And a mighty angel took up a stone like a great millstone, and cast it into the sea, saying, Thus with violence shall that great city Babylon be thrown down, and shall be found no more at all."

This will occur as Jeremiah also prophesied: "And Jeremiah said to Seraiah, When thou comest to Babylon, and shalt see, and shalt read all these words; Then shalt thou say, O LORD, thou hast spoken against this place, to cut it off, that none shall remain in it, neither man nor beast, but that it shall be desolate for ever. And it shall be, when thou hast made an end of reading this book, that thou shalt bind a stone to it, and cast it into the midst of Euphrates: And thou shalt say, Thus shall Babylon sink, and shall not rise from the evil that I will bring upon her: and they shall be weary. Thus far are the words of Jeremiah" (Jeremiah 51:61-64). Economic Europe, the kingdom of the Antichrist, will be annihilated forever.

(22) "And the voice of harpers, and musicians, and of pipers, and trumpeters, shall be heard no more at all in thee; and no craftsman, of whatsoever craft he be, shall be found any more in thee; and the sound of a millstone shall be heard no more at all in thee;"

Various forms of social leisure, characterized by music and enjoyment, will pass away. Craftsmen and other professional workers, the so called pillars of society, will be no more, as prophesied by Isaiah: "Therefore hath the curse devoured the earth, and they that dwell therein are desolate: therefore the inhabitants of the earth are burned, and few men left. The new wine mourneth, the vine languisheth, all the merryhearted do sigh. The mirth of tabrets ceaseth, the noise of them that rejoice endeth, the joy of the harp ceaseth" (Isaiah 24:6-8).

(23) "And the light of a candle shall shine no more at all in thee; and the voice of the bridegroom and of the bride shall be heard no more at all in thee: for thy merchants were the great men of the earth; for by thy sorceries were all nations deceived."

All those who will have adulterously deviated from the Lord Jesus will have nothing but eternal darkness as their portion: "They shall never see light" (Psalm 49:19). Every man who leaves this world without having repented and asked forgiveness from the Lord Jesus will see neither light of sun nor any other illumination forever and ever. This is why you should not turn to the riches of the world; rather, you should come to the Lord Jesus and receive forgiveness of sins, eternal life, and everlasting light with him in heaven: "And they that be wise shall shine as the brightness of the firmament; and they that turn many to righteousness as the stars for ever and ever" (Daniel 12:3). For: "Eye hath not seen, nor ear heard, neither have entered into the heart of man, the things which God hath prepared for them that love him" (1 Corinthians 2:9).

(24) "And in her was found the blood of prophets, and of saints, and of all that were slain upon the earth."

Babylon's plan is to plunge into trade and into the exploitation of men, driven by the love of money and the desire to accumulate it. Driven by that lust, Babylon's plan will be to kill God's children who do not share this wicked mind-set with her; she who seeks to draw people away from the love of the Lord Jesus. The Lord Jesus deserves all our worship, and bowing before him in reverence and adoration is for our own good.

The Lord's goal is to punish traditional Christianity because its purpose springs from Satan, who hates the salvation of souls. Be alert of your own destiny, for: "If thou be wise, thou shalt be wise for thyself: but if thou scornest, thou alone shalt bear it" (Proverbs 9:12).

19

RETURN OF THE KING OF KINGS TO EARTH – CALL TO THE MARRIAGE SUPPER OF THE

(1) "And after these things I heard a great voice of much people in heaven, saying, Alleluia; Salvation, and glory, and honour, and power, unto the Lord our God:"

After the destruction of economic, or commercial Babylon, John hears a sound of celebration coming from heaven. It is the celebration of the saints on high, acclaiming the destruction of every facet of the kingdom of the Antichrist: (i) political, (ii) military, (iii) religious, and now (iv) commercial. She will fall and be wiped out from existence: "Thou sawest till that a stone was cut out without hands, which smote the image upon his feet that were of iron and clay, and brake them to pieces. Then was the iron, the clay, the brass, the silver, and the gold, broken to pieces together, and became like the chaff of the summer threshingfloors; and the wind carried them away, that no place was found for them" (Daniel 2:34-35).

Now the Lord Jesus will return from heaven to carry out his sentence on this kingdom. He will arrest of the Antichrist and the False prophet, crush their kingdom, and cast them both in the eternal fires of hell, prepared for Satan and his associates. Then, the Lord Jesus will establish his kingdom in fulfilment of

Daniel's prophesy: "And the stone that smote the image became a great mountain, and filled the whole earth" (Daniel 2:35).

Therefore all thanks, glory, honour, and praise be to the Lord Jesus Christ, the all powerful – omnipotent God. It was comforting to us to read at the end of the last chapter: "Rejoice over her, thou heaven, and ye holy apostles and prophets; for God hath avenged you on her" (Revelation 18:20).

And now in this verse, it is also comforting to us to read the desired response: "And after these things I heard a great voice of much people in heaven, saying, Alleluia; Salvation, and glory, and honour, and power, unto the Lord our God" (Revelation 19:1).

It is refreshing for us to note that here we see a bridge which connects Revelation chapter 4, where heaven opens up and the church is lifted up thereto, and here Revelation chapter 19, where heaven opens again for the church to descend with the Lord Jesus. The church is not mentioned from Revelation chapter 5 to Revelation chapter 18. During the period covered by these chapters, the church is not present on the earth. Here in chapter 19, the book of Revelation suddenly returns to mentioning the church, which will have been raptured 7 years previously.

(2) "For true and righteous are his judgments: for he hath judged the great whore, which did corrupt the earth with her fornication, and hath avenged the blood of his servants at her hand."

The Lord Jesus is the just Judge who recompenses each wicked man according to his wickedness: "God judgeth the righteous, and God is angry with the wicked every day" (Psalms 7:11). To the one who shed the blood of saints, he gave blood to drink. To the one who sold the Lord in pursuit of commercial gain and worldly prosperity, he gave everlasting destruction and eternal fire.

(3) "And again they said, Alleluia. And her smoke rose up for ever and ever."

Why do the saints say "Alleluia" again? The first "Alleluia" expresses gratitude for their salvation. The second "Alleluia" is related to the fact that Babylon has received her punishment from the Lord. The saints confirm that its torment will indeed be eternal.

(4) "And the four and twenty elders and the four beasts fell down and worshipped God that sat on the throne, saying, Amen; Alleluia."

The pivotal characters who surround the throne of God and of the Lord Jesus are the cherubims and the twenty-four elders. They participate in this heavenly celebration.

(5) "And a voice came out of the throne, saying, Praise our God, all ye his servants, and ye that fear him, both small and great."

All who are in heaven, angels, archangels, and the redeemed of the human race who have passed on to glory, also participate in this praise.

(6) "And I heard as it were the voice of a great multitude, and as the voice of many waters, and as the voice of mighty thunderings, saying, Alleluia: for the Lord God omnipotent reigneth."

- And I heard as it were the voice of a great multitude, and as the voice of many waters, and as the voice of mighty thunderings - These are the voices of vast multitudes of people and the voices of many angels before the Divine Presence. They joyfully join together in acclamation of adoration that fills heaven because the Lord Jesus has judged Babylon, the kingdom of the Antichrist.

It is true that the heavens rejoice in the salvation of souls: "I say unto you, that likewise joy shall be in heaven over one sinner that repenteth, more than over ninety and nine just persons, which need no repentance" (Luke 15:7); but also heaven rejoices in the destruction of the enemy of our souls.

- Saying, Alleluia: for the Lord God omnipotent reigneth - Acclamation of praise is mentioned four times in the first few verses of this chapter:

(i) In verse 1, the righteous of the great tribulation will praise the Lord because they have received deliverance and salvation.

(ii) In verse 2, heaven shouts "Alleluia" for the Lord has avenged his children.

(iii) In verse 4, the twenty four elders join with the four cherubims in acclamation.

(iv) In verse 6, all of heaven, the angelic beings and the saints of the Old and New Testament, join in on this praise.

This acclamation of praise focuses on the fact that salvation is then complete. The kingdom of the Antichrist is crushed; and the true king, Jesus, is come to establish his kingdom founded on righteousness, justice, peace, and prosperity.

(7) "Let us be glad and rejoice, and give honour to him: for the marriage of the Lamb is come, and his wife hath made herself ready."

Now the tribulation is past and it is time for the joy of the Kingdom of Christ, which will be inaugurated by the marriage of Christ to his bride, the Church. The Lord Jesus Christ will reign, and his Church, the righteous of the New Testament who have believed and been baptized in the name of Jesus, will reign with him under his authority. The Church is composed of the saints of the New Testament and does not include the saints of the Old Testament, who are the guests of the wedding and the friends of the Bridegroom: "Verily I say unto you, Among them that are born of women there hath not risen a greater than John the Baptist: notwithstanding he that is least in the kingdom of heaven is greater than he" (Matthew 11:11); "He that hath the bride is the bridegroom: but the friend of the bridegroom, which standeth and heareth him, rejoiceth greatly because of the bridegroom's voice: this my joy therefore is fulfilled" (John 3:29). The church does include the saved of the tribulation, according to:; "It is a faithful saying: For if we be dead with him, we shall also live with him: If we suffer, we shall also reign with him" (2 Timothy 2:11-12); "And I saw thrones, and they sat upon them, and judgment was given unto them: and I saw the souls of them that were beheaded for the witness of Jesus, and for the word of God, and which had not worshipped the beast, neither his image, neither had received his mark upon their foreheads, or in their hands; and they lived and reigned with Christ a thousand years." (Revelation 20:4).

This is the church which will have:

(i) First raptured to heaven at the beginning of chapter four: "After this I looked, and, behold, a door was opened in heaven: and the first voice which I heard was as it were of a trumpet talking with me; which said, Come up hither, and I will shew thee things which must be hereafter. And immediately I was in the spirit: and, behold, a throne was set in heaven, and one sat on the throne" (Revelation 4:1-2).

(ii) Second, stood before the judgment seat of Christ and gave an account to him: "For we must all appear before the judgment seat of Christ; that every one may receive the things done in his body, according to that he hath done, whether it be good or bad" (2 Corinthians 5:10); "And hast made us unto our God kings and priests: and we shall reign on the earth" (Revelation 5:10); "For I am jealous over you with godly jealousy: for I have espoused you to one husband, that I may present you as a chaste virgin to Christ" (2 Corinthians 11:2).

(iii) Third, has spent seven years of preparation in heaven.

(iv) Fourth, is now ready for the marriage, the marriage supper, and reigning with Christ.

(8) "And to her was granted that she should be arrayed in fine linen, clean and white: for the fine linen is the righteousness of saints."

In the parable of the marriage of the king's son, the Lord Jesus teaches us that participation in the marriage supper requires correct attire: "And when the king came in to see the guests, he saw there a man which had not on a wedding garment: And he saith unto him, Friend, how camest thou in hither not having a wedding garment? And he was speechless. Then said the king to the servants, Bind him hand and foot, and take him away, and cast him into outer darkness; there shall be weeping and gnashing of teeth" (Matthew 22:11-13).

The wedding garment is the works of righteousness which we do here upon the earth. So take up your cross daily and follow Christ. Sacrifice and bear burdens for the sake of the name of the Lord Jesus! The Christian life without sacrifice does not enjoy the full blessings of the Holy Spirit; the Christian life with sacrifice receives the wonderful joy of the Holy Spirit: "If ye be reproached for the name of Christ, happy are ye; for the spirit of glory and of God resteth upon you" (1 Peter 4:14).

(9) "And he saith unto me, Write, Blessed are they which are called unto the marriage supper of the Lamb. And he saith unto me, These are the true sayings of God."

- And he saith unto me, Write, Blessed are they which are called unto the marriage supper of the Lamb. Indeed, as was said in the gospel of Luke, "Blessed is he that shall eat bread in the kingdom of God" (Luke 14:15), for the master of the marriage is Jesus, the bridegroom, and the church is his bride. All the righteous of the Old Testament will have a role in the kingdom: "And the Lord my God shall come, and all the saints with thee" (Zechariah 14:5).

- And he saith unto me, These are the true sayings of God - The angel desires here to affirm that what he says is from heaven and is supported by the Bible; thus it is our duty to be obedient faithful servants of the Lord Jesus.

It might be good for us to pause at this verse and recall that the church will ascend in the rapture to heaven and will stand before the judgment seat of Christ for rewards, which will be given according to our faithfulness and consecration while on the earth: "For other foundation can no man lay than that is laid, which is Jesus Christ. Now if any man build upon this foundation gold, silver, precious stones, wood, hay, stubble; Every man's work shall be made manifest: for the day shall declare it, because it shall be revealed by fire; and the fire shall try every man's work of what sort it is. If any man's work abide which he hath built thereupon, he shall receive a reward. If any man's work shall be burned, he shall suffer loss: but he himself shall be saved; yet so as by fire" (1 Corinthians 3:11-15); "For we must all appear before the judgment seat of Christ; that every one may receive the things done in his body, according to that he hath done, whether it be good or bad" (2 Corinthians 5:10); "If we suffer, we shall also reign with him: if we deny him, he also will deny us" (2 Timothy 2:12).

Every believer must stand before the judgment seat of Christ to receive rewards according to what he has done, whether it be good or bad. Every believer will receive rewards according to the quality of his service, whether wood and hay or gold, silver, and precious stones. Every believer will be rewarded according to his motives and according to the extent of his sacrifices. As for he who receives no reward, he shall be saved, but as if it were from fire. He will stand empty handed, being saved from hellfire and being present in heaven, but without any crowns or eternal rewards or treasures.

In heaven, we will wear fine linen which symbolizes the righteousness of the saints, that is, the good works we have done for the glory of the name of the Lord Jesus, the Lord of glory.

So the text asks us to rejoice and be glad, for the marriage of the Lamb is ready and the bride, the Church, has prepared herself, putting on the fine linen of good works.

Every work which we do for the Lord Jesus will remain with

us forever. Our prayers that we pray are like incense before the throne of God. All we have to do is minister spiritual services as unto the Lord Jesus, a sweet smelling odour before him, so that he looks favourably upon us. In the text, the church is chaste, that is, it did not betray the Lord Jesus, and now has come the day of her marriage to the Lamb, the Lord Jesus.

This scene leads us to an important theological question: where does the marriage take place, in heaven or on the earth? A wedding or marriage refers to a unity of two partners that care for each other in a unique way, as we see in the Isaiah's description of Jerusalem: "And thy land shall be married. For as a young man marrieth a virgin, so shall thy sons marry thee: and as the bridegroom rejoiceth over the bride, so shall thy God rejoice over thee" (Isaiah 62:4-5). The logic of the passage and its content leads to the conclusion that the marriage and the marriage supper will take place upon the earth because:

(i) First, according to the apostle Matthew, the marriage takes place on the earth: "And while they went to buy, the bridegroom came; and they that were ready went in with him to the marriage" (Matthew 25:10).

(ii) Second, a marriage cannot take place until after judgment is brought upon the world of iniquity at the return of Jesus to earth, until after judgment is brought upon the Antichrist: "And I saw heaven opened, and behold a white horse; and he that sat upon him was called Faithful and True, and in righteousness he doth judge and make war....And the beast was taken, and with him the False prophet that wrought miracles before him, with which he deceived them that had received the mark of the beast, and them that worshipped his image. These both were cast alive into a lake of fire burning with brimstone. And the remnant were slain with the sword of him that sat upon the horse, which sword proceeded out of his mouth: and all the fowls were filled with their flesh" (Revelation 19:11, 20-

21). There can be no marriage while war is raging and while the Antichrist makes havoc with souls.

(iii) Third, in heaven we will prepare ourselves to return with the Lord Jesus to the earth. The actual marriage will take place upon the earth, which is where invitations to the supper will be given out. These invitations automatically include the marriage and the marriage supper. With the supper on the earth, the marriage should also be upon the earth.

(iv) Fourth, the marriage of the Lamb will be upon the earth at the beginning of the millennium. The wedding which joins the Lamb and his betrothed wife will be blessed, and the marriage supper will be most splendid and exceedingly beautiful. Both will be upon the earth, for the church will be the bride of Christ on earth. The new Jerusalem will be the bride of Christ in in heaven: "The city of my God, which is new Jerusalem, which cometh down out of heaven" (Revelation 3:12); "And I John saw the holy city, new Jerusalem, coming down from God out of heaven, prepared as a bride adorned for her husband" (Revelation 21:2). The church is the bride of Christ upon the earth at the beginning of the millennium, and the heavenly Jerusalem is the bride of Christ in heaven at the beginning of eternity.

(v) Fifth, the events described in this verse are preparatory in their nature, preparatory steps for the descent after 4 verses of the Lord Jesus to earth and joy of enjoying the marriage and the marriage supper. In the parable of the ten virgins, the gospel of Matthew points to the marriage occurring on the earth after the return of the bridegroom: "Behold, the bridegroom cometh … .the bridegroom came; and they that were ready went in with him to the marriage" (Matthew 25:6, 10).

(10) "And I fell at his feet to worship him. And he said unto me, See thou do it not: I am thy fellowservant, and of thy brethren that have the testimony of Jesus: worship God: for the testimony of Jesus is the spirit of prophecy."

- And I fell at his feet to worship him. And he said unto me, See thou do it not: I am thy fellowservant, and of thy brethren that have the testimony of Jesus: worship God - The Lord Jesus does not allow drifting away from him to worship angels. This is clear in the Bible and is the opposite of what is taught by traditional Christianity. The Bible exhorts us believers in the Lord Jesus to preserve our elves from worshiping idols: "For, lo, they that are far from thee shall perish: thou hast destroyed all them that go a whoring from thee" (Psalms 73:27); "Little children, keep yourselves from idols" (1 John 5:21). For all worship is for the Lord Jesus and him alone who: "humbled himself, and became obedient unto death, even the death of the cross. Wherefore God also hath highly exalted him, and given him a name which is above every name: That at the name of Jesus every knee should bow, of things in heaven, and things in earth, and things under the earth; And that every tongue should confess that Jesus Christ is Lord, to the glory of God the Father" (Philippians 2:8-11).

- For the testimony of Jesus is the spirit of prophecy - The focal point of all worship is the Lord Jesus Christ, the son of the living God, who is the Lord of glory who receives all prostration and worship. He is the pivotal point of every prophesy, testimony, and evangelical outreach. Jesus is at the center of the entire Bible.

(11) "And I saw heaven opened, and behold a white horse; and he that sat upon him was called Faithful and True, and in righteousness he doth judge and make war."

Heaven opens twice in the book of Revelation. The first time, it opens to receive the church, the second time, in this verse, for the return of Christ and all the saints with him. They are:

(i) The righteous of the Old Testament: "And the Lord my God shall come, and all the saints with thee" (Zechariah 14:5)),

(ii) The righteous of the New Testament, who are the

Church: "When Christ, who is our life, shall appear, then shall ye also appear with him in glory" (Colossians 3:4)),

(iii) The righteous of the Great Tribulation: "And I saw thrones, and they sat upon them, and judgment was given unto them: and I saw the souls of them that were beheaded for the witness of Jesus, and for the word of God, and which had not worshipped the beast, neither his image, neither had received his mark upon their foreheads, or in their hands; and they lived and reigned with Christ a thousand years" (Revelation 20:4)).

This is now the second coming of Christ! In his first coming, Jesus Christ was born in a manger and suffered humiliation, insult, and pain upon the cross for redemption of mankind. In his second coming, the Lord Jesus will establish his kingdom on the earth for 1,000 years. He will have victory over Satan; he will bind him and cast him into the bottomless pit for a period of a thousand years, as we will see in the next chapter.

In his first coming, Jesus said to Peter, "Behold, Satan hath desired to have you, that he may sift you" (Luke 22:31); but in his second coming, he will send his angels to sift the wicked so that only the righteous will enter into the millennium. And at that time, the saints will greatly rejoice, as Isaiah says, "Oh that thou wouldest rend the heavens, that thou wouldest come down, that the mountains might flow down at thy presence" (Isaiah 64:1).

The Lord Jesus will come in great light and glory, as the Bible says: "For as the lightning cometh out of the east, and shineth even unto the west; so shall also the coming of the Son of man be ... And then shall appear the sign of the Son of man in heaven: and then shall all the tribes of the earth mourn, and they shall see the Son of man coming in the clouds of heaven with power and great glory" (Matthew 24:27, 30); "For the powers of heaven shall be shaken. And then shall they see the Son of man coming in a cloud with power and great glory" (Luke 21:26-27).

(12) "His eyes were as a flame of fire, and on his head were many crowns; and he had a name written, that no man knew, but he himself."

- His eyes were as a flame of fire - The Lord Jesus returns to destroy the wicked. He is the Judge and righteous Magistrate of all the earth: "A king that sitteth in the throne of judgment scattereth away all evil with his eyes" (Proverbs 20:8).

- And on his head were many crowns - In his first coming, Jesus accepted a crown of thorns, by virtue of which he rules in our hearts. Now and then, he wears many crowns because he is the King of kings and the Lord of lords: "That at the name of Jesus every knee should bow, of things in heaven, and things in earth, and things under the earth; And that every tongue should confess that Jesus Christ is Lord, to the glory of God the Father" (Philippians 2:10-11).

- And he had a name written, that no man knew, but he himself - The Lord Jesus will make all things new; he will even have a new name that no one knows. It is beautiful to note that every one of God's children will also have a new name: "He that hath an ear, let him hear what the Spirit saith unto the churches; To him that overcometh will I give to eat of the hidden manna, and will give him a white stone, and in the stone a new name written, which no man knoweth saving he that receiveth it" (Revelation 2:17).

Every faithful believer will have the new names of Jesus and Jerusalem: "Him that overcometh will I make a pillar in the temple of my God, and he shall go no more out: and I will write upon him the name of:

(i) My God,

(ii) And the name of the city of my God, which is new Jerusalem, which cometh down out of heaven from my God:

(iii) And I will write upon him my new name" (Revelation 3:12). Jerusalem is going to have a new name. This was seen by Isaiah too: "For Zion's sake will I not hold my peace, and for Jerusalem's sake I will not rest, until the righteousness thereof go forth as brightness, and the salvation thereof as a lamp that burneth. And the Gentiles shall see thy righteousness, and all kings thy glory: and thou shalt be called by a new name, which the mouth of the LORD shall name" (Isaiah 62:1-2).

(13) "And he was clothed with a vesture dipped in blood: and his name is called The Word of God."

- And he was clothed with a vesture dipped in blood - In other words, the basis of justice and of his judgment is his innocent blood, which was poured out upon the wood of the cross in order to:

(i) Satisfy God's holiness,

(ii) Fulfil divine justice,

(iii) Save our souls, and

(iv) Purchase the earth's deed of ownership, as we discussed in chapter 5.

- And his name is called The Word of God - "Jesus Christ the same yesterday, and to day, and for ever" (Hebrews 13:8). He is the one who, from the beginning, is the Logos, the Word: "In the beginning was the Word, and the Word was with God, and the Word was God ... And the Word was made flesh, and dwelt among us, (and we beheld his glory, the glory as of the only begotten of the Father,) full of grace and truth" (John 1:1, 14).

He is the faithful witness, who demands, at all times, that we be faithful to his word: "I ... was in the isle that is called Patmos, for the word of God, and for the testimony of Jesus Christ" (Revelation 1:9); "Thou ... hast kept my word, and hast not denied my name" (Revelation 3:8); "I saw under the altar the souls of them that were slain for the word of God" (Revelation 6:9); "And they overcame him by the blood of the Lamb, and by the word of their testimony; and they loved not their lives unto the death" (Revelation 12:11); "And I saw thrones, and they sat upon them, and judgment was given unto them: and I saw the souls of them that were beheaded for the witness of Jesus, and for the word of God" (Revelation 20:4).

The word of the Lord Jesus is so important that he has magnified it over his name: "Thou hast magnified thy word above all thy name" (Psalm 138:2).

(14) "And the armies which were in heaven followed him upon white horses, clothed in fine linen, white and clean."

These armies consist of the righteous angels, who follow Jesus upon white horses, a symbol of their holiness and of the fact that they fight with him: "For whosoever shall be ashamed of me and of my words, of him shall the Son of man be ashamed, when he shall come in his own glory, and in his Father's, and of the holy angels" (Luke 9:26); "These shall make war with the Lamb, and the Lamb shall overcome them: for he is Lord of lords, and King of kings: and they that are with him are called, and chosen, and faithful" (Revelation 17:14). Additionally we the raptured church, will participate in the return as we shall be part of these armies: "The LORD my God shall come, and all the saints with thee" (Zechariah 14:5); "When Christ, who is our life, shall appear, then shall ye also appear with him in glory" (Colossians 3:4).

We are at a point in the sequence of events when the second rapture takes place here.

(15) "And out of his mouth goeth a sharp sword, that with it he should smite the nations: and he shall rule them with a rod of iron: and he treadeth the winepress of the fierceness and wrath of Almighty God."

- And out of his mouth goeth a sharp sword, that with it he should smite the nations - The sharp sword is the sword of the Spirit, which is the word of God's justice: "But with righteousness shall he judge the poor, and reprove with equity for the meek of the earth: and he shall smite the earth with the rod of his mouth, and with the breath of his lips shall he slay the wicked" (Isaiah 11:4): "The sword of the Spirit, which is the word of God" (Ephesians 6:17); "For the word of God is quick, and powerful, and sharper than any twoedged sword, piercing even to the dividing asunder of soul and spirit, and of the joints and marrow, and is a discerner of the thoughts and intents of the heart" (Hebrews 4:12); "And he had in his right hand seven stars: and out of his mouth went a sharp twoedged sword: and his countenance was as the sun shineth in his strength" (Revelation 1:16).

- And he shall rule them with a rod of iron: and he treadeth the winepress of the fierceness and wrath of Almighty God - The returning Christ will enforce impose justice upon the earth. He will destroy the wicked, and will reign: "Ask of me, and I shall give thee the heathen for thine inheritance, and the uttermost parts of the earth for thy possession. Thou shalt break them with a rod of iron; thou shalt dash them in pieces like a potter's vessel" (Psalm 2:8-9); "But those mine enemies, which would not that I should reign over them, bring hither, and slay them before me" (Luke 19:27); "And she brought forth a man child, who was to rule all nations with a rod of iron: and her child was caught up unto God, and to his throne" (Revelation 12:5).

These passages add to a description which we have already seen; "And another angel came out from the altar, which had power over fire; and cried with a loud cry to him that had the sharp sickle, saying, Thrust in thy sharp sickle, and gather the clusters of the vine of the earth; for her grapes are fully ripe. And the angel thrust in his sickle into the earth, and gathered the vine of the earth, and cast it into the great winepress of the wrath of God. And the winepress was trodden without the city, and blood came out of the winepress, even unto the horse bridles, by the space of a thousand and six hundred furlongs" (Revelation 14:18-20).

(16) "And he hath on his vesture and on his thigh a name written, KING OF KINGS, AND LORD OF LORDS."

This title is drawn from the Old Testament: "For the LORD your God is God of gods, and Lord of lords" (Deuteronomy 10:17); "O give thanks unto the God of gods: for his mercy endureth for ever. O give thanks to the Lord of lords: for his mercy endureth for ever" (Psalm 136:2-3). In this title, we see the inability of language to express the extent of the greatness of Jesus. The event here has been described previously in the book of Revelation: "And the seventh angel sounded; and there were great voices in heaven, saying, The kingdoms of this world are become the kingdoms of our Lord, and of his Christ; and he shall reign for ever and ever" (Revelation 11:15).

(17) "And I saw an angel standing in the sun; and he cried with a loud voice, saying to all the fowls that fly in the midst of heaven, Come and gather yourselves together unto the supper of the great God;"

The fact that the angel stands in the sun shows us that the angels are, in their essence, glorious spirit beings, similar in nature to the glorified body of the Lord Jesus. Their glorified bodes are not subject to laws of physics. So will our glorified bodies:

(i) New: "So also is the resurrection of the dead. It is sown in corruption; it is raised in incorruption: It is sown in dishonour; it is raised in glory: it is sown in weakness; it is raised in power: It is sown a natural body; it is raised a spiritual body. There is a natural body, and there is a spiritual body" (1 Corinthians 15:42-44);

(ii) Glorified for we shall be like unto him: "⁷But if the ministration of death, written and engraven in stones, was glorious, so that the children of Israel could not stedfastly behold the face of Moses for the glory of his countenance; which glory was to be done away: ⁸How shall not the ministration of the spirit be rather glorious? ⁹For if the ministration of condemnation be glory, much more doth the ministration of righteousness exceed in glory. ¹⁰For even that which was made glorious had no glory in this respect, by reason of the glory that excelleth. ¹¹For if that which is done away was glorious, much more that which remaineth is glorious", "¹⁸But we all, with open face beholding as in a glass the glory of the Lord, are changed into the same image from glory to glory, even as by the Spirit of the Lord"; "¹⁷For our light affliction, which is but for a moment, worketh for us a far more exceeding and eternal weight of glory;" (2 Corinthians 3:7-11, 18; 4:17); "Beloved, now are we the sons of God, and it doth not yet appear what we shall be: but we know that, when he shall appear, we shall be like him; for we shall see him as he is" (1 John 3:2).

The fact that the angel stands in the sun also shows us that he speaks with great, heavenly power and authority. The angel calls the birds, which must understand the language of heaven because they speak to heaven: "Then shall the trees of the wood sing out at the presence of the Lord, because he cometh to judge the earth" (1 Chronicles 16:33); "Who provideth for the raven his food? when his young ones cry unto God, they wander for lack of meat" (Job 38:41); "These wait all upon thee; that thou mayest give them their meat in due season" (Psalm 104:27).

(18) "That ye may eat the flesh of kings, and the flesh of captains, and the flesh of mighty men, and the flesh of horses, and of them that sit on them, and the flesh of all men, both free and bond, both small and great."

The birds of the air are called to eat the flesh of men. From the point of view of the Bible, this fact speaks of the severity of God in punishing the wickedness of this earth. "And thy carcase shall be meat unto all fowls of the air, and unto the beasts of the earth, and no man shall fray them away" (Deuteronomy 28:26). "And, thou son of man, thus saith the Lord GOD; Speak unto every feathered fowl, and to every beast of the field, Assemble yourselves, and come; gather yourselves on every side to my sacrifice that I do sacrifice for you, even a great sacrifice upon the mountains of Israel, that ye may eat flesh, and drink blood.

Ye shall eat the flesh of the mighty, and drink the blood of the princes of the earth, of rams, of lambs, and of goats, of bullocks, all of them fatlings of Bashan. And ye shall eat fat till ye be full, and drink blood till ye be drunken, of my sacrifice which I have sacrificed for you. Thus ye shall be filled at my table with horses and chariots, with mighty men, and with all men of war, saith the Lord GOD. And I will set my glory among the heathen, and all the heathen shall see my judgment that I have executed, and my hand that I have laid upon them" (Ezekiel 39:17-21).

Normally man used to offer animals as sacrifices to the Lord; but it is a fearful punishment when God offers man as a sacrifice to animals. Indeed it is a fearful thing to fall in the hands of the Lord: "It is a fearful thing to fall into the hands of the living God" (Hebrews 10: 31).

(19) "And I saw the beast, and the kings of the earth, and their armies, gathered together to make war against him that sat on the horse, and against his army."

This is the war of Armageddon: "And the sixth angel poured out his vial upon the great river Euphrates; and the water thereof was dried up, that the way of the kings of the east might be prepared. And I saw three unclean spirits like frogs come out of the mouth of the dragon, and out of the mouth of the beast, and out of the mouth of the False prophet. For they are the spirits of devils, working miracles, which go forth unto the kings of the earth and of the whole world, to gather them to the battle of that great day of God Almighty. Behold, I come as a thief. Blessed is he that watcheth, and keepeth his garments, lest he walk naked, and they see his shame. And he gathered them together into a place called in the Hebrew tongue Armageddon" (Revelation 16:12-16).

All the nations of the world and all their armies together with the evil spirits will gather against Israel to do harm to Jerusalem: "And it shall come to pass in that day, that I will seek to destroy all the nations that come against Jerusalem" (Zechariah 12:9).

It is strange that the kings and rulers of the world, though gathering to make battle against each other in the plain of Armageddon, are all in agreement against Christ, rejecting his authority and his rule over them. The Lord will destroy them, as we shall see in the following two verses.

(20) "And the beast was taken, and with him the False prophet that wrought miracles before him, with which he deceived them that had received the mark of the beast, and them that worshipped his image. These both were cast alive into a lake of fire burning with brimstone."

Finally, the Lord will overcome the Antichrist and the False prophet. He will capture them, bind them, and cast them alive into eternal hellfire, where they will be tormented forever and ever.

(21) "And the remnant were slain with the sword of him that sat upon the horse, which sword proceeded out of his mouth: and all the fowls were filled with their flesh."

The sword is a symbol which represents divine justice! However, the military instrument which will actually be used is the atomic bombs and nuclear missiles: "And this shall be the plague wherewith the LORD will smite all the people that have fought against Jerusalem; Their flesh shall consume away while they stand upon their feet, and their eyes shall consume away in their holes, and their tongue shall consume away in their mouth" (Zechariah 14:12).

The Lord Jesus will kill all the rulers and armies of the world. They will descend into hell to the inner belly of the earth as did the rich man mentioned in Luke: "The rich man also died, and was buried; And in hell he lift up his eyes, being in torments" (Luke 16:22-23). There they will remain until they stand before God's great white throne for judgment, to be cast thereafter into eternal hellfire: "And I saw a great white throne, and him that sat on it, from whose face the earth and the heaven fled away; and there was found no place for them. And I saw the dead, small and great, stand before God; and the books were opened: and another book was opened, which is the book of life: and the dead were judged out of those things which were written in the books, according to their works. And the sea gave up the dead which were in it; and death and hell delivered up the dead which were in them: and they were judged every man according to their works. And death and hell were cast into the lake of fire. This is the second death" (Revelation 20:11-14).

Due to the greatness of their evil, the Antichrist and the False prophet are cast directly into hell without a trial. As for the rest of the wicked, their portion will be the more common judicial arrangement. With the end of this verse and this chapter, we reach the end of the great tribulation. In the next chapter, we will learn about the millennium- the kingdom of the Lord Jesus upon the earth. Finally, in chapters 21 & 22, we enter into the description of eternity!

20
THE MILLENNIUM – GOG AND MAGOG –

(1) "And I saw an angel come down from heaven, having the key of the bottomless pit and a great chain in his hand."

- And I saw an angel come down from heaven, having the key of the bottomless pit - After the judgment of the False prophet and the Antichrist, it is now time for the judgment of their leader, Satan.

A mighty angel descended from heaven in Revelation chapter 10 and swore by the one who lives forever and ever : "that there should be time no longer" (Revelation 10:6). Then an angel with great authority cried with a powerful voice in Revelation chapter 18, saying: "Babylon the great is fallen, is fallen" (Revelation 18:2). Also, a glorious angel stood in the sun in Revelation chapter 19 and called all the fowls that fly in the midst of heaven saying: "Come and gather yourselves together unto the supper of the great God" (Revelation 19:17). Now comes a fourth angel and appears on the heavenly scene to bind Satan and to imprison him in the pit.

- And a great chain in his hand - Since angels are spirits, we should understand that this chain is not literal. Rather, it is a symbol of the authority and ability of this angel to restrict

Satan's freedom and to prevent his movement. This is similar to what we read about Job's experience: "And the Lord said unto Satan, Behold, all that he hath is in thy power; only upon himself put not forth thine hand ... And the Lord said unto Satan, Behold, he is in thine hand; but save his life" (Job 1:12; 2:6). There are similar situations which are described in other passages of the Bible: "For if God spared not the angels that sinned, but cast them down to hell, and delivered them into chains of darkness, to be reserved unto judgment" (2 Peter 2:4): "And the angels which kept not their first estate, but left their own habitation, he hath reserved in everlasting chains under darkness unto the judgment of the great day" (Jude 1:6).

Likewise in a positive context we read of the experience of Paul who was bound: "In the bonds of the gospel" (Philemon 13). So we can see that this description is symbolic and exceeds our limited human understanding of physics. A spiritual entity cannot be bound by a physical limitation, so we should accept it with the understanding eye of our human limitations.

(2) "And he laid hold on the dragon, that old serpent, which is the Devil, and Satan, and bound him a thousand years,"

Satan is a monster and a dragon in regard to his savagery, a snake in his cunning, and to the likeness of an angel of light with regard to his imitating; for he is very evil. He is a lion in his ferocity: "Be sober, be vigilant; because your adversary the devil, as a roaring lion, walketh about, seeking whom he may devour" (1 Peter 5:8). He is a snake, as he spreads his harmful venom: "But I fear, lest by any means, as the serpent beguiled Eve through his subtilty, so your minds should be corrupted from the simplicity that is in Christ" (2 Corinthians 11:3). He has the likeness of an angel of light in his harmful cheating deceit: "And no marvel; for Satan himself is transformed into an angel of light" (2 Corinthians 11:14). What is significantly important is that in every shape or form, Satan is the enemy of souls.

Chronologically, three and a half years earlier, Satan was

cast out of heaven to earth, where he had wreaked havoc: "And the great dragon was cast out, that old serpent, called the Devil, and Satan, which deceiveth the whole world: he was cast out into the earth, and his angels were cast out with him" (Revelation 12:9). Now the time has come for him to be cast into the pit in the depths of the interior of the earth, a place of burning flames of fire: "As for the earth, out of it cometh bread: and under it is turned up as it were fire" (Job 28:5); "The rich man also died, and was buried; And in hell he lift up his eyes, being in torments" (Luke 16:22-23).

As for geographical location of the lake of brimstone and fire, we have no knowledge of it now, maybe in the belly of the earth, but it will be made manifest to us in the last days: "And they shall go forth, and look upon the carcases of the men that have transgressed against me: for their worm shall not die, neither shall their fire be quenched; and they shall be an abhorring unto all flesh" (Isaiah 66:24).

Now, at the end of the great tribulation, the Lord Jesus Christ returns to the earth to establish his kingdom. Satan will be bound from activity for the duration of the millennium. Isaiah describes this situation from a parallel point of view which emphasizes the extent of God's authority: "In that day the LORD with his sore and great and strong sword shall punish leviathan the piercing serpent, even leviathan that crooked serpent; and he shall slay the dragon that is in the sea" (Isaiah 27:1).

(3) "And cast him into the bottomless pit, and shut him up, and set a seal upon him, that he should deceive the nations no more, till the thousand years should be fulfilled: and after that he must be loosed a little season."

- And cast him into the bottomless pit, and shut him up, and set a seal upon him, that he should deceive the nations no more, till the thousand years should be fulfilled. Satan during this time is:

(a) Cast away,
(b) Confined,
(c) Sealed securely.

All three imply that he will be ineffective or dysfunctional for the thousand year period.

This is what Isaiah the prophet also saw eight hundred years before this prophecy was given to John the apostle: "And it shall come to pass in that day, that the LORD shall punish the host of the high ones that are on high, and the kings of the earth upon the earth. And they shall be gathered together, as prisoners are gathered in the pit, and shall be shut up in the prison, and after many days shall they be visited. Then the moon shall be confounded, and the sun ashamed, when the LORD of hosts shall reign in mount Zion, and in Jerusalem, and before his ancients gloriously" (Isaiah 24:21-23). Praise the Lord and praise the truthfulness of his Word!

- And after that he must be loosed a little season. After that, Satan is released for the war of Gog and Magog. Subsequently, all his activity and impact come to an end when he is doomed and cast irrevocably and eternally in the lake of fire and brimstone.

(4) "And I saw thrones, and they sat upon them, and judgment was given unto them: and I saw the souls of them that were beheaded for the witness of Jesus, and for the word of God, and which had not worshipped the beast, neither his image, neither had received his mark upon their foreheads, or in their hands; and they lived and reigned with Christ a thousand years."

- And I saw thrones, and they sat upon them, and judgment was given unto them: and I saw the souls of them that were beheaded for the witness of Jesus, and for the word of God, and which had not worshipped the beast, neither his image, neither had received his mark upon their foreheads, or in their hands - This is the commencement of the millennium, an event that is described in many Bible passages: "Then shall the kingdom of heaven be likened unto ten virgins, which took their lamps, and went forth to meet the bridegroom. And five of them were wise, and five were foolish. They that were foolish took their lamps, and took no oil with them: But the wise took oil in their vessels with their lamps. While the bridegroom tarried, they all slumbered and slept. And at midnight there was a cry made, Behold, the bridegroom cometh; go ye out to meet him. Then all those virgins arose, and trimmed their lamps And the foolish said unto the wise, Give us of your oil; for our lamps are gone out. But the wise answered, saying, Not so; lest there be not enough for us and you: but go ye rather to them that sell, and buy for yourselves. And while they went to buy, the bridegroom came; and they that were ready went in with him to the marriage: and the door was shut" (Matthew 25:1-10).

The Lord Jesus is inaugurating his kingdom by offering thrones to the righteous to rule with him. As we have seen before, these righteous come from the:

(a) New Testament,
(b) Old Testament,
(c) Great Tribulation.

All they will reign with Christ in his kingdom, as he promised them in both the Old and New Testaments: "And ye shall be unto me a kingdom of priests, and an holy nation" (Exodus 19:6); "And Jesus said unto them, Verily I say unto you, That ye which have followed me, in the regeneration when the Son of man shall sit in the throne of his glory, ye also shall sit upon twelve thrones, judging the twelve tribes of Israel" (Matthew 19:28); "If we suffer, we shall also reign with him" (2 Timothy 2:12); "But ye are a chosen generation, a royal priesthood" (1 Peter 2:9).

The events described in this verse are the inauguration of the amazing 1,000 years rule of Jesus Christ. We see several descriptions of this commencement in the Bible: "And he shall judge among the nations, and shall rebuke many people: and they shall beat their swords into plowshares, and their spears into pruninghooks: nation shall not lift up sword against nation, neither shall they learn war any more" (Isaiah 2:4); "Of the increase of his government and peace there shall be no end, upon the throne of David, and upon his kingdom, to order it, and to establish it with judgment and with justice from henceforth even for ever. The zeal of the Lord of hosts will perform this" (Isaiah 9:7); "The wolf also shall dwell with the lamb, and the leopard shall lie down with the kid; and the calf and the young lion and the fatling together; and a little child shall lead them. And the cow and the bear shall feed; their young ones shall lie down together: and the lion shall eat straw like the ox. And the sucking child shall play on the hole of the asp, and the weaned child shall put his hand on the cockatrice' den. They shall not hurt nor destroy in all my holy mountain: for the earth shall be full of the knowledge of the Lord, as the waters cover the sea. And in that day there shall be a root of Jesse, which shall stand for an ensign of the people; to it shall the Gentiles seek: and his rest shall be glorious" (Isaiah 11:6-10); "But they shall sit every man under his vine and under his fig tree; and none shall make them afraid: for the mouth of the LORD of hosts hath spoken it" (Micah 4:4); "The kingdom of heaven is like unto a certain king, which made a marriage for his son, And sent forth his servants to call them that were bidden to the wedding: and they would not come. Again, he sent forth other servants, saying, Tell them which are bidden, Behold, I have prepared my dinner: my oxen and my fatlings are killed, and all things are ready: come unto the marriage" (Matthew 22:2-4); "And when one of them that sat at meat with him heard these things, he said unto him, Blessed is he that shall eat bread in the kingdom of God" (Luke 14:15). "Because the creature itself also shall be delivered from the bondage of corruption into the glorious liberty of the children of God. For we know that the whole creation groaneth and travaileth in pain together until now. And not only they, but ourselves also, which have the firstfruits of the Spirit, even we ourselves groan within ourselves, waiting for the adoption, to wit, the redemption of our body" (Romans 8:21-23); "Behold, I stand at the door, and knock: if any man hear my voice, and open the door, I will come in to him, and will sup with him, and he with me. To him that overcometh will I grant to sit with me in my throne, even as I also overcame, and am set down with my Father in his throne" (Revelation 3:20-21); "Alleluia: for the Lord God omnipotent reigneth. Let us be glad and rejoice, and give honour to him: for the marriage of the Lamb is come, and his wife hath made herself ready. And to her was granted that she should be arrayed in fine linen, clean and white: for the fine linen is the righteousness of saints. And he saith unto me, Write, Blessed are they which are called unto the marriage supper of the Lamb" (Revelation 19:6-9).

All these texts bring joy and comfort to the heart and the hope of anticipating what the Lord Jesus has promised us, that joy and gladness and harmony shall prevail over the globe and all creation. Even the animals will become tame, and there will be no harm from plants. The peace of the Lord Jesus will dominate the whole world.

The Lord Jesus will rule the world from Jerusalem, its capital; he will rule from Mount Zion, and we will rule with him: "Beautiful for situation, the joy of the whole earth, is mount Zion, on the sides of the north, the city of the great King" (Psalm 48:2).

Revelation 19:9 describes Jerusalem as "the beloved city". In the Millennium, Jerusalem will be the glory of the cities and capitals of the world, as it once was in the past. Jeremiah referred to Jerusalem as the "Princess among the provinces" (Lamentations 1:1) and "The perfection of beauty, the joy of the whole earth" (Lamentations 2:15). It will once again be "the great city" (Revelation 16:19), the city of the King of glory, the

Lord Jesus Christ. It will be become the most beautiful city of all the cities of the world. All of the land of Canaan will become like the Garden of Eden under Christ's rule in the millennium: "Awake, awake; put on thy strength, O Zion; put on thy beautiful garments, O Jerusalem, the holy city: for henceforth there shall no more come into thee the uncircumcised and the unclean" (Isaiah 52:1); "And they shall say, This land that was desolate is become like the garden of Eden" (Ezekiel 36:35).

Springs will burst forth in Jerusalem. Great rivers will flow through it, as in her days of glory: "So there was gathered much people together, who stopped all the fountains, and the brook that ran through the midst of the land, saying, Why should the kings of Assyria come, and find much water?" (2 Chronicles 32:4); At that time, Jerusalem was the ornament of all inhabited cities. It will return to and exceed that preeminent beauty and glory in the light of the reign of Christ: "Arise, shine; for thy light is come, and the glory of the Lord is risen upon thee ... but the Lord shall arise upon thee, and his glory shall be seen upon thee. And the Gentiles shall come to thy light, and kings to the brightness of thy rising ... and thine heart shall fear, and be enlarged; because the abundance of the sea shall be converted unto thee, the forces of the Gentiles shall come unto thee ... The glory of Lebanon shall come unto thee, the fir tree, the pine tree, and the box together, to beautify the place of my sanctuary; and I will make the place of my feet glorious ... Thy people also shall be all righteous: they shall inherit the land for ever, the branch of my planting, the work of my hands, that I may be glorified" (Isaiah 60:1-3, 5, 13, 21).

Two great rivers will flow from Jerusalem, one west to the Mediterranean Sea, and the other will flow east to the Dead Sea; the waters in that area will live and will be filled with fish: "Afterward he brought me again unto the door of the house; and, behold, waters issued out from under the threshold of the house eastward: for the forefront of the house stood toward the east, and the waters came down from under from the right side of the house, at the south side of the altar. Then brought he me out of the way of the gate northward, and led me about the way without unto the utter gate by the way that looketh eastward; and, behold, there ran out waters on the right side. And when the man that had the line in his hand went forth eastward, he measured a thousand cubits, and he brought me through the waters; the waters were to the ankles. Again he measured a thousand, and brought me through the waters; the waters were to the knees. Again he measured a thousand, and brought me through; the waters were to the loins. Afterward he measured a thousand; and it was a river that I could not pass over: for the waters were risen, waters to swim in, a river that could not be passed over. And he said unto me, Son of man, hast thou seen this? Then he brought me, and caused me to return to the brink of the river. Now when I had returned, behold, at the bank of the river were very many trees on the one side and on the other. Then said he unto me, These waters issue out toward the east country, and go down into the desert, and go into the sea: which being brought forth into the sea, the waters shall be healed. And it shall come to pass, that every thing that liveth, which moveth, whithersoever the rivers shall come, shall live: and there shall be a very great multitude of fish, because these waters shall come thither: for they shall be healed; and every thing shall live whither the river cometh. And it shall come to pass, that the fishers shall stand upon it from Engedi even unto Eneglaim; they shall be a place to spread forth nets; their fish shall be according to their kinds, as the fish of the great sea, exceeding many. But the miry places thereof and the marishes thereof shall not be healed; they shall be given to salt" (Ezekiel 47:1-11);"And it shall be in that day, that living waters shall go out from Jerusalem; half of them toward the former sea, and half of them toward the hinder sea: in summer and in winter shall it be. And the LORD shall be king over all the earth: in that day shall there be one LORD, and his name one" (Zechariah 14:8-9).

Jerusalem will be a land of "gardens and orchards" (Ecclesiastes 2:5) and more beautiful because Jesus is greater than Solomon: "A greater than Solomon is here." (Luke 11:31).

Days of gladness and joy await us when Jesus comes again! Alleluia!

Now, at the beginning of the millennium, there will be no wicked men. Those who enter the millennium will be the righteous who survived the great tribulation, who are still alive at the end of that 7 year tribulation period. However, there are a couple of "red lights" which we should be aware of:

(i) First, even though Satan is bound in the millennium, sin, the curse, and death remain in the picture: "The child shall die an hundred years old; but the sinner being an hundred years old shall be accursed" (Isaiah 65:20). The average lifespan of a person will be hundreds of years: "For as the days of a tree are the days of my people" (Isaiah 65:22).

(ii) Second, the righteous of the earth will marry; those who survived the great tribulation and entered the millennium in their human bodies. They will marry and bring forth children! But these children will be, at birth, unregenerate sinners, not saved by the blood of the Lord Jesus. So there be a newly born generation of the human race, and a large number of them will reject the salvation of Christ even though they were born and they live in the days of Christ, the blessed King. These new generations will rise up in an insurrection against the Lord Jesus, who will rule them with a rod of iron: "Ask of me, and I shall give thee the heathen for thine inheritance, and the uttermost parts of the earth for thy possession. Thou shalt break them with a rod of iron; thou shalt dash them in pieces like a potter's vessel" (Psalm 2:8-9).

This is the true reality of man's nature. This revolt will demonstrate the depth of man's fallen and depraved state, for even though Satan will be bound, man will still continue to commit sin. The degree of man's depravity will become evident in the millennium, when, with the devil bound and confined, man will rise up against Jesus Christ.

We thank the Lord Jesus that this thousand year reign is not actually eternity, but rather it is the completion of a certain stage of God's dealings with man. A study of the genealogies of Adam in the Bible leads to the conclusion that mankind's time upon the earth has been around 6,000 years. After six thousand years of mankind's travail on the earth, mankind will experience 1,000 years of rest on the earth. The millennium is the "last day of the week" of man's 7,000 year history on this earth. After that we shall enter eternity with God.

- And they lived - It is at this point specifically that the second rapture occurs – the rapture which we explained when discussing the three raptures in our exposition of (Revelation 14:15).

- And reigned with Christ a thousand years - All the righteous of Christ, from Adam and Eve and other individuals that we read about in the Bible such as righteous Abel and Enoch and Abraham and Sarah and Moses and the 12 disciples of Christ and their wives and Lydia and Stephen and Antipas, down to the last convert saved at the end of the great tribulation; we will all together rule with the Lord Jesus Christ for one thousand years.

(5) "But the rest of the dead lived not again until the thousand years were finished. This is the first resurrection."

All the wicked of the human race, from Cain to the Antichrist, will remain in death at this time. They have no part in the first resurrection, which is a resurrection of the just unto everlasting life with the Lord Jesus Christ, the Lord of glory. The portion of all the wicked of mankind is the second resurrection, which leads to the second death, as we will see in verses (11 – 13) of this chapter.

(6) "Blessed and holy is he that hath part in the first resurrection: on such the second death hath no power, but they shall be priests of God and of Christ, and shall reign with him a thousand years."

The Bible teaches us that there is a first birth and a second birth, a first death and a second death, a first resurrection and a second resurrection.

The first birth is medically called the "water birth". It is when the fetus is formed in the womb of its mother and lives in a sack of fluids for nine months. This is the first birth that we see Jesus comparing to Nicodemus with the "second birth": "except a man be born of water and of the Spirit, he cannot enter into the kingdom of God" (John 3:5).

The first fleshly birth does not qualify one to enter Heaven, because we need the second birth which is the "spiritual birth". The first birth is physical, but the second birth is spiritual: "That which is born of the flesh is flesh; and that which is born of the Spirit is spirit. Marvel not that I said unto thee, Ye must be born again. The wind bloweth where it listeth, and thou hearest the sound thereof, but canst not tell whence it cometh, and whither it goeth: so is every one that is born of the Spirit" (John 3: 6-8).

Just as there is a first and second birth in the Bible, which is the Word of God, so there is a first death and a second death. When the body dies, man dies, and this is the first death, physical death. As for the second death, it is a spiritual death where the sinner is cast away from God forever into the fire of hell. A man who is saved by the blood of the Lord Jesus has a second birth, a spiritual birth, and he will not see the second death because he is born again for then he has "passed from death unto life" (John 5:24).

The man who rejects the forgiveness and salvation of the Lord JESUS CHRIST has his sins remained unpardoned and therefore his punishment will be the second death which ends up sending him down to hell to the: "everlasting fire, prepared for the devil and his angels" (Matthew 25:41). "This is the second death. And whosoever was not found written in the book of life was cast into the lake of fire" (Revelation 20:14-15).

In the beginning of creation, the Lord God said to Adam: "Of every tree of the garden thou mayest freely eat: But of the tree of the knowledge of good and evil, thou shalt not eat of it: for in the day that thou eatest thereof thou shalt surely die" (Genesis 2: 16-17). The Bible says that Adam and Eve ate of the fruit of the tree and died both physically and spiritually. Physically, they died after a long period of time after hundreds of years: "And all the days that Adam lived were nine hundred and thirty years: and he died" (Genesis 5:5). But spiritually they had both died instantaneously the moment they ate from the tree of the knowledge of good and evil, as they were both separated from fellowship with the Lord Jesus Christ.

Spiritual death is separation from God; and spiritual birth is the reopening of the channel of the fellowship between you and God. What separates a person from God is sin. So, the channel of fellowship reopens or you get born spiritually again when your sins are forgiven by washing them in the blood of Jesus for: "without shedding of blood is no remission" (Hebrews 9:22).

The whole Bible teaches that salvation is not by works but by faith, by believing in the blood of the Lord Jesus Christ being shed on the Cross for the remission of your sins and mine and the entire human race: "Being justified freely by his grace through the redemption that is in Christ Jesus: Whom God hath set forth to be a propitiation through faith in his blood" (Romans 3:24-25).

We also find in Scripture that just as there is a first birth and a second birth, a first death and a second death, there is a first resurrection and a second resurrection!

The first resurrection is for everyone justified by the blood of Christ, for all the righteous of mankind: "the Lord my God shall come, and all the saints with thee" (Zechariah 14: 5). The resurrection of the righteous people of the Old Testament and the righteous people of the New Testament is the first rapture at the end of the church age where: "We shall be caught up together with them in the clouds, to meet the Lord in the air" (1 Thessalonians 4:17)

The second rapture is that of the righteous of the Great Tribulation at its end, when: "Then shall two be in the field; the one shall be taken, and the other left" (Matthew 24: 40); at the beginning of the Millennial reign and rule of the Lord Jesus: "and they lived and reigned with Christ a thousand years. But the rest of the dead lived not again until the thousand years were finished. This is the first resurrection. "Blessed and holy is he that hath part in the first resurrection: on such the second death hath no power" (Revelation 20:4-6).

This is the fate and destiny of everyone who has had a second birth in Christ, as the Lord Jesus tells us: "Verily, verily, I say unto you, He that heareth my word, and believeth on him that sent me, hath everlasting life, and shall not come into condemnation; but is passed from death unto life"; "I am the resurrection, and the life: he that believeth in me, though he were dead, yet shall he live" (John 5:24; 11:25).

All the wicked of the human race from Cain up to the false Christ or Antichrist, are spiritually dead and will remain physically dead without a first resurrection. Their fate is the second resurrection for judgement which is the second death.

At the end of the Millennium, the Lord Jesus will judge them according to their evil and wicked deeds. Then they all will be thrown into the lake of fire and brimstone, along with Satan, the false Christ, the False prophet and the evil angels, where the suffering of every one is according to their evil work.

Dear reader, is your destiny Hell or Heaven? This is the most serious question in life! If you do not come to Jesus and accept him as your Lord and Saviour, then in reality you are rejecting him and your destiny will be in the lake of fire. By your acceptance of Christ, your reward is eternal life and you will go to the paradise of bliss in the 3rd heaven: "I knew a man in Christ above fourteen years ago, whether in the body, I cannot tell; or whether out of the body, I cannot tell: God knoweth; such an one caught up to the third heaven. And I knew such a man, whether in the body, or out of the body, I cannot tell: God knoweth; How that he was caught up into paradise, and heard unspeakable words, which it is not lawful for a man to utter" (2 Corinthians 12: 2-4).

So if you do not have in your heart the assurance of salvation then come to Jesus and open your heart to Him and surrender to Him the ownership of your life and say unto Him: "Lord Jesus, I am a sinner. I come to You today. I repent of my sins and I accept You as Lord and Savior of my life. I surrender the title deed of my life to You. Cleanse me and wash my sins away with Your blood that was shed in my place on the cross. I thank you for forgiving my sins and giving me eternal life with you, Lord Jesus! Amen.

If you have prayed this prayer to Jesus then your fate is Heaven where: "Eye hath not seen, nor ear heard, neither have entered into the heart of man, the things which God hath prepared for them that love him" (1 Corinthians 2:9).

(7) "And when the thousand years are expired, Satan shall be loosed out of his prison,"

As mentioned under verse (4), at the end of the millennium, the world will be filled with wicked men born during the millennial reign. These men will reject the rule of the Lord Jesus, even though he is present in their midst, ruling over them in peace, joy, gladness, righteousness, and holiness. Man's nature is fallen, wicked, and corrupt in its structure and composition; it is loathed with sin. Today, people blame the devil for their problems, but during the millennium the devil will be bound; still with the devil out of the picture, people will rebel and reject Jesus. Therefore, at the end of the millennium, the Lord Jesus will briefly release the devil from his imprisonment as part of his eternal purpose to free mankind and earth from the oppression of sin and its loathsomeness and its consequences.

(8) "And shall go out to deceive the nations which are in the four quarters of the earth, Gog and Magog, to gather them together to battle: the number of whom is as the sand of the sea.

Satan's nature does not change. He continues to hate the Lord Jesus, the Lord of glory. He also continues with his old habits of rebellion against the Lord: "For thou hast said in thine heart, I will ascend into heaven, I will exalt my throne above the stars of God: I will sit also upon the mount of the congregation, in the sides of the north: I will ascend above the heights of the clouds; I will be like the most High" (Isaiah 14:13-14). Satan will gather all his associates one last time in an attempt to overthrow the Jewish people and to revolt against Christ.

(9) "And they went up on the breadth of the earth, and compassed the camp of the saints about, and the beloved city: and fire came down from God out of heaven, and devoured them."

Here, the powers of Russia along with an alliance of all the nations of the world join in making war in a "Second Battle of Armageddon", meaning to occupy Jerusalem. In this second Armageddon, there is no Antichrist, no False prophet, no revived Roman Empire, but the countries of the north, Gog and Magog, that is Russia and its allies according to the table of nations in Genesis chapter 10, will be used by Satan to make war against the nation of Israel. It is their intent to occupy Jerusalem and to plunder its riches, as Jerusalem will be the richest city in the world in the millennium, for "the abundance of the sea shall be converted unto thee, the forces of the Gentiles shall come unto thee" (Isaiah 60:5).

The Lord Jesus will intervene and send down his fire from

on high. The fire of the Lord will come down from heaven and destroy them: "And I will plead against him with pestilence and with blood; and I will rain upon him, and upon his bands, and upon the many people that are with him, an overflowing rain, and great hailstones, fire, and brimstone. Thus will I magnify myself, and sanctify myself; and I will be known in the eyes of many nations, and they shall know that I am the Lord" (Ezekiel 38:22-23); "Therefore, thou son of man, prophesy against Gog, and say, Thus saith the Lord God; Behold, I am against thee, O Gog, the chief prince of Meshech and Tubal: And I will turn thee back, and leave but the sixth part of thee, and will cause thee to come up from the north parts, and will bring thee upon the mountains of Israel: And I will smite thy bow out of thy left hand, and will cause thine arrows to fall out of thy right hand. Thou shalt fall upon the mountains of Israel, thou, and all thy bands, and the people that is with thee: I will give thee unto the ravenous birds of every sort, and to the beasts of the field to be devoured. Thou shalt fall upon the open field: for I have spoken it, saith the Lord God. And I will send a fire on Magog, and among them that dwell carelessly in the isles: and they shall know that I am the Lord. So will I make my holy name known in the midst of my people Israel; and I will not let them pollute my holy name any more: and the heathen shall know that I am the Lord, the Holy One in Israel ... And it shall come to pass in that day, that I will give unto Gog a place there of graves in Israel, the valley of the passengers on the east of the sea: and it shall stop the noses of the passengers: and there shall they bury Gog and all his multitude: and they shall call it The valley of Hamongog. And seven months shall the house of Israel be burying of them, that they may cleanse the land" (Ezekiel 39:1-7, 11-12).

(10) "And the devil that deceived them was cast into the lake of fire and brimstone, where the beast and the False prophet are, and shall be tormented day and night for ever and ever."

This is Satan's final destruction when he will be cast in the lake of fire and brimstone forever. Ultimately, Satan, the Antichrist, and the False prophet will be brought together, experiencing punishment and torment eternally in hell. Additionally, hell will be the portion of all sinful people, "Hell fire: Where their worm dieth not, and the fire is not quenched" (Mark 9:47-48); "And they shall go forth, and look upon the carcases of the men that have transgressed against me: for their worm shall not die, neither shall their fire be quenched; and they shall be an abhorring unto all flesh" (Isaiah 66,24).

(11) "And I saw a great white throne, and him that sat on it, from whose face the earth and the heaven fled away; and there was found no place for them."

- And I saw a great white throne, and him that sat on it - This is the most important scene in all the Bible, and it occurs at the end of the world in the presence of the Father, the Son, and the Holy Spirit. We saw this very clearly in chapter 5: "And I beheld, and, lo, in the midst of the throne and of the four beasts, and in the midst of the elders, stood a Lamb as it had been slain, having seven horns and seven eyes, which are the seven Spirits of God sent forth into all the earth" (Revelation 5:6). The vision of the heavenly throne and the presence of God and the Lord Jesus together is a common scene throughout the Bible from Genesis to Revelation: "And God said, Let us make man in our image, after our likeness ... let us go down, and there confound their language" (Genesis 1:26; 11:7); "I beheld till the thrones were cast down, and the Ancient of days did sit, whose garment was white as snow, and the hair of his head like the pure wool: his throne was like the fiery flame, and his wheels as burning fire. A fiery stream issued and came forth from before him: thousand thousands ministered unto him, and ten thousand times ten thousand stood before him: the judgment was set, and the books were opened ... I saw in the night visions, and, behold, one like the Son of man came with the clouds of heaven, and came to the Ancient of days, and they brought him near before him. And there was given him dominion, and glory, and a kingdom, that all people, nations, and languages, should serve him: his dominion is an everlasting dominion, which shall not pass away" (Daniel 7:9-10, 13-14); "To him that overcometh will I grant to sit with me in my throne, even as I also overcame, and am set down with my Father in his throne ... And every creature which is in heaven, and on the earth, and under the earth, and such as are in the sea, and all that are in them, heard I saying, Blessing, and honour, and glory, and power, be unto him that sitteth upon the throne, and unto the Lamb for ever and ever ... And said to the mountains and rocks, Fall on us, and hide us from the face of him that sitteth on the throne, and from the wrath of the Lamb ... After this I beheld, and, lo, a great multitude, which no man could number, of all nations, and kindreds, and people, and tongues, stood before the throne, and before the Lamb, clothed with white robes, and palms in their hands; And cried with a loud voice, saying, Salvation to our God which sitteth upon the throne, and unto the Lamb ... And I saw no temple therein: for the Lord God Almighty and the Lamb are the temple of it. And the city had no need of the sun, neither of the moon, to shine in it: for the glory of God did lighten it, and the Lamb is the light thereof ... And he shewed me a pure river of water of life, clear as crystal, proceeding out of the throne of God and of the Lamb ... And there shall be no more curse: but the throne of God and of the Lamb shall be in it; and his servants shall serve him" (Revelation 3:21; 5:13; 6:16; 7:9-10; 21:22-23; 22:1, 3). Here the Lord Jesus Christ appears in his role as the just Judge before the presence of God.

There are three seats of the judgement of Christ, and each individual shall stand before one of them:

(i) BEMA Seat of Christ in heaven for the redeemed in Christ; right after the Rapture to be rewarded for their faithfulness and service to the Lord Jesus. It is a resurrection for rewards: "¹⁰Blessed are they which are persecuted for righteousness' sake: for theirs is the kingdom of heaven. ¹¹Blessed are ye, when men shall revile you, and persecute you, and shall say all manner of evil against you falsely, for my sake. ¹²Rejoice, and be exceeding glad: for great is your reward in heaven" (Matthew 5:10-12); "¹³Every man's work shall be made manifest: for the day shall declare it, because it shall be revealed by fire; and the fire shall try every man's work of what sort it is. ¹⁴If any man's work abide which he hath built thereupon, he shall receive a reward. ¹⁵If any man's work shall be burned, he shall suffer loss: but he himself shall be saved; yet so as by fire" (1 Corinthians 3:13-15); "¹⁰For we must all appear before the judgment seat of Christ; that every one may receive the things done in his body, according to that he hath done, whether it be good or bad" (2 Corinthians 5:10); "¹¹It is a faithful saying: For if we be dead with him, we shall also live with him: ¹²If we suffer, we shall also reign with him: if we deny him, he also will deny us: ¹³If we believe not, yet he abideth faithful: he cannot deny himself" (2 Timothy 2:11-13).

(ii) Throne of Christ the King on earth to judge all the living at the end of the Great Tribulation, to purge his kingdom from the sinners and begin the 1,000 years reign of his monarchy: "When the Son of man shall come in his glory, and all the holy angels with him, then shall he sit upon the throne of his glory: And before him shall be gathered all nations: and he shall separate them one from another, as a shepherd divideth his sheep from the goats: And he shall set the sheep on his right hand, but the goats on the left. Then shall the King say unto them on his right hand, Come, ye blessed of my Father, inherit the kingdom prepared for you from the foundation of the world: For I was an hungred, and ye gave me meat: I was thirsty, and ye gave me drink: I was a stranger, and ye took me in: Naked, and ye clothed me: I was sick, and ye visited me: I was in prison, and ye came unto me. Then shall the righteous answer him, saying,

Lord, when saw we thee an hungred, and fed thee? or thirsty, and gave thee drink? When saw we thee a stranger, and took thee in? or naked, and clothed thee? Or when saw we thee sick, or in prison, and came unto thee? And the King shall answer and say unto them, Verily I say unto you, Inasmuch as ye have done it unto one of the least of these my brethren, ye have done it unto me. Then shall he say also unto them on the left hand, Depart from me, ye cursed, into everlasting fire, prepared for the devil and his angels: For I was an hungred, and ye gave me no meat: I was thirsty, and ye gave me no drink: I was a stranger, and ye took me not in: naked, and ye clothed me not: sick, and in prison, and ye visited me not. Then shall they also answer him, saying, Lord, when saw we thee an hungred, or athirst, or a stranger, or naked, or sick, or in prison, and did not minister unto thee? Then shall he answer them, saying, Verily I say unto you, Inasmuch as ye did it not to one of the least of these, ye did it not to me" (Matthew 25:31-45).

(iii) The Great White throne of the judgement of God in heaven at the end of the Millennium and the end of the world: "[11]And I saw a great white throne, and him that sat on it, from whose face the earth and the heaven fled away; and there was found no place for them. [12]And I saw the dead, small and great, stand before God; and the books were opened: and another book was opened, which is the book of life: and the dead were judged out of those things which were written in the books, according to their works. [13]And the sea gave up the dead which were in it; and death and hell delivered up the dead which were in them: and they were judged every man according to their works. [14]And death and hell were cast into the lake of fire. This is the second death. [15]And whosoever was not found written in the book of life was cast into the lake of fire" (Revelation 20:11-15). This judgment at the end of the millennium will happen when the Lord Jesus sends out his angels throughout his kingdom to gather up all the unbelieving sinners: "The harvest is the end of the world; and the reapers are the angels. As therefore the tares are gathered and burned in the fire; so shall it be in the end of this world. The Son of man shall send forth his angels, and they shall gather out of his kingdom all things that offend, and them which do iniquity; And shall cast them into a furnace of fire: there shall be wailing and gnashing of teeth. Then shall the righteous shine forth as the sun in the kingdom of their Father" (Matthew 13:39-43). The redeemed born again believers of Christ are present in this scene here but they will be in glorified bodies with the Lord Jesus to judge:

(a) Wicked people: "Do ye not know that the saints shall judge the world?" (1 Corinthians 6:2);

(b) Angels: "Know ye not that we shall judge angels? how much more things that pertain to this life?"(1 Corinthians 6:3); "And the angels which kept not their first estate, but left their own habitation, he hath reserved in everlasting chains under darkness unto the judgment of the great day" (Jude 6).

Coinciding with this judgment is the promise of the Apostle Peter: "Seeing then that all these things shall be dissolved, what manner of persons ought ye to be in all holy conversation and godliness, Looking for and hasting unto the coming of the day of God, wherein the heavens being on fire shall be dissolved, and the elements shall melt with fervent heat? Nevertheless we, according to his promise, look for new heavens and a new earth, wherein dwelleth righteousness" (2 Peter 3:11-13).

- From whose face the earth and the heaven fled away; and there was found no place for them - He then will end the history of the human race and admit the righteous, whose names are in the book of life, into eternity. On this day of the Lord, prophecies of Isaiah, Haggai, Peter the apostle, and Paul the apostle come to pass: "Behold, the day of the Lord cometh, cruel both with wrath and fierce anger, to lay the land desolate: and he shall destroy the sinners thereof out of it. For the stars of heaven and the constellations thereof shall not give their light: the sun shall be darkened in his going forth, and the moon shall not cause her light to shine. And I will punish the world for their evil, and the wicked for their iniquity; and I will cause the arrogancy of the proud to cease, and will lay low the haughtiness of the terrible. I will make a man more precious than fine gold; even a man than the golden wedge of Ophir. Therefore I will shake the heavens, and the earth shall remove out of her place, in the wrath of the Lord of hosts, and in the day of his fierce anger" (Isaiah 13:9-13); "For thus saith the Lord of hosts; Yet once, it is a little while, and I will shake the heavens, and the earth, and the sea, and the dry land; And I will shake all nations, and the desire of all nations shall come: and I will fill this house with glory, saith the Lord of hosts" (Haggai 2:6-7); "Whose voice then shook the earth: but now he hath promised, saying, Yet once more I shake not the earth only, but also heaven. And this word, Yet once more, signifieth the removing of those things that are shaken, as of things that are made, that those things which cannot be shaken may remain" (Hebrews 12:26-27); "Looking for and hasting unto the coming of the day of God, wherein the heavens being on fire shall be dissolved, and the elements shall melt with fervent heat? Nevertheless we, according to his promise, look for new heavens and a new earth, wherein dwelleth righteousness" (2 Peter 3:12-13).

(12) "And I saw the dead, small and great, stand before God; and the books were opened: and another book was opened, which is the book of life: and the dead were judged out of those things which were written in the books, according to their works."

All the dead of the human race shall gather in the presence of God. If we want to divide the Word of truth rightly, then they are all unsaved sinners, for the saved believers of the Old Testament and the New Testament and the Great Tribulation and the Millennium have all risen in the three raptures. This is the well known and fearful day of the Lord: "Alas for the day! for the day of the Lord is at hand, and as a destruction from the Almighty shall it come ... The sun shall be turned into darkness, and the moon into blood, before the great and terrible day of the Lord come" (Joel 1:15; 2:31); "the great and notable day of the Lord come ... Because he hath appointed a day, in the which he will judge the world in righteousness by that man whom he hath ordained; whereof he hath given assurance unto all men, in that he hath raised him from the dead" (Acts 2:20; 17:31).

It is the day of the Lord's anger and judgment: "Behold, the day of the Lord cometh, cruel both with wrath and fierce anger, to lay the land desolate: and he shall destroy the sinners thereof out of it" (Isaiah 13:9).

All of creation will be gathered here in the presence of God, and the born again redeemed of the Lord will be taking part in judging: "Know ye not that we shall judge angels? how much more things that pertain to this life?"(1 Corinthians 6:3);

Note that the book of life is different and independent from the rest of the books. The book of life is the book of all believers in Jesus and shall not come into condemnation because they have shall already passed from death unto life in Christ. This includes all believers, including the righteous of the millennium, whose portion will be with all other saints. Every unsaved sinner shall stand before the Lord Jesus and the book of his life on earth will be opened up and he will be judged according to it. Billions of books will be opened, and each book will reveal what its owner has done and how he had lived from the cradle to the coffin.

(13) "And the sea gave up the dead which were in it; and death and hell delivered up the dead which were in them: and they were judged every man according to their works."

All the dead of the human race who have not experienced

God's forgiveness and the salvation of the Lord Jesus will be judged at this time, whether they be small or great, women or men. All the sinful seed of Adam and Eve will be called to account whatever their nationality or race and irrespective of how and when they died. All will be brought, in trembling, before God's Great White Throne to be sentenced for eternal punishment.

One by one, each will be judged according to the wickedness of his deeds and his thoughts; each one will be punished in the fires of hell. The Word of God warns of such a terrible fate: "The Son of man indeed goeth, as it is written of him: but woe to that man by whom the Son of man is betrayed! good were it for that man if he had never been born" (Mark 14:21); "Then said he unto the disciples, It is impossible but that offences will come: but woe unto him, through whom they come! It were better for him that a millstone were hanged about his neck, and he cast into the sea, than that he should offend one of these little ones" (Luke 17:1-2).

(14) "And death and hell were cast into the lake of fire. This is the second death."

All the physically and spiritually dead are now temporarily in prison in the place of torment in the belly of the earth in hell. Then they shall stand before God's great white throne, and then all the sinful people and hell itself will be cast into the lake of fire and brimstone eternally. The second death and the lake of fire are twins both speaking to the final condition that awaits all unsaved sinners.

In the second death, sinners will be given corrupt, cursed bodies that never die and are full of worms: "And they shall go forth, and look upon the carcases of the men that have transgressed against me: for their worm shall not die, neither shall their fire be quenched; and they shall be an abhorring unto all flesh" (Isaiah 66:24); "And if thy hand offend thee, cut it off: it is better for thee to enter into life maimed, than having two hands to go into hell, into the fire that never shall be quenched: Where their worm dieth not, and the fire is not quenched" (Mark 9:43-44).

They will not die and they will not cease to exist; for they will "be tormented day and night for ever and ever" (Revelation 20:10). Their suffering will know no end.

As we explained in verse six, this is the second death which is eternal separation from Jesus Christ, the living Son of God.

(15) "And whosoever was not found written in the book of life was cast into the lake of fire."

The second death is spending eternity of torment in hell, and it is the lot of every individual whose name is not written in the book of the Lamb, the Lord Jesus.

The consolation of every person who has repented of his sins and accepted Jesus as Lord and Saviour of his life and his name is written in the Lamb's book of life: "Notwithstanding in this rejoice not, that the spirits are subject unto you; but rather rejoice, because your names are written in heaven" (Luke 10:20); "Those women which laboured with me in the gospel, with Clement also, and with other my fellowlabourers, whose names are in the book of life" (Philippians 4:3); "He that overcometh, the same shall be clothed in white raiment; and I will not blot out his name out of the book of life, but I will confess his name before my Father, and before his angels ...And all that dwell upon the earth shall worship him, whose names are not written in the book of life of the Lamb slain from the foundation of the world ...And they that dwell on the earth shall wonder, whose names were not written in the book of life from the foundation of the world ... And there shall in no wise enter into it any thing that defileth, neither whatsoever worketh abomination, or maketh a lie: but they which are written in the Lamb's book of life" (Revelation 3:5; 13:8; 17:8; 21:27).

What is the lake of fire? The Lord Jesus spoke about hell more than any other person did, since he does not want you to go there. The lake of fire is hell; its various features are mentioned in several Bible passages:

(i) Its streams are of pitch and brimstone, like burning volcanic lava: "And the streams thereof shall be turned into pitch, and the dust thereof into brimstone, and the land thereof shall become burning pitch" (Isaiah 34:9).

(ii) Worms eat you continuously: "Where their worm dieth not, and the fire is not quenched" (Mark 9:44).

(iii) A place of crying, tears, and gnashing of teeth: "Wailing and gnashing of teeth" (Matthew 13:42).

(iv) A place of torment in the flames of fire; "I am tormented in this flame" (Luke 16:24).

(v) A place of thick darkness in which you will not see light forever: "They shall never see light" (Psalm 49:19).

(vi) You will have an eternally corrupt body which constantly produces worms: "And they shall go forth, and look upon the carcases of the men that have transgressed against me: for their worm shall not die, neither shall their fire be quenched; and they shall be an abhorring unto all flesh" (Isaiah 66:24).

(vii) A place of never quenched fire: "Everlasting fire, prepared for the devil and his angels" (Matthew 25:41).

(viii) A place of eternal torment: "And the smoke of their torment ascendeth up for ever and ever: and they have no rest day nor night" (Revelation 14:11).

There is no joy in this world like the joy of forgiveness of sins and knowing that your name is written in heaven in the book of life of the Lord Jesus Christ, the Son of the living God: "But rather rejoice, because your names are written in heaven" (Luke 10:20).

Behold, his hand is reaching forth to you: "Come unto me, all ye that labor and are heavy laden, and I will give you rest. Take my yoke upon you, and learn of me; for I am meek and lowly in heart: and ye shall find rest unto your souls. For my yoke is easy, and my burden is light" (Matthew 11:28-30).

Open your heart to him. Give him the title deed to your life, and you will live forever.

Thus ends the story of man upon the earth. In the last two chapters, we will see a quick glimpse, faster than lightning, of the joyful eternity that awaits all of us who love the Lord Jesus, the Lord of glory. Blessed be his name Jesus, Saviour, Emmanuel God with us!

21

THE NEW JERUSALEM AND ENTERING ETERNAL JOY

(1) "And I saw a new heaven and a new earth: for the first heaven and the first earth were passed away; and there was no more sea."

- And I saw a new heaven and a new earth: for the first heaven and the first earth were passed away - In spite of the great beauty of the millennium, still it is not God's final plan for us. Rather, he has an ideal world in store for us.

After the millennium, after Satan's rebellion and final judgment, and after the demise of the earth and stars and planets and moons and the sun, and after sin and death cease to exist, a new heaven and earth will appear as the Lord Jesus promised in the Bible: "Nevertheless we, according to his promise, look for new heavens and a new earth, wherein dwelleth righteousness" (2 Peter 3:13).

So beginning with this verse, we leave behind the old life and old world, and enter a utopic world of a new ideal heaven and a new ideal righteous earth.

- And there was no more sea - In our world today, three quarters of the globe is covered with water. However, in the new earth there will be no sea, which has a connection to Satan.

In studying the Bible, we find that where there is a sea, or seas, or lakes, or an abundance of water, satanic activity increases. The earth is a symbol of good in the Bible, like the promise of the land of Canaan, whereas the sea is a symbol of evil: "Am I a sea, or a whale, that thou settest a watch over me?" (Job 7:12); "In that day the Lord with his sore and great and strong sword shall punish leviathan the piercing serpent, even leviathan that crooked serpent; and he shall slay the dragon that is in the sea" (Isaiah 27:1). The country of the Gadarenes' population lived by the sea: "And they came over unto the other side of the sea, into the country of the Gadarenes. And when he was come out of the ship, immediately there met him out of the tombs a man with an unclean spirit" (Mark 5:1-2). When the Lord Jesus allowed the evil spirits to enter into the swine, the spirits led the swine into the water so that they may rest, killing the animals: "And forthwith Jesus gave them leave. And the unclean spirits went out, and entered into the swine: and the herd ran violently down a steep place into the sea, (they were about two thousand;) and were choked in the sea" (Mark 5:13).

Also Satan used the sea to try to attack Jesus: "Now it came to pass on a certain day, that he went into a ship with his disciples: and he said unto them, Let us go over unto the other side of the lake. And they launched forth. But as they sailed he fell asleep: and there came down a storm of wind on the lake; and they were filled with water, and were in jeopardy" (Luke 8:22-23). In the gospels of Matthew and Luke, an evil spirit goes out of a man to search for water, and not finding any water, he returns: "When the unclean spirit is gone out of a man, he walketh through dry places, seeking rest; and finding none, he saith, I will return unto my house whence I came out" (Luke 11:24). The devil tried to kill Paul the Apostle at sea: "But not long after there arose against it a tempestuous wind, called Euroclydon. And when the ship was caught, and could not bear up into the wind, we let her drive" (Acts 27:14-15). Even when the Lord saved him: "Saying, Fear not, Paul" (Acts 27:24), Satan got a snake to bite Paul after the rains in Malta: "And when Paul had gathered a bundle of sticks, and laid them on the fire, there came a viper out of the heat, and fastened on his hand" (Acts 28:3). We also saw previously that the Antichrist came from the sea: "And I stood upon the sand of the sea, and saw a beast rise up out of the sea" (Revelation 13:1). So we see a link between the sea, or water, and Satan's increased violence. We see this with the demon possessed boy that Jesus healed: "And ofttimes it hath cast him into the fire, and into the waters, to destroy him" (Mark 9:22). I think that the profound reason is that most of the surface of the earth is covered with water, and Satan has authority over it because he was given this authority when he fell. This will last until the Lord Jesus takes back the title deed to earth from him as we expounded in chapter five. We thank that Lord that we stand on the shore of safety in Jesus, for he alone is the rock and every thing he does is perfect: "He is the Rock, his work is perfect: for all his ways are judgment: a God of truth and without iniquity, just and right is he" (Deuteronomy 32:4). The Lord Jesus is our rock and our refuge; he is our firm security throughout eternity!

(2) "And I John saw the holy city, new Jerusalem, coming down from God out of heaven, prepared as a bride adorned for her husband."

- And I John saw - John mentions his personal name with an adjective 5 times in

the book of Revelaion:

(i) "The Revelation of Jesus Christ, which God gave unto him, to shew unto his servants things which must shortly come to pass; and he sent and signified it by his angel unto his servant John" (Revelation 1:1).

(ii) "John to the seven churches which are in Asia" (Revelation 1:4).

(iii) "I John, who also am your brother, and companion in

tribulation, and in the kingdom and patience of Jesus Christ" (Revelation 1:9).

(iv) "And I John saw the holy city, new Jerusalem, coming down from God out of heaven" (Revelation 21:2).

(v) "And I John saw these things, and heard them" (Revelation 22:8).

In each statement, John emphasizes the importance, seriousness, and credibility of that which he sees and what he testifies of. John here bears witness that he sees a new Jerusalem that is a real heavenly city.

There are also five women mentioned in the book of Revelation, one of which is this new heavenly Jerusalem:

(i) Jezebel, the heretical member of the church of Thyatira: "Notwithstanding I have a few things against thee, because thou sufferest that woman Jezebel, which calleth herself a prophetess, to teach and to seduce my servants to commit fornication, and to eat things sacrificed unto idols" (Revelation 2:20).

(ii) The woman clothed with the sun, the moon, and the planets- a symbol of the nation of Israel: "And there appeared a great wonder in heaven; a woman clothed with the sun, and the moon under her feet, and upon her head a crown of twelve stars" (Revelation 12:1).

(iii) Babylon: "So he carried me away in the spirit into the wilderness: and I saw a woman sit upon a scarlet coloured beast, full of names of blasphemy, having seven heads and ten horns" (Revelation 17:3).

(iv) The church, the bride of Christ: "Let us be glad and rejoice, and give honour to him: for the marriage of the Lamb is come, and his wife hath made herself ready" (Revelation 19:7).

(v) The heavenly Jerusalem, the bride of God in Revelation 21:2, our current verse.

We see a woman as a person, or a nation, or a group of people. In this verse, we see her as a magnificent glittering brilliant city.

The number five is the number of grace or death in the Bible:

(a) Positively, Benjamin took five portions from Joseph, and the temple had five porches.

(b) Negatively, in the fifth verse of the fifth chapter of the fifth book of the New Testament, the book of Acts, a liar drops dead at the feet of the Apostle Peter (Acts 5:5).

Five times a man is mentioned in Revelation, namely the Apostle John, and five times different women are mentioned. This connection speaks to the completeness of the story of redemption.

The number five is the number of Jesus' wounds on the cross, but these wounds were the source of Jesus' grace for our salvation and our eternal fellowship with him. The Lord Jesus loves to fellowship with us. We see this mentioned five times in the Bible:

(i) In the garden of Eden, the Lord Jesus enjoyed fellowship with Adam and Eve before the fall;

(ii) In the Old Testament, the Lord lived with his people in the temple, in the holiest of holies;

(iii) In the age of grace the Lord resides in the midst of his church;

(iv) In the millennium, the Lord lives with his bride, the church;

(v) In eternity we see the Lord Jesus in eternal fellowship with the fifth and final woman, the perfect bride of God, the heavenly Jerusalem.

- The holy city, new Jerusalem, coming down from God out of heaven, prepared as a bride adorned for her husband - Here, we see the new heavenly Jerusalem descend as an eternal bride for the son of the living God.

As we said in our explanation of Revelation (12:5), the

church is Jesus' bride on earth in the Millennium, while the new Jerusalem is Jesus' bride in heaven in eternity.

(3) "And I heard a great voice out of heaven saying, Behold, the tabernacle of God is with men, and he will dwell with them, and they shall be his people, and God himself shall be with them, and be their God."

The heavenly Jerusalem will be our dwelling place with God throughout eternity. It is our eternal home, the abode of all the righteous, the habitation of all the children of the Lord Jesus: "But Jerusalem which is above is free, which is the mother of us all" (Galatians 4:26). Abraham, the father of believers, saw it: "For he looked for a city which hath foundations, whose builder and maker is God" (Hebrews 11:10). The new Jerusalem was promised to us by the Lord Jesus in the gospel of John: "In my Father's house are many mansions: if it were not so, I would have told you. I go to prepare a place for you. And if I go and prepare a place for you, I will come again, and receive you unto myself; that where I am, there ye may be also" (John 14:2-3).

(4) "And God shall wipe away all tears from their eyes; and there shall be no more death, neither sorrow, nor crying, neither shall there be any more pain: for the former things are passed away."

Sin has brought sadness, crying, tears, pain, and death. But the Lord Jesus will bring an end to all these things. He will wipe away the tears of the past. Our former lives here upon the earth will be as a dream which has passed away: "As a dream when one awaketh" (Psalm 73:20). The Lord Jesus will make us forget our first life, which will no longer "come into mind" (Isaiah 65:17).

(5) "And he that sat upon the throne said, Behold, I make all things new. And he said unto me, Write: for these words are true and faithful."

Indeed, when we got saved and received the new birth, we were given a new spiritual nature, a new destiny, and a new eternity which exceeds imagination and description: "Eye hath not seen, nor ear heard, neither have entered into the heart of man, the things which God hath prepared for them that love him" (1 Corinthians 2:9). Beauty, radiance and splendor await us; such magnificence as baffles our minds and thoughts. Therefore God and the Son himself assure us that these words are true, faithful, and reliable.

(6) "And he said unto me, It is done. I am Alpha and Omega, the beginning and the end. I will give unto him that is athirst of the fountain of the water of life freely.'

God's program for man is then complete, and so we will enter eternity. The one uttering these things is God, who sits upon the throne, the giver of everlasting life that springs from him; the giver of living water that quenches all thirst as a free gift by the grace of Christ who sits at the right hand of the throne.

(7) 'He that overcometh shall inherit all things; and I will be his God, and he shall be my son."

Each individual who receives the Lord Jesus as Saviour overcomes in him, and Jesus is his God. We are his children and his heirs: "And if children, then heirs; heirs of God, and joint-heirs with Christ" (Romans 8:17).

(8) "But the fearful, and unbelieving, and the abominable, and murderers, and whoremongers, and sorcerers, and idolaters, and all liars, shall have their part in the lake which burneth with fire and brimstone: which is the second death."

This describes all the sinners who were afraid to take a stand for the Lord Jesus and did not believe in him, who chose rather to defile themselves with the filthiness of the flesh. They participated in the evils of Satan, such as murder, fornication, sorcery, idolatry, and lying, their portion will be hell, the lake of fire that burns with fire and brimstone. They will be separated eternally from the Lord Jesus Christ, which is spiritual death, the second death.

Note in this verse the phrase "all liars", for Satan is a murderer, a liar, and the father of lies. In like manner, man has artistic achievements in the area of lying, being the inventor of white lies and black lies, as well as April's fool's day's lies. The important thing to the unsaved is to lie, to avoid honesty and truth because Jesus is truth: "Jesus saith unto him, I am the way, the truth, and the life: no man cometh unto the Father, but by me ... Pilate therefore said unto him, Art thou a king then? Jesus answered, Thou sayest that I am a king. To this end was I born, and for this cause came I into the world, that I should bear witness unto the truth. Every one that is of the truth heareth my voice. Pilate saith unto him, What is truth? And when he had said this, he went out again unto the Jews, and saith unto them, I find in him no fault at all" (John 14:6; 18:37-38).

(9) "And there came unto me one of the seven angels which had the seven vials full of the seven last plagues, and talked with me, saying, Come hither, I will shew thee the bride, the Lamb's wife."

There is a hidden wisdom in connecting this angel with the seven vials. One of this group of angels proclaimed the fall of the city of wickedness, Babylon: "And there came one of the seven angels which had the seven vials, and talked with me, saying unto me, Come hither; I will shew unto thee the judgment of the great whore that sitteth upon many waters" (Revelation 17:1). Now, one of these angels will also proclaim the descent of the city of righteousness, the heavenly Jerusalem.

(10) "And he carried me away in the spirit to a great and high mountain, and shewed me that great city, the holy Jerusalem, descending out of heaven from God,"

- And he carried me away in the spirit to a great and high mountain. This angel took John the Beloved to a great, blessed mountain! This is the heavenly Mount Zion, the Mount Zion of God: "Great is the LORD, and greatly to be praised in the city of our God, in the mountain of his holiness. Beautiful for situation, the joy of the whole earth, is mount Zion, on the sides of the north, the city of the great King" (Psalm 48:1-2); "Out of Zion, the perfection of beauty, God hath shined" (Psalm 50:2); "They go from strength to strength, every one of them in Zion appeareth before God" (Psalm 84:7); "And I looked, and, lo, a Lamb stood on the mount Sion, and with him an hundred forty and four thousand, having his Father's name written in their foreheads" (Revelation 14:1).

- And shewed me that great city, the holy Jerusalem, descending out of heaven from God - The Lord gave John the opportunity to see the new heavenly Jerusalem descending in its beauty from the third heaven, the throne of God. John here had the same experience which Paul the Apostle previously enjoyed: "How that he was caught up into paradise, and heard unspeakable words, which it is not lawful for a man to utter"(2 Corinthians 12:4). John had the same experience as our father Abraham, who knew of a coming city not built or made by human hand: "For he looked for a city which hath foundations, whose builder and maker is God" (Hebrews 11:10).

(11) "Having the glory of God: and her light was like unto a stone most precious, even like a jasper stone, clear as crystal;"

The heavenly Jerusalem is a holy city whose glory baffles the mind and whose radiance overwhelms the eyes. It shines like a brilliantly glittering crystal. It shines brighter than pure diamond.

(12) "And had a wall great and high, and had twelve gates, and at the gates twelve angels, and names written thereon, which are the names of the twelve tribes of the children of Israel:"

The heavenly Jerusalem is shaped like a cube according to verse 16. Along its length and breadth, it has a total of twelve gates, according to the number of the tribes of Israel. On each of the gates is written the name of one of the tribes of Israel and each gate has its own guardian angel.

(13) "On the east three gates; on the north three gates; on the south three gates; and on the west three gates."

The gates are symmetrically and evenly distributed. On each side, there are three gates, each bearing the name of one of the twelve sons of Jacob, in accordance with the familiar norm of the Law of Moses: East, North, South, and West.

(14) "And the wall of the city had twelve foundations, and in them the names of the twelve apostles of the Lamb."

The walls of the heavenly Jerusalem, with the names of the tribes of Israel, are built upon and stand upon the foundations of the city, which bear the names of the twelve disciples of the Lord Jesus.

There is an everlasting marriage between Church and Israel. According to the Bible, they are one, as each is the seed of Abraham: Physical one, that is, Israel, and the other spiritual, that is the Church. There is a joint plan for the two, for one is grafted into the other: "And if some of the branches be broken off, and thou, being a wild olive tree, wert grafted in among them, and with them partakest of the root and fatness of the olive tree" (Romans 11:17). We see this plan in practice in the harmony of the new Jerusalem.

(15) "And he that talked with me had a golden reed to measure the city, and the gates thereof, and the wall thereof."

Measurements are always important as far as the Lord Jesus is concerned, such as the measurement of Jerusalem during the millennium: "I lifted up mine eyes again, and looked, and behold a man with a measuring line in his hand. Then said I, Whither goest thou? And he said unto me, To measure Jerusalem, to see what is the breadth thereof, and what is the length thereof" (Zechariah 2:1-2). And so we are given the measurements of the heavenly city of Jerusalem, our eternal home.

(16) "And the city lieth foursquare, and the length is as large as the breadth: and he measured the city with the reed, twelve

thousand furlongs. The length and the breadth and the height of it are equal."

It is a huge and colossal city, firmly established. Its length is 1,375 miles, its width is 1,375 miles, and its height is 1,375 miles. Each dimension is about the distance between New York and Dallas, with 1,375 miles in height. These dimensions baffle the human mind for the size of a city. Blessed be the name of JESUS!

(17) "And he measured the wall thereof, an hundred and forty and four cubits, according to the measure of a man, that is, of the angel."

The vastness of this city is seen in the thickness of its wall around 44 miles.

(18) "And the building of the wall of it was of jasper: and the city was pure gold, like unto clear glass."

The wife of the lamb, the everlasting, heavenly Jerusalem, was seen by the psalmist as "standing in gold": "Upon thy right hand did stand the queen in gold of Ophir" (Psalm 45:9). John sees matters here more clearly; he sees the walls of the city made of diamonds, and its streets made of pure gold. Nothing compares to its dazzling richness nor the purity of its beauty. The text here uses descriptive words like jasper and gold, but the reality is that our human languages are ill equipped to describe the beauty of the heavenly Jerusalem city.

(19) "And the foundations of the wall of the city were garnished with all manner of precious stones. The first foundation was jasper; the second, sapphire; the third, a chalcedony; the fourth, an emerald;"

- And the foundations of the wall of the city were garnished with all manner of precious stones. The foundations of the city are decorated with precious stones, each more beautiful than the other: "O thou afflicted, tossed with tempest, and not comforted, behold, I will lay thy stones with fair colours, and lay thy foundations with sapphires. And I will make thy windows of agates, and thy gates of carbuncles, and all thy borders of pleasant stones. And all thy children shall be taught of the LORD; and great shall be the peace of thy children" (Isaiah 54:11-13). These foundations are as follows:

(i) The first is jasper- a clear crystal.

(ii) The second is blue sapphire- a bluish purple.

(iii) The third is chalcedony- a deep, pure white.

(iv) The fourth is emerald- a dark, translucent green.

(20) "The fifth, sardonyx; the sixth, sardius; the seventh, chrysolite; the eighth, beryl; the ninth, a topaz; the tenth, a chrysoprasus; the eleventh, a jacinth; the twelfth, an amethyst."

(v) The fifth is sardonyx- a dark orange similar to the colour to the setting sun.

(vi) The sixth is sardius- a deep red similar to the colour of blood.

(vii) The seventh is chrysolite- a bright green similar to the colour of grass.

(viii) The eighth is beryl- a glowing, dark green.

(ix) The ninth is a topaz- a bright yellow.

(x) The tenth is chrysoprasus- a dark, olive green.

(xi) The eleventh is jacinth- a pure gold-like yellow.

(xii) The twelfth is amethyst- purple.

If you put the colours of these stones side by side, you will obtain a beautiful panorama of colours better in harmony than the colours of a rainbow.

(21) "And the twelve gates were twelve pearls; every several gate was of one pearl: and the street of the city was pure gold, as it were transparent glass."

Although we read that each gate bears the name of one of the tribes of God's Israel, the gates themselves are each composed of one pearl. Pearls come from unclean sea animals. A pearl is a symbol of the church, which is composed of Jews and Gentiles. This confirms what the Lord Jesus said to Peter:

"What God hath cleansed, that call not thou common" (Acts 10:15).

Each gate of the new Jerusalem is one, huge pearl. There are no appropriate words to use, and all languages fail to capture or express the wondrous beauty of the heavenly city of Jerusalem.

(22) "And I saw no temple therein: for the Lord God Almighty and the Lamb are the temple of it."

There will be no need for a temple in the heavenly Jerusalem, for we will be in the presence of the Lord God constantly forever and ever, and this is the grand feature of this city. The fabulous distinction in the heavenly Jerusalem is that we shall dwell with God the Father and the Son. Jesus will lead us like a Shepherd, bringing us to fountains of living water. We will dwell and live with the Lord Jesus and with God forever!

The triune God and the Lord Jesus Christ are one: "I and my Father are one" (John 10:30); "For in him dwelleth all the fulness of the Godhead bodily" (Colossians 2:9); "Whosoever transgresseth, and abideth not in the doctrine of Christ, hath not God. He that abideth in the doctrine of Christ, he hath both the Father and the Son" (2 John 1:9); "I am Alpha and Omega, the beginning and the ending, saith the Lord, which is, and which was, and which is to come, the Almighty ... I am the first and the last: I am he that liveth, and was dead; and, behold, I am alive for evermore" (Revelation 1:8, 17-18). This is why our text says God and the Lamb are both, jointly, the temple of heaven.

We obtain all these privileges and glory because Jesus paid the price for our salvation on the cross of Golgotha. He died and rose again to purchase our redemption and bring us this everlasting glory: "Jesus, when he had cried again with a loud voice, yielded up the ghost ...And the angel answered and said unto the women, Fear not ye: for I know that ye seek Jesus, which was crucified. He is not here: for he is risen, as he said" (Matthew 27:50; 28:5-6); "If in this life only we have hope in Christ, we are of all men most miserable. But now is Christ risen from the dead, and become the firstfruits of them that slept. For since by man came death, by man came also the resurrection of the dead. For as in Adam all die, even so in Christ shall all be made alive" (1 Corinthians 15:19-22); "But we all, with open face beholding as in a glass the glory of the Lord, are changed into the same image from glory to glory, even as by the Spirit of the Lord" (2 Corinthians 3:18); "Whereunto he called you by our gospel, to the obtaining of the glory of our Lord Jesus Christ" (2 Thessalonians 2:14).

(23) "And the city had no need of the sun, neither of the moon, to shine in it: for the glory of God did lighten it, and the Lamb is the light thereof."

As we expounded in Revelation (16:8), light ultimately comes from God for: "God is light" (1 John 1:5); He dwells in "light which no man can approach unto" (1 Timothy 6:16). The Bible also bears witness to the light of Christ: "And after six days Jesus taketh Peter, James, and John his brother, and bringeth them up into an high mountain apart, And was transfigured before them: and his face did shine as the sun, and his raiment was white as the light" (Matthew 17:1-2). Paul said, "At midday, O king, I saw in the way a light from heaven, above the brightness of the sun, shining round about me and them which journeyed with me" (Acts 26:13). John said: "And his countenance was as the sun shineth in his strength" (Revelation 1:16). When we enter eternity, the light of God and the light Christ will shine more brightly than the sun shines during the day. The splendour and glory of God and the Lamb are not only the temple of the new Heaven, but also provide its light: "So shall it be in the end of this world. The Son of man shall send forth his angels, and they shall gather out of his kingdom all things that offend, and them which do iniquity; And shall cast them into a furnace of fire: there shall be wailing and gnashing of teeth. Then shall the righteous shine forth as the sun in the kingdom of their Father" (Matthew 13:40-43).

(24) "And the nations of them which are saved shall walk in the light of it: and the kings of the earth do bring their glory and honour into it."

Several verses in the Bible indicate that in eternity there will be some sort of a connection or correlation among people and individuals according to what ties they had while on earth. For example, the Bible places value on the burial of a man and his wife in the same tomb as was the case for Abraham and Sarah, Isaac and Rebecca, and Jacob and Leah: "And he charged them, and said unto them, I am to be gathered unto my people: bury me with my fathers in the cave that is in the field of Ephron the Hittite, In the cave that is in the field of Machpelah, which is before Mamre, in the land of Canaan, which Abraham bought with the field of Ephron the Hittite for a possession of a burying place. There they buried Abraham and Sarah his wife; there they buried Isaac and Rebekah his wife; and there I buried Leah. The purchase of the field and of the cave that is therein was from the children of Heth. And when Jacob had made an end of commanding his sons, he gathered up his feet into the bed, and yielded up the ghost, and was gathered unto his people" (Genesis 49:29-33).

There is a blessing associated with the burial of a person at the grave-site of his fathers, as we see in the example of Barzillai the Gileadite: "Let thy servant, I pray thee, turn back again, that I may die in mine own city, and be buried by the grave of my father and of my mother" (2 Samuel 19:37). There is also a curse when this does not happen as was the case with the prophet that came from Judea to Samaria: "But camest back, and hast eaten bread and drunk water in the place, of the which the Lord did say to thee, Eat no bread, and drink no water; thy carcase shall not come unto the sepulchre of thy fathers" (1 Kings 13:22).

There is blessing and a spiritual foresight associated with burying a person with his people or with his kin: "And thou shalt go to thy fathers in peace; thou shalt be buried in a good old age" (Genesis 15:15); "Behold therefore, I will gather thee unto thy fathers, and thou shalt be gathered into thy grave in peace; and thine eyes shall not see all the evil which I will bring upon this place" (2 Kings 22:20); "For David, after he had served his own generation by the will of God, fell on sleep, and was laid unto his fathers, and saw corruption" (Acts 13:36). ; "These all died in faith, not having received the promises, but having seen them afar off, and were persuaded of them, and embraced them, and confessed that they were strangers and pilgrims on the earth. For they that say such things declare plainly that they seek a country. And truly, if they had been mindful of that country from whence they came out, they might have had opportunity to have returned. But now they desire a better country, that is, an heavenly: wherefore God is not ashamed to be called their God: for he hath prepared for them a city" (Hebrews 11:13-16).

All this comes, I think blended in with our spiritual life here on earth, for each of us has a father in the faith who won us to the Lord Jesus. Also we too have spiritual children whom we in turn won to the Lord Jesus. There is an eternal spiritual bond here:"For though ye have ten thousand instructors in Christ, yet have ye not many fathers: for in Christ Jesus I have begotten you through the gospel" (1 Corinthians 4:15); "Unto Timothy, my own son in the faith: Grace, mercy, and peace, from God our Father and Jesus Christ our Lord" (1 Timothy 1:2); "To Titus, mine own son after the common faith: Grace, mercy, and peace, from God the Father and the Lord Jesus Christ our Saviour" (Titus 1:4); " I beseech thee for my son Onesimus, whom I have begotten in my bonds" (Philemon 1:10). Also too each of us in his spiritual association with the church where he was baptized into and given gifts of the spirit to serve in with that particular congregation: "[7]But the manifestation of the Spirit is given to every man to profit withal....[11]the same Spirit; dividing to every man severally as he will. [12]For as the body is one, and hath many members, and all the members of that one body, being many, are one body: so also is Christ. ¹³For by one Spirit are we all baptized into one body, whether we be Jews or Gentiles, whether we be bond or free; and have been all made to drink into one Spirit." (1 Corinthians 12:7,11-14). This is mere speculation.

From reading these references, I tend to think that people in eternity will be living in communities and families as they did when they were in the flesh. Without marriage we will coexist like angels do. There will be righteous kings that will lead these righteous peoples, kings that were faithful in the flesh. They will worship and serve the Lord Jesus in his monarchy over the world of eternity.

At the end of the millennium all the redeemed of the entire human race will enter eternity the new earth in bright shining glorified bodies: "And they that be wise shall shine as the brightness of the firmament; and they that turn many to righteousness as the stars for ever and ever" (Daniel 12:3); "The Son of man shall send forth his angels, and they shall gather out of his kingdom all things that offend, and them which do iniquity; And shall cast them into a furnace of fire: there shall be wailing and gnashing of teeth. Then shall the righteous shine forth as the sun in the kingdom of their Father" (Matthew 13:41-43).

In the new eternal earth, peoples will be distributed perfectly in accordance with God's original plan for Adam and Eve. All righteous people and their kings and we as believers will walk and live in the shadow of the light of God, the glory of the heavenly Jerusalem.

(25) "And the gates of it shall not be shut at all by day: for there shall be no night there."

There will be no need to closed gates. They will remain open for ever for Satan will no more be present, nor evil nor fear. We will be able to come and go through these gates, just like we saw in our earlier exposition of Isaiah chapter 66.

(26) "And they shall bring the glory and honour of the nations into it."

Many questions come to mind here and there is minute information there but it is clear that the worship of the Lord Jesus is prevalent in the universe and it will continue forever.

(27) "And there shall in no wise enter into it any thing that defileth, neither whatsoever worketh abomination, or maketh a lie: but they which are written in the Lamb's book of life."

This does not mean that eternity will include some defilement, with this defilement being denied entrance to the heavenly Jerusalem. Rather, the gates of the city are open forever, since no defilement exists of any kind. No sin of any type pollutes eternity. All the wicked have been cast into the lake of fire and brimstone. Those freely enter and exit the city are solely the redeemed, who have been bought by the blood of the Lord Jesus. Blessed be his name JESUS !

22
THE RIVER OF LIFE AND ENTERING ETERNAL JOY

(1) "And he shewed me a pure river of water of life, clear as crystal, proceeding out of the throne of God and of the Lamb."

When a person dreams of rest, happiness, and well-being, he dreams of gardens, paradises, parks, resorts, and shoreline picnics banks of brooks and rivers. So shall we be in eternity in eternal bliss and joyful relaxation in praise to the Lord Jesus. Even in service, there will be, according to verse 3, no toil for there will be no sin.

At the beginning of the book of Genesis, Adam and Eve lived in such an environment. After the fall and redemption, the righteous descendants of Adam and Eve will live in joyful tranquillity. That is where the repentant thief on the cross resides today: "And Jesus said unto him, Verily I say unto thee, To day shalt thou be with me in paradise" (Luke 23:43). Also while alive, Paul the apostle saw this place: "Eye hath not seen, nor ear heard, neither have entered into the heart of man, the things which God hath prepared for them that love him" (1 Corinthians 2:9); "He was caught up into paradise, and heard unspeakable words, which it is not lawful for a man to utter" (2 Corinthians 12:4).

There is a blessed heavenly river, whose streams paradise in its entirety, even as it was in the garden of Eden: "And a river went out of Eden to water the garden; and from thence it was parted, and became into four heads. The name of the first is Pison: that is it which compasseth the whole land of Havilah, where there is gold; And the gold of that land is good: there is bdellium and the onyx stone. And the name of the second river is Gihon: the same is it that compasseth the whole land of Ethiopia. And the name of the third river is Hiddekel: that is it which goeth toward the east of Assyria. And the fourth river is Euphrates" (Genesis 2:10-14).

That heavenly river is blessed, pure, and refreshing; and we shall rest on its banks in bliss and tranquillity and peace and gladness in conditions that exceed our imagination. This is coupled with blessed health, life, youth, and eternal glory.

(2) "In the midst of the street of it, and on either side of the river, was there the tree of life, which bare twelve manner of fruits, and yielded her fruit every month: and the leaves of the tree were for the healing of the nations."

As in the case of beautiful mountainous country village, the new Jerusalem will have a main market street at its heart, running along both sides of the river.

It might be that this is the tree of life that appeared in the garden of Eden in the book of Genesis: "And out of the ground made the LORD God to grow every tree that is pleasant to the sight, and good for food; the tree of life also in the midst of the garden, and the tree of knowledge of good and evil"; "So he drove out the man; and he placed at the east of the garden of Eden Cherubims, and a flaming sword which turned every way, to keep the way of the tree of life" (Genesis 2:9; 3:24). Its leaves will not be for healing from sickness because the next verse says that there will be no curse. Its fruit will be for giving health, vigor, and enjoyment when it is eaten. The tree of life gives 12 fruits per month or 144 fruits every year. And there is fruit year-round. Does this means that there will be time? Of course not. Does this mean that there will sickness? Of course not. We do not know what is meant by this text, but at least, we do understand that there will be a permanent state of health and wellness.

The marketplace in the middle of the city is not for commerce, but rather for strolls, picnics, gatherings, dancing, and other leisurely activities. The prophet Zechariah describes it as follows: "Thus saith the Lord; I am returned unto Zion, and will dwell in the midst of Jerusalem: and Jerusalem shall be called a city of truth; and the mountain of the Lord of hosts the holy mountain. Thus saith the Lord of hosts; There shall yet old men and old women dwell in the streets of Jerusalem, and every man with his staff in his hand for very age. And the streets of the city shall be full of boys and girls playing in the streets thereof" (Zechariah 8:3-5).

There is very little detail but it is a great text, so we should be happy and comforted with it. What is certain is that there is a:

(a) River
(b) Marketplace
(c) Main street
(d) Tree of life

(3) "And there shall be no more curse: but the throne of God and of the Lamb shall be in it; and his servants shall serve him:"

There are no hardships, nor calamities, nor any tears in heaven. There is no sadness, nor any wicked thing. Instead, there are bounties and blessings that flow from the throne of heaven, as we serve God and the Lord Jesus who shall be present with us as Ezekiel says: "And the name of the city from that day shall be, The Lord is there" (Ezekiel 48:35). What is most important is that the Lord Jesus be present with us as the psalmist Asaf expresses in his psalm: "Whom have I in heaven but thee? and there is none upon earth that I desire beside thee" (Psalms 73:25). We shall be in glorified bodies as we live in the shadow of his presence, serving and worshiping him. It is an honour that passes understanding that we the born again believers shall be in the presence of the Father, the Son, and the Holy Spirit in the heavenly Jerusalem, in the presence of the Lord Jesus Creator of the heavens and stars and galaxies and planets and all heavenly bodies and the entire universe.

(4) "And they shall see his face; and his name shall be in their foreheads."

- And they shall see his face - It is not possible for man to see the glory of God, not even for a moment: "Thou canst not see my face: for there shall no man see me, and live" (Exodus 33:20); "Who is the blessed and only Potentate, the King of kings, and Lord of lords; Who only hath immortality, dwelling in the light which no man can approach unto; whom no man hath seen, nor can see" (1 Timothy 6:15-16); "No man hath seen God at any time" (1 John 4:12). But we being then glorified, we shall see him; "Beloved, now are we the sons of God, and it doth not yet appear what we shall be: but we know that, when he shall appear, we shall be like him; for we shall see him as he is" (1 John 3:2). Thanks be to the Lord Jesus, who has promised and who will keep his promise: "Blessed are the pure in heart: for they shall see God" (Matthew 5:8).

- And his name shall be in their foreheads - Jesus promised the church of Philadelphia that he would write upon us three names, the name of:

(i) His God,

(ii) City of his God,

(iii) His new name (Revelation 3:12; 19:12). We are reckoned as his own, and this is the greatest distinction which can be bestowed upon us, an everlasting privilege which is ours in Christ Jesus, the Lord of glory!

(5) "And there shall be no night there; and they need no

candle, neither light of the sun; for the Lord God giveth them light: and they shall reign for ever and ever."

- And there shall be no night there; and they need no candle, neither light of the sun; for the Lord God giveth them light - Just as we saw in the last chapter, the light of God, the light of the Lord Jesus, and the light of we the redeemed will illumine the new heavenly universe in its entirety. That exactly similar to how our present world is illuminated by the sun, moon, and stars, each of which derive their light from God. In eternity, the bright radiant dazzling light of the Lord Jesus will shine constantly in an everlasting dawn, and propagated through us as well: "And they that be wise shall shine as the brightness of the firmament; and they that turn many to righteousness as the stars for ever and ever" (Daniel 12:3).

- And they shall reign for ever and ever - After the millennial kingdom, we will once again rule with the Lord Jesus forever: "But the saints of the most High shall take the kingdom, and possess the kingdom for ever, even for ever and ever ... Until the Ancient of days came, and judgment was given to the saints of the most High; and the time came that the saints possessed the kingdom" (Daniel 7:18, 22).

In verses 1-5 of this chapter, we find seven glories which await us in the heavenly Jerusalem:

(i) There is no curse anymore. No more sin, but utter full holiness.

(ii) The throne of God and the Lamb reign therein. There will be neither chaos nor oppression anymore, but justice, equality, and freedom.

(iii) We will serve Christ in his kingdom. There will be neither laziness nor boredom. We will have blessed joy, royal tasks in the regal service of our Lord and Saviour Jesus Christ in his reign over the universe.

(iv) It will be an indescribable honour for us to behold the face of the Lord Jesus Christ forever, which is the yearning to be fulfilled desire of every believer today: "But blessed are your eyes, for they see: and your ears, for they hear. For verily I say unto you, That many prophets and righteous men have desired to see those things which ye see, and have not seen them; and to hear those things which ye hear, and have not heard them" (Matthew 13:16-17).

(v) The name of the Lord will be upon our foreheads. We will be his possession forever. What consolation, security, peace, exaltation, and privilege is our portion since we are the children of the wealthiest king in the universe.

(vi) Everlasting light, which is eternal joy, gladness, and health.

(vii) We will reign eternally. We will be kings and priests forever under the monarchy of Christ, and we will be in continual fellowship with him!

(6) "And he said unto me, These sayings are faithful and true: and the Lord God of the holy prophets sent his angel to shew unto his servants the things which must shortly be done."

- And he said unto me, These sayings are faithful and true - The angel affirms to John that what he has seen is real. It is not a figment of his imagination; it is not a collection of symbols or a set of dreams. It is a realistic, futuristic truth whose beauty exceeds description. The Lord Jesus himself is careful to fulfil that which he has declared to John and to us through his Holy Spirit: "But God hath revealed them unto us by his Spirit: for the Spirit searcheth all things, yea, the deep things of God" (1 Corinthians 2:10).

- And the Lord God of the holy prophets sent his angel to shew unto his servants the things which must shortly be done - All the sayings which the Lord Jesus had given to the prophets of old have been fulfilled in their every detail. This constitutes conclusive proof that the Lord will also keep this prophecy in its specifics and its particulars.

The prophecies of John will soon be fulfilled. We have

already seen that several signs point to the reality that we are on the doorstep of the end times. The Lord Jesus might return at any moment now and take us home to heaven.

(7) "Behold, I come quickly: blessed is he that keepeth the sayings of the prophecy of this book."

- Behold, I come quickly. Here, the Lord Jesus himself enters in on the declarations of the angel, in order to affirm the featured the words of the angel. He confirms the credibility and accuracy of all that the angel proclaimed. That is why three times in this chapter Jesus says: "I come quickly":

(i) "Behold, I come quickly: blessed is he that keepeth the sayings of the prophecy of this book" (v. 7).

(ii) "And, behold, I come quickly; and my reward is with me, to give every man according as his work shall be" (v. 12).

(iii) "Surely I come quickly" (v. 20).

Thus the Lord Jesus affirms the inevitability and the imminence of these events.

- Blessed is he that keepeth the sayings of the prophecy of this book – Just like in the beginning of the book of Revelation given to John the Beloved, there was a blessing was promised to every individual who reads, hears, and keeps the words of this book: "Blessed is he that readeth, and they that hear the words of this prophecy, and keep those things which are written therein: for the time is at hand" (Revelation 1:3). So also here, at the end of the book the Lord Jesus emphasizes the importance of studying, keeping, and applying this book. How many times have lives of believers been changed by virtue of studying this book?! On the opposite end of the spectrum, how many believers today are lukewarm spiritually because they do not study the prophecies of the return of Christ, which are the right hand of all enthusiasm, activity and spiritual zeal in our lives and world today.

(8) "And I John saw these things, and heard them. And when

I had heard and seen, I fell down to worship before the feet of the angel which shewed me these things."

This is the second time that John the Beloved, weakens and bows before the overwhelming greatness of the visions and the greatness of the glories that await us, we whom God fashioned from a handful of dirt:

(i) John bowed down the first time before chapter (19) before the great honours of the Church, the Bride of Christ, in the Millennium: "And he saith unto me, Write, Blessed are they which are called unto the marriage supper of the Lamb. And he saith unto me, These are the true sayings of God. And I fell at his feet to worship him. And he said unto me, See thou do it not: I am thy fellowservant, and of thy brethren that have the testimony of Jesus: worship God: for the testimony of Jesus is the spirit of prophecy" (Revelation 19:9-10).

(ii) The second time in this verse, John bows down before the honours of the Church, the Bride of Christ, in Eternity.

(9) "Then saith he unto me, See thou do it not: for I am thy fellowservant, and of thy brethren the prophets, and of them which keep the sayings of this book: worship God."

Once again the angel rebukes John, instructing him that worship should not be directed to any man, angel, or any being that is created like him, no matter how great he may be.

Worship should be directed to God in the person of the Lord Jesus Christ alone; he is the Creator: "That at the name of Jesus every knee should bow, of things in heaven, and things in earth, and things under the earth; And that every tongue should confess that Jesus Christ is Lord, to the glory of God the Father" (Philippians 2:10-11); "Who is gone into heaven, and is on the right hand of God; angels and authorities and powers being made subject unto him" (1 Peter 3:22).

(10) "And he saith unto me, Seal not the sayings of the prophecy of this book: for the time is at hand."

In the past, the Lord said to Daniel that the fulfilment of the prophecies he received would happen in the distant future: "But thou, O Daniel, shut up the words, and seal the book, even to the time of the end: many shall run to and fro, and knowledge shall be increased" (Daniel 12:4). Now the prophecies are at the door, and their fulfilment is nigh. The Lord spoke of "knowledge increasing" as if he is encouraging his children to seek more Biblical, prophetic knowledge: "Seal not" indicates that additional understanding of the subject in question is possible. "The time is at hand" indicates that this is the subject of the hour.

(11) "He that is unjust, let him be unjust still: and he which is filthy, let him be filthy still: and he that is righteous, let him be righteous still: and he that is holy, let him be holy still."

This statement is very much in agreement with what the Lord Jesus said to Daniel: "Many shall be purified, and made white, and tried; but the wicked shall do wickedly: and none of the wicked shall understand; but the wise shall understand" (Daniel 12:10). These two sayings interpret each other, for there is plenty of information in the Bible that is plenty sufficient to lead a man to repentance from iniquity unto righteous living. But the problem is that man, although capable of distinguishing right from wrong, chooses darkness and defilement. Those who choose the way of righteousness are driven by their knowledge to a growing determination to live holier even more. Solomon urges us in this direction when he writes: "Rejoice, O young man, in thy youth; and let thy heart cheer thee in the days of thy youth, and walk in the ways of thine heart, and in the sight of thine eyes: but know thou, that for all these things God will bring thee into judgment" (Ecclesiastes 11:9).

(12) "And, behold, I come quickly; and my reward is with me, to give every man according as his work shall be."

The one who lives according to his whims will ultimately pay the price. The one who lives for the Lord Jesus will in the end receive a heavenly reward. During his earthly ministry, this is what the Lord Jesus Christ challenged us to strive for.

So now has come the time to receive the reward from the King of Glory JESUS!

(13) "I am Alpha and Omega, the beginning and the end, the first and the last."

This description we have in this verse refers to both God and Jesus Christ at the same time: "Who hath wrought and done it, calling the generations from the beginning? I the Lord, the first, and with the last; I am he ... Ye are my witnesses, saith the Lord, and my servant whom I have chosen: that ye may know and believe me, and understand that I am he: before me there was no God formed, neither shall there be after me ... Thus saith the Lord the King of Israel, and his redeemer the Lord of hosts; I am the first, and I am the last; and beside me there is no God ... Hearken unto me, O Jacob and Israel, my called; I am he; I am the first, I also am the last. Mine hand also hath laid the foundation of the earth, and my right hand hath spanned the heavens: when I call unto them, they stand up together" (Isaiah 41:4; 43:10; 44:6; 48:12-13). "I am Alpha and Omega, the beginning and the ending, saith the Lord, which is, and which was, and which is to come, the Almighty ... I was in the Spirit on the Lord's day, and heard behind me a great voice, as of a trumpet, Saying, I am Alpha and Omega, the first and the last: and, What thou seest, write in a book, and send it unto the seven churches which are in Asia ... And he that sat upon the throne said, Behold, I make all things new. And he said unto me, Write: for these words are true and faithful. And he said unto me, It is done. I am Alpha and Omega, the beginning and the end. I will give unto him that is athirst of the fountain of the water of life freely" (Revelation 1:8, 10-11; 21:5-6).

This verse testifies that Jesus is God the Creator of all things. He is the one who decides. He is the one who has authority over all things in the universe. He is the one who dispenses rewards!

(14) "Blessed are they that do his commandments, that they may have right to the tree of life, and may enter in through the gates into the city."

The word "Blessed" means "fortuned from heaven". Blessed are all those who love Jesus Christ and obey him, for he will give them the right to the tree of life. He will give them an entrance befitting kings through the doors of his blessed, heavenly, eternal city: "For so an entrance shall be ministered unto you abundantly into the everlasting kingdom of our Lord and Saviour Jesus Christ" (2 Peter 1:11). The one who loves the Lord Jesus hearkens to his commandments, obeying and applying them: "He that hath my commandments, and keepeth them, he it is that loveth me: and he that loveth me shall be loved of my Father, and I will love him, and will manifest myself to him" (John 14:21). The one who loves the Lord Jesus sanctifies his life in holy living in anticipation of meeting him: "And every man that hath this hope in him purifieth himself, even as he is pure" (1 John 3:3).

(15) "For without are dogs, and sorcerers, and whoremongers, and murderers, and idolaters, and whosoever loveth and maketh a lie."

Outside are "dogs", a metaphor used in the Bible for all that are unclean, defiled, corrupt, ignoble, and valueless. The word dog is used to refer to Sodomites: "Thou shalt not bring the hire of a whore, or the price of a dog, into the house of the LORD thy God for any vow: for even both these are abomination unto the LORD thy God" (Deuteronomy 23:18). It is also used to refer to the degenerate. "Give not that which is holy unto the dogs, neither cast ye your pearls before swine, lest they trample them under their feet, and turn again and rend you" (Matthew 7:6). It can also be used to refer to the lazy: "His watchmen are blind: they are all ignorant, they are all dumb dogs, they cannot bark; sleeping, lying down, loving to slumber" (Isaiah 56:10).

Generally, the word "dog" applies to every sinful practice

mentioned in this verse such as sorcery, fornication, murder, idolatry in the heart, and lying in its many forms.

All who bear any of the dishonourable titles enumerated in this verse will be deprived forever from entering into the heavenly city of Jerusalem. It will be a great loss, a loss beyond measure or compensation to miss out and losee all the glories which are being prepared for us by the Lord Jesus; for: "The sufferings of this present time are not worthy to be compared with the glory which shall be revealed in us" (Romans 8:18).

Do not pass up the opportunity but, rather, learn the lesson from Esau: "Lest there be any fornicator, or profane person, as Esau, who for one morsel of meat sold his birthright. For ye know how that afterward, when he would have inherited the blessing, he was rejected: for he found no place of repentance, though he sought it carefully with tears" (Hebrews 12:16-17).

(16) "I Jesus have sent mine angel to testify unto you these things in the churches. I am the root and the offspring of David, and the bright and morning star."

Jesus identifies himself here by his own name. What a consolation for us that it is Jesus himself who bears witness to the trustworthiness of the book of Revelation. The word of the Lord Jesus is directed fundamentally to the seven churches but ultimately to all who have "ears to hear."

Also, this is the first mention of the Church since chapter 3. This gap provides further evidence of the fact that the true Church, the Body of Christ, will not pass through the great tribulation but will be raptured before it, as we have studied previously. Jesus is the king of the Jews and the hope of Israel. He is also the bridegroom of the Church and the bright and morning star who dispels the darkness of night for all creation. This is true in the Old Testament; it is true in the New Testament; and it will be true during the Great Tribulation, during the Millennium, and throughout Eternity. Jesus is the lot of every believer, as he promised the church of Thyatira: "And I will give him the morning star. He that hath an ear, let him hear what the Spirit saith unto the churches" (Revelation 2:28-29). Jesus is the Sun of righteousness: "But unto you that fear my name shall the Sun of righteousness arise with healing in his wings" (Malachi 4:2). He is the healing physician: "I am the Lord that healeth thee" (Exodus 15:26).

(17) "And the Spirit and the bride say, Come. And let him that heareth say, Come. And let him that is athirst come. And whosoever will, let him take the water of life freely."

- And the Spirit and the bride say, Come. And let him that heareth say, Come. The invitation extended here is an individual summons from the bridegroom himself, the Lord Jesus Christ, to the living Church.

The relationship with the Lord Jesus is individual, immediate, and very personal. The Spirit is the Holy Spirit- the Spirit of Christ. This is the Spirit who lived in the hearts of the prophets of old, and who now lives in the hearts of believers. It is the spirit in us who yearns for the coming of Christ Jesus in glory: "Searching what, or what manner of time the Spirit of Christ which was in them did signify, when it testified beforehand the sufferings of Christ, and the glory that should follow" (1 Peter 1:11); "That good thing which was committed unto thee keep by the Holy Ghost which dwelleth in us" (2 Timothy 1:14).

The Bride is the Church, and the important question is: "Are you part of this bride?" Can you join your voice to this invitation and say: "Amen. Even so, come, Lord Jesus"? Or are you identified with nominal churches which are drowning in traditions that have no spirit, no life, no love, and no hope in waiting for Christ's return from heaven? If you hear his voice, call upon him and ask him to forgive your sins. Ask him to make your portion with him in the new Jerusalem and in heavenly glory. And to those who follow other religions that cannot solve the problem of sin, Jesus nailed sin to the cross. He has opened the door of forgiveness and is calling to you: "Come unto me, all ye that labour and are heavy laden, and I will give you rest" (Matthew 11:28).

- And let him that is athirst come. And whosoever will, let him take the water of life freely. But you cannot come if you have no spiritual thirst. The one who issues this invitation is the Lord Jesus Christ, who is the source of everlasting life: "And he said unto me, It is done. I am Alpha and Omega, the beginning and the end. I will give unto him that is athirst of the fountain of the water of life freely" (Revelation 21:6).

Accept Jesus' call to you, and you will be celebrating ecstatically for ever in heaven: "In the last day, that great day of the feast, Jesus stood and cried, saying, If any man thirst, let him come unto me, and drink. He that believeth on me, as the scripture hath said, out of his belly shall flow rivers of living water. But this spake he of the Spirit, which they that believe on him should receive: for the Holy Ghost was not yet given; because that Jesus was not yet glorified" (John 7:37-39).

Our love for the Lord Jesus produces spiritual thirst and motivates our hearts to desire his quick return: The expression "let him" appears three times in this verse:

(i) "Let him that heareth",

(ii) "Let him that is athirst",

(iii) "Whosoever will, let him take."

The one who hears will receive a thirst which draws him to Christ, which lets him accept the Lord Jesus. And thus his thirst will be quenched by the Holy Spirit of the Lord. Thus we see the connection between the one who hears, who is athirst, and who desires to obtain salvation.

(18) "For I testify unto every man that heareth the words of the prophecy of this book, If any man shall add unto these things, God shall add unto him the plagues that are written in this book:"

Tampering with God's word is a trap and a peril, and an evil. This has been true from the beginning of mankind, for God's word to Adam and Eve was: "But of the tree of the knowledge of good and evil, thou shalt not eat of it" (Genesis 2:17). But Eve, out of fear or maybe a sense of excessive piety, decided to add a couple of words to the Lords statement: by adding: "neither shall ye touch it" (Genesis 3:3). So Satan overcame her, and she brought great sorrow upon herself and the entire human race.

There is a clear, continual divine injunction against adding to or subtracting from God's word: "Ye shall not add unto the word which I command you, neither shall ye diminish ought from it" (Deuteronomy 4:2); "Every word of God is pure: he is a shield unto them that put their trust in him. Add thou not unto his words, lest he reprove thee, and thou be found a liar" (Proverbs 30:5-6). These warnings are reiterated here at the end of the Bible, for Jesus is putting his seal on it. If anyone adds to it, the Lord God will add to him the plagues written in this book.

(19) "And if any man shall take away from the words of the book of this prophecy, God shall take away his part out of the book of life, and out of the holy city, and from the things which are written in this book."

The unbeliever, or the wicked man who tampers with God's word loses his opportunity to be saved, for salvation is through that word: "For in Christ Jesus I have begotten you through the gospel" (1 Corinthians 4:15); "Of his own will begat he us with the word of truth" (James 1:18). Such an one loses the hope of everlasting life and forfeits the opportunity of living in the heavenly Jerusalem.

(20) "He which testifieth these things saith, Surely I come quickly. Amen. Even so, come, Lord Jesus."

This is the last time the Lord Jesus speaks to us through his Word. He is careful to make the closing statement in the Bible himself, as this verse also contains the last recorded words uttered by man in the Bible. In these words, the Church expresses its yearning for the bridegroom, the Lord Jesus.

The very first statement made by fallen man and recorded in the Bible is: "I heard thy voice in the garden, and I was afraid, because I was naked; and I hid myself" (Genesis 3:10). The last statement made by man and recorded in the Bible is, "Amen. Even so, come, Lord Jesus."

(21) "The grace of our Lord Jesus Christ be with you all. Amen."

My believing brother, we must be faithful and say, "Amen. Even so, come, Lord Jesus." Thank you, my Lord Jesus! Amen.

The book of Revelation is a refreshing, invigorating book; it revives and rejuvenates our hope and expectation that the Lord Jesus is coming very soon. It revitalizes our determination to live in holiness and in anticipation of the return of the Lord Jesus. Let us always remember the words of the Apostle Peter: "Knowing this first, that there shall come in the last days scoffers, walking after their own lusts, And saying, Where is the promise of his coming? for since the fathers fell asleep, all things continue as they were from the beginning of the creation. For this they willingly are ignorant of, that by the word of God the heavens were of old, and the earth standing out of the water and in the water: Whereby the world that then was, being overflowed with water, perished: But the heavens and the earth, which are now, by the same word are kept in store, reserved unto fire against the day of judgment and perdition of ungodly men. But, beloved, be not ignorant of this one thing, that one day is with the Lord as a thousand years, and a thousand years as one day. The Lord is not slack concerning his promise, as some men count slackness; but is longsuffering to us-ward, not willing that any should perish, but that all should come to repentance. But the day of the Lord will come as a thief in the night; in the which the heavens shall pass away with a great noise, and the elements shall melt with fervent heat, the earth also and the works that are therein shall be burned up. Seeing then that all these things shall be dissolved, what manner of persons ought ye to be in all holy conversation and godliness, Looking for and hasting unto the coming of the day of God, wherein the heavens being on fire shall be dissolved, and the elements shall melt with fervent heat? Nevertheless we, according to his promise, look for new heavens and a new earth, wherein dwelleth righteousness. Wherefore, beloved, seeing that ye look for such things, be diligent that ye may be found of him in peace, without spot, and blameless" (2 Peter 3:3-14).

BLESSED BE THE NAME:

JESUS CHRIST SON OF GOD

JESUS' Light dazzles
- His Beauty is indescribable
- His Grace is pure
- His Kindness is overflowing
- His Warmth radiates
- His Love is unrestrained
- His Mercy is everlasting
- His compassion heals the soul
- His Salvation is Heavenly Eternal

In Biology JESUS CHRIST was born of a virgin.

In Chemistry He turned water into wine.

In Physics He opposed the law of gravity when ascended to heaven.

In Economics he fed 5,000 with 5 loaves and 2 fish.

In Medicine He healed the sick, gave sight to the blind, and raised the dead.

In History He is the beginning and the end.

In Government he is wonderful, counselor, the Prince of Peace.

In Religion He is the Holy Son of God.
In Salvation He is the Truth the Way and the Life.

JESUS had no slaves, but they called him master.

He did not get academic degrees, but they called him teacher.

He did not use any medicine, but he healer the sick and raised the dead.

He had no army, but the kings feared him.

He did not declare wars, but he conquered the world.

JESUS CHRIST is the Son of God, Lord of Heaven,
Saviour of the world.

JESUS CHRIST was crucified, buried, risen, ascended to heaven, and coming back again to earth

JESUS CHRIST forgives sins

JESUS CHRIST is the Prince of Peace

JESUS CHRIST is the most unusual man, greater than all men. At JESUS' name every knee shall bow. So come to him and bow down your knees to Him now and ask him to forgive your sins and save your soul and give you eternal life. Make him your Lord and Saviour and master of your life. He is Trustworthy, come to Him now and have life in Him.

I feel proud to serve JESUS CHRIST, the King of kings and Lord of Lords, who loved me and redeemed me with his blood. To him all glory be.

"No weapon that is formed against thee shall prosper; and every tongue that shall rise against thee in judgment thou shalt condemn. This is the heritage of the servants of the Lord, and their righteousness is of me, saith the Lord" (Isaiah 54:17).

www.ingramcontent.com/pod-product-compliance
Lightning Source LLC
Chambersburg PA
CBHW030101170426
43198CB00009B/443